"In the age of TikTok and Instagram, the examination of digital advocacy is more critical than ever. This volume does a masterful job of capturing the different elements of political communication processes through quantitative and qualitative approaches. It not only identifies key challenges but also offers pathways forward in an increasingly fragmented and polarized political environment."

—Dr. Daniela Dimitrova,
LAS Dean's Professor, Greenlee School of Journalism & Communication,
Iowa State University, USA
Editor-in-Chief, *Journalism & Mass Communication Quarterly*

"Distinguished scholars John Allen Hendricks and Dan Schill have assembled a team of top senior and emerging scholars that provide powerful chapter-based analyses of digital advocacy and political communication. The chapters provide a wealth of knowledge and insights along the themes of political rhetoric and electoral engagement, political misinformation and disinformation, political partisanship and polarization, and political communication strategies. Collectively the authors adroitly navigate the complexities with in-depth studies in numerous applications, contexts, and use of digital strategies. This collection is a superb volume of research that illuminates where we have been and where we are headed in terms of the use and impact of social and digital media in politics. This book needs to be on the shelves for anyone who teaches, studies, or is interested in the ever evolving and dynamic world of political communication."

—Robert E. Denton, Jr.
W. Thomas Rice Chair Emeritus and Professor Emeritus of Communication,
Virginia Tech University, USA

Political Communication and Digital Advocacy

Mitchell S. McKinney and Mary E. Stuckey
General Editors

Vol. 53

Political Communication and Digital Advocacy

Strategies and Implications

Edited by
John Allen Hendricks and
Dan Schill

PETER LANG
New York · Berlin · Bruxelles · Chennai · Lausanne · Oxford

Library of Congress Cataloging-in-Publication Data

Names: Hendricks, John Allen, editor. | Schill, Dan, editor.
Title: Political communication and digital advocacy : strategies and
   implications / edited by John Allen Hendricks and Dan Schill.
Description: New York, NY : Peter Lang, [2025] | Series: Frontiers in
   political communication, 1525-9730 ; volume 53 | Includes
   bibliographical references and index.
Identifiers: LCCN 2024061298 (print) | LCCN 2024061299 (ebook) |
   ISBN 9783034355643 (paperback ; alk. paper) |
   ISBN 9783034356435 (hardback ; alk. paper) |
   ISBN 9783034355667 (ebook) |
   ISBN 9783034355674 (epub)
Subjects: LCSH: Communication in politics–United States—History—21st
   century. | Political participation –Technological innovations – United
   States. | Mass media – Political aspects – 21st century. | Internet and
   Activism – United States – 21st century. | Social media and
   Society – United States. | Democracy – Technological innovations--United
   States.
Classification: LCC JA85.2.U6 P635 2025 (print) | LCC JA85.2.U6 (ebook) |
   DDC 320.97301/4 – dc23/eng/20250203
LC record available at https://lccn.loc.gov/2024061298
LC ebook record available at https://lccn.loc.gov/2024061299
DOI 10.3726/b22642

Bibliographic information published by the Deutsche Nationalbibliothek. The German National Library lists this publication in the German National Bibliography; detailed bibliographic data is available on the Internet at <http://dnb.d-nb.de>.

Cover credit © iStock: natasaadzic

Cover design by Peter Lang Group AG

ISSN 1525-9730 (print)
ISBN 9783034355643 (paperback)
ISBN 9783034356435 (hardback)
ISBN 9783034355667 (ebook)
ISBN 9783034355674 (epub)
DOI 10.3726/b22642

© 2025 Peter Lang Group AG, Lausanne
Published by Peter Lang Publishing Inc., New York, USA
info@peterlang.com—www.peterlang.com

All rights reserved.
All parts of this publication are protected by copyright.
Any utilization outside the strict limits of the copyright law, without the permission of the publisher, is forbidden and liable to prosecution.
This applies in particular to reproductions, translations, microfilming, and storage and processing in electronic retrieval systems.

This publication has been peer reviewed.

CONTENTS

List of Figures		ix
List of Tables		xi
Acknowledgments		xiii

Section I: Political Rhetoric and Electoral Engagement

1	Trust, Truth, and Technology: Political Communication in Polarized Times *John Allen Hendricks and Dan Schill*	3
2	Polysyndeton, Social Media, and the Presidency: Digital Culture & Rhetorical Style in the 2020 Election *Randall Fowler*	25
3	Trump and Twitter: A Study of Parasocial Interaction, Identification, and Social Presence *Kalah Kemp and Myrna Roberts*	45

| 4 | The Citizen-Fan: The Impact of Social Media and Fandom on Contemporary Political Engagement Online
Emily Sauter | 67 |

Section II: Political Misinformation and Disinformation

5	Knowledge Gaps and Misinformation: Social Media Engagement, Ideology, and Elections *Ben Wasike*	101
6	Sowing Seeds of Distrust: Investigating the Spread of Mis- and Disinformation by Exploring the Pathways for Rural Americans to News *Todd R. Vogts and Jacob Groshek*	121
7	theDonald.win: Electoral Fraud and a Nation in Crisis *Tyler Martinez and Majia Nadesan*	157

Section III: Political Partisanship and Polarization

8	Streaming Entertainment into Political Pandemonium: Examining (Even More) Partisanship and Polarization in the 2020 Campaign *Sarah Krongard and Jacob Groshek*	183
9	The Influence of Partisan Cues on Social Media: Acceptance of the 2020 Presidential Election Results *Madeleine Montgomery, Freddie J. Jennings, Kathleen Coyle, Ariana Aquino, and Malloree Murdock*	209
10	The Moderating Effect of Racial Resentment and Ambivalent Sexism on Partisanship and Thought Listing after Viewing the 2020 Vice Presidential Debate *Xavier Scruggs and Benjamin R. Warner*	229

Section IV: Political Communication Strategies

11	Shared Blindness in Filter Bubbles: Political Messages in Social Media *Yanjun Zhao*	253
12	When Election Lies Go Viral: How Social Media Platforms Amplified Cable News Networks' Defamatory Comments about Dominion Voting Systems and Smartmatic Corporation *Juliet Dee*	271
13	Normalizing New Identities in Political Roles: An Examination of the Social Media of Pete and Chasten Buttigieg *Christopher J. McCollough*	295
14	Hashtag Politics: #StopTheSteal as Rhetorical Strategy *Joseph P. Zompetti*	323

About the Editors — 349
About the Contributors — 351
Index — 357

FIGURES

Figure 4.1:	Screenshot of Sofie.Holland TikTok Post	74
Figure 4.2:	Selfie of Shiyinglu with Andrew Yang	74
Figure 4.3:	Examples of 2020 memes in support of Donald Trump	87
Figure 5.1:	Twitter meme depicting elections-related misinformation	106
Figure 5.2:	Elections information knowledge test	108
Figure 5.3:	Social media engagement and interpersonal discussion questions	109
Figure 9.1:	Hypothesized model of the direct and indirect influence of partisan identification and attitudinal congruence	217
Figure 9.2:	Final model of the direct and indirect influence of partisan identification and attitudinal congruence	220
Figure 10.1:	Correlation between hostile sexism and racial resentment	240
Figure 10.2:	Interactions of racial resentment, hostile sexism, and digital communication environment on evaluations of Kamala Harris's debate performance	241

TABLES

Table 3.1:	Summary of HLR analysis for variables examining Trump's tweets' influence on voter behavior	57
Table 3.2:	Correlation between perceptions of Trump's tweets and perceptions of Trump's credibility	57
Table 3.3:	Summary of HLR analysis for variables examining Trump's tweets' influence on perceptions of Donald Trump's policies	58
Table 5.1:	Elections-related knowledge and social media engagement means	111
Table 5.2:	OLS regression predicting elections-related knowledge	111
Table 5.3:	OLS regression predicting social media engagement with elections-related misinformation	112
Table 6.1:	Interview participants	134
Table 7.1:	Emergent themes on theDonald.win	166
Table 8.1:	Hierarchical linear regression of online political participation	194
Table 8.2:	Hierarchical linear regression of offline political participation	195
Table 8.3:	Hierarchical linear regression of online political talk	197
Table 8.4:	Hierarchical linear regression of perspective-taking	199

Table 8.5:	Hierarchical linear regression of empathic concern	200
Table 10.1:	Effects of racial resentment and hostile sexism on evaluations of Harris's debate	239
Table 10.2:	Effects of communication environment on Harris's debate	242
Table 12.1:	Dominion and smartmatic defamation suits related to the 2020 election	272
Table 13.1:	Pete Buttigieg tweets, January 20, 2021–January 20, 2022	306
Table 13.2:	Chasten Buttigieg tweets, January 20, 2021–January 20, 2022	312

ACKNOWLEDGMENTS

The field of political communication emerged soon after World War II and steadily grew into an established field of study within the Communication discipline. From the field's beginning, it was clear that better understanding the role of and influence of political rhetoric (or political communication) was important, especially due to the rapidly escalating technological developments that were utilized by politicians to campaign for votes.

Each scholar who contributed to this book is interested in understanding political communication's role in the political process and, especially, within a democratic society. For all the time and effort put forth by each of the contributors to this collection, the editors are most appreciative.

The Peter Lang Group is a well-respected international academic and scholarly publisher and has been patient and helpful throughout the process of this book's development. The editors are indebted to Dr. Elizabeth Howard, Acquisitions Editor at Peter Lang, for her assistance directing the manuscript through the concluding stages of publication. Appreciation is owed to Sweetlin Ajitha, of Peter Lang, for her assistance in the final stages. The editors wish to acknowledge the role of and express appreciation to Niall Kennedy, Senior Acquisitions Editor for Media and Communication, who enthusiastically supported this book idea and worked with us at the beginning of the project.

The editors also wish to acknowledge Muralidharan Pattabiraman and the production team at Peter Lang Private Limited in India for the appearance of the finished product, including the book's cover design.

Importantly, the editors wish to express gratefulness to Dr. Mary E. Stuckey, the Edwin Erle Sparks Professor of Communication Arts & Sciences at The Pennsylvania State University, and Dr. Mitchell S. McKinney, Dean and Professor of the Buchtel College of Arts & Sciences at the University of Akron. Mary and Mitchell are well-respected scholars in the political communication field, and they supported this work from the beginning. Their input from the peer review process vetting this project's initial proposal, indeed, improved this book. The editors are honored they chose the project to be included in their "Frontiers in Political Communication" book series.

John Allen Hendricks is indebted to, Dr. Stacy Hendricks, his wife of more than 30 years. He wishes to recognize the support of Stephen F. Austin State University (SFA), a member of the University of Texas System. SFA has been a wonderful academic home.

Dan Schill remains deeply thankful for Jessica, Ellie, and Bennett. He would also like to recognize his colleagues at James Madison University for their continued collegiality, encouragement, and strong support for research and teaching.

Section I
Political Rhetoric and Electoral Engagement

· 1 ·

TRUST, TRUTH, AND TECHNOLOGY: POLITICAL COMMUNICATION IN POLARIZED TIMES

John Allen Hendricks and Dan Schill

Effectively communicating with the electorate is arguably the most important task a candidate for political office must master to get elected. Clear and persuasive communication helps candidates connect with voters, build trust and credibility, frame the issues and influence public opinion, navigate media scrutiny, respond to crises, and mobilize supporters to volunteer, donate, and vote. In addition to mastering effective communication, political candidates certainly must also have a firm grasp of policy issues, but, without doubt, if the candidate does not get elected due to poor communication skills and strategies, then knowledge and experience of the issues is irrelevant. Hackenburg et al. (2023) explained: "At the very heart of elections in a representative democracy lies the art of rhetoric. As Aristotle observed, effective rhetoric can offer political advocates significant electoral influence" (para. 3). Further, communication is not just about speaking eloquently but also about listening, empathizing, and adapting messages to diverse audiences. Communication is a fundamental skill that allows candidates to connect, persuade, and lead effectively in a complex and competitive media environment.

At the national level, communicating effectively with the electorate becomes much more complicated due to the multiple and fragmented mediums in which communication occurs combined with the vast diversity and competing interests of a national audience. Communicating effectively with a nationwide audience demands not only precision and clarity, but also cultural competence, adaptability across a fragmented media ecosystem, and the ability to navigate complex issues while maintaining trust with the citizenry. McNair (2011) explained:

> Brave (and probably doomed to failure) is the organization which ventures into the contemporary political arena without a more or less sophisticated understanding of how the media work and the professional public relations machinery capable of putting that knowledge to good use. For all political actors, from presidents and prime ministers to trade union leaders and terrorists, this is now recognized to be a major prerequisite of successful intervention in public debate and governmental decision-making. (pp. xiv-xv)

Further elaborating on the importance and role of communication in the political process, Denton and Kuypers (2008) asserted that communication is foundational to social cohesion, issue discussion, and legislative enactment: "the essence of politics is talk or human interaction. Such interaction is formal and informal, verbal and nonverbal, public and private—but always persuasive in nature, causing us to interpret, to evaluate, and to act" (p. xii).

While the fundamentals of political communication go back to Aristotle and before, in recent years, political communication has become more dynamic, personalized, and complex over the past decade, driven by technological advancements, changing media landscapes, and shifts in political strategy. Among many other changes, digital and social media platforms like Facebook, X/Twitter, Instagram, YouTube, and TikTok have become central to political communication. Candidates and parties use these platforms to directly reach voters, share their messages, mobilize supporters, and respond to criticism in real-time. Digital tools also allow for highly targeted advertising based on demographics, interests, and behaviors. The 24/7 news cycle driven by online news platforms and social media has increased the speed and intensity of political communication as political events and statements spread rapidly and reach a global audience almost instantly. There has been a shift towards more visual and interactive content in political communication, such as infographics, short-form videos, live streams, podcasts, and interactive websites. Social media has empowered citizens to participate in political discourse through user-generated content and citizen journalism and new platforms have diversified the sources of political news and information. At the same time, the decline of legacy media and institutional trust have contributed to the prevalence of misinformation and fake news. Thus, the purpose of this book is to more closely examine the role of communication in the political process and how communication has evolved on digital and social media platforms in recent years. This book studies these issues through the lens of the 2020 election cycle in the United States, however these trends will continue in the future and, just as political communication now extends beyond national borders, the findings in this book apply to other countries and contexts. So while each chapter necessarily looks to the recent past, each contribution will speak to the future and how candidates and leaders must adapt their communication capabilities to navigate the challenges and opportunities of modern political discourse.

Political Communication as an Evolving Discipline

With a basis in the existing disciplines of political science, speech communication, and journalism, political communication emerged as a distinct area in a limited manner in the 1950s and was established as a field of study in the 1980s (Nimmo & Sanders, 1981). While analyzing the emergence of this new field of study and its multidisciplinary origins, Nimmo and Sanders (1981), in a seminal work, asserted political communication "defies neat characterization" due to its multidisciplinary nature (p. 28). Elaborating on the pluralistic background from which the study of political communication emerged, Nimmo and Sanders traced the origins of the field to "rhetorical analysis, propaganda analysis, attitude change studies, voting studies, studies of the government and news media, functional and systems analysis, and studies of the influence of technological change in the field" (p. 671). As noted, from the beginning, scholars of political communication have examined the intersection of technology and politics. For example, scholars have investigated how communication technologies such as the printing press, telegraph, photography, radio, and television have influenced political discourse, participation, and power dynamics. In the decades following the 1990s, political discourse found itself being filtered through even more technological inventions such as the Internet, social media, big data, and artificial intelligence that required adjustments in theoretical and methodological approaches.

In 1990, a decade after Nimmo and Sanders (1981), Denton and Woodward defined political communication as "pure discussion about the allocation of public resources (revenues), official authority (who is given the power to make legal, legislative and executive decision), and official sanctions (what the state rewards or punishes)" (p. 14). Building upon that definition, Denton and Kuypers (2008) elaborated on political discourse by contending:

> politics is conversation, discussion, and argument; human communication is the vehicle for political thought, debate, and action. It is a practical, process-centered, decision-oriented activity. Because it is dependent on the approval of specific audiences, its utility is strongly restricted by time and by the willingness of the political media to make its messages accessible. (p. 17)

The emergence of this field of study occurred because it was evident that political rhetoric and political communication, in general, needed more scrutiny because of its importance in political campaigning. It was especially important to understand the influence and effects of political communication on the political process in a democratic society, such as public opinion formation, political behavior, and electoral outcomes.

Normatively, democratic societies are premised upon basic tenets that promote and preserve the basic right to self-govern. To do so, there must be an informed and educated electorate to determine who would be best to govern. Recently, the rapid spread of technological advancements in communication has made it difficult for voters to clearly determine the best leaders for our nation. Additionally, the combination of traditional media and digital media has complicated the communication process. McQuade (2024) explained:

> In a democracy, the people need a shared set of facts as a basis to debate and make decisions that advance and secure their collective interests. Differences of opinion, and even propaganda, have always existed in the United States, but now, enemies of democracy are using disinformation to attack our sovereign right to truthful information, intellectual integrity, and the exercise of the will of the people. Online disinformation is particularly insidious because of its immediacy, its capacity to deceive, and its ability to reach its target. (para. 9)

Social media companies such as X (formerly known as Twitter), Instagram, Facebook, and others have wielded considerable influence in recent elections' political discourse. These platforms have enacted policies that have exacerbated issues related to creating and perpetuating confusing messages that undermine democracy. For example, Meta (the parent company of Facebook and Instagram) created a policy that allowed political candidates to post advertising that perpetuated the inaccurate assertion that significant voter fraud occurred in past elections (Zahn, 2023). Zahn (2023) stated: "The move raises concerns about the spread of false election-denial ads on Instagram and Facebook that could erode the public's trust in U.S. democracy" (para. 5).

Trust in the American democratic process is vital to its future. Shea (2022) underscored just how fragile democratic societies are by sharing that "70% of the world's population now lives in non-democratic states; in 2021, 33 countries veered towards authoritarianism while only 5 moved towards democracy, or at least more tolerance of democratic practices and strengthening of democratic institutions" (para. 7). This trend reflects a broader global challenge where the resilience of democratic values and practices is increasingly tested. It prompts reflection on the factors driving this shift, including geopolitical dynamics, internal governance challenges, and societal attitudes towards democratic norms. Such developments underscore the critical need for robust efforts to safeguard and promote democratic principles worldwide. One of these principles is the core idea that active citizen engagement and informed decision-making are fundamental to maintaining a healthy and responsive government and that an informed populace serves as a safeguard against governmental abuses and inefficiencies. President Thomas Jefferson (1789), and one of the nation's Founding Fathers, explained the importance of an informed electorate: "wherever the people are well informed, they can be trusted with their own government; that whenever things get so far wrong as to attract their notice, they may be relied on to set them to rights" (Bains, n.d., para. 1). Further explaining the importance of an informed electorate and how it delineates democracies from autocracies, McNair (2011) explained: "The importance of an informed, knowledgeable electorate dictates that democratic politics must be pursued in the public arena (as distinct from the secrecy characteristics of autocratic regimes)" (p. 17). To obtain an informed electorate, all citizens must have access to reliable information that is dispensed via trustworthy outlets. In recent American elections, the reliability of information on trustworthy outlets has rightfully been questioned by the electorate because of the increasingly partisan tone of political rhetoric on both traditional and digital media outlets.

Partisan News Outlets

Recent elections have revealed that news outlets have lost the trust of the American electorate. Specifically, Malik and Peterson (2021) suggested that trust in traditional media declined during the 2020 election. They shared that a Gallup survey found:

the percentage of Americans with no trust in the mass media hit a record high in 2020: only nine percent of respondents said they trust the mass media "a great deal" and a full 60 percent said they have little to "no trust at all" in it. (para. 2)

As trust in traditional media wanes, it raises critical questions about the future of public information consumption and the role of media in democratic societies.

Political polarization contributes significantly to the electorate's lack of trust in the mass media. Malik and Peterson (2021) stated: "The American media landscape has become increasingly polarized over the last few decades" (para 3). When political discourse becomes highly polarized, individuals tend to seek out media sources that align with their existing beliefs and values. This phenomenon, known as selective exposure, leads people to consume news that reinforces their ideological perspectives while dismissing or distrusting information that contradicts them. Demonstrating the polarization of American politics, 95 percent of Democrats watch MSNBC while 93 percent of Republicans watch Fox News according to the Pew Research Center (Grieco, 2020). Without much debate among media observers, MSNBC is a left-leaning news organization while Fox News is a right-leaning news organization. In a polarized political environment, media outlets may cater to specific partisan audiences to maintain viewership or readership. This can result in biased reporting or selective framing of news stories that align with the ideological leanings of their target audience. As a consequence, audiences on both ends of the political spectrum perceive mainstream media as either favoring the opposing side or failing to represent their own views accurately. Further, political polarization often leads to heightened levels of suspicion and scrutiny towards media organizations. Partisans may accuse media outlets of bias, distortion, or outright fabrication of facts to advance a particular political agenda. The data bear this out. For example, Brenan (2022) found that there has been a consistent decline in the trust Americans hold toward the media. Brenan asserted: "There has been a consistent double-digit gap in trust between Democrats and Republicans since 2001, and that gap has ranged from 54 to 63 percentage points since 2017" (para. 6). Moreover, McGreal (2022) shared: "The Reuters Institute revealed last month that 42% of Americans actively avoid the news at least some of the time because it grinds them down or they just don't believe it. Fifteen percent said they disconnected from news coverage altogether" (para. 2). The lack of trust the electorate holds toward the media has consistently declined over recent decades. Brenan (2022) stated: "The current level of public trust in media's full, fair, and accurate reporting of the news is the second lowest on record" (para. 9). When the citizenry cannot trust the media outlets, they migrate to sources they do trust creating political polarization.

Political Polarization

Political polarization is when voters are strongly divided along ideological lines. Nivola (2005) characterized this phenomenon as sorting into clear and opposite factions: "polarization of U.S. politics reflects a sorting of political convictions by either the mass public or ruling elites, or both, into roughly two distinct camps: persons inclined to support the Democratic or the Republican parties' policies and candidates for elective office" (para. 7). In 2024, the Pew Research Center (2024) found that the nation was evenly divided among the political parties. The study showed that 49% of registered voters were Democrats and 48% were Republicans. The Pew Research Center noted: "The partisan and ideological composition of voters is relatively unchanged over the last five years" (para. 9). Thus, there is little room for political apathy. That is, either you are a Democrat or a Republican, and you vote accordingly. There are fewer "independent" voters with a willingness to see both sides of the political spectrum, suggesting a landscape where party affiliation strongly influences voting behavior. Political polarization also shapes broader societal dynamics and governance. As ideological divisions deepen, partisan identities become more entrenched, leading to heightened levels of political tribalism. This tribalism manifests in various ways, including increased hostility towards opposing viewpoints, greater resistance to compromise, and a tendency to perceive political issues in stark black-and-white terms without nuance or complexity.

As far back as 2014, the Pew Research Center observed this sharp division along ideological lines stating, "Republicans and Democrats are more divided along ideological lines—and partisan antipathy is deeper and more extensive—than at any point in the last two decades" (2014, para. 1). The depth of partisan antipathy highlighted suggests not only a polarization of political beliefs but also a heightened emotional intensity in the way individuals perceive and interact with members of the opposing party. Another way to view the polarization, according to Kleinfeld (2023), is that Americans are less "politically" polarized and more "emotionally" polarized. To put it simply, Kleinfeld explained that Americans "do not like members of the other party. Americans harbor strong dislike for members of the other party" (para. 9). As a result of this dislike for those of the other party, individuals often distance themselves from others who hold differing opinions (Kelly, 2021). When individuals distance, or isolate themselves from people in political parties different from their own, they no longer are exposed to differing beliefs, opinions, and values, thus skewing and limiting their political knowledge. Instead, they are only exposed to information that reinforces already held beliefs. This distancing that occurs creates "echo chambers" and "filter bubbles."

Echo Chambers/Filter Bubbles

As noted, the political distancing creates echo chambers that perpetuate political polarization and digital environments can intensify political polarization by reinforcing individuals' existing beliefs while isolating them from opposing viewpoints. Travers (2023) explained the "echo chamber" concept:

> An echo chamber is a social environment or platform where individuals are exposed to information, opinions, and viewpoints that align with their preexisting beliefs and perspectives exclusively. It's a place where dissenting voices are muffled or entirely absent and where biases are confirmed rather than challenged. (para. 1)

Hobolt et al. (2023) asserted: "It is often argued that partisan 'echo chambers' are one of the drivers of both policy and affective polarization" (p. 1). When individuals are predominantly exposed to information that validates their beliefs, they are less likely to consider alternative viewpoints or engage in meaningful discourse across ideological lines. This polarization not only affects political attitudes but also deepens emotional divisions between different partisan groups. Elaborating on filter bubbles, also called "media bubbles," Benson (2023) explained:

> If people are only hearing opinions they already agree with or seeing stories that align with their worldview, they may become more entrenched in their beliefs, whether or not their beliefs reflect the real world. They may also become easier to manipulate and more extreme (para. 1).

With media bubbles, "people can start to believe they're the only ones with the facts and that the other side is illegitimate" (para. 6). This personalized content consumption can lead individuals to become more entrenched in their beliefs, detached from objective reality, and susceptible to manipulation or radicalization. Further, Avin et al. (2024) explained:

> On a basic level, an echo chamber is 'an environment in which somebody encounters only opinions and beliefs similar to their own, and does not have to consider

alternatives.' By communicating and repeating beliefs within a closed system or network insulated from rebuttal, echo chambers amplify or reinforce beliefs. (para. 2)

Echo chambers and media bubbles have tendencies to perpetuate misinformation and disinformation. Travers (2023) said: "More often than not, such environments become a medium for the rampant spread of misinformation" (para. 1). In environments where alternative viewpoints are scarce, false or misleading information can circulate unchecked, further polarizing public discourse and undermining trust in reliable sources of information.

Misinformation/Disinformation

The distinction between misinformation and disinformation is crucial in understanding their respective impacts on public discourse and democracy. Ruiz and Nilsson (2022) explained: "Misinformation refers to information quality in terms of flawed, misleading, or inaccurate information, and misinformation is unintentional, whereas disinformation is intentional" (p. 20). Misinformation results from errors or misunderstandings and can propagate through well-meaning individuals who unknowingly share false or flawed information. On the other hand, disinformation is deliberate and strategic falsehoods spread with malicious intent. Bennett and Livingston (2018) characterize disinformation as intentional deception aimed at advancing specific agendas, whether political, economic, or ideological. This deliberate manipulation often involves the use of credible-seeming news stories or simulated documentary formats to deceive audiences and undermine trust in factual reporting. Furthermore, Ruiz and Nilsson (2022) proclaimed disinformation as "an adversarial campaign that weaponizes multiple rhetorical strategies and forms of knowing—including not only falsehoods but also truths, half-truths, and value-laden judgments—to exploit and amplify identity-driven controversies" (p. 29). This exploitation of social and political tensions can polarize communities, deepen distrust in institutions, and erode democratic norms. Stated another way, McQuade (2024) explained:

> Disinformation is the deliberate use of lies to manipulate people, whether to extract profit or to advance a political agenda. Its unwitting accomplice, misinformation, is spread by unknowing dupes who repeat lies they believe to be true. In America today, both forms of falsehood are distorting our perception of reality. (para. 8)

In an environment already polarized along ideological lines, these falsehoods can reinforce existing beliefs, making it harder for individuals to discern truth from fiction. Concerning this, Ruiz and Nilsson (2022) emphasized that individuals who are exposed to disinformation do more than just *disseminate* the misleading arguments, they begin *creating* the disinformation. Ruiz and Nilsson explained: "Consumers of disinformation do not just repeat or reverberate it because they do more than passively consume [information]. Instead, they co-create an adversarial fantasy, constructing antagonists to wage culture wars, which is a highly engaging activity" (p. 29). Again, the continuance of political polarization poses threats to democracy.

The misinformation and disinformation that is spread in echo chambers or filter bubbles contributes to polarization and divisiveness. The divisiveness is damaging, and Hobolt et al. (2023) asserted: "democracy suffers when such conflict solidifies and political identities crystallize into polarized groups who are unwilling to engage respectfully with each other" (p. 1). This solidification of political identities into opposing groups can hinder constructive dialogue and compromise, essential components of democratic governance. Similarly, Ruiz and Nilsson (2022) found that democracy was threatened by disinformation. They declared: "Disinformation threatens democratic institutions because it stokes and amplifies the divisions that polarize society, antagonizing groups that hold a different worldview" (p. 18). By exacerbating societal divisions and antagonizing groups with differing worldviews, disinformation undermines trust in democratic processes and institutions. The deliberate amplification of divisive narratives through disinformation campaigns can heighten social tensions and diminish the willingness of individuals to engage respectfully with those holding different political beliefs. For example, Malik and Peterson (2021) found: "that polarization and the increasing alienation from mainstream media among parts of the American population contributed to the convictions that drove the deadly Jan. 6 riot on Capitol Hill" (para. 13). During the 2020 election, much of the political rhetoric flowed through social media platforms, particularly Twitter, since Donald Trump had more than 88 million followers (Beer, 2020). Social media platforms played a role in escalating the political polarization, too. Overgaard and Woolley (2022) clearly stated that their review of literature revealed "recent research suggests that social media can inflame polarization" (para. 1).

Social Media and Political Communication

The rapid expansion and pervasive influence of social media have transformed how information is disseminated and consumed, particularly in the realm of politics. With over 5 billion users worldwide by 2023, and over 300 million in the United States alone, social media platforms wield immense power as conduits of political discourse (Dixon, 2023). Due to the scale, social media platforms must be responsible stewards during elections because, as discussed, the electorate is turning away from traditional news outlets. Traditional news consumption is declining while social media usage is increasing. Social media platforms are uniquely designed to allow individuals with similar views and interests to gather. Gao et al. (2023) explained: "Social media has three main features that make it the perfect environment for echo chambers: no geographical restrictions, no social cost to sharing fringe beliefs, and fellow believers can be found no matter how fringe" (para. 2). In a review of the literature concerning echo chambers, filter bubbles, and polarization, Arguedas et al. (2022) found "that exposure to like-minded political content can potentially polarize people or strengthen the attitudes of people with existing partisan attitudes and that cross-cutting exposure can potentially do the same for political partisans" (para. 8).

While social media platforms have been credited with empowering individuals by providing platforms for self-expression, raising awareness about societal issues, and facilitating political mobilization, their impact on democracy remains contested. In 2022, the Pew Research Center found that most people surveyed across 19 nations thought social media had "both a constructive and destructive component of political life, and overall most believe it has actually had a positive impact on democracy" (Wike et al., 2022, para. 2). Overall, the survey found that 57% viewed social media platforms as a "good thing" for democracy with the United States being an outlier with only 37% of Americans finding social media to be a "good thing" for the political process (Wike et al., 2022). Americans clearly found social media to be "divisive" (Wike et al., 2022, para. 3). The negative perception among the American electorate toward social media's role in the political process is due to its ability to create political polarization through echo chambers and filter bubbles, as has been discussed. For Americans, the 2020 presidential election (and its immediate aftermath) demonstrated a stark example of the negative role social media can play in the democratic process. Social media platforms were utilized to stoke anger and division that led to the attempted insurrection of the United States Capitol as former President Donald Trump pushed false narratives that the election had been stolen. Allcott et al. (2024) said: "Concerns about the integrity of the electoral process were widely aired on social media, including concerns about fraud and vote-by-mail, and social media played an important role in the events following the election, including the 'Stop the Steal' movement questioning the election outcome and the storming of the U.S. Capitol on January 6" (para. 1). Again, not all view social media as a negative player in the political process. Wike et al. (2022) found that social media have the ability to (1) inform the individuals; (2) accomplish political goals such as bringing awareness to important societal issues; and (3) serve as a conduit for self-expression.

Moving forward, addressing the negative implications of social media on democracy requires balancing the benefits of increased connectivity and information dissemination with mitigating the risks of polarization and misinformation. Clearly, promoting media literacy, enhancing transparency in content moderation, and fostering platforms that encourage diverse viewpoints and civil discourse are important steps toward harnessing the potential of social media as a positive force in democratic governance. Studying and better understanding these complex and interrelated concepts can also work towards a more informed and resilient democratic system, which is the goal of this book. The book proceeds in four sections: political rhetoric and electoral engagement, political misinformation and disinformation, political partisanship and polarization and political communication strategies.

Political Rhetoric and Electoral Engagement

In the evolving landscape of contemporary politics, the influence of social media on political discourse and voter behavior has become increasingly pronounced. The 2020 presidential campaign exemplified this transformation, where platforms like Twitter, Facebook, TikTok, and YouTube played pivotal roles in shaping public perception and mobilizing voter support. Together, the chapters in this section illuminate the complex dynamics where social media platforms not only amplify political messages but also redefine how citizens engage with and perceive political leadership in the digital age.

The 2020 campaign demonstrated how the norms of social media discourse have permeated political rhetoric. The endless scroll of social media feeds, with their constant barrage of updates and information, creates a rhythm of constant connectivity and amplified importance. This environment encourages a rhetorical style where issues are presented in a continuous stream, each one seemingly as critical as the next. In Chapter 2, Randall Fowler finds that the 2020 campaign—especially the rhetorical styles of Donald Trump and Joe Biden—provides a compelling case study on the use of polysyndeton, a rhetorical device characterized by the repetition of conjunctions in close succession. With its ability to link multiple issues and amplify their collective importance, Fowler argues that polysyndeton serves as a master trope and has become a defining feature of contemporary political discourse, reflecting the dynamics of modern digital communication and the broader political culture. Platforms like X/Twitter, Facebook, TikTok, and YouTube have popularized a communication style characterized by rapid, associative links between topics that creates a sense of urgency and collective importance among various issues, asserting that they cannot be addressed in isolation and for the necessity of major political change.

Donald Trump's use of Twitter played a significant role in influencing the 2020 presidential election in several ways: Trump used Twitter as a direct communication channel with his supporters, bypassing traditional media filters; Trump's tweets often served to mobilize his base and rally support for his campaign; Trump's prolific use of Twitter allowed him to set the agenda for media coverage and dominate the news cycle; and Trump frequently used Twitter to attack his political opponents. Aiming to understand the complex relationship between Trump's Twitter activity and public perception, Kalah Kemp and Myrna Roberts conduct a survey of American Twitter users in Chapter 3. The chapter shows that perceptions of Trump's tweets significantly influenced voter behavior, particularly among Republican voters. Parasocial interaction and identification with Trump were strong predictors of voting for him, suggesting that individuals who felt emotionally connected to Trump through his tweets were more likely to support him. This research highlights the importance of understanding the psychological mechanisms underlying social media interactions with political leaders.

Fandom, traditionally associated with sports and pop culture, has become a powerful force in political participation and communication with supporters displaying behaviors akin to fan culture such as wearing merch, attending events, and vocally supporting candidates. This convergence has intensified with the rise of social and digital media creating a landscape where political figures are treated as celebrities on Reddit, Facebook, and TikTok. Donald Trump's "MAGA" supporters, Vice President Kamala Harris's "KHive," Bernie Sanders's "Bernie Bros," and Andrew Yang's "Yang Gang" exemplify this trend. In Chapter 4, Emily Sauter examines the communication, narratives, tensions, and common themes within these citizen-fan communities. Sauter deduces that citizen-fans bring emotional investment, specialized knowledge, and community-driven participation to the political sphere, reshaping traditional civic engagement. No doubt, the convergence of fandom and politics has transformed how Americans engage in democracy and talk politics.

Political Misinformation and Disinformation

As discussed, in the realm of contemporary politics and media studies, understanding the dynamics of misinformation and disinformation is crucial amidst increasing political polarization and distrust in traditional media sources. In total, these chapters highlight the interwoven complexities of media consumption, political beliefs, and the dissemination of misinformation, providing valuable perspectives on the evolving landscape of current political communication.

A classic media effects theory is the Knowledge Gap Hypothesis, which states that segments of the population with higher socioeconomic status tend to acquire mass media information at a faster rate than those with lower socioeconomic status, perpetuating differences in knowledge and, consequently, disparities in societal power and influence. In Chapter 5, Ben Wasike employs the Knowledge Gap Hypothesis to explore the impact of socioeconomic status and political ideology on knowledge about elections, as well as the likelihood of engaging with elections-related misinformation on social media. Based on survey data, this chapter shows that in 2020 higher socioeconomic status, indicated by income and education, was positively associated with greater knowledge about elections and negatively related to engagement with misinformation. Further, the chapter determines that conservative-leaning individuals were more susceptible to misinformation and that interpersonal discussion on social media increased the likelihood of engaging with misinformation.

When considering social and digital media impacts, it is important to recognize that "media" is a plural noun and that "media" encompasses a diverse array of communication channels, each with its own characteristics, audience, and effects. Relatedly, media effects are conditional, meaning that the influence of media on individuals is not uniform or universal. Instead, it varies depending on a variety of conditions or factors, including characteristics of the media content itself, such as its format, tone, and source, as well as individual differences among audience members, such as their demographics, beliefs, attitudes, and prior experiences. Against the backdrop of increasing political polarization and distrust in media, especially fueled by partisan news sources, in Chapter 6, Todd R. Vogts and Jacob Groshek aim to understand the news consumption patterns of rural Americans and their susceptibility to misinformation. Based on in-depth interviews of rural residents in Kansas, the study finds that news consumption plays a significant role in the daily lives of rural residents, including radio, television, newspapers, news websites, and social media. In the interviews, participants expressed a pervasive lack of trust in national media outlets, attributing bias, sensationalism, and political agendas to them. Opinions varied on the severity of mis- and disinformation as a societal problem and many attributed its spread to political polarization, biased news outlets (both conservative and liberal), and the influence of social media. Additionally, the study suggests that efforts to combat mis- and disinformation must consider the specific news consumption behaviors of rural populations, which may differ from urban or suburban counterparts.

The January 6, 2021, assault on the U.S. Capitol shocked the nation and made manifest the deep political and social polarization in the country. In Chapter 7, Tyler Martinez and Majia Nadesan examine the motivations and perceptions of Trump supporters on the online platform "theDonald.win" that led to such an unprecedented action. This chapter concludes that the online activities and discussions on platforms like theDonald.win contributed to the radicalization of Trump supporters by reinforcing narratives of electoral fraud, media censorship, and existential threats. Correspondingly, these narratives fostered a sense of urgency and justification for extreme actions, culminating in the Capitol assault. This chapter emphasizes the powerful influence of online platforms in fostering political fandom and reinforcing conspiratorial narratives.

Political Participation and Polarization

From binge watching to debates, the third section of the book delves deeper into various aspects of political participation, polarization, and media influence. These studies collectively discuss the complexities of political participation in a media-saturated environment, where diverse media diets and partisan affiliations intersect to shape public discourse and democratic engagement.

Watching television and movies was the most common strategy Americans used to cope with the unprecedented stress and uncertainty of the coronavirus outbreak (Pew Research Center, 2020). Roughly 3 out of 4 (73%) said they watched TV daily to cope and another 16% said they watched video programming weekly. Two out of three Americans (67%) said they frequently binge-watched shows, defined as watching several episodes of the same TV show back-to-back (Yeomans, 2021). In Chapter 8, Sarah

Krongard and Jacob Groshek delve into the social and civic dimensions of binge watching. Their survey finds a statistically significant, albeit modest, positive relationship between binge-watching and both online and offline political participation. Notably, binge-watching news and informational programming emerged as a particularly strong predictor of political engagement. While binge-watching was not directly associated with political discourse, specific genres such as horror and news/informational programming were significant predictors of online political talk. Interestingly, discussing binge-watched TV programs emerged as a strong predictor of both online and offline political discourse. This chapter sheds light on the potential impacts of pop culture on civic engagement.

Going back to at least *The American Voter* (Campbell et al., 1960), scholars have long recognized the important role of party identification in shaping individual's political behaviors. In Chapter 9, Madeleine Montgomery, Freddie J. Jennings, Kathleen Coyle, Ariana Aquino, and Malloree Murdock conduct an experiment to understand how partisan cues in media messages influence individuals' attitudes and beliefs against the backdrop of significant societal changes in 2020, including the COVID-19 pandemic, protests against racial inequality, and heightened political polarization. Drawing on theories such as the Elaboration Likelihood Model, Social Identity Theory, and Motivated Reasoning, this chapter establishes that partisan cues significantly influence both the degree and valence of elaboration, with individuals exhibiting greater positively valenced elaboration when exposed to messages from their own party and vice versa for opposing party messages. The chapter reminds us of the powerful influence of partisan cues in political communication.

Debates were again a focal point in 2020 and millions of Americans watched the contests on both legacy and digital and social media platforms. Alongside the two presidential debates, the vice-presidential debate between Vice President Mike Pence and Senator Kamala Harris was the second most-watched VP debate in TV history with 57.9 million people tuning in on television alone (Fischer, 2020). While presidential debates have received considerable scholarly attention, vice presidential debates have been relatively overlooked. However, the 2020 election introduced Kamala Harris as the first African American and South Asian woman nominated for vice president by a major party, offering a unique opportunity to explore the role of race and gender in perceptions of campaign communication. In Chapter 10, Xavier Scruggs and Benjamin R. Warner investigate how attitudes about race (i.e., racial resentment) and gender (i.e., hostile sexism) influenced viewers' perceptions of Harris's debate performance. Additionally, the chapter examines the impact of the communication environment, particularly the presence of homogeneous or mixed chat settings during the debate. Scruggs and Warner show that racial resentment significantly influenced negative assessments of Harris's debate performance, even after considering partisanship. Hostile sexism, however, did not directly impact perceptions of Harris. Moreover, homogeneous chat environments, particularly among Republicans, resulted in more negative evaluations of Harris's debate performance, indicating a polarization effect. These findings underscore the importance of considering attitudes about race and gender in understanding how viewers interpret political communication, particularly for historically marginalized candidates like Kamala Harris. Additionally, the study highlights the impact of the communication environment on shaping perceptions of candidates, with homogeneous environments potentially exacerbating polarization.

Political Communication Strategies

This final section explores how political communication strategies shaped the 2020 U.S. presidential election. Viewed as a whole, these chapters show how digital media and political rhetoric influenced public perception, democratic engagement, and legal battles by reinforcing ideological echo chambers, amplifying disinformation, and providing a platform for political figures and surrogates to advance narratives and mobilize support.

Artificial intelligence and algorithms have not only changed how we consume political culture and information, but also which content and culture gets made in the first place. In Chapter 11, Yanjun Zhao analyzes how social media algorithms affect both the diversity and quality of content by prioritizing content that reinforces users' preferences, leading to an "echo chamber" effect where diverse perspectives are underrepresented. Additionally, algorithms may amplify anger-inducing, sensational, and extreme content making political discussions more contentious and less constructive, undermining the foundation of informed democratic participation. The chapter proposes several ways forward, such as developing media literacy and critical thinking, regulatory and platform-level interventions that prioritize a healthy information environment and viewpoint-neutral news exposure, and creating online spaces for balanced debates and dialogue across ideological perspectives.

One impact of the widespread disinformation in the 2020 political media-politics ecosystem was the high-profile defamation suits filed by Dominion

Voting Systems and Smartmatic Corporation. In Chapter 12, Juliet Dee focuses on the defamatory claims made by Fox News, Newsmax, and One America News Network and how they were extensively echoed on social media platforms like Twitter, Facebook, YouTube, Instagram, Parler, and Rumble, leading to widespread belief in the election fraud narrative among Trump supporters. By examining these cases, this chapter explains the significant role social media played in propagating false narratives and amplifying disinformation, ultimately influencing public perception and behavior during the post-2020 election period.

Mirroring society, political communication is constantly evolving. One notable development in 2020 was the candidacy and rhetoric of Pete Buttigieg. Pete Buttigieg's campaign for president in 2020 was notable for several reasons. Buttigieg went from being relatively unknown on the national stage to becoming a top-tier candidate in the Democratic primary race. His ability to gain traction and compete with more established politicians, despite being the mayor of a midsize city (South Bend, Indiana), was impressive. Buttigieg's campaign was also historic as he was the first openly gay candidate to launch a major campaign for the presidency of the United States. This represented a significant milestone in LGBTQ+ representation in American politics. While he didn't secure the nomination, Buttigieg went on to be one of the most prominent surrogates as Joe Biden's Secretary of Transportation. Like other well-known political spouses, Buttigieg's husband, Chasten, was also active on social media, focusing on LGBTQ+ advocacy. In Chapter 13, Christopher J. McCollough analyzes the tweets of Pete and Chasten Buttigieg to understand their approaches to political surrogacy and issue advocacy. The chapter highlights the effective use of Twitter by Pete Buttigieg as a political surrogate for the Biden administration's infrastructure and policy agendas and Chasten Buttigieg's advocacy for LGBTQ+ rights demonstrates the potential of political spouses to engage in issue advocacy on social media platforms. The study underscores the importance of representation in political communication and reveals that political figures and their spouses play a crucial role in normalizing diversity in political and public life.

The January 6, 2021, attack on the U.S. Capitol was not spontaneous. It was a result of the "Stop the Steal" movement, a months-long disinformation campaign, promoted by President Donald Trump and incorporating a wide range of supporting groups. The movement's central claim was that the election had been stolen from Trump through widespread voter fraud, despite a lack of evidence supporting this assertion. In Chapter 14, Joseph P. Zompetti investigates how the "Stop the Steal" movement evolved and functioned as a rhetorical strategy to challenge the legitimacy of the 2020 presidential election results. Through a systematic analysis of social media posts using the #StopTheSteal hashtag, the chapter identifies how Trump supporters spread their beliefs in widespread election fraud, used appeals to patriotism and to defending democracy, framed the opposition as enemies, and justified potential violence during the January 6 rally. This chapter is another example of the deep divisions within American society and the potential for online platforms to exacerbate conspiracy theories and polarization by reinforcing ideological echo chambers.

Conclusion

While the fundamentals of political communication remain rooted in persuasion and engagement, the dynamics of modern media demand continuous adaptation, innovation, and examination. Looking ahead to future U.S. presidential elections, these principles are more relevant than ever. The advent of digital and social media platforms continues to reshape political discourse, offering unprecedented opportunities for direct voter engagement and mobilization. However, this digital era also brings challenges such as echo chambers, filter bubbles, and the proliferation of misinformation and disinformation. These factors have contributed to heightened political polarization, where individuals increasingly gravitate towards information that confirms their existing beliefs, leading to a fragmented media landscape and a more polarized electorate. In the 2020 election cycle, social media platforms played a pivotal role in disseminating political messages, mobilizing supporters, and shaping public opinion. Yet, they also amplified divisions and misinformation, culminating in events like the January 6 Capitol insurrection, fueled in part by false narratives of election fraud spread online. Addressing these issues becomes imperative for safeguarding democratic processes and fostering informed civic engagement. Looking forward, political communication will continue to evolve alongside technological advancements and shifts in media consumption habits.

References

Allcott, H., Gentzkow, M., & Tucker, J. A. (2024, May 13). The effects of Facebook and Instagram on the 2020 election: A deactivation experiment. *PNAS*, *121*(21), Article e2321584121. https://doi.org/10.1073/pnas.2321584121

Arguedas, A. R., Robertson, C. T., Fletcher, R., & Nielsen, R. K. (2022, January 19). Echo chambers, filter bubbles, and polarisation: A literature review. *Reuters Institute, University of Oxford*. https://reutersinstitute.politics.ox.ac.uk/echo-chambers-filter-bubbles-and-polarisation-literature-review

Avin, A., Daltrophe, H., & Lotker, Z. (2024). On the possibility of breaking the echo chamber effect in social media using regulation. *Scientific Reports*. *14*, Article 1107. https://doi.org/10.1038/s41598-023-50850-6

Beer, T. (2020, December 15). Trump suddenly loses 220,000 Twitter followers—First big drop in 5 years. *Forbes*. https://www.forbes.com/sites/tommybeer/2020/12/05/trump-suddenly-loses-220000-twitter-followers-first-big-drop-in-5-years/

Bennett, W. L., & Livingston, S. (2018). The disinformation order: Disruptive communication and the decline of Democratic institutions. *European Journal of Communication*, *33*(2), 122–139. https://doi.org/10.1177/0267323118760317

Benson, T. (2023, January 20). The small but mighty danger of echo chamber extremism. *Wired.com*. https://www.wired.com/story/media-echo-chamber-extremism/

Brenan, M. (2022, October 18). Americans' trust in media remains near record low. *Gallup*. https://news.gallup.com/poll/403166/americans-trust-media-remains-near-record-low.aspx

Campbell, A., Converse, P. E., Miller, W. E., & Stokes, D. E. (1960). *The American voter*. John Wiley & Sons.

Denton, R. E., Jr., & Kuypers, J. A. (2008). *Politics and communication in America: Campaigns, media, and governing in the 21st century*. Waveland Press.

Denton, R. E., Jr., & Woodward, G. C. (1990). *Political communication in America*. Praeger.

Dixon, S. J. (2023, July 26). Social media – Statistics & facts. *Statista*. https://www.statista.com/topics/1164/social-networks/

Fischer, S. (2020, October 8). 57.9 million people watched the VP debate on television. *Axios*. https://www.axios.com/2020/10/08/vp-debate-tv-ratings

Gao, Y., Liu, F., & Gao, L. (2023). Echo chamber effects on short video platforms. *Scientific Reports*, *13*, Article 6282. https://doi.org/10.1038/s41598-023-33370-1

Grieco, E. (2020, April 1). Americans' main sources for political news vary by party and age. *Pew Research Center*. https://www.pewresearch.org/short-reads/2020/04/01/americans-main-sources-for-political-news-vary-by-party-and-age/

Hackenburg, K., Brady, W. J., & Tsakiris, M. (2023). Mapping moral language on U.S. presidential primary campaigns reveals rhetorical networks of political division and unity. *PNAS Nexus*, *2*(6). https://doi.org/10.1093/pnasnexus/pgad189

Hobolt, S. B., Lawall, K., & Tilley, J. (2023). The polarizing effect of partisan echo chambers. *American Political Science Review*, 1–16. https://doi.org/10.1017/S0003055423001211

Jefferson, T. (1789, January 8). Thomas Jefferson to Richard Price. *Library of Congress.* https://www.loc.gov/exhibits/jefferson/60.html

Kelly, M. (2021, December 9). Political polarization and its echo chambers: Surprising new, cross-disciplinary perspectives from Princeton. *Princeton University.* https://www.princeton.edu/news/2021/12/09/political-polarization-and-its-echo-chambers-surprising-new-cross-disciplinary

Kleinfeld, R. (2023, September 5). Polarization, democracy, and political violence in the United States: What the research says. *The Carnegie Endowment for International Peace.* https://carnegieendowment.org/research/2023/09/polarization-democracy-and-political-violence-in-the-united-states-what-the-research-says

Malik, S. & Peterson, S. (2021, March 28). How U.S. media lost the trust of the public. *Canadian Broadcasting Corporation.* https://www.cbc.ca/news/world/media-distrust-big-news-1.5965622

McQuade, B. (2024, March 4). Disinformation is tearing America apart. *TIME.* https://time.com/6837548/disinformation-america-election/

McGreal, C. (2022, July 17). Broken and distrusting: Why Americans are pulling away from the daily news. *The Guardian.* https://www.theguardian.com/us-news/2022/jul/16/americans-avoid-news-reuters-survey

McNair, B. (2011). *An introduction to political communication* (5th ed.). Routledge.

Nimmo, D. D. & Sanders, K. R. (Eds.). (1981). *Handbook of political communication.* Sage.

Nivola, P. S. (2005, January 1). Thinking about political polarization. *The Brookings Institute.* https://www.brookings.edu/articles/thinking-about-political-polarization/

Overgaard, C. S. B., & Woolley, S. (2022, December 21). How social media platforms can reduce polarization. *The Brookings Institute.* https://www.brookings.edu/articles/how-social-media-platforms-can-reduce-polarization/

Pew Research Center. (2020, August 7). Americans oppose religious exemptions from coronavirus-related restrictions. https://pewrsr.ch/3gD8OYR

Pew Research Center. (2014, June 12). Political polarization in the American public. http://pewrsr.ch/1mHUL02

Pew Research Center. (2024, April 9). The partisanship and ideology of American voters. https://www.pewresearch.org/?p=45265

Ruiz, C. D., & Nilsson, T. (2022). Disinformation and echo chambers: How disinformation circulates on social media through identity-driven controversies. *American Marketing Association, 42*(1), 18–35. https://doi.org/10.1177/07439156221103852

Shea, J. (2022, April 19). Autocracies versus democracies: 7-3 at halftime, but a lot can still happen in the second half. *Friends of Europe.* https://www.friendsofeurope.org/insights/autocracies-versus-democracies-7-3-at-halftime-but-a-lot-can-still-happen-in-the-second-half/

Travers, M. (2023, November 21). How to break out of the echo chamber. *Psychology Today.* https://www.psychologytoday.com/us/blog/social-instincts/202311/how-to-break-out-of-the-echo-chamber

Wike, R., Silver, L., Fetterolf, J., Huang, C., Austin, S., Clancy, L., & Gubbala, S. (2022, December 6). Social media seen as mostly good for democracy across many nations, but

U.S. is a major outlier. *Pew Research Center.* https://www.pewresearch.org/global/2022/12/06/social-media-seen-as-mostly-good-for-democracy-across-many-nations-but-u-s-is-a-major-outlier/

Yeomans, A. (2021, December 1). Can traditional broadcasters lure audiences back from SVoD services? *Ampere Analysis.* https://www.ampereanalysis.com/insight/can-traditional-broadcasters-lure-audiences-back-from-svod-services

Zahn, M. (2023, November 20). 'Really worried': Meta decision allowing 2020 election-denial ads risks distrust, extremism, experts say. *ABC News.* https://abcnews.go.com/Business/worried-meta-decision-allowing-2020-election-denial-ads/story?id=104985165

· 2 ·

POLYSYNDETON, SOCIAL MEDIA, AND THE PRESIDENCY: DIGITAL CULTURE & RHETORICAL STYLE IN THE 2020 ELECTION

Randall Fowler

On an August 17 stage in Mankato, Minnesota, Donald Trump listed the dangers a Democratic presidency would pose to the country before a crowd of electrified supporters. "Joe Biden is the puppet of left-wing extremists," Trump (2020a) proclaimed, "trying to erase our borders, eliminate our police, indoctrinate our children, vilify our heroes, [and] take away our energy" (para. 2). Biden, he continued, would bring about a litany of disasters: "Destroy our second amendment, attack the right to life and replace American freedom with left wing fascism . . . [a] future of crime and chaos, corruption, and economic collapse that puppet Joe Biden would unleash on America" (para. 2). At this occasion, the third rally Trump held during the general election stretch of the 2020 campaign, the president invoked countless dangers presented by the Democrats ranging from the "China virus" to "fake news" to American cities being set "ablaze" by "the radical left." Weaving together innumerable issues, this performance exemplifies the rhetorical pattern Trump followed in the sixty-five additional rallies between then and election day. He enumerated an endless parade of horribles that would ensue should Biden win, which meant Americans should vote Republican.

Not to be outdone, three days later Biden (2020a) responded in his nomination acceptance address at the Democratic National Convention. Trump's tenure had created the "perfect storm," he roared:

> The worst pandemic in over 100 years. The worst economic crisis since the Great Depression. The most compelling call for racial justice since the 60's. And the undeniable realities and accelerating threats of climate change .... That's all on the ballot. (paras. 26–28, 41)

Biden then asserted that rather than address these problems, the sitting president had unleashed calamities upon the American people:

> Just judge this president on the facts. 5 million Americans infected with COVID-19. More than 170,000 Americans have died. By far the worst performance of any nation on Earth. More than 50 million people have filed for unemployment this year. More than 10 million people are going to lose their health insurance this year. Nearly one in 6 small businesses have closed this year. (paras. 44–50)

Biden closed by projecting these fears into the future:

> If this president is re-elected we know what will happen. Cases and deaths will remain far too high. More mom and pop businesses will close their doors for good. Working families will struggle to get by, and yet, the wealthiest one percent will get tens of billions of dollars in new tax breaks. And the assault on the Affordable Care Act will continue until it's destroyed. (paras. 53–55)

Like Trump, Biden direly forecasted that an untold number of catastrophes—each adding to the agony of the others—would afflict the nation if Trump won and "this chapter of American darkness" continued (para. 176).

While it may be tempting to dismiss these statements as the caustically over-the-top campaign rhetoric Americans have come to expect, they reflect deeper realities about each campaign and the communicative norms that inform U.S. politics. Whether measured in terms of their vitriol, threats, warnings, advertisements, or vocal delivery, Trump and Biden reached a new maximum volume during the 2020 campaign. Indeed, total money spent on the presidential race alone nearly tripled from 2016, to say nothing of congressional contests, inundating Americans in campaign messaging and negative advertisements (Schwartz, 2020). Whatever else they did, Trump and Biden seemingly achieved a new level of *amplification*, or an increase in the intensity of meaning associated with an appeal to maximize its rhetorical impact on an audience. Each of these performances and presidential campaigns comprised pure amplification.

Not only this, but both candidates activated a specific rhetorical device to amplify their appeals: *polysyndeton*. Polysyndeton is defined as the repetition of conjunctions in close succession for rhetorical effect; it produces an overwhelming sensation through its use of connectives in rapid sequence (e.g., "here and there and everywhere"). It stands in contrast to *asyndeton*, the deliberate omission of conjunctions (e.g., "reduce, reuse, recycle"), as well as *auxesis*, in which words are ordered according to an ascending gradient of force (e.g., "he dribbles, he shoots, he scores!"). Polysyndeton, in other words, links issues, refuses prioritization, and amplifies overtures. It thus not only suffused the rhetoric of the Trump and Biden 2020 presidential campaigns, but also reflects the inner logic of a communicative culture saturated with social media to the extent that it is becoming a new master trope of American political discourse.

Social Media, Polysyndeton, and Political Culture

The 2020 presidential election confirmed that the advent of social media has profoundly reshaped U.S. political culture by offering new pathways for presidents and their teams to reach critical audiences. As Colin Delany (2023) wrote,

> A couple of decades ago, American politics doesn't look like it does now .... Nowadays, the political machine includes tech companies, data vendors, ad platforms, ad buyers, creative agencies and independent expenditure orgs aplenty, plus the staff and consultants who've grown up professionally trying to run them all. (para. 2)

Big tech, especially social media, has radically transformed the political landscape of campaigning, voting, and governing in the twenty-first century United States.

Yet as impactful as they are, the power of platforms such as Twitter/X, YouTube, Facebook, and TikTok extends beyond their ability to circumvent legacy media outlets and channel information directly to voters. Their collective influence surfaces perhaps most clearly in the ways that communication "in real life" progressively adopts the norms of online discourse. To detect these more subtle changes requires a close attunement to language, the shifts of which rarely map on neatly to cause-effect relationships. Following Marshall McLuhan, then, whose famous maxim admonishes scholars to "look beyond the obvious and seek the non-obvious changes or effects that are enabled, enhanced, accelerated or extended by the new thing," this chapter aims to show how the communicative norms of social media filtered into presidential campaign rhetoric during the 2020 elections writ large (Federman, 2004, p. 2, see also, McLuhan 1964).

Specifically, this study argues that polysyndeton operated as a master trope for both the Biden and Trump presidential campaigns. Polysyndeton comprises an excess of connective conjunctions, typically expressed as an overabundance of the word "and." For example, in his speech *The Strenuous Life*, Theodore Roosevelt (1889) called on men "to dare *and* endure *and* to labor" and praised "all men and women who are themselves strong *and* brave *and* high-minded" (para. 3). Thanks to his use of polysyndeton, Roosevelt's language did not arrange these attributes in ascending order but rather packaged them collectively. Joan Didion (1968) similarly used polysyndeton to juxtapose disparate sensations in her description of eating fruit in uptown Manhattan: "I could taste the peach *and* feel the soft air blowing from a subway grating on my legs *and* I could smell lilac *and* garbage *and* expensive perfume" (p. 336). Polysyndeton connects discrete phenomena, ideas, or issues and delivers them to an audience as a singular mass of undifferentiated experience.

Polysyndeton is consequently a device that conveys amplification while also defying hierarchical organization. It slows comprehension, drawing attention to each phrase or word joined together. It devotes, in the words of George Campbell (1801), "a deliberate attention to every circumstance, as being of importance" (p. 368). For example, the King James Version translation of Genesis 1 contains 99 instances of the word "and." This repetition, according to Phillips (1980), "is used to slow us down" as readers and "to have us weigh each word and phrase" (p. 35). Whether it appears in scripture, speeches, or journalism, polysyndeton challenges audiences by screaming "this is important!" while pointing at multiple referents. It joins distinct phenomena, directs attention toward them, and transmits them as an assemblage of issues linked by the word "and."

Because it does these things, polysyndeton reflects the dynamics of online digital culture. The "endless scroll" of a Twitter or Facebook homepage amount to an endlessly deferred "and," inviting users to look at this-and-this-and-this ad infinitum as they keep scrolling down. Unless the search terms are highly specified, Google's search function provides a practically unending menu of answers to whatever query users may input, implicitly telling readers that there's always additional information—an "and"—simply waiting to be discovered. Indeed, the internet itself is composed of an ever-expanding number of websites, by one count almost two billion (Wise, 2022). Social media platforms like TikTok, Twitter, Facebook, and Instagram literally construct their content by grouping the inputs of millions of users into a repackaged stream organized by an algorithm and consumed by other users; to use these platforms is to lose untold hours of time viewing just one more video, image, or post (and then another, and then another, and then . . .).

In all these ways, digital culture not only echoes polysyndeton but relies on this trope as a logic of arrangement and articulation. If, as Leslie Hahner (2017) argued, "tropes serve an ontological and epistemological function—a mode of representation that . . . becomes a way of organizing and constituting human expression and knowledge" (p. 23), then polysyndeton serves as *the* dominant trope of online digital culture, such that it not only organizes but also constitutes human experiences of social media and the internet. Stated otherwise, tropes structure the expression of thought, particular tropes organize the epistemic logic of a public culture, and polysyndeton constitutes experiences of online digital culture. And so, to the extent that American political discourse *also* begins to adopt polysyndeton as a master trope, it is a sign that the communicative norms that obtain in social media are architectonically shifting the rhetorical practices of U.S. political actors. The 2020 presidential campaign provides a prime case study to demonstrate that such a shift is indeed underway.

Although there are specific instances of Trump and Biden each deploying polysyndeton as a figurative device in their speeches, the tropological logic of polysyndeton—linking issues together, refusing to prioritize one issue over another, and asserting that all issues implicate all other issues—suffused the rhetorical style of each campaign, as the following analysis shows.

Polysyndeton and the Trump Presidential Campaign

President Trump's 2020 reelection campaign manifested the logic of polysyndeton in three main ways. First, the most obvious display of this trope in Trump's campaign rhetoric can be found in the opening paragraph of this chapter. Namely, Trump created impromptu lists in almost every rally address he delivered, using these moments to energize the crowd by tallying enemies, touting accomplishments, or issuing promises for his next presidential term. Polysyndeton served as a crucial organizational and amplification device for Trump's rally speeches, as he literally catalogued things periodically throughout these addresses at strategic points.

Trump's September 10 address in Freeland, Michigan, illustrates this tendency. Near the end of the rally, Trump launched into the climax of his speech. He cast a vision for his second term, enumerating the many ways in which he and his supporters would "keep on winning, winning, winning." He declared (conjunctions italicized):

> We will make America into the manufacturing superpower of the world, *and* we will end our reliance on China once *and* for all .... We will make our medical supplies right here in the United States, *and* right here in Michigan. We will enact fair trade deals that create American jobs *and* grow American wages. We will rapidly return to full employment, soaring incomes, *and* record prosperity, *and* that's already happening. We will hire more police, increase penalties for assaults on law enforcement— surge federal prosecutors into high-crime communities, *and* we will ban sanctuary cities. We will appoint prosecutors, judges, *and* justices who believe in enforcing the law, not their own political agenda. We will ensure equal justice for citizens of every race, color, religion, *and* creed. We will defend the dignity of work *and* the sanctity of life. We will uphold religious liberty, free speech, *and* the right to keep *and* bear arms.

These sentences display the ample use of polysyndeton at the most powerful moment of Trump's speech. Referencing various topics, Trump proclaimed that his leadership would restore U.S. manufacturing and end "reliance on China" and revitalize Michigan and grow prosperity and restore law and order and preserve equal rights and maintain American freedoms. By linking each of these issues with an "and" rather than structuring his discussion of them through cause-effect relationships, storytelling, or other organizational devices, Trump invited his audience to embrace his appeals as a single rallying cry. He continued this charge as he concluded:

> We will strike down terrorists who threaten our citizens, *and* we will keep out people, keep them out, of these horrible, horrible situations where they hurt our country, they hurt the people of our country, *and* we're also going to be staying out of the endless, ridiculous foreign wars in countries that you've never even heard of. We will build the most powerful missile *and* cyber defense. We've already got it, pretty much. *And* we will maintain peace through strength .... We will protect Medicare *and* Social Security, *and* we will always protect our patients .... America will land the first woman on the moon, *and* the United States will be the first nation to land an astronaut on Mars. We will restore patriotic education, you know what I mean by that—*and* we will teach our children to love our country, honor our history, *and* always respect our great American flag. *And* we will live by the timeless words of our national motto, "In God we trust."

Beyond the issues he had previously mentioned, Trump now raised a plethora of additional topics ranging from space exploration to terrorism to entitlement programs. By grouping these various issues, Trump articulated the logic of polysyndeton as he associated numerous issues on an equal footing. Perelman and Olbrechts-Tyteca (1969) argued that rhetorical strategies of association "bring separate elements together and allow us to establish a unity among them" (p. 190). Trump's use of polysyndeton in the midst of this address functioned exactly in this manner, uniting distinct topics into a rhetorical whole to amplify his appeals with the combined salience of all these various issues. He frequently deployed polysyndeton in this way to conclude his rallies; like a resounding orchestra, this device enabled Trump to end his speeches at fortissimo forte volume.

Second, Trump broached a bewildering number of issues, personalities, events, and policies in each of his rally addresses. Displaying a tremendous topical range, Trump brought up issues that might appear utterly unrelated, yet he inserted them into his speeches nonetheless. Viewed as an overall performance, Trump's speeches thus followed the organizational logic of polysyndeton. His speeches followed the pattern of him speaking about this-and-this-and-this-and-this and so on. Critically, he did not develop clear lines of hierarchy under which to organize these topics, but simply connected issue after issue in a manner that presented them all on relatively equal footing until he concluded each rally. Regardless of whether he actually deployed polysyndeton as a rhetorical device during each speech, polysyndeton operated as a structural logic arranging Trump's campaign addresses at his rallies.

For example, at his September 3 rally in Latrobe, Pennsylvania, Trump (2020b) invoked roughly 50 topics over the course of his address. While he circled back to several topics such as Nancy Pelosi's leadership, he more or less brought up each of these individual issues in this order:

1. Violence of summer protest rioters
2. Islamic State caliphate "obliterated"
3. Job numbers
4. Operation Warp Speed
5. Biden is a puppet
6. Sizes of crowds at Trump rallies
7. Election polls meant to depress GOP voter turnout
8. China "ripping off" United States in trade deals
9. Portland and Seattle anarchists

10. Trump ordering national guard to disperse rioters
11. Prison sentences for statue topplers
12. Radical left agenda
13. Bernie Sanders [I-VT]
14. Anti-fracking Democrats
15. Anti-gun Democrats
16. Democrat radical prosecutors
17. Law-abiding citizens in Texas, Florida, Ohio, and the Carolinas
18. Biden giving jobs to China
19. Biden basement campaign ("Joe Hiding")
20. Paris Climate Accord
21. Democrats want to "blow up" Mount Rushmore
22. Italian New Yorkers defending Christopher Columbus statues
23. Beto O'Rourke [D-TX]
24. Plastic straw bans
25. Green New Deal
26. Rumors about Trump's health
27. CNN = fake news
28. Nancy Pelosi [D-CA]
29. Conor Lamb [D-PA]
30. Mitt Romney [R-UT]
31. Steel tariffs on Brazil and Mexico
32. COVID-19 lethality rates
33. Border Patrol clash with MS-13
34. Iran Nuclear Deal
35. Moving U.S. embassy to Jerusalem
36. United Arab Emirates signing Abraham Accords
37. Russian and North Korean hostility
38. Biden's voting record
39. Mail-in ballot strategy
40. U.S. COVID-19 China travel ban
41. Suicide and depression rates from pandemic isolation
42. Blue state COVID-19 lockdowns
43. European response to COVID-19
44. Ventilator production
45. Swine flu
46. Russiagate
47. Ukraine (Trump impeachment)

48. Hospital price transparency
49. NASA (promise to reach Mars and put woman on the Moon)
50. George Washington being desecrated

This list demonstrates two points. First, Trump broached a wide span of issues in this speech, adding to the perception that his addresses achieved amplification by the sheer accumulation of topics he associated through his rhetoric. Second, the rough chronological sequencing of this list reveals the relative lack of hierarchy or organizational structure guiding the address. This shows how Trump tended to jump from one set of issues to another in relatively haphazard fashion. Trump leaped topic to topic within sentences and paragraphs for hours on end, thus illustrating how polysyndeton (this-and-this-and-this) operated as the organizational logic behind this speech and Trump's overall campaign rhetoric.

Finally, the 2020 Trump presidential campaign also exhibited the logic of polysyndeton through its use of presence. As Perelman and Obrechts-Tyteca (1969) stated, presence comprises "the thing on which the eye dwells, that which is best or most often seen," so it "acts directly on our sensibility ... The thing that is present to the consciousness assumes thus an importance that the theory and practice of argumentation must take into consideration." Adept rhetors, they wrote, generate presence "to enhance the value" of their arguments and so recognize how it provides "an essential element in argumentation" (pp. 116–117). By the same token, Patricia-Roberts-Miller (2017) observed that demagogic rhetoric manipulates an audience's sense of presence "by keeping the attention" (p. 55) on a subject matter the rhetor has strategically chosen, whether that be to distract listeners from the rhetor's shortcomings or to generate outrage by fixing attention on the scandal of a political rival. Trump displayed a masterful ability to steer audience attention during the 2020 campaign through the sheer number of events he held—a dizzying 45 rallies in the three weeks before election day—as well as his constant presence in news coverage and online. He was, in tropological terms, here-and-there-and-everywhere over the course of the campaign.

To be sure, Trump's penchant for generating presence as a means to direct audience attention was not new to this race. Over the 2016 campaign, for instance, Trump received nearly $5 billion in earned media coverage as news agencies dissected his every speech, post, and election rally (Saba, 2016). In the words of communication scholar Stephanie A. Martin (2017), Trump employed his garrulous Twitter account "to make news, to react to news, and to object to news" (p. xiv) in a manner that rendered his words nigh omnipresent. More than perhaps any other politician at the time, Trump understood how to deploy his boisterous personality to generate presence on-and-offline, growing to become a practically inescapable persona across all channels of news media. As Scacco and Coe remarked in The Ubiquitous Presidency (2021), Trump gained "visibility not through traditional means but by going directly to the public via Twitter" (p. 119). The consequence was a presidency that maximized visibility and message control at the cost of antagonizing news outlets and unfriendly audiences, thus constraining Trump's political appeal to a wide swath of the electorate while increasing his overall presence among all audiences.

Trump's constant media presence and fecundity of speaking engagements generated a similar effect in the 2020 presidential campaign. By holding so many rallies, his physical appearances complemented his ubiquitous presence online and in traditional news media, working to create the rhetorical impression of a political candidate who was here *and* there *and* everywhere. In this way the Trump presidential effort of 2020 attempted to duplicate the almost suffocating sense of presence he achieved during the 2016 race, complementing Trump's tactical use of lists in his speeches and his broader tendency to invoke innumerable topics over the course of his rallies. In the process, his campaign yet again recapitulated the logic of its rhetorical master trope. If polysyndeton joins numerous phenomena, delivers them to audiences as an undifferentiated mass, and proclaims their collective importance, then Trump's campaign—from his speeches to his platform to his daily schedule—embodied polysyndeton from start to finish.

Polysyndeton and the Biden Presidential Campaign

Joe Biden's 2020 presidential campaign was not known for his boisterous performances, inescapable presence across media platforms, raucous rallies, or punishing schedule. Indeed, critics attacked Biden constantly for his lack of energy; *National Review* writer Victor Davis Hanson (2020) argued in June that the campaign's strategy was to "hide Biden in the basement till Election Day" (p. 1). Kyle Smith (2020) pointed out on September 23 that Biden had "called a lid"—a colloquial term for ending the candidate's campaign events for the day—before noon on eight different mornings that month, including the day before, a "bizarrely somnolent campaign strategy.... Who calls it a day at 9:22 a.m. besides Homer Simpson?" (para. 2). Rather than a constant, ubiquitous presence, Biden seemingly tried to stay out of the spotlight, perhaps as a model of the "normalcy" his campaign promised to restore to American politics. His campaign team accordingly promoted his candidacy through press releases, paid election advertisements, friendly interviews, and rhetorical surrogates such as Kamala Harris or Jill Biden rather than virtuoso performances from the presidential candidate himself. As a result, one might justifiably wonder what the Biden presidential campaign had to do with polysyndeton.

Yet while this trope might not be an appropriate tool to diagnose the rhythm of Biden's speeches, his jumps between topics in a standalone address, or the ambition of his campaign schedule, polysyndeton dominated the ideational content of Biden's campaign rhetoric. Namely, Biden's rhetoric consistently emphasized that the nation was experiencing not just one emergency, but several crises unfolding at the same time and whose effects could not be compartmentalized from each other. This premise informed every major address Biden gave on the 2020 campaign trail.

For example, on July 21 Biden delivered a speech outlining the economic component of his "Build Back Better" agenda. Biden (2020b) began this speech supposedly about the economy by claiming that Trump had not done enough to address the disruptive effects of COVID-19:

> We are in a child care emergency. It didn't have to be this way. That's why I'm calling on the President to get these facilities the resources and equipment they need—now. Enough. Each day the pandemic's death toll grows. Each day, in some states, more people test positive than the day before. Each day too many Americans are still out of work, losing hope. (paras. 14–18)

Having portrayed Trump's COVID-19 leadership as a disaster, Biden then announced his verdict: "Donald Trump fails the most important test of being the American President: the duty to care" (para. 20). Biden's speech conveyed a simple narrative of Americans suffering because Trump had not done enough to counteract the pandemic. One might expect him to next specify how he would have handled the situation differently and promise to change things once in office. Yet at this juncture Biden finally pivoted from healthcare to economics: "We can't deal with our economic crisis without solving the public health crisis" (para. 23). He then reiterated his overall economic vision, detailing how his "Build Back Better" agenda would address the myriad challenges of automation, globalization, and climate change through the development of clean energy, infrastructure modernization, and increased unionization before again returning to public health. Linking all these issues together, he used the language of crisis to assert a relationship among all these problems: "We are trapped in a caregiving crisis within an economic crisis within a public health crisis" (para. 48). Biden spent the rest of the speech propounding the ways his agenda would help health workers, which he argued would expand early childhood education and also create "shovel-ready jobs" for Americans due to the interlinked nature of the problems facing the nation. He thus promised to use "common-sense steps" to solve the crises at hand.

A week later, Biden (2020c) performed a similar maneuver in speech on the theme of racial justice. As he declared (italics added),

> I've proposed a criminal justice reform and policing reform agenda *and* I'm committed to working with the Congress to seeing it through as President. It's also about jobs. Good-paying jobs, financial stability, *and* building wealth for families of color and passing it down to their kids. It's about economic growth for our country, *and* outcompeting the world. *And* it's also about dignity for working people and the middle class . . . . Build Back Better will deal with systemic racism *and* advance racial equity in our economy. (paras. 49–52, 56)

Here again Biden asserted that the challenges facing the country were bonded together, such that by passing legislation to reduce racial discrimination and police violence his administration would also create "economic growth for our country" that would enable the United States to outcompete its geopolitical rivals.

These two speeches illustrate a broader pattern in Biden's campaign rhetoric. His "Build Back Better" platform, according to him, would solve all the nation's crises because all the nation's crises were interconnected on a policy level. Consequently, Biden's rhetorical pivoting from the pandemic to healthcare to jobs programs to racial inequality to economic growth all made sense within the internal, everything-is-everything logic of his campaign speeches. While more conceptually complex than Trump's slapdash hurdles from topic to topic, Biden's speeches presented a similar picture to audiences of a wide range of issues all coupled together into an epic "battle for the soul of this nation." (Biden 2020d, para. 49).

Viewed tropologically, Biden's rhetoric echoed the symbolic logic of polysyndeton on the levels of problem and solution. On the first level, all the crises facing the United States were interlinked and equally challenging for the country. This reading of the political situation posed that this-problem-and-this-problem-and-this-problem were all connected, urgent, and cataclysmic. In other words, under Biden's framing racial injustice and jobs growth and the pandemic response were all related to climate change (and vice versa). All these crises were—at least rhetorically—a singular set of interconnected problems that could not be independently addressed in isolation.

By the same token, all the solutions Biden presented for those problems were interdependent as well. Under this rubric, to address climate change was to address racial injustice, create jobs, and so on. The Build Back Better plan would solve each issue equally, in Biden's telling, such that Trump's poor handling of the pandemic = racial injustice = bad economic policy, and Biden's proposals = good pandemic policy = racial justice = good economic planning. Biden's platform reflected the logic of polysyndeton insofar as it promised to solve multiple national crises (this-and-this-and-this) without placing one policy priority above another.

From an audience standpoint, Biden's speeches functioned as a rhetorical plea to support him on healthcare and racial justice and economic policy and climate change and the pandemic response because each issue was inextricably linked to the others. This formula structurally mirrored the symbolic movement of polysyndeton. He associated numerous issues, refused to differentiate among them, and delivered them to his audience as one singular mass appeal.

On a strategic level, the language of crisis Biden used to associate these topics had three clear advantages. First, the invocation of a crisis is typically a presidential rhetorical act (Stogsdill, 2013; Windt 1973), so Biden may have appeared more presidential to the electorate by declaring the existence of these crises. Second, the rhetoric of crisis forestalls criticism; as Jim Kuypers (1997) noted, the declaration of a crisis amounts to a request by the leader "for his decision to be supported, not for debate upon what should be done" (p. 8). Lastly, crisis rhetoric operates as an amplification device, calling urgent attention to the rhetor's demands. As Denise Bostdorff (1994) observed, "The word *crisis*, for instance, defines an issue as especially threatening, which helps an advocate focus the attention of citizens . . . The ominous character of crisis also encourages auditors to unite in support of a policy that will bring the crisis to an end" (p. 5). In this case, Biden's rhetoric of crisis worked to amplify fears over the political situation and called on citizens to vote for him to solve the national crisis. By proclaiming the existence of multiple interconnected crises—relying on an implicit level on polysyndeton—his words elevated the stakes of the election to a deafening roar.

Biden (2020e) followed this rhetorical formula throughout the fall. On August 31, he declared,

> We need justice in America. And we need safety in America. We are facing multiple crises–crises that, under Donald Trump, keep multiplying. COVID. Economic devastation. Unwarranted police violence. Emboldened white nationalists. A reckoning on race. Declining faith in a bright American future. The common thread? An incumbent president who makes things worse, not better. (paras. 18–27).

Biden's speech blamed Trump for the lack of justice *and* safety *and* equality *and* health *and* faith in the nation, framing these issues as interlocked calamities demanding urgent action at the voting booth.

His reliance on polysyndeton as an organizational logic for his 2020 campaign rhetoric also came across clearly in a September 14 address on climate. Biden (2020f) proclaimed,

> And none of this happens in a vacuum. A recent study showed air pollution is linked with an increased risk of death from COVID-19. Our economy can't recover if we don't build back with more resiliency to withstand extreme weather—extreme weather that will only come with more frequency. The unrelenting impact of climate change affects every single one of us. But too often the brunt falls disproportionately on communities of color, exacerbating the need for environmental justice. These are the interlocking crises of our time. (paras. 37–41)

Each negative aspect of the national situation (this-and-this-and-this) was inextricably connected to all the others; racial injustice, economic growth, and COVID-19 were all part of the climate crisis (and vice versa) according to Biden.

This theme appeared in Biden's campaign rhetoric no matter where he was speaking, as a pair of October speeches illustrates. In Florida, Biden (2020g) connected jobs policy and social justice and economic growth and climate change:

> But true justice is also about economic justice: schools, housing, access to capital, good-paying jobs with at least a $15 an hour minimum wage, financial stability .... Combating climate change means jobs. We can unleash American ingenuity and manufacturing to build a stronger and more climate-resilient nation, creating millions of new, high-paying union jobs. (paras. 57, 80–81)

Biden (2020h) associated even more issues in an address delivered in Flint, Michigan, working to assert linkages among support for the military, climate change, racial justice, infrastructure policy, jobs, and pollution:

> We must support our military. Let's vote for them. And we have to vote to meet the climate crisis. Donald Trump calls it a hoax. I see it as jobs and health and safety.

The impacts of climate change too often fall disproportionately on communities of color. We'll make sure these communities benefit from hundreds of billions in federal investments in infrastructure and climate change. That will create local jobs to rebuild roads, fill the sidewalk cracks, install broadband, and create spaces to live, work, and play safely. To modernize infrastructure so you can turn on the faucet, and clean water comes out and what happens in Flint never happens again . . . I will also hold polluters accountable with the most ambitious environmental justice agenda ever. And we will act to deliver racial justice in America. (paras. 93–101)

Polysyndeton is impossible to ignore in these passages. Biden promised to do this-and-this-and-this, which he declared would solve that-and-that-and-that. More crucially, however, Biden and his campaign team continually formulated their appeals using the rhetoric of crisis to assert a relationship among all these issues. In doing so, Biden interpreted each plank of his platform as an interrelated response to an overarching emergency whose deleterious effects could not be addressed in isolation, thus imploring voters to support him not for just one issue but all issues. Each problem, Biden asserted, was a part of each other problem, which his platform would solve.

Conclusion

The 2020 election will not be remembered for the eloquent words of these presidential aspirants. Their campaigns remain rhetorically significant nonetheless. Not only did each candidate offer a vision for the nation that found deep resonance with swaths of the country, but both Trump and Biden relied heavily on digital technology to reach and motivate supporters. Trump's Twitter account no less than Biden's videoconferencing signal the ways that political communication is changing in the Internet age. But as this chapter shows, the impact of social media on presidential campaign rhetoric takes more subtle forms as well. The foregoing analysis reveals three points of import for political campaign communication.

To start, polysyndeton is virtually omnipresent in digital culture; its logic informs everything from the interface of ChatGPT to the infinite scroll of a Facebook landing page. It equally saturated the rhetoric of the 2020 presidential campaign. Though each candidate's messaging evinced polysyndeton in different ways, this trope organized the core of both Trump and Biden's campaign appeals. To the extent contemporary political rhetoric has internalized the discursive norms that obtain online, it indicates a consilience between political and digital culture that may yet have far reaching effects for how democracy functions in the United States and elsewhere. In that sense, the 2020 race might furnish the opening act to a much larger shift in rhetorical norms as the political world adapts to the rapid advance of the internet in virtually every arena of life. While the 2024 presidential campaign remains underway as of this writing, this interplay between digital culture and political rhetoric signals how the symbolic logics that dominate life online progressively establish norms for discourse in other domains. One might expect not only the role of influencers, social media, and entertainment media in political campaigning to grow in the coming years but also for politicians and their communication teams to adopt the tropes of online discourse in their messaging as they seek to reach an ever more digitally native electorate. These dynamics suggest scholars of communication should expect political campaign rhetoric that is as unpredictable as the shifting tides of social media.

Second, the rise of polysyndeton as a master trope of political as well as digital discourse could help explain the affective intensity as well as exhaustion many Americans feel toward national politics. Rita Kirk's (2017) work on disruptive technology serves as an apt point of comparison. She built on the concept of "narcotizing dysfunction" introduced by Paul Lazarsfeld and Robert K. Merton (2000), which held that the overabundance of information produced by a mass media society would breed passivity and "unthinking conformism" in the minds of most media consumers. Yet, Kirk argued, "rather than being narcotized by so much information that the public becomes inert, current users have become so engaged in responding to information that they experience frenetic dysfunction: a need to respond without time for contemplation" (p. 26). Technology today, social media most of all, cultivates a public not that "is passive but that is overactive." In an era where persuasion is measured by response in the form of clicks, donations, screentime, and retweets, audiences are barraged with constant demands for attention and action. This, in turn, cultivates frenetic dysfunction, or "much action with little reflection ... too much talking and not enough listening and dialogue" (pp. 45–46) To the extent that political discourse mirrors the impatient dynamics of digital culture, it may be reproducing the same problems, leading to the extreme levels of both voter burnout and negative affective polarization—along with distrust in institutions and sources of official information—that define so much of the political landscape.

Lastly, the Biden and early second Trump presidencies suggest that polysyndeton will continue to operate as a master trope of political discourse into the foreseeable future. While there is not space here to fully explore the continuation of the trends analyzed in this chapter, examples abound of ways that Biden's rhetoric and proposals continue to be animated by the logic of polysyndeton. He spent his first summer in office laboring to pass a $3.5 trillion spending bill that would reform higher education, childcare, energy policy, immigration, healthcare, housing, family leave, K-12 education, and eldercare, opting to bundle all these issues into a single congressional proposal. He similarly touted the Inflation Reduction Act in the 2023 State of the Union address, crediting the law with not only reducing inflation but also decreasing prescription drug prices in addition to "lowering utility bills, creating American jobs, leading the world to a clean energy future" as "the most significant investment ever in climate change—ever." In foreign affairs, the Biden White House depicts conflicts in Gaza, Yemen, Ukraine, and Taiwan as linked theaters of a battle between democracy and its enemies. Biden's presidential record is complex, to be sure. But the insistence on packaging numerous legislative or foreign policy issues together and defending them as interchangeable parts of an interlinked whole reveals an implicit reliance on polysyndeton as a tool of statecraft in the White House, a reliance echoed in Trump's frontloading the entire legislative agenda for his second term in a single congressional reconciliation bill. Whether the rest of Biden's presidency follows the same pattern remains to be seen. What seems certain, however, is that the discursive norms of social media will continue to shape political rhetoric—including U.S. presidential campaigns—in impalpable and unanticipated ways.

References

Biden, J. R. (2020a, August 20). Address accepting the Democratic presidential nomination in Wilmington, Delaware. *American Presidency Project*. https://www.presidency.ucsb.edu/documents/address-accepting-the-democratic-presidential-nomination-wilmington-delaware

Biden, J. R. (2020b, July 21). "Build back better" remarks by Vice President Joe Biden on the caregiving and education workforce in New Castle, Delaware. *American Presidency Project*. https://www.presidency.ucsb.edu/documents/build-back-better-remarks-vice-president-joe-biden-the-caregiving-and-education-workforce

Biden, J. R. (2020c, July 28). "Build back better" remarks by Vice President Joe Biden on racial economic equity in Wilmington, Delaware. *American Presidency Project*. https://www.presidency.ucsb.edu/documents/build-back-better-remarks-vice-president-joe-biden-racial-economic-equity-wilmington

Biden, J. R. (2020d, August 12). Remarks by Vice President Joe Biden introducing Kamala Harris as his vice presidential running mate in Wilmington, Delaware. *American Presidency*

Project. https://www.presidency.ucsb.edu/documents/remarks-vice-president-joe-biden-introducing-kamala-harris-his-vice-presidential-running

Biden, J. R. (2020e, August 31). Remarks by Vice President Joe Biden in Pittsburgh, Pennsylvania. *American Presidency Project.* https://www.presidency.ucsb.edu/documents/remarks-vice-president-joe-biden-pittsburgh-pennsylvania

Biden, J. R. (2020f, September 14). Remarks by Vice President Joe Biden in Wilmington, Delaware on climate change. *American Presidency Project.* https://www.presidency.ucsb.edu/documents/remarks-vice-president-joe-biden-wilmington-delaware-climate-change

Biden, J. R. (2020g, October 29). Remarks by Vice President Joe Biden in Broward County, Florida. *American Presidency Project.* https://www.presidency.ucsb.edu/documents/remarks-vice-president-joe-biden-broward-county-florida

Biden, J. R. (2020h, October 31). Remarks by Vice President Joe Biden in Flint, Michigan. *American Presidency Project.* https://www.presidency.ucsb.edu/documents/remarks-vice-president-joe-biden-flint-michigan

Bostdorff, D. A. (1994). *The Presidency and the rhetoric of foreign policy crisis.* University of South Carolina Press.

Campbell, G. (1801, 1963). *The Philosophy of rhetoric,* (L. F. Bitzer, Ed.). Southern Illinois Press.

Delany, C. (2023, January 4). It's 2023. Consultants, welcome to the machine. *Campaigns & Elections.* https://campaignsandelections.com/campaigntech/its-2023-consultants-welcome-to-the-machine/

Didion, J. (1968). *Slouching towards Bethlehem.* Farrar, Status and Giroux.

Federman, M. (2004). What is the meaning of the medium is the message? University of Toronto, https://transformationdesignfall2021.wordpress.com/wp-content/uploads/2021/10/mcluhan-meaning-of-the-medium-is-the-message_highlighted.pdf

Hahner, L. A. (2017). *To become an American: Immigrants and Americanization campaigns of the early twentieth century.* Michigan State Press.

Hanson, V. (2020, June 30). The strategies of dementia politics. *National Review.* https://www.nationalreview.com/2020/06/joe-biden-campaign-strategy-hide-biden-stoke-chaos-obstruct-recovery/

Kirk, R. (2017). Revisiting narcotizing dysfunction: New media, interactivity, and rapid response in presidential communication. In S. A. Martin (Ed.), *Columns to characters: The presidency and the press enter the digital age* (pp. 25–49). Texas A&M Press.

Kuypers, J. (1997). *Presidential crisis rhetoric and the press in the post-cold war world.* Praeger.

Lazarsfeld, P., & Merton, R. (2000). Mass communication, popular taste and organized social action. In P. Marris & S. Thornham (Eds.), *Media studies: A reader* (pp. 18–30). New York University Press.

Martin, S. A. (2017). On Trump. In S. A. Martin (Ed.), *Columns to characters: The presidency and the press enter the digital age* (pp. xiii–xvi). Texas A&M University Press.

McLuhan, M. (1964). *Understanding media: The extensions of man.* McGraw Hill.

Perelman, C., & Olbrechts-Tyteca, L. (1969). *The new rhetoric: A treatise on argumentation*, (J. Wilkinson & P. Weaver, Trans.). Notre Dame University Press.

Phillips, J. (1980). *Exploring genesis: An expository commentary*. Kregel Publications.

Roberts-Miller, P. (2017). *Demagoguery and democracy*. The Experiment.

Roosevelt, T. (1889). The strenuous life. *Theodore Roosevelt Association*. https://www.theodoreroosevelt.org/content.aspx?page_id=22&club_id=991271&module_id=339361

Saba, J. (2016, September 30). Breaking views: Trump's $4.6 billion in free media. CNBC. https://www.nationalreview.com/2020/06/joe-biden-campaign-strategy-hide-biden-stoke-chaos-obstruct-recovery/

Scacco, J. M., & Coe, K. (2021). *The Ubiquitous presidency: Presidential communication and digital democracy in tumultuous times*. Oxford University Press.

Schwartz, B. (2020, October 28) Total 2020 election spending to hit nearly $14 billion, more than double 2016's sum. CNBC. https://www.cnbc.com/2020/10/28/2020-election-spending-to-hit-nearly-14-billion-a-record.html

Smith, K. (2020, September 23). Hidin' Biden and the invisible woman. *National Review*. https://www.nationalreview.com/corner/hidin-biden-and-the-invisible-woman/

Stogsdill, S. (2013). FDR and the victor-in-waiting strategy: Posturing oneself during a campaign as the candidate who has already won. *American Communication Journal, 15*(2), 29–43.

Trump, D. J. (2020a, August 17). Remarks at a 'Make America Great Again' rally in Mankato, Minnesota. *American Presidency Project*. https://www.presidency.ucsb.edu/documents/remarks-make-america-great-again-rally-mankato-minnesota

Trump, D. J. (2020b, September 3). Remarks at a 'Make America Great Again' rally in Latrobe, Pennsylvania. *American Presidency Project*. https://www.presidency.ucsb.edu/documents/remarks-make-america-great-again-rally-latrobe-pennsylvania

Windt, T. O., Jr. (1973). The presidency and speeches on international crises: Repeating the rhetorical past. *Speaker and Gavel, 11*(1), 6–14.

Wise, J. (2022, November 29). How many websites are there in 2023? *EarthWeb*. https://earthweb.com/how-many-websites-are-there/

· 3 ·

TRUMP AND TWITTER: A STUDY OF PARASOCIAL INTERACTION, IDENTIFICATION, AND SOCIAL PRESENCE

Kalah Kemp and Myrna Roberts

Considering former President Trump's use of Twitter in his first 50 days in office, this study explores how perceptions of his tweets influenced perceptions of his leadership. The results of this study attempt to explain Trump's appeal using blended media communication theories. This study also seeks to understand how Mr. Trump's Twitter use influenced the 2020 election, and by extension, the subsequent confrontation on January 6 at the U.S. Capitol. Other researchers have explored how tweets have impacted the Trump's presidency (e.g., Gross & Johnson, 2016; Lee & Shin, 2014; Rutenberg, 2016; Xu, 2018). The controversial nature of Trump's tweets merit investigation of how perceptions of his tweets influence other perceptions. This study begins with an overview of Trump's celebrity background, presidency, and credibility to contextualize the significance of his communication through Twitter.

Donald J. Trump's Background

Donald J. Trump, as a political figure, was influenced by his background as a businessperson and celebrity. Since the 1960s, some voters have accused U.S. politicians of self-serving corruptness (Dalton, 2005; Fukuyama, 2016), while others, including political pundits, have maintained polarized partisan orthodoxies (Fukuyama, 2016; Meyerson, 2013). These concerns help to define a political atmosphere where representatives are concertedly disjointed from voters in practice and ideology (Fukuyama, 2016). Trump's presidential candidacy in 2015 was a resounding answer for public distrust. While candidate Trump had never served in a political office, he had established a celebrity persona through his successful career in real estate and subsequent hosting of a long-running reality television show, The Apprentice. He therefore appealed to voters because: (1) a large section of American voters believed that candidate Trump was performing an important duty by provocatively tearing down the established order in Washington (Fukuyama, 2016; Morrongiello, 2016); and (2) candidate Trump's employment of Twitter drove social trust and community engagement (Ahmadian et al., 2017; Fukuyama, 2016), among other factors.

As a wealthy businessman and celebrity, Trump's 2015 announcement for the presidency was initially viewed as narcissistic and insincere (Ahmadian et al., 2017; Morrongiello, 2016), and his ability to handle the media was vastly underestimated (Kellner, 2016). His style was unlike the conventional methods of presidential politics where media elites served as gatekeepers and granted privileged access to the public and news agencies (Rozell & Mayer, 2008). Rather, Trump interacted with the public by using his previously established personal brand equity and by informally tweeting in relatively high volumes with a celebrity tone. The prevalence of his informal, celebrity-styled tweets was used to drive political news cycles (Ahmadian et al., 2017; Gross & Johnson, 2016). Together, this trend of his brand and tweets produced millions of dollars in media exposure for Trump's campaign, depriving his opponents of similar media coverage (Ahmadian et al., 2017). This was heralded as a key to his Republican Party nomination in early 2016 (Rutenberg, 2016). Consequently, Trump changed the tide of the 2016 election, overcoming sixteen professional politicians, to claim the Republican presidential nomination, and the presidency thereafter.

Trump's Presidency

Mr. Trump's primary campaign slogan for the 2016 election, "Make America Great Again" (MAGA) evoked a sense of nostalgia for a bygone era when, in the minds of many of Trump's supporters, America was more prosperous, powerful, and respected on the global stage, and at the same instance, a time in which White people were dominant over people of color in the United States

(Gonzalez, 2019; Scheurich, 2017). Many voters saw Trump as an outsider who would disrupt the political establishment and bring about much-needed change. The slogan conveyed a message of defiance against the perceived failures of the political elite and promised a return to a time when American leaders prioritized the needs of ordinary citizens. The slogan tapped into feelings of nationalism and patriotism, framing Trump's campaign as a movement to restore America's greatness and prioritize the interests of Americans over those of other countries. In that respect, political pundits were correct in their connotations that the MAGA rhetoric was a symbolic dog whistle of returning to a more oppressive time for marginalized people (Filimon, 2016; Weimann & Am, 2020). After winning the election President Trump did not abandon his MAGA campaign slogan. He continued to use MAGA to energize his fans and followers: "In Nashville, Tennessee! Let's MAKE AMERICA GREAT AGAIN" was tweeted by @realDonaldTrump on March 15, 2017. This March 15 tweet, posted by Trump as a private individual, was then immediately retweeted by the president, levying unprecedented communicative prowess, a shining example of how Mr. Trump exponentially raised his own personal power dynamic by using Twitter's platform engagement currency.

During his first 50 days in office, President Trump's Twitter usage accelerated, wherein he issued insults to those who disagreed with his executive orders, fired federal executives, criticized the Affordable Care Act, and vowed to defend the Second Amendment. He vowed to make America great again, despite later praising Russian President Putin, North Korean dictator Kim Jong-un, and other unsavory characters, all on Twitter. President Trump so overwhelmed the world's news cycles that the masses grew weary and cried for a return to normalcy.

Trump's Credibility

Perceptions of Donald Trump's credibility varied significantly among American voters, leading to stark divisions in public opinion (Pew Research Center, 2020). While many voters found Trump' unfiltered, often brash communication style to be authentic and refreshing, Trump's history of making controversial statements, often via social media, led many to question his temperament and judgment and allegations of unethical behavior, including accusations of fraud, sexual misconduct, and conflicts of interest related to his business dealings, cast doubt on Trump's integrity in the eyes of some voters (Pew Research Center, 2020). Factors informing this study that affected

Trump's credibility as a national leader include: (1) the fact that the election results in 2016 did not align with the popular vote; (2) his accusatory tweets that the news media provides fake news (Davis & Grynbaum, 2017); (3) his employment of family members and fellow industrialists in presidential cabinet positions (Liptak, 2017); (4) his insults of America's military allies and domestic intelligence agencies (Rucker & Miller, 2017); (5) his cordial rhetoric toward the Russian Prime Minister (Kutner & Saul, 2017); (6) his unprecedented abuse of, and attacks on the rule of law (Kravis & Liu, 2021; Ramirez & Clem, 2021); and (7) the overwhelming number of inaccuracies imbedded in the information dispersed within his tweets causing the constant need for fact checking (Rich et al., 2020). Despite Trump's loyalty to the U.S.'s historical enemies and his retweeting of falsehoods, several White House officials continued to defend Trump's sharing of disinformation and alternative facts (Riechmann & Sullivan, 2017). These inconsistencies, coupled with his lack of experience in a political office, merit critical discourse about Trump's credibility during his presidency and in the 2020 election.

Theoretical Framework and Construct

In addition to his credibility, Trump's celebrity influence is also a reason to consider his Twitter use. Employing a breadth of social influence theories, this study applies parasocial interaction (PSI), identification (IDT), and social presence (SPT) theories to discern factors that shape perceptions of Trump's Twitter use. This literature review reveals the main contentions of PSI, IDT, and SPT, how these theories have been used in recent scholarship, and how they have been examined in conjunction with credibility. Since Twitter has become an influential tool for political campaigns and presidential communication, PSI, IDT, and SPT shed light on how perceptions of Trump's credibility were influenced by his Twitter use.

Parasocial Interaction

PSI is defined as becoming emotionally and psychologically involved with popular media personalities because of repeated exposure to media programming (Brown et al., 2003). These interactions are characteristically one-sided and not necessarily related to logical discussion, ideas, and opinions. PSI is an imaginary, unreciprocated involvement with media celebrities or personae (Hartmann & Goldhoorn, 2011).

Over the last fifty years, political science scholars have described celebrity influence in politics as a gateway to elected offices for actors like Ronald Reagan, Arnold Schwarzenegger, and Clint Eastwood. Wood et al. (2016) defined "everyday political celebrities" as individuals who: (1) use two-way media such as reality shows with viewer interaction or social media; (2) are receptive to more spontaneous interactions as compared to planned, scripted interactions; and (3) are constructed as authentic, yet flawed individuals in their political roles. Former President Trump's well-developed media persona and use of Twitter classify him as a *celebrity politician*.

Recent studies in mediated effects have explored PSI and repeated exposure to new media. (Ruoyun et al., 2016). For example, Ruoyun et al. (2016) found that Twitter users had higher intimacy in one-sided relationships with persons who tweeted more frequently about intimate, entertaining, and informative content. In a study of Chinese social media users, Yuan et al. (2016) similarly found that social networking sites positively affect attitudes in parasocial relationships. Another study by Chung and Cho (2014) measured how audiences build parasocial relationships with reality TV characters through social media. They found that reality TV leads people to perceive media characters as having a heightened sense of reality and are therefore more approachable. Trump's hosting of a reality television show, status as a celebrity politician, and social media use warrant investigation through the lens of PSI.

Identification

Identification theory (IDT) is considered because when an individual sees similarity or likeness with another person, persuasion is likely to follow (Kelman, 1961). That is, whenever someone attempts to persuade, identification is sought first. IDT was considered herein because both IDT and PSI describe forms of audience involvement. PSI explains perceived relationships with celebrities, but it does not extend beyond psychological attachment (Brown & de Matviuk, 2010). IDT, on the other hand, describes how individuals integrate celebrity values, beliefs, and behaviors into their own lives. Lasswell (1935) described identification in terms of symbols, those used by a person who perceives similarities between herself or himself and someone or something else. Symbols may be verbal or non-verbal representations, such as the way one would say "American" or reference symbols for it (Lasswell, 1935, pp. 36–39). Further, Kelman (1961) found identification occurs "when an individual adopts behavior derived from another person or a group because this behavior is associated with a self-defining relationship," forming "part of a person's self-image" (pp. 63–65).

It is important to note that while often studied together, IDT and PSI describe two distinctively different processes (Brown et al., 2003). In differentiating PSI from IDT, Cohen (2001) explained "identification lacks an interactional component" due to a lack of self-awareness in the process (p. 253). In addition to their PSI measure, Brown and Bocarnea (2007a) developed the celebrity-persona scale to test identification with celebrities. Brown (2012) suggested identification can reinforce "existing cognitions, emotions, and behavior shared with the persona, or the adoption of new cognitions, emotions, and behavior modeled by the persona" (p. 271). Relatedly, Cohen's (2001) descriptions are especially useful in identification within politics, where political ideologies may positively or negatively influence perceptions of Trump's presidency.

Social Presence Theory

Short et al. (1976) developed social presence theory (SPT) to describe how new media affect communication and perceptions of closeness, discussing "the degree of salience of the other person in the interaction and the consequent salience of the interpersonal relationships" (p. 65). Since Twitter is computer-mediated, interactive partners develop perceptions about each other's personae and closeness. If partners perceive encounters through Twitter as impersonal or distant, then communication becomes more individualistic and stifles relationship-building. SPT is most frequently used to describe educational, intercultural, and organizational communication (Kahn & Williams, 2016; Stephans et al., 2013; Wei et al., 2012). Further, the theory addresses how media influence individuals' perceptions of one another's identity, and therefore informs this study.

Researchers have applied SPT to explore how journalists use Twitter, the effects of politicians' Twitter communication, selective exposure to politicians, and how politicians may use Twitter to build social presence. First, Littau and Jahng (2016) found journalists with elevated levels of self-disclosure on their Twitter profiles were more likely to be interactive, predicting higher perceptions of credibility. Second, Lee and Shin (2014) discovered that when individuals followed a politician on Twitter and visited their profile, social presence increased, which in turn led to positive impressions of both the politician and their policies. Third, Lee and Shin's (2012) study used survey research to explore how social presence increased as politicians interacted with the Twitter community and influenced voting behavior. This research informed the present study, and hence, SPT was selected to determine whether individuals perceived President Trump as *real* based on his tweets. Fourth, Messing and Westwood (2012), specifically found that news gathering from social media led to heightened social presence and increased partisanship. Research has yet to intersect PSI, IDT, and SPT, so this study seeks to discern ways in which the three theories interact with one another pertaining to perceptions of Trump's tweets.

Credibility

Aristotle contended that it is necessary to establish credibility as a speaker in order for the audience to be open to persuasion. Credibility as a framework has been examined in recent media effects research and credibility is a construct often used to measure leadership (Gaur et al., 2012; Ohanian, 1990). Early experimental designs modified source characteristics to measure people's willingness to alter their attitudes based on opinion leaders (Hovland, 1953). Weimann (1994) found that opinion leaders are perceived as more qualified in their respective circles, and, over time, perceived credibility and source expertise promote reliance by audience members on these sources. Source credibility is a multidimensional construct. McCroskey and Teven's (1999) study of political and public figures measured competence, trustworthiness, and goodwill/caring. Similarly, this study uses Ohanian's (1990) credibility semantic differential measures across three dimensions—trustworthiness, attractiveness, and expertise.

Credibility and Social Media. Recently scholars have explored Twitter's influence on credibility. Jendoubi et al. (2017) found that Twitter's structure may have effects on user influence mediated by: (1) the number of Twitter followers; (2) the popularity of the user's tweets; and (3) the number of times the user was mentioned in others' tweets. Additionally, Ledbetter and Redd's (2016) study found that posting frequency influenced perceived celebrity credibility. This study builds on the aforementioned research to explore how individuals engage with Trump through Twitter. Understanding the implications of the link between social media and celebrity credibility is necessary for politicians to explore. To further understand this relationship, it is important to discuss Trump's Twitter use in the first 50 days as president.

President Trump's Use of Twitter

Trump's use of Twitter before and after taking office sheds light on ways that he used his celebrity persona to influence public support of his presidency and policies. Trump brought his Twitter savvy and millions of followers with him to the White House in 2016. Upon swearing in as president, he inherited the presidential Twitter account, @POTUS, which was established by former President Barack Obama, who posted 342 tweets in his last two years of office. President Trump grew the followership of @POTUS by 6 million within his first 50 days, totaling 26.3 million followers (Trackalytics, 2017). He set the tone for his Twitter use during that time, tweeting 300 times. Tweeting, he noted, "is working," and he was confident that his tweets would continue to become "breaking news" (FOX News Insider, 2017).

Throughout Trump's presidency, he tweeted 23,585 times, averaging 16 tweets per day (Madaminov, 2020). During the 2020 election, Trump's @realdonaldtrump account had 88.9 million followers whereas his presidential account, @POTUS had 32.8 million followers. Trump increased his use of @realdonaldtrump leading up to the 2020 election, often expressing concerns about the integrity of the election and accusations of voting falsehoods (Qui, 2020). Trump significantly changed presidential communication through his use of Twitter (Xu, 2018) and used divisive rhetoric to reframe American values (Kemp, 2019).

In this study of Donald Trump and Twitter, the expectation was that public involvement with him occurred through (1) PSI, relating to Trump as a celebrity politician with approachability; (2) IDT, assuming his political ideology would influence perception with likeminded supporters; (3) SPT would increase partisanship; all blended seamlessly with; and (4) social media credibility, which is etched deeply with frequent posting on the platform. Restated, it was expected that people who perceived Trump as someone they knew and cared about would also perceive him as credible and behave favorably toward his policies.

Based on the review of literature, the following research questions were explored:

RQ1: How did perceptions of Trump's tweets influence voter behavior?
RQ2: In what ways did perceptions of Trump's tweets influence perceptions of his credibility?
RQ3: How did Trump's use of Twitter impact Americans' perceptions of his policies?

Method

To examine the research questions outlined, investigators employed Amazon's Mechanical Turk (MTurk) to solicit on-line survey participants from March 10 through the 28, 2017. MTurk is a crowdsourcing website used by businesses and researchers to hire "workers" remotely to perform tasks. In 2021, Aguinis, Villamor, and Ramani explored MTurk to review its role in research and recommended best practices. They found that while there is skepticism about the validity of data, if MTurk researchers set appropriate qualifications of workers (survey participants), increase sample size, and carefully screen data, then they may benefit from the large and diverse participant database. The authors of this study sought a large sample size and carefully screened the data. They embedded a SurveyMonkey.com hyperlink into MTurk. Database parameters within the MTurk system and initial survey questions screened voluntary participants, selecting American residents with Twitter accounts. Participants initially were compensated forty cents; however, like a study by Buhrmester et al. (2011), higher pay hastened respondents' willingness to participate. Therefore, later participants were compensated fifty cents per completed survey.

Survey Questions

The seventy-four-item survey included questions that were forced-choice and scaled measures, encouraging participants to be attentive to the differences between the measures and stimulate thinking about their attitudes. Scaled questions assessed PSI, IDT, SPT, and credibility. One question requested participants to reveal who they voted for in the 2016 presidential election. Twitter-specific questions investigated participants' Twitter use and engagement with Donald Trump. Further, four general social media use and nine demographic questions were included.

Measurements

Parasocial Interaction

Brown and Bocarnea's (2007b) celebrity-persona PSI scale was used to assess participants' level of PSI with Donald Trump including twelve 5-point Likert scale measures. Each scale in this study was composited into one variable, and to assess the reliability of each measurement scale, the Cronbach's alpha coefficient was used. Reliability for the PSI scale was high (α = .911). Examples of these scaled questions were: "I would like to meet President Trump in person," "I feel I understand the emotions President Trump experiences," and "Whenever I am unable to get news about President Trump, I really miss it."

Identification

A second scale from Brown and Bocarnea (2007a), the celebrity-persona identification scale, was used to measure participants' identification with Donald Trump. Researchers chose 12 of the scale's 20 variables to use as five-point Likert-scaled questions. Reliability for the composited IDT variable is high (α = .969). Scaled items included, "What is important to Donald Trump is important to me," "I support those who support Donald Trump," and, "The things that make Donald Trump upset make me upset."

Social Presence

The social presence scale, developed by Lee and Shin (2012), was used to measure individuals' perceived closeness with Donald Trump. This composite variable comprised of a four-item, five-point Likert scale questionnaire, and was reliable (α = .842). Scaled items included, "I feel as if Donald Trump was speaking directly to me," "I feel like I am in the same room with Donald Trump," and, "I can imagine Donald Trump vividly."

Credibility

Ohanian's (1990) 12-item scale was adapted from a semantic differential scale into Likert questions to measure the perceived credibility of Donald Trump. For each of Ohanian's three constructs—attractiveness, trustworthiness, and expertise—four questions were asked. All dimensions were reliable (credibility-trustworthiness α = .982, credibility-attractiveness α = .920, and credibility-expertise α = .967). Questions included, "I think President Trump is stylish," "I think President Trump is honest," and, "I think President Trump is qualified."

Trump's Twitter Use

Six Likert-scaled questions were used to analyze perceptions of Trump's Twitter use. The Cronbach's alpha coefficient for perceptions of Trump's Twitter (PTT) was high at α = .963. Questions included, "I like to see President Trump using

Twitter;" "I like the ways in which President Trump uses Twitter;" and, "I like the frequency of President Trump's tweets on Twitter."

Twitter Behavior and Political Issues

Participants were asked about their Twitter engagement with @realDonaldTrump and @POTUS. One in three people followed @realDonaldTrump (34%) and one in four followed @POTUS (23.6%). Participants were also asked about their perceptions of Trump's issues including immigration, the environment, national security, and attitude toward the news media. The Cronbach's alpha coefficient for the issues (ISS) composite variable was reliable ($\alpha = .958$).

Results

Once the preliminary analysis was completed to form reliable composite variables, a Pearson correlation analysis and two hierarchical linear regressions were conducted to address the research questions. Each of these tests considered demographic variables, including age, biological sex, household income, ethnicity, education level, and political party affiliation of the survey participants.

Survey Participants

There were 470 participants, ranging in age from 19 to 71, with a mean age of 39.10 ($N = 468$), who successfully completed the survey. The participants were primarily women (56.81%, $n = 267$), and the participants identified their ethnicity as Caucasian (77.45%, $n = 364$), African American (9.57%, $n = 45$), Asian (4.26%, $n = 20$), Latino/Hispanic (4.26%, $n = 20$), and multiple races (3%, $n = 14$). Regarding political affiliation, 26.81% ($n = 126$) identified as Republican, 42.77% ($n = 201$) as Democrat, 26.81% ($n = 126$) as Independent, and 3.62% as something else. A moderate percentage, 47.66% ($n = 224$), voted for the presidential Democratic candidate, while 31.49% ($n = 148$) voted for the Republican candidate. A small minority voted for the Libertarian candidate (4.69%, $n = 20$), and 4.89% ($n = 23$) for the Green Party candidate. Approximately one in nine (10.85%, $n = 51$) did not vote.

Table 3.1, below, reveals the hierarchical linear regression (HLR) analysis used to examine perceptions of Trump's tweets and voter behavior. Voter behavior (presidential candidate for which the participant voted in 2016) was the dependent variable, and demographics, parasocial interaction (PSI), identification (IDT), social presence (SPT), and perceptions of Trump's tweets (PTT) were the independent variables. All the theoretical constructs were added to this model to discern whether they may account for variances in the data. This model explains 35.8% of the variance in responses based on demographics (R^2 change = .033), PSI, IDT, SPT (R^2 change = .317), and PTT (R^2 change = .343), where significance is at the $p < .001$ level (see Table 3.1). The strongest indicators of voter behavior were party affiliation, along with perceptions of Trump's tweets. Biological sex, age, annual household income, ethnicity, and education level were insignificant predictors.

In the second and third blocks, party affiliation remained significant. In other words, those who identified with the Republican Party were more likely than those who did not identify with that party to vote for Trump ($\beta = .048$, $p < .05$). When PSI, IDT, and SPT were considered, those who experienced parasocial interaction with Trump ($\beta = -.189, p < .05$) and identified with him ($\beta = .790, p < .001$) tended to vote for Trump. Perceptions of Trump's social presence had no significant effect. Further, in block 3, when perceptions of Trump's tweets were considered, those who had experienced PSI ($\beta = -.225$, $p < .05$) or IDT ($\beta = .459, p < .001$) with Trump were more likely to vote for Trump. Similarly, individuals were more likely to vote for Trump based on their positive perceptions of his tweets ($\beta = .366, p < .001$). This indicated that party affiliation, along with Trump's use of Twitter, influenced PSI, IDT, and voter behavior.

To consider the relationship between perceptions of Trump's tweets and perceptions of his credibility, a Pearson correlation analysis was conducted (See Table 3.2). The analysis revealed that correlations were all significant at a $p < .001$ level. This two-tail analysis revealed that positive perceptions of Trump's tweets were correlated with positive perceptions of his trustworthiness ($r = .899$), expertise ($r = .959$), and attractiveness ($r = .780$), all significant at the $p < .001$ level. Those who perceived Trump's tweets positively also perceived him to be trustworthy, hold expertise, and be attractive.

Finally, a second HLR analysis was used to uncover ways in which Trump's use of Twitter impacted American residents' perceptions of his policies (See Table 3.3). In this model, perceptions of Trump's policies as the dependent variable onto demographic variables in block 1, SPT, IDT, and SPT in block 2, and perceptions of Trump's tweets in block 3. The adjusted R square for block 1 was .155, block 2 was .828, and block 3 was .852. Compared with

Table 3.1: Summary of HLR analysis for variables examining Trump's tweets' influence on voter behavior

Variables	Step 1 B	Step 1 SE B	Step 1 β	Step 2 B	Step 2 SE B	Step 2 β	Step 3 B	Step 3 SE B	Step 3 β
Sex	-.321	.168	-.091	-.001	.143	.000	.013	.141	.004
Age	-.005	.007	-.036	-.006	.006	-.044	-.008	.006	-.056
Income	-.078	.056	-.069	-.057	.047	-.051	-.054	.046	-.048
Ethnicity	-.060	.056	-.052	-.029	.047	-.026	-.037	.046	-.032
Education	-.137	.082	-.083	-.013	.070	-.008	-.012	.069	-.007
Party	-.299	.103	-.139*	.149	.094*	.070	.102	.092	.048*
Parasocial Identification				-.334	.143	-.189*	-.398	.141	-.225*
Social Presence				1.201	.122	.790**	.697	.169	.459**
				-.146	.121	-.078	-.071	.120	-.038
Tweet Perceptions							.471	.112	.366**
R^2	.426			.331			.358		
R^2 change	.033			.317			.343		
F for change in R^2	3.44*			59.76**			17.72**		

Note: DV is Voter Behavior; *$p < .05$; **$p < .001$.

Table 3.2: Correlation between perceptions of Trump's tweets and perceptions of Trump's credibility

	1	2	3	4
Tweet Perceptions	-			
Trust	.899**	-		
Expertise	.899**	.959**	-	
Attractiveness	.739**	.770**	.780**	-

Note: *$p < .05$; **$p < .001$.

the first HLR analysis in Table 3.1, this model explains 85.6% of variance in responses regarding perceptions of Trump's policies and attitude toward the media. Demographics like sex (β = -.151), education level (β = -.107), and party affiliation (β = -.346) were all significant at the $p < .05$ level. Demographics were the weakest predictors of attitudes toward Trump's policies. Nevertheless, men, individuals with a lower education level, and those who identified with the Republican Party thought positively of Trump's policies. At the same time, women, individuals with a higher education level, and those who affiliated with other parties than Republican thought negatively of Trump's policies.

In the PSI, IDT, SPT block, age (β = .039) and income (β = .045) were significant at the $p < .05$ level. So, despite perceptions of Trump's tweets, older individuals and those with a high household income thought positively about Trump's policies. Once PSI, IDT, and SPT were considered, party affiliation no longer accounted for significant answer variations. Both IDT (β = .989, $p < .001$) and SPT (β = -.147, $p < .05$) were significant as well. This implies that individuals who identified with Trump perceived his policies positively, and those who experienced a high level of social presence with Trump perceive his policies positively.

Finally, in the third block, age (β = .040, $p < .05$) and household income (β = .047, $p < .05$) were significant. Perceptions of Trump's tweets were the strongest predictor of those who supported his policies. IDT (β = .677) and

Table 3.3: Summary of HLR analysis for variables examining Trump's tweets' influence on perceptions of Donald Trump's policies

Variables	Step 1			Step 2			Step 3		
	B	SE B	β	B	SE B	β	B	SE B	β
Sex	-.456	.135	-.151*	-.025	.062	-.008	-.014	.057	-.005
Age	.010	.006	.081	.006	.003	.039*	.005	.002	.040*
Income	.013	.045	.013	.043	.020	.045*	.046	.019	.047*
Ethnicity	-.043	.045	-.044	.001	.020	.001	-.005	.019	-.005
Education	-.152	.066	-.107*	-.013	.030	-.009	-.013	.028	-.009
Party	-.639	.083	-.346*	-.020	.040	-.011	-.059	.038	-.032
Parasocial Identification				.033	.061	.022	-.020	.057	-.013
				1.293	.052	.989**	.885	.069	.677**
Social Presence				-.236	.052	-.147**	.383	.046	.346**
Tweet Perceptions							.383	.046	.346**
R^2	.166			.832			.856		
R^2 change	.155			.828			.852		
F for change in R^2	14.01**			550.79**			70.19**		

Note: DV is Perceptions of Donald Trump's Policies; *$p < .05$; **$p < .001$.

SPT (β = .346) remained significant at the $p < .001$ level. This means that respondents who identified with Trump or who had experienced high social presence with him were more likely to support his policies. Also, individuals who think positively about Trump's tweets (β = .346) were likely to support his policies.

Discussion

In response to calls for more studies analyzing politicians through Twitter (Ledbetter & Redd, 2016; Lee & Shin, 2012), the primary goal of this study was to examine the relationship between President Trump's Twitter use on perceptions of his credibility. This study is significant to scholarship as it explores how PSI, IDT, and SPT mediate today's digital, political climate. The results in this study indicate that Trump's use of Twitter partially shaped perceptions of his presidency—influencing voter behavior, Twitter engagement with politicians, proclivity to support his attitude toward issues—and, in turn, swayed the ways in which Trump built his political celebrity persona. This study adds to current research insights into PSI, IDT, SPT, and credibility for celebrity politicians.

Theoretical Analysis

Parasocial Interactions

The results of this study show the relationship between PSI, IDT, and SPT as it relates to voter behavior and support of a celebrity politician's policies. Previous research has found that PSI predicts identification (Brown et al., 2003), but only correlation was found in this study. Trump's use of Twitter adds to a study by Yuan et al. (2016), as it shows that social media engagement leads to higher perceptions of PSI. The results of this study also support a relationship between PSI and IDT. Future research should explore how differing levels of PSI impact perceptions of Trump's candidacy in 2024.

Identification Theory

Positive perceptions of former President Trump's Twitter use increased identification as evidenced by voter behavior and policy support. Specifically, Trump's tweets significantly influenced Republican voters who experienced identification and perceived connection with Trump. Individuals who supported Trump's policies were influenced by identification with President Trump. This supports Lee and Shin's (2014) contention that when individuals follow politicians on Twitter, they are more likely to have positive impressions of both the politician and her or his policies. Additionally, Brown (2012) suggested that identification may reinforce existing attitudes and behavior, which is supported by the influence of political party affiliation and perceptions of Trump's tweets. This investigation found that identification and parasocial interaction with Trump were significant attributes affecting voter behavior. Further, this study revealed that identification with Trump, along with social presence predicted one's support of political issues.

Social Presence Theory

The next area of analysis was to explore how perceptions of Trump's psychological closeness influenced perceptions of his credibility. Social presence influenced individuals' support of Trump's political issues and attitude toward the media. It is important to note that while Mr. Trump's social presence is what made him popular in the 2016 election, it is also what antagonized many Americans during his presidency. Table 3.3 reveals a dynamic split in the second block where the beta went from negative ($\beta = -.147$) to positive ($\beta = .346$) in the third block on SPT, suggesting that affluent, men, or Republicans believed his policies were somehow unconventional, but chose to support the policies due to Trump's tweets. This study shows a strong correlation between PSI, IDT, and SPT and perceptions of Trump's tweets, yet, SPT seemed to be the least significant variable to explain voting behavior. More research is needed to investigate the relationship and interactions between these theories of social influence.

Credibility

Finally, Trump's credibility was explored. The results of this study parallel Littau and Jahng's (2016) findings that journalists with high levels of self-disclosure through Twitter predicted higher perceptions of credibility. Trump's tweets correlated with perceptions of social presence, identification, and credibility as well. This investigation also supports studies by Jendoubi et al. (2017) and Ledbetter and Redd (2016). Since Trump continued to increase followership of his Twitter handles, increase media attention, audience engagement, and tweet frequency, his Twitter use had a high influence on perceptions of his credibility. Though most participants did not like the frequency of Trump's tweets or his use of Twitter, perceptions of Trump were heavily influenced by his tweets. Perceptions of Trump's tweets was the most significant predictor of supporting Trump's political issues and influenced voter behavior as well. Future studies should investigate positive and negative engagement with Trump's Twitter accounts to discern the influence of engagement on perceived credibility.

Limitations

While the findings of this study are significant, there are several limitations the authors faced. First, the sample size is relatively small, making it difficult to determine the extent of which they describe the whole population. Second, while this cross-sectional study explores a topic through various theoretical lenses, it is limited to uncovering correlations and does not discern cause-and-effect relationships. In other words, while it considers variables that influence attitudes, it does not fully explain or predict voter behavior. A longitudinal study that hypothesizes about these variables throughout several election cycles might shed light on the implications of these intersecting theories and celebrity-politicians' communication. Finally, each measured construct was kept short to seek better data quality. Experimental studies examining one to two of these variables at a time would yield results that would add to these social theories.

This study contributes as an empirical analysis of Mr. Trump's success in establishing a world where tweets rang supreme over formal methods of communicating via executive orders and policymaking. Based on the high correlation between Trump's tweets and perceptions of his credibility, his publicity-styled tweets strengthened his relationship with voters. Restated, this study found that for celebrities all publicity may be good, but for politicians and their constituents, it matters whether the notoriety is good or bad.

Finally, researchers here found that people who perceived Trump as someone they knew and cared about would also perceive his policies as credible, channeled through PSI, SPT, IDT, and credibility constructs. Further research on celebrity politicians' usage of social media messaging should be done with a concentration on inaccurate and untrue statements rapidly disseminated throughout the biosphere. Situations where identification through symbolic discourse are quantifiably predictable, signaling that the blended scale established here is generalizable. It is imperative that scholars continue to explore aggregate effects of celebrity-politician communication through social media to better understand cascading implications on the future elections and future political climates.

References

Aguinis, H., Villamor, I., & Ramani, R. S. (2021). MTurk research: Review and recommendations. *Journal of Management, 47*(4), 823–837. https://doi.org/10.1177/0149206320969787

Ahmadian, S., Azarshahi, S., & Paulhus, D. L. (2017). Explaining Donald Trump via communication style: Grandiosity, informality, and dynamism. *Personality and Individual Differences, 107*, 49–53. https://doi.org/10.1016/j.paid.2016.11.018

Brown, W. J. (2012). Examining four processes of audience involvement with media personae: Transportation, parasocial interaction, identification, and worship. *Communication Theory, 25*(3), 259–283. https://doi.org/10.1111/comt.12053

Brown, W. J., & Bocarnea, M. C. (2007a). Celebrity-persona identification scale. In R. A. Reynolds, R. Woods, & J. D. Baker (Eds.), *Handbook of research on electronic surveys and Measurements* (pp. 302–308). Idea Group Reference.

Brown, W. J., & Bocarnea, M. C. (2007b). Celebrity-persona parasocial interaction scale. In R. A. Reynolds, R. Woods, & J. D. Baker (Eds.), *Handbook of research on electronic surveys and measurements* (pp. 309–315). Idea Group Reference.

Brown, W. J., Basil, M. D., & Bocarnea, M. C. (2003). Social influence of an international celebrity: Responses to the death of Princess Diana. *Journal of Communication, 53*(4) 587–605.

Brown, W. J., & de Matviuk, M. A. (2010). Sports celebrities and public health: Diego Maradona's influence on drug use prevention. *Journal of Health Communication, 15*(4) 358–373. https://doi.org/10.1080/10810730903460575

Buhrmester, M., Kwang, T., & Gosling, S. D. (2011). Amazon's mechanical turk: A new source of inexpensive, yet high-quality, data? *Perspectives on Psychological Science, 6*(1), 3–5. https://doi.org/10.1177/1745691610393980

Chung, S., & Cho, H. (2014). Parasocial relationship via reality TV and social media: Its implications for celebrity endorsement. *VX '14: Proceedings of the ACM International Conference on Interactive Experiences for TV and Online Video*. https://doi.org/10.1145/2602 299.2602306

Cohen, J. (2001). Defining identification: A theoretical look at the identification of audiences with media characters. *Mass Communication & Society, 4*(3), 245–264. https://doi.org/10.1207/S15327825MCS0403_01

Dalton, R. J. (2005). The social transformation of trust in government. *International Review of Sociology, 15*(1), 133–154. https://doi.org/10.1080/03906700500038819

Davis, J. H., & Grynbaum, M. M. (2017, February 24). Trump intensifies his attacks on journalists and condemns F.B.I. 'leakers'. *The New York Times*. https://www.nytimes.com/2017/02/24/us/politics/white-house-sean-spicer-briefing.html

Field, A. (2013). *Discovering statistics using IBM SPSS statistics*. Sage.

Filimon, L. M. (2016). From the dog whistle to the dog scream: The Republican party's (ab) use of discriminatory speech in electoral campaigns and party politics. *Romanian Journal of Society and Politics, 11*(2), 25–48.

FOX News Insider (2017, January 16). Report: Donald Trump to continue using @RealDonaldTrump Twitter account as President. *Fox News.* http://insider.foxnews.com/2017/01/16/trump-continue-using-personal-twitter-account-realdonaldtrump-president-not-potus

Fukuyama, F. (2016). *American political decay or renewal?: The meaning of the 2016 election.* Council on Foreign Relations, Inc.

Gaur, S. S., Tiwari, S. P., & Bathula, H. (2012). Ohanian's celebrity endorsers' credibility scale: evaluation and validation in the context of an emerging economy. *International Journal of Indian Culture and Business Management, 5*(2), 152–161. https://doi.org/10.1504/IJICBM.2012.045642

Pew Research Center. (2020, October 9). Amid campaign turmoil, Biden holds wide leads on Coronavirus, unifying the country. https://www.pewresearch.org/politics/2020/10/09/amid-campaign-turmoil-biden-holds-wide-leads-on-coronavirus-unifying-the-country/

Gonzalez, E. (2019). Stereotypical depictions of Latino criminality: U.S. Latinos in the media during the MAGA campaign. *Democratic Communiqué, 28*(1). https://doi.org/10.7275/democratic-communique.1688

Gross, J. H., & Johnson, K. T. (2016). Twitter taunts and tirades: Negative campaigning in the age of Trump. *PS: Political Science & Politics, 49*(4), 748–754. https://doi:10.1017/S1049096516001700

Hartmann, T., & Goldhoorn, C. (2011). Horton and Wohl revisited: Exploring viewers' experience of parasocial interaction. *Journal of Communication, 61*(6), 1104–1121. https://doi.org/10.1111/j.1460-2466.2011.01595.x

Hovland, C. I. (1953). *Communication and persuasion; Psychological studies of opinion change.* Yale University Press.

Jendoubi, S., Martin, A. Liétard, L., Hadji, A. B., & Yaghlanec, B. B. (2017). Two evidential data-based models for influence maximization in Twitter. *Knowledge-Based Systems, 121,* 58–70. https://dx.doi.org/10.1016/j.knosys.2017.01.014

Kahn, A. S., & Williams, D. (2016). We're all in this (game) together. *Communication Research, 43*(4), 487–517. https://doi.org/10.1177/0093650215617504

Kellner, D. (2016). *American nightmare: Donald Trump, media spectacle, and authoritarian populism.* Sense Publishers.

Kelman, H. C. (1961). Processes of opinion change. *Public Opinion Quarterly, 25*(1), 57–78. https://doi.org/10.1086/266996

Kemp, K. (2019). NFL national anthem protests: A cluster analysis of President Trump's tweets. In S. D. Perry (Ed.), *Pro football and the proliferation of protest: Anthem posture in a divided America* (pp. 115–128). Rowman and Littlefield.

Kravis, J., & Liu, J. K. (2021). The Justice Department and the rule of law. *Notre Dame Journal of Law, Ethics & Public Policy, 35,* 699–721.

Kutner, M., & Saul, J. (2017, April). Can FBI director James Comey untangle the Trump-Russia allegations? *Newsweek*. http://www.newsweek.com/2017/04/21/fbi-director-james-comey-russia-investigation-583154.html

Lasswell, H. D. (1935). *World politics and personal insecurity*. Whittlesey House (McGraw-Hill Book Company).

Ledbetter, A. M., & Redd, S. M. (2016). Celebrity credibility on social media: A conditional process analysis of online self-disclosure attitude as a moderator of posting frequency and parasocial interaction. *Western Journal of Communication*, 80(5), 601–618. https://doi.org/10.1080/10570314.2016.1187286

Lee, E. J., & Shin, S. Y. (2014). Are they talking to me? Cognitive and affective effects of interactivity in politicians' Twitter communication. *Cyberpsychological Behavior Social Network*, 15(10), 515–520. https://doi.org/10.1089/cyber.2012.0228

Lee, E. J., & Shin, S. Y. (2012). When the medium is the message: How transportability moderates the effects of politicians' Twitter communication. *Communication Research*, 41(8), 1088–1110. https://doi.org/10.1177/0093650212466407

Liptak, K. (2017, April 3). Trump's secretary of everything: Jared Kushner. *CNN*. http://www.cnn.com/2017/04/03/politics/jared-kushner-donald-trump-foreign-policy/

Littau, J., & Jahng, M. R. (2016). Interactivity, social presence, and journalistic use of Twitter. *#ISOJ Journal*, 6(1). https://isoj.org/research/interactivity-social-presence-and-journalistic-use-of-twitter/

Madaminov, A. (2020, November 24). All the President's tweets. President Trump sent 23,858 tweets. *Medium.com*. https://medium.com/swlh/all-the-presidents-tweets-e7d31fd1dbc6

McCroskey, J. C., & Teven, J. J. (1999). Goodwill: A re-examination of the construct and its measurement. *Communication Monographs*, 66(1), 90–103. https://doi.org/10.1080/03637759909376464

Meyerson, H. (2013, October 15). A tea party purge among the GOP. *The Washington Post*. https://www.washingtonpost.com/opinions/harold-meyerson-a-tea-party-purge-among-the-gop/2013/10/15/727ef4e8-35a8-11e3-8a0e-4e2cf80831fc_story.html

Messing, S., & Westwood, S. J. (2012). Selective exposure in the age of social media: Endorsements Trump partisan source affiliation when selecting online news. *Communication Research*, 41(8), 1042–1063. https://doi.org/10.1177/0093650212466406

Morrongiello, G. (2016, November 9). Trump triumphs, calls on Americans to unite: 'It is time for us to come together'. *The Washington Examiner*. http://www.washingtonexaminer.com/trump-triumphs-calls-on-americans-to-unite-it-is-time-for-us-to-come-together/

Ohanian, R. (1990). Construction and validation of a scale to measure celebrity endorsers' perceived expertise, trustworthiness, and attractiveness. *Journal of Advertising Research*, 19(3), 39–52. https://doi.org/10.1080/00913367.1990.10673191

Qui, L. (2020, November 16). Trump has amplified voting falsehoods in over 300 tweets since election night. *The New York Times*. https://www.nytimes.com/2020/11/16/technology/trump-has-amplified-voting-falsehoods-in-over-300-tweets-since-election-night.html

Ramirez, D., & Clem, G. (2021). Fortifying the rule of law: Filling the gaps revealed by the Mueller report and impeachment proceedings. *Northeastern University Law Review*, 13(1). https://nulawreview.org/volume-13-issue-1-preview/fortifying-the-rule-of-law

Rich, T. S., Milden, I., & Wagner, M. T. (2020). Research note: Does the public support fact-checking social media? It depends on who and how you ask. *The Harvard Kennedy School Misinformation Review*. https://doi.org/10.37016/mr-2020-46

Riechmann, D., & Sullivan, E. (2017, March 30). Russian experts paint sinister picture of Russian meddling. AP News. https://apnews.com/article/3aa5e6ab89f84bcbb01722f04810354f. https://www.washingtonpost.com/politics/federal_government/senate-intel-leaders-pledge-russia-probe-cooperation/2017/03/29/caea64ea-14df-11e7-bb16-269934184168_story.html

Rozell, M. J., & Mayer, J. D. (Eds.). (2008). *Media power, media politics*. Rowman & Littlefield.

Rucker, P., & Miller, G. (2017, January 21). Trump visits CIA headquarters after sharply criticizing the intelligence community. *The Washington Post*. https://www.washingtonpost.com/news/post-politics/wp/2017/01/21/trump-to-visit-cia-headquarters-after-sharply-criticizing-the-intelligence-community/

Ruoyun, L., Levordashka, A., & Utz, S. (2016). Ambient intimacy on Twitter. *Cyberpsychology*, 10(1), 72–87. https://doi.org/10.5817/CP2016-1-6

Rutenberg, J. (2016, July 29). Clinton's convention was made for TV. Trump's was made for Twitter. *The New York Times*. B1–B7.

Scheurich, J. J. (2017). Trump is the mask torn off of who we white people are and have been. *International Journal of Qualitative Studies in Education*, 30(10), 1053–1059. https://doi.org/10.1080/09518398.2017.1312612

Short, J., Williams, E., & Christie, B. (1976). *The social psychology of telecommunications*. John Wiley & Sons.

Stephans, K. K., Barrett, A. K., & Mahometa, M. J. (2013). Organizational communication in emergencies: Using multiple channels and sources to combat noise and capture attention. *Human Communication Research*, 39(2), 230–251. https://doi.org/10.1111/hcre.12002

Trackalytics. (2017, January 20). @POTUS. Trackalytics. http://www.trackalytics.com/twitter/followers/widget/potus/

Trump, D. J. [@realDonaldTrump]. (2017, March 15). In Nashville, Tennessee. Let's MAKE AMERICA GREAT AGAIN! [Tweet]. https://twitter.com/realDonaldTrump/status/842164356297175040

Wei, C., Chen, N., & Kinshuk (2012). A model for social presence in online classrooms. *Educational Technology Research and Development*, 60(3), 529–545. https://doi.org/10.1007/s11423-012-9234-9

Weimann, G. (1994). *The influentials: People who influence people*. State University of New York Press.

Weimann, G., & Am, A. B. (2020). Digital dog whistles: The new online language of extremism. *International Journal of Security Studies*, 2(1), Article 4.

Wood, M., Corbett, J., & Flinders, M. (2016). Just like us: Everyday celebrity politicians and the pursuit of popularity in an age of anti-politics. *British Journal of Politics & International Relations*, 18(3), 581–598. https://doi.org/10.1177/1369148116632182

Xu, Z. (2018). The rise of Twitter in presidential communication: An examination of the relationship between President Trump's Twitter feed and the media coverage of his first 100 days

[Doctoral dissertation, The University of Texas at Arlington]. *UTA ResearchCommons.* http://hdl.handle.net/10106/27670

Yuan, C. L., Kim, J., & Kim, S. J. (2016). Parasocial relationship effects on customer equity in the social media context. *Journal of Business Research*, 69(9), 3795–3803. https://doi.org/10.1016/j.jbusres.2015.12.071

· 4 ·

THE CITIZEN-FAN: THE IMPACT OF SOCIAL MEDIA AND FANDOM ON CONTEMPORARY POLITICAL ENGAGEMENT ONLINE

Emily Sauter

Fandom has provided fans with a number of skills for political participation—the ability to organize across broad swathes of people, tools for debate and deliberation, technical skills, leadership experience, and public speaking skills—all evidence that fans are primed to engage productively in the public sphere. In fact, there can be little doubt as to the efficacy of fans to engage in politics. For example, K-pop fans have been making headlines in recent years with their engagement in Black Lives Matter, from signing up for tickets to Trump's political rallies to keep real attendance low to signing petitions for a number of social justice issues. Looking deeper we can see fans working in any number of ways to improve their communities, whether that is donating money, creating content, or just bringing attention to a cause. There are many reasons to be hopeful that fandom can stand as a new avenue for people to participate in politics, especially in light of fading involvement in traditional institutions that have historically facilitated civic participation. Membership in churches, political groups, and other extracurriculars is at an all-time low (Jeffrey, 2019; van Biezen & Poguntke, 2014), and a growing concern is that with social isolation will come a loss of interest in civic participation (Putnam, 2000). Instead, we can see that fandom is one such avenue that has helped people fill that gap.

Many politicians have used the trappings of fandom to motivate fans—from Hillary Clinton's "May the Force be with you" sign-off at the end of the third Democratic Primary debate to MoveOn.org's Harry Potter political ads—and this, in turn, has influenced fans to think of politics in terms of fandom behavior. Certainly, a type of fandom has long been a part of presidential elections; people choose a candidate or party and throw themselves into supporting them—wearing buttons, stickers, and t-shirts; attending rallies; and exhausting friends and family members with their full-throated support. Yet with the advent of the Internet, political adaptations of popular culture slogans and icons, and modern fan behavior, we have seen a turn from supporting a politician to becoming full-on fans, and the consequences have the potential to fundamentally change how Americans engage in politics. Vice President Kamala Harris's fans formed the "KHive," Bernie Sanders' supporters formed the "Bernie Bros," members of Andrew Yang's "Yang Gang" still linger on the Internet, and, of course, the "MAGA" fans of former President Trump are ever-present. Members of these clubs do not include just fans but are also comprised of "stans," a term defined by Merriam-Webster (n.d.) as "an overzealous or obsessive fan, especially of a particular celebrity." For "stans," fandom and support of a political candidate becomes part of their identity. In a prescient article for *The New York Times*, Amanda Hess (2019) argued:

> We are witnessing a great convergence between politics and culture, values and aesthetics, citizenship and commercialism. Here, civic participation is converted seamlessly into consumer habit. Political battles are waged through pop songs and novelty prayer candles and evocative emoji. Elizabeth Warren is cast as a "Harry Potter" character and Kamala Harris is sliced into a reaction GIF. This is democracy reimagined as celebrity fandom, and it is now a dominant mode of experiencing politics. (para. 1)

What does this mean for modern American politics? Using 2020 as a case study we can see that this behavior encourages voters to think of their preferred politician not as a potential political representative but instead as a celebrity with whom they have an intense parasocial relationship and represents much more than just a political figure. In this chapter, I explore the connections between fans and politics by comparing fan behavior to contemporary American political behavior, explore the anti-fan side of political fandom, and discuss the potential impacts on future elections.

This chapter explores online fan behavior by analyzing social media-based texts, including threads, hashtags, videos, and other political content on Twitter/X, Reddit, Facebook, and TikTok, referencing four major political figures of the 2020 election: Donald Trump and MAGA supporters, Bernie Sanders and Bernie Bros, Kamala Harris and the KHive, and Andrew Yang and the Yang Gang. Taken together, these textual fragments reveal the multiplicity of fan communities surrounding these political candidates, the tensions and frictions between fan-based narratives, and the circulation of commonplace topoi taken up in different spaces and places.

I introduce the term "citizen-fan" to describe people who are fans of politicians and relate to them not just as politicians but as celebrities around whom to build a fandom world, in the same ways they build a fandom world around traditional popular culture artifacts, thus motivating them not solely as citizens, but as fans. I first examine the work done on celebrity politicians and the celebritization of politics, current studies on the intersection of fandom and politics, and then discuss fan behavior towards politicians using examples from the 2020 election to showcase how some fans not only created a celebrity community around their politician of choice, but elevated their actions from fan behavior to stan behavior. Finally, I close this chapter by discussing the implications of this behavior on forthcoming elections and possible directions for future research.

Celebrity, Fans, Fandom, and Politics

The field of celebrity politics has focused on the relationship between celebrity and politics over the better part of the past two decades (Bennett, 2011; Blake, 2016; Chatterjee, 2004; Cooper, 2008; Lin & Zhao, 2020; McKernan, 2011; Moon, 2020; Mukherjee, 2004; van Zoonen, 2006; Wheeler, 2012; Zwarun & Torrey, 2011). The foundation of celebrity politics is that the celebrity politician is importantly different from a traditional politician, so it follows that much of the literature examines how and in what ways the politician is different. A seminal work in the field of celebrity politics, Darrell West and John Orman's (2003) book *Celebrity Politics* focused largely on the overarching harm that is done to society as a result of celebrity culture in politics. John Street (2004) countered with a more neutral overview of celebrity politics and offered a simplified set of definitions where he argued for a distinction between the celebrity *politician*, a traditional politician who engages "with the world of popular culture in order to advance their pre-established political functions and goals" (p. 437), and the *celebrity* politician, an "entertainer who pronounces on politics and claims the right to represent people and causes, but who does so without seeking or acquiring elected office" (p. 439). David

Marsh et al. (2010) generated their own definition of celebrity politician by examining the nature of the political work in which they engaged. Critics of this position argued that Marsh and his fellow writers did not fully explore the "celebrity" in celebrity politics in that their categories were "between kinds of political engagement, not of celebrity enactment" (Street, 2019, p. 5). In response to this criticism, Wood et al. (2016) introduced the concepts of the "everyday" celebrity politician and the "superstar" celebrity politician to explore "the differentiated and often contradictory ways in which 'celebrity' is constructed" (p. 583).

These studies focus on the actions of celebrity politicians and how they build celebrity, yet the other side of this equation is equally important—celebrities must have fans. A fan is someone with "an intense engagement with a fan-object" (Hinck, 2019, p. 9), and fans and supporters are a fundamental aspect of the celebrity politician, without whom there would be no fame for politicians to capitalize upon. Fans allow a politician to gain celebrity *as a* politician, rather than a celebrity who becomes a politician. Importantly, supporters of these celebrity politicians must be understood as citizen-fans who engage in the political process not as supporters of a politician but as fans of a celebrity. As a result, political action and engagement then mirror the behaviors we see fans engaging in.

Traditionally, in modern democracies, political participation has been understood as a process in which citizens interact directly with the institutions of a nation-state, confining how citizenship and political agency are enacted. Verba et al. (1995), for example, noted that "political participation affords citizens in a democracy an opportunity to communicate information to government officials about their concerns and preferences and put pressure on them to respond" (p. 37). However, scholars across disciplines believe that the idea of "cultural citizenship" provides a wider framework from which to understand political participation (Cohen, 2010; Jenkins, 2009, 2012, 2018; Levine, 2015; Livingstone, 2005; Lopez, 2016). Brough and Shresthova (2012) argued that "over the last several decades, younger generations in particular have become civically and politically engaged in new and different ways, related less to electoral politics or government or civic organizations and more to personal interests, social networks, and cultural or commodity activism" (para. 3.2). Instead, younger people have turned towards the kinds of political participation that are focused around or based in online communities that are "informal, noninstitutionalized, [and] nonhierarchical" (Brough & Shresthova, 2012, para. 3.2). In these spaces, civic skills are often cultivated as a result of low barriers to entry and the participatory nature of contemporary popular culture. In his book *Convergence Culture*, Henry Jenkins (2006) argued that as early as the 2004 election citizens applied behavior learned as consumers of popular culture in their political activism. He wrote, "popular culture influenced the way the [2004] campaigns courted their voters—but more importantly, it shaped how the public processed and acted upon political discourse" (2006, p. 219).

Fandom scholars have taken up this thread in their work to understand the link between politics and fandom. "Fandom is not often seen as political, and particularly not in traditionally civic ways" argued Mel Stanfill (2020), and that though "research does not often bring the tools of fan studies to bear on politics," a traditional academic understanding of political behavior that does not acknowledge and include the power of fandom "cannot explain large swaths of social activity" (p. 123). Fan scholars first had to address the negative connotation of "fans" as illogically fanatical outcasts dwelling on the fringes of society (Duffet, 2013; Fiske, 2002; Jenson, 1992; Jenkins, 1992; 2006). Fandom instead, scholars of fandom have argued, should be understood as a cornerstone of contemporary life, and "as such the study of fans is now ... arguably, one of the most important devices for understanding the driving force behind what defines the conversation of topical issues" (Le Clue, 2023, p. 2) As Jenkins noted, where fans were "once silent and invisible" they "are now noisy and public" (Jenkins, 2006, p. 19), and we must acknowledge and understand the intersections of fans, fandom, and politics.

There has been a spate of recent research exploring these links in a variety of academic fields (Stanfill, 2020; Reinhard & Miller, 2020; Dean & Andrews, 2021; Allen & Moon, 2023; Le Clue, 2023) but I turn to Ashley Hinck's (2019) theory of fan-based citizenship, and Rob Asen's (2004) discourse theory of citizenship, as guiding works to examine how people have taken normative fan practices and thinking and applied them to politicians. Hinck's (2019) work is useful here in that it provides a strong foundation for examining fan-based citizenship practices in the digital world—where many of the fandom-based practices we witnessed in 2020 were located. In particular, Hinck (2019) illustrates how people choose fandom and popular culture to guide their civic actions in a new mode of citizenship that she calls "fan-based citizenship," which is defined as "public engagement that emerges from a commitment to a fan-object" (p. 6). Fan-based citizenship is rooted in one's experience as a fan and fan's motivations are tied to the deeply held love of the object of their fandom.

This builds on Asen's (2004) work on citizenship, which allows us to recognize these fan practices *as* citizenship practices. Asen (2004) argues that citizenship is "a mode of public engagement," which frames citizenship as "a process that recognizes the fluid, multimodal, and quotidian enactments of citizenship in a multiple public sphere" (p. 191). Using these two frameworks I argue that we can understand that the fan behavior demonstrated in 2020—the unwavering support, the near fanatic loyalty, the deep parasocial relationships—as a new type of political behavior, the citizen-fan, in which the objects of fandom are the politicians themselves and fans' political behaviors towards their objects of fandom are adapted from traditional fan-based behavior.

The Citizen-Fan

Catering to fan behavior by politicians or by political parties still does not quite acknowledge the behavior of the citizen *as* a fan. In fandom studies there is an agreement that "political practices are like fandom" (Stanfill, 2020, p. 127), in that common fan practices like discussion, activism, and community-building are foundational to democracy. In fact, Jonathan Dean (2017) found that "fandom is now an established feature of contemporary politics" (p. 409). In examining Barack Obama's 2008 presidential campaign, Cornel Sandvoss (2012) suggested that some "forms of political engagement ... are not *like* forms of fandom, but that *are* a form of fandom" (p. 69). Traditionally fandom has been understood to be centered around a fan-object that is some sort of popular culture artifact, such as books, television shows, video games, movies, sports teams, and celebrities (Le Clue, 2023). However, fan studies scholars now widen this category to include politicians as fan-objects, arguing that "fandom can attach itself to any source material, not only those drawn from the spheres of popular and high culture" (Allen & Moon, 2023, p. 1506). Hinck (2019) lays out four categories that define the fan experience and serve as the foundation for fan-based citizenship, which in turn also helps make sense of the experiences of the citizen-fan and undergirds their performances of citizenship. These categories are: (1) fans experience deeply held emotional and affective relationships towards their fan-object; (2) fans develop specialized knowledge about their fan-object; (3) fans participate in a fandom community made up of other fans of the same fan-object; and (4) fans engage in creating material products around their fan-object. Citizen-fans easily fit into these categories, proving that there is a growing group of contemporary voters whose civic performances are based on fandom-learned behavior, and we must understand this new civic behavior in order to make sense of the contemporary political landscape. The next section will discuss these categories and how citizen-fans interacted with their chosen political fandom in 2020.

Emotional and Affective Relationships

Affect is one of the characteristics that "most clearly define fandom" (Hills, 2002, p. 76). Many definitions of fandom across fan studies identify the emotional and affective elements of identity as key, including Sandvoss's (2005) definition of fandom as the "regular, emotionally involved consumption of a given popular narrative or text" (p. 16). Affect not only internally connects a fan to their fan-object but also results in material external performances as a way for fans to showcase their emotional tie to the object of their fandom. For example, in a TikTok video posted by @BernieBro69 (2020), the user lip-synced to a 54-second-long video clip of Bernie Sanders from the 10th Democratic primary debate held on February 5, 2020. In the clip facing the camera, she held up a computer with a video of Bernie Sanders answering a question about the economy. She perfectly lip-synced his reply in the clip, mimicking his hand movements, facial expressions, and body language. This user presents the memorized answer as a script to be performed in homage to Bernie Sanders. In another TikTok video, a user showed herself meeting Bernie Sanders in-person at a rally and being overcome with tears. She stands with a hand over her mouth and tears in her eyes and then briefly leans in towards Sanders, visibly choking back sobs (Kath Anne, 2020). As shown in Figure 4.1, another user shows herself sobbing on camera, talking about how much she loves Bernie Sanders, before ending by saying "and I'm CANADIAN!!" (Holland, 2021). Similarly, in the subreddit /r/YangGang, user shiyinglu (2020) posted a selfie she took with Andrew Yang in New York (see Figure 4.2). In response, other users wrote: "That's a dream come true!"; "No way, that's a dream of mine for sure"; and "OMG! You are so lucky!!!!" (shiyinglu, 2020).

Affect is performed not just through emotional displays, but through bodily performance as well, such as cosplay, which serve as a physical demonstration of fandom based on one's affective state (Lamerichs, 2018). In a viral tweet, user @ErinnFHarley shared a short video of her 11-year-old daughter dressed up as Kamala Harris for Halloween (Harley-Lewis, 2020). In the

Figure 4.1: Screenshot of Sofie.Holland TikTok Post
Source: https://www.tiktok.com/@sofie.holland/video/6916002062081723654

Figure 4.2: Selfie of Shiyinglu with Andrew Yang
Source: /https://www.reddit.com/r/YangGang/comments/kn61du/
guess_who_i_randomly_ran_into_yesterday_in_a/?rdt=58308

video the girl wears her mother's blue blazer, a string of pearls, and heels, topping off the ensemble with Harris's trademark sleek bob. Waving, she walks towards her house, pausing when her mother asks her if she has any words for her audience and responding, "When I become vice president, I want to help all the American people. I want to deliver health care for all, equality and justice under the law" (Harley-Lewis, 2020). In another Halloween post, user @mariebabyyyyy_ (2019) posted a photo of her toddler dressed as Donald Trump. Posing on the front stoop with pumpkins in the background, he is dressed in a black suit, a crisp white collared shirt, and a bright red tie with a Trump 2020 pinned to the lapel and has Trump's characteristic wispy, messy blonde hair. It is through fan practices such as these, Lamerichs (2018) argued, that affect is "nourished, created, and performed" (p. 227). Taking the performativity of affect into account, it is easy to see the emotional ties displayed by fans of politicians.

These bodily displays of affect are also important ways of showing the investment of the fan's identity with their chosen fan-object. Jenkins (1992) argued that "fans have chosen these media products from the total range of available texts precisely because they seem to hold special potential as vehicles for expressing the fans' pre-existing social commitments and cultural interests" (p. 34) and that there is an important relationship between people's identities and beliefs and the texts they choose to associate with and consume. Identity is not just a symbolic practice but an embodied one in which people literally enact their identity through material objects or physical participation. And cosplay is a particular fan practice that enables the citizen-fan to not only showcase their fan fervor but literally merge their identity with their favorite politician. Whether dressing up, memorizing dialogue, or posing for pictures, these intense affective and emotional bonds citizen-fans form with their favorite politician are behaviors learned from traditional modes of connecting with popular culture artifacts and transferred to contemporary performances of citizenship.

Specialized Fan Knowledge

When entering a new fandom one of the biggest barriers to entry is lack of knowledge, whether that be all the lyrics from an album, the stats of the starting pitcher for the 1923 New York Yankees, the type of TARDIS Doctor Who travels in, or the number of Oscars the movie *Titanic* won in 1997. "Wanting to know more is at the heart of fandom," wrote Thomas Brett (2015), and "fans often share a fascination with the details of the object of their fandom" (p. 10). Indeed, fans are often "excessive readers" (Fiske, 2010, p. 116) who ascribe "new and original significance" to texts that extends beyond mere enjoyment of a fan-object (Grossberg, 1992, p. 52). This "critical significance of information" (Hills, 2002, p. 140) not only acts as a tool for gatekeeping but allows fans information to construct the boundaries of their fandom. As fandom moves away from a focus on static texts such as a book, television series, or movie to "media whose textuality is both more ephemeral and limitless, audiences are required to formulate textual boundaries at the point of consumption" (Sandvoss, 2012, p. 71).

With each of these campaigns running between one to three years, a 24-hour news cycle, and constant social media coverage, fans had an overwhelming and seemingly limitless amount of information to know. The 2020 presidential campaign run by Andrew Yang began when Yang filed with the Federal Election Commission to participate in the Democratic primaries on November 6, 2017, and ended on February 11, 2020, the night of the New Hampshire primary. Bernie Sanders did not announce his bid for the 2020 presidential election until February 19, 2019, but stayed in the running until April 8, 2020, when he suspended his campaign following a string of losses to Joe Biden. Kamala Harris announced her run on January 21, 2019, with an announcement on *Good Morning America*. Harris officially withdrew from the race on December 3, 2019, but stayed very much in the public eye when it was announced she would be Joe Biden's running mate on August 11, 2020. Then-President Donald Trump officially announced his reelection campaign on June 18, 2019, and though he has not officially acknowledged his loss in 2020, in a video posted to Twitter account on January 7, 2021, he stated that a "new administration" would succeed his (Reuters, 2021; Trump, 2021).

As a result of this overload of information, specialized and detailed knowledge becomes one of the defining characteristics of the citizen-fan. While the specific knowledge required to be a citizen-fan of a certain politician varies from group to group, there are three particular genres of specialized knowledge that emerge when studying these citizen-fandom communities: (1) backstory and history; (2) policy details; and (3) personal information.

For Bernie Sanders citizen-fans, his backstory and history are particularly important when building an argument for Sanders as a lifelong progressive and defender of civil rights. For example, in his 2016 campaign, a photo from the *Chicago Tribune*'s archives surfaced of Sanders being carried by two police officers during a 1963 protest against school segregation on the South Side of

Chicago, which went viral. In 2020, coverage of that same photo continued to circulate, and fans used it as proof of his authenticity as a proponent of human rights as well as a jumping off point to talk more in-depth about his past policy stances. In a YouTube video posted by CNN discussing the photo, one user commented, "Bernie was also in favor of gay marriage back in the 80s on record. Unlike all the other candidates" (CNN, 2016). In response to that commenter, a user wrote, "70s actually," and yet another responded, "Bernie has always been on the right side of issues from the get go contrary to Hillary who is for gay marriage since 2013" (CNN, 2016). In 2020, nearly four years after the original video was uploaded, a user wrote, "#Bernie for president 2020 and he was frontline at the I have a dream speech as well" (CNN, 2016). In a TikTok video submitted to berniesanders.com and posted on the official Sanders TikTok account, a young supporter dances in front of a collage of photos of Sanders as a young man protesting or getting arrested at various rallies in the past while the lyrics in the background affirm there is no one she would vote for over Bernie Sanders, the implication being that this is in part because of his long history of engagement with civil and human rights movements. Bernie's past becomes part of a present canon of knowledge that fans use to situate his current political beliefs and actions and ascribe new significance to his past actions. As a result of Bernie's past, the fandom boundaries are wide—fans not only *can* pull from material as far back as the 1970s, but *should* pull from his background. This not only serves as a performance of devotion to Sanders—much as knowing the minutiae of an athlete's stats—but also acts as a gatekeeping tool, to determine who is a Bernie supporter versus a Bernie fan.

As one of the other older candidates, Trump also had a long history to pull from, but his fans focused on his record of success in business rather than in politics. For example, in a thread posted to the subreddit /r/sales/ (a business-focused subreddit popular amongst Trump supporters), comments discussed in-depth his business history, particularly his successes in the 1980s and 1990s and failures in the 2000s. User Trainer_Red99 (2020) started the conversation by posing the question, "Is / was Donald Trump really a good salesman or just good at branding himself as a 'lifestyle' . . . All politics aside. Was he a good salesman or only good at marketing himself as a luxury icon?" Many attributed his early successes in part to family money and the advantage of starting off wealthy. User Bodacious_Dad_Bod (2020) argued that "Trump was blessed by having an enormous advantage in life that 99% of the population could never have those resources" but that, "It's extremely doubtful that Trump would be nearly as successful in 2020 as he was back in the day."

Other commenters pushed back on the idea that he was no longer a successful businessman and argued that his past success was proof that he had the persuasive skills and business acumen to have earned his position as President. User doublecremeoreo (2020) retorted, "Of course he's good at selling. He's the fucking President of United States of America. If that's not proof of quite an advanced sales skill-set, I don't know what is." In an older post about Trump's business past, users detailed his investments in real estate, casinos, and hotels and his ability to build a brand name known worldwide (alexgarcia55, 2016). Even before his 2020 run, Trump fans delved deep into his history and used that knowledge to argue in favor of Trump and prove their devotion to him. With any of the candidates with a long public history, fans use that to curate specialized knowledge that sets fans apart, especially the die-hard fans.

Kamala Harris and Andrew Yang were much younger candidates and have had shorter histories in politics in general, and as such fans have had to work harder to build up a specialized knowledge based on backstory. Much of the information wielded by fans at this time focused on both Harris and Yang as "firsts" and what they argued was the newness of their policy positions. For example, in the comments section of a *New York Times* article (Stevens, 2019) on Andrew Yang, the top comments centered around his new ideas and how he was different than the other candidates:

> Yang's appeal for me comes down to the fact that he's radically different than Trump ... He offers solutions that are new and different, and that will tend to build unity.
>
> I've been an Andrew Yang supporter since reading his book *The War on Normal People*. He's got a plan that would have an immediate positive impact for individuals ... that is revolutionary, and quite fitting our the [sic] brave new world.
>
> I was an early supporter when Yang was trying to hit $200k ... his new ways of thinking about the economy, automation, the people left behind, etc. really resonated. I also liked that he was constructive and forward thinking while others were all about anti-Trumpism or single issue (Medicare for all).

For "Yang Gang" supporters it was important that his policies and actions were not just different from the other candidates in the field but seemingly different from any candidate ever. His history of business was relevant only in that it informed his policy beliefs like universal basic income. Harris fans had somewhat more political history to pull from than Yang's, but the KHive emphasized her as a historical candidate—both as a possible president and then as a vice president. For instance, Twitter user Stardust tweeted on November 28, 2019, "@SenKamalaHarris #KamalaHarris2020 #Khive YES we need a woman to be elected for President in 2020 and her name is @KamalaHarris ♡" (Hartley, 2019). On November 7, 2019, a Twitter user similarly wrote, "I don't know who needs to hear this but let's elect a woman president" (Bengtson, 2019), to which the official KHive account responded, "I don't know who needs to hear this but let's elect Kamala Harris president" (The KHive, 2019). In the comments of that post, user @OnePageWriter seconded the need to vote for a woman but specifically for Kamala Harris, "The nation owes itself a shot of gender reparations. We have other injustices to correct too but after #metoo and stealing President Hillary's victory, gender justice is a deserved first step. Plus, @KamalaHarris is a twofer!" (Happy PerpWalk Day, 2019). In this comment the user was focusing on Harris as a doubly historic first should she win the election—the first woman to be president and also the first woman of color to be president.

The specialized knowledge of the citizen-fan is also particularly policy based. Much like a passionate fan of Star Wars knows the details about the politics of the Galactic Empire, so too the citizen-fan understands many of the intricacies of the policies of their favorite politician and are eager to discuss the finer points with one another as well as with the candidates themselves. For example, in the subreddit /r/YangForPresidentHQ, Andrew Yang did an "AMA" (Ask Me Anything) where users posted questions in a forum, and he answered them within the hour. While some of the questions were of a lighter nature, like "What was your favorite Race and Class to play in D&D?", most questions focused on policy. One user asked, "You've talked about how the US only accounts for 15% of global emissions, so any real solution to climate change needs to be global, not just American, solution. What kind of policies/diplomacy would a Yang presidency implement to achieve this?" (AndrewyangUBI, 2019). Another asked, "What are the specifics of your plan for the VAT? . . . [and] How do you plan to combat the current $20 Trillion deficit alongside your Freedom Dividend?" (AndrewyangUBI, 2019). Many of the questions centered around the question of a universal basic income, which was a cornerstone policy of his campaign. In a similar AMA on the subreddit /r/SandersForPresident, users likewise focused on policy questions, though many chimed in with details after Sanders had posted his answer. For example, one user asked, "I'm curious what your plan is to both raise taxes on corporations and the top 1% while at the same time doing everything to make sure these businesses and people don't move out of the country" (bernie-sanders, 2019). Sanders responded with a generic answer, "There is no rational reason why a corporation like Amazon, owned by the wealthiest person in America, paid NOTHING in federal income taxes last year ... Large corporations must become good corporate citizens. They have every right to make a profit but they also must pay their fair share of taxes, treat their workers with respect and protect our environment" (bernie-sanders, 2019). In the replies to that, commenters pushed for more specifics using detailed knowledge of previous policy positions held by Sanders or brought up other policies from other candidates. For example, user WhyYouAreVeryWrong brought up Elizabeth Warren's proposed plan as a counter to Sanders' argument about Amazon:

> Elizabeth Warren has proposed a wealth tax that would affect someone like Mr. Bezos. I have not actually seen a proposal from you that would affect Amazon or Mr. Bezos. Your 2016 tax plan proposed increasing income and capital gains taxes, but neither of those would affect Mr. Bezos in this case. How specifically would you tax someone like Jeff Bezos, who doesn't get income taxes (low pay) and doesn't take his capital gains (never triggering taxes)? (bernie-sanders, 2019)

In response, user kemisage provided more details about Sanders' policy position on taxation:

> [The] wealth tax was originally proposed by Bernie in 2017 as part of the white paper for financing options for M4A: 1% annual wealth tax on the top 0.1% which was $21.5 million, I think, in 2017 and is about $32 million now. At that time, Warren's aides didn't even want to comment on whether she supports it as well. Anyway, Bernie also intends to increase tax on dividends (same as capital gains) for the top 1%. (bernie-sanders, 2019)

This kind of policy detailed knowledge can be found as a core part of the fandom for almost any popular political candidate. Beyond a supporter who might settle for more generic information or promises from a candidate, fans are invested in the details (Brett, 2015). One profile on Harris fans—the KHive—wrote, "The #KHive could talk your ear off about Harris's efforts to better the lives of Americans: the LIFT Act tax credit for middle-class families, the Rent Relief Act, the Maternal CARE Act to address the high rates of maternal mortality among Black women, and more" (Gontcharova, 2019, para. 5).

For the citizen-fan, knowledge of policy is a key part of the canon (the source material for a given fan-object) and essential for setting the bounds of the fandom. Policy is one of the primary focuses of the candidates as well, and as a result there are large amounts of information on policy positions on candidates' websites, laid out in stump speeches, repeated in debates, and found in some of their legislative records. Creating boundaries around the fandom becomes difficult as citizen-fans sift through the available information in order to form a coherent picture of their favorite candidate's positions. This often becomes a point of contention within the fandom, whether that is arguing about the accuracy of details, gatekeeping admittance to the fandom, or arguing about the relevance to a candidate's identity. Agreeing on specialized knowledge is key to building a fandom community, in that the narratives built "unites people around not just a shared sense of identity, but a shared story and the idea that they're building that story together" (Romano, 2024). However, "by treating politics as a fandom treating politics as a fan-object raises barriers to engagement by necessitating the mastering of a complex rulebook before one can play" writes Paul Allen and David Moon (2023), and that those who want to engage with politics becomes "limited to those with specialist knowledge" (p. 1508).

Finally, specialized knowledge also falls into a category about knowing personal information about the candidates. The affordances and norms of social media encourage a deeper parasocial relationship with candidates in that it is a medium built for personalization, and fans use this to build a sense of identity and personality for the candidates that becomes, in many ways, "fanon" knowledge. If canon is source material—quotes from a candidate, policy from a website, a social media post from a candidate—then "fanon" is information about a fan-object that is largely speculation from fans and that has become so widely circulated that it is accepted as truth ("Fanon," n.d.). While most citizens understand that a candidate's image is managed and manufactured, there is still a belief that fans can "know" a candidate, whether that is information about their personal life, their relationships, or their personality. On TikTok there are a string of videos of Kamala Harris cooking. In one video originally posted by Harris's niece on TikTok (Harris, n.d.), subsequently deleted, but then re-posted by a Harris supporter on TikTok, commenters affectionately talk about Harris almost like a family member: "She's so funny, we love your Auntie so much," "a great cook," "She's always so happy love it about her," "I know she gives the best hugs," and "Always white wine also!!!" (Queen-Kamalaa, 2020). In a Quora forum, a user posed the question, "Do you think that Donald Trump is a good father?" Fans of Trump defended him as "An amazing father . . . [who] raised good, productive, responsible kids that know how to work and aren't afraid to get their hands dirty" (Bello, 2020). One user compared Trump to their own father: "my father was the most amazing father in the world . . . But he was not a touchy-feely guy. He said 'I love you' every day but not with words or touch. I think Donald is that type of man" (Saxon, 2020). In a video posted to Twitter by a user claiming to be his grandson, Bernie Sanders appears to be playfully interacting with his family. Users applauded his "Grandpa energy" and said that "he's actually a normal person. He isn't a rich snob who only wants money just like the other candidates" and that "[Sanders] seems like a funny grandpa lmao" and is "Such a wholesome grandpa" (Donk, 2020). Citizen-fans often build a parasocial relationship and develop a sense of intimacy, perceived friendship, and identification with their candidate of choice (Horton & Wohl, 1956), and "social media are perfect platforms for promoting parasocial relationships" (Chung & Cho, 2017, p. 483) because of the platforms' ability to create a sense of authentic reality and two-sided communication (Aw & Chuah, 2021; Labrecque, 2014).

Fan Communities

Specialized knowledge is not built in a vacuum, however; it is created and shared within a fan community. Fandom is a "mode of participation" (Cavicchi, 1998, p. 4) wherein fans contribute their knowledge to a common pool of information to form a "community of imagination" that "constitutes itself through a common affective engagement" (Hills, 2002, p. 179). Fans can more easily participate in fandom communities because of the access granted by the Internet, argue Leora Hadas and Limor Shifman (2013). In the past, fans had to invest "time, effort, and sometimes money to . . . buy series guides, photocopy fanzines, and attend conventions . . . Yet, with a plethora of means to easily discover and pass along information . . . knowledge is now within the easy reach of any internet user" (p. 277). As a result of this ease of access, fans can build communities in which anyone can interact, and fan sites thrive across social media platforms. Supporters of Bernie Sanders have been considered some of the most vocal citizen-fans of the 2020 election and have gathered in numbers across platforms. Besides popular subreddits like /r/politics and /r/all/, Sanders fans can choose from three different subreddits dedicated to the Vermont Senator: /r/SandersForPresident, /r/WayOfTheBern, and /r/BernieSanders. Andrew Yang fans also have a number of subreddits to gather on: /r/YangForPresidentHQ, /r/YangForPresident, and /r/YangGang. Fans of Donald Trump have a more complicated relationship with this particular website. Initially MAGA fans created a subreddit called /r/The_Donald in 2015, which grew to over 790,000 subscribers and became one of the most active communities on Reddit (Jackson, 2016). However, the subreddit was banned in June 2020 for violating Reddit rules on harassment and targeting, and fans were forced to find other means of digital gathering and community building. Twitter had about 347 million users at the time, and Donald Trump's account had some 80 million followers to whom he tweeted 25,000 times during his presidency. Though Trump's accounts were eventually suspended from most major social media platforms like Twitter, Instagram, and Facebook in 2021, supporters remained on those sites as well as some less mainstream sites like 4Chan. Like the others, Kamala Harris fans could be found on many of the major social media platforms, though there was no dedicated subreddit to Harris. Instead, Harris fans could be largely found on Twitter using the hashtag #TheKHive. During her presidential run in 2019 (as opposed to her run as a vice-presidential candidate), 38,000 Twitter accounts had used the hashtag and "accrued an estimated 360 million impressions" (Zhou, 2019, para. 7).

With many of these popular candidates came the common fandom practice of acquiring a community name. MAGA fans were among the first fan group to gain a popular name, largely attributed to Donald Trump's 2016 campaign and his slogan "Make America Great Again." However, the name has roots in a number of previous elections, starting with Ronald Reagan in his 1980 presidential campaign and his slogan "Let's Make America Great Again." Bill Clinton used a similar phrase throughout his 1992 presidential run and during a radio promotion during Hillary Clinton's 2008 presidential run (Boys, 2021; Syphilis Two, 2016). Shortly after Mitt Romney lost the 2012 presidential election to Barack Obama, Trump signed an application with the U.S. Patent and Trademark Office for exclusive rights to the phrase "Make America Great Again." In an interview with *The Washington Post*, Trump discussed the process of coming up with the slogan:

> I said, "We'll make America great." And I had started off "We Will Make America Great." That was my first idea, but I didn't like it. And then all of a sudden it was going to be "Make America Great." But that didn't work because that was a slight to America because that means it was never great before. And it has been great before. So I said, "Make America Great Again." I said, "That is so good." I wrote it down. I went to my lawyers. I have a lot of lawyers in-house. We have many lawyers. I have got guys that handle this stuff. I said, "See if you can have this registered and trademarked." (Tumulty, 2017)

As Trump supporters become more visible in the public eye the slogan began to attach to that community and shortened to be simply "MAGA." This spawned a wide array of merchandise with the slogan prominently displayed, such as flags, the iconic bright red hats, t-shirts, a variety of home goods like cups, carpets, and drapes, and more. Physical items became an important way to signal their participation in the Trump fandom in offline spaces as well, particularly at rallies. While many Trump supporters might attend a rally, it was the Trump *fans* who would deck themselves out in MAGA. Additionally, the term became a popular hashtag for social media that has endured well beyond that of the 2020 election. It can be found on almost any popular social media site such as Twitter, TikTok, Instagram, Facebook, Snapchat, and even LinkedIn. While all of the candidates had merchandise in some capacity or another, it was the MAGA fandom that overwhelmingly created, distributed, and consumed this physical proof of their fandom.

Supporters of Bernie Sanders were also identified before the 2016 election as "Bernie Bros" or "Berniebros." These terms were first used in an article in *The Atlantic* by Robinson Meyer (2015) to describe the young male supporters of Sanders and remained a consistent moniker in the 2020 election. For Meyers, the term "Bernie Bro" described obnoxious supporters of Sanders comprised of young men who are "white; well-educated; middle-class (or, delicately, 'upper middle-class'); and aware of NPR podcasts and jangly bearded bands" and voted for Barack Obama in 2012 (Meyer, 2015, para. 10). The Sanders campaign did not embrace this new fan community the way the Trump campaign did. Sanders distanced himself from the Bernie Bros after being asked about the group's seeming propensity for sexist attacks. Of this group of supporters he said, "It's disgusting ... Anybody who is supporting me and who is doing sexist things, we don't want them. I don't want them. That is not what this campaign is about" (Cohen, 2016; Shastry, 2016). Sanders tried to rehabilitate the group in 2020 by claiming that the negative comments posted were a result of Russian intervention (Stein & Rawnsley, 2020), though there was little evidence to support this claim (Feiner & Javers, 2020).

Kamala Harris supporters became known as members of the "KHive" as early as 2017 after the airing of an MSNBC panel led by anchor Joy Reid, though the term gained popularity in 2019 as she began her bid for the White House. In an early profile by Natalie Gontcharova (2019) for *Refinery29*, she writes that the KHive is a fitting parallel to Beyoncé fans who call themselves the BeyHive. "Harris is their Beyoncé in a suit and pearls, the one who can make political history while putting on one hell of a performance," writes Gontcharova (2019), "the term #KHive also acknowledges all the firsts she's achieved as a Black and South Asian woman—and the breathtaking, historic potential of seeing her elected president" (para. 2). The term was a grassroots label that came from ardent supporters but was quickly adapted by Harris campaign staffers and even added to the Twitter biography of her husband Douglas Emhoff (Zhou, 2019). For fans of Harris, this term became a way to identify other members of their community, says Julie Zebrak, the co-founder of @Mamas4Kamala, a group focused on rallying moms to back Harris, "It's just kind of code, for we're in the club, we're all in for Kamala" (Zhou, 2019, para. 14).

Though he launched his campaign in 2017, Andrew Yang's profile and his group of fans, known as members of the "Yang Gang," did not become popular until early 2019 after he appeared on the Joe Rogan podcast, *The Joe Rogan Experience* (Fisher, 2020). In an article for *Business Insider*, Anthony Fisher (2020) interviewed Elisa and Russell Peterson who discovered Yang after listening to his interview with Joe Rogan and subsequently "quit their jobs and hit the campaign trail with their four-year-old son. While on the road, they launched the 'GrassRoots #YangGang' YouTube channel, where they livestream[ed] nearly every Yang campaign event and provided regular commentary throughout the day to more than 10,000 subscribers" (para. 4). Some media articles attributed Yang's continued prominence in the 2020 campaign to the sustained Internet presence of the Yang Gang (Johnson et al., 2019; Roose, 2019; Stevens, 2019). "Yang's ascent from anonymity has been instantaneous in a way that can only exist in the age of social media," wrote Johnson et al. (2019), "Digital media shapes Yang's worldview and his self-presentation ... He is an emblem of the everyman thinkers of the Internet age" (para. 10). As political campaigns increasingly rely on social media to reach voters, it is likely this trend of online digital communities as a tool to make or break a campaign will likely not just continue but grow.

Fan Materials

The final category that defines the fan experience and serves as the foundation for not just fan-based citizenship, but the citizen-fan is the creation of material objects by fans around their chosen fan-object. This is a broad category that includes writing fanfiction and making memes, remixes, and videos of their favorite candidate. As discussed earlier, it could be embodied or material practices like creating cosplays and making signs, shirts, banners, and hats. Fans could make TikTok or YouTube videos; moderate forums; post support to Twitter, Facebook, or Reddit; or provide literature at in-person fan gatherings.

Scholars understand this fan practice as either transformative or affirmational (Hinck, 2019). Transformational engagement "aggressively alters and transforms the source text, changing and manipulating it to the fans own desires" (Stein & Busse, 2012, p. 16). For example, user lotsofmoxiee posted a TikTok video of herself lip-syncing to Harris's viral moment in her debate against Mike Pence when she says "Mr. Vice President I'm speaking . . . I'm speaking," which then transitions into the lyrics of *Girls in the Hood* by Megan Thee Stallion (lotsofmoxiee, 2020). This transformational engagement takes a brief quote from Harris and transforms it in such a way as to serve the needs of the fan and the fan community, that is, affirming that Harris is indeed a strong woman who would not allow a man to speak over her. Other examples of transformational engagement were two fan-made documentaries focused on Andrew Yang and the rise of the Yang Gang: *Andrew Yang's 2020 Presidential Campaign: The Official Yang Gang Documentary* (The Matt Skidmore Show, 2021) and *My Yang Gang Diary* (Juhl, 2021). Though they were released in 2021, they documented the rise and fall of Yang's 2020 presidential campaign and ended by presenting the case for a 2024 presidential run for him. The documentaries included videos of Yang taken at in-person events and media appearances, as well as moments important to the fans themselves in their relationship with Yang and other supporters.

Affirmational engagement, on the other hand, "analyzes and interprets the source text, creating shared meaning and characterizations" (Stein & Busse, 2012, p. 16). For example, a TikTok video posted by user veganhater2000 in February 2020 starts with a simple close-up of the young supporter with the words "Why you should support bernie sanders" and then changes to a series of photos of Sanders over the years protesting and marching, most notably with Martin Luther King, Jr. (veganhater2000, 2020). The user did not alter the images except to circle Sanders in a crowd but otherwise lets the text speak for itself. Another method of affirmational engagement is cosplay, in which people who dress up work to make their costumes as accurate as possible. As discussed above, fans mimic their favorite politician's appearance by finding suits that match theirs, styling their hair as similarly as possible, or even buying wigs to maintain accuracy. Images of their fan-object are scrutinized for details, like what jewelry they might be wearing, brands they might favor, preferred pins and placements, and types of shoes. Videos are likewise examined so that fans can capture the nonverbal idiosyncrasies of a candidate, including speech patterns, particular movements or gestures, and how they laugh and smile. While popular parodies can be seen mocking the candidates

Figure 4.3: Examples of 2020 memes in support of Donald Trump
Source: Meme 1: https://twitter.com/tamileefortney
Meme 2: https://imgflip.com/i/xrqqh
Meme 3: https://imgflip.com/memetemplate/48772652/Trump-Pepe

as they do on Saturday Night Live, fans use these costumes to connect with and represent their fan-object to the best of their ability as an homage, not a mockery. Paul Booth (2015) notes that "fan practices hover between these categories, enacting them not as absolute polarities but as shifting interpretations and identities" (p. 13).

Donald Trump was one of the candidates whose fans created wide-spread fan content across platforms, particularly memes, so much so that "there is little question they changed [the] tone" of the 2016 election (Schreckinger, 2017, para. 7). Started during Trump's first presidential run, MAGA fandom argued, and many agreed with them, that their fandom actually managed to meme Trump into the White House (Ohlheiser, 2016). In 2020 the fandom attempted to re-create the magic, sending pepe the frog and trump train memes out to millions of people, yet were ultimately unsuccessful in their second attempt to utilize fandom to win an election (Figure 4.3 depicts several Trump memes from 2020). Despite the loss, it is clear that fan material plays an integral role in the world of the citizen-fan, whether someone creates content themselves or consumes it as a type of communion in homage to their chosen politician.

The Citizen-Stan

One particular kind of fan behavior that has become commonplace in political action is the act of "stanning" someone. The term "stan" comes from Eminem and Dido's hit 2000 song "Stan," which tells the story of a fan whose obsession drives him to violence. The term took on a pejorative meaning for an obsessive fan—rather than the name of the fan himself—in a 2001 song by Nas (Blistein, 2019). The term is both a noun and a verb according to Merriam-Webster; as a noun, a "stan" is defined as "an extremely or excessively enthusiastic and devoted fan," while as a verb it is defined as "to exhibit fandom to an extreme excessive degree" (Merriam-Webster, n.d.). As the citizen-fan has learned how to engage in politics through the behavior of fandom we must consider how the negative sides of fandom—like stanning—have become common practices in people's political engagement. In the case of many political fandom communities, the citizen-stan separates themselves from the citizen-fan by their anti-fan behavior. Anti-fans are "those who hate or dislike a given text, personality, or genre" and "spend consider-able time discussing why a given text makes them angry to the core" (Gray, 2005, pp. 840–841). Fandom studies have in the past focused largely on the positive aspects of fandom—how it brings people together, creates a space for those who lack a voice, provides community, etc., but Jonathan Gray (2005) argued that "hate or dislike of a text can be just as powerful as can a strong and admiring, affective relationship with a text, and they can produce just as much activity, identification, meaning, and ... serve just as powerfully to unite and sustain a community" (p. 841). For the citizen-stan, anti-fandom is as much a part of their identity as is their positive affective relationship with a fandom, that is, for the citizen-stan it is not enough to like a candidate, they also must actively dislike or even hate other candidates and their fans.

Popular media has noted the effects of this trend, writing headlines like "Politicians dread the sting of #KHive, the fervent online fans of Kamala Harris" (Bierman, 2021); "What it's like to be swarmed by Sanders supporters" (CNN, 2020); and "Trump says 'treason.' His fans invoke violence" (Stanley-Becker, 2019) or describing online fans as "rabid" (Smith, 2019) or as members of a "cult" (Kroll, 2019). Writers note how fans attack those who do not support their candidate and that the attacks are often very personal. For example, when the Working Families Party (WFP) endorsed Elizabeth Warren for president, some Sanders fans reacted by calling for counter events, spying on the WFP to take it down, and sending hundreds of messages on social media calling them "corrupt," "shameless," and "bloodless scumbag hacks" (Devine et al., 2020). One WFP spokesperson revealed the content of messages she had received that hoped she and her colleagues would "all get cancer you are f**king trash." She also said they received private messages saying "eat sh*t and die" and "drop dead dumb c*nts" (Devine et al., 2020). A subreddit account was created called /r/Enough_Sanders_Spam/ where people gathered to discuss the toxic behavior of Sanders supporters. The top fourth post of all time for the subreddit (which has 28,252 subscribers and was founded six years ago) is a post titled "I'm done. I quit. These people are insane," in which the poster talks about how the "movement has become the very thing we sought to destroy. Instead of dismantling the far right and exposing their hypocrisy we're now trafficking in the same types of baseless smears, disinformation campaigns, personal attacks, edited videos, and crazy conspiracies as they do" and that the former supporter "want[s] nothing to do with Bernie Sanders or his brand ever again" (Bern_2020, 2020).

There is also a growing concern that fans who have turned to standom have left themselves open to a much darker path. While fandom is "a source of great creativity, playfulness, and mobilization of social and political movements" (Petersen et al., p. 2), it has also been a resource for "revolutionaries, reactionaries, and racists alike" (Jenkins, 2006, p. 221). For example, in "the Great Meme Wars" of 2016, the memes created in favor of Donald Trump soon turned hateful and racist and in September of that year, Pepe the Frog was classified as a hate symbol by the Anti-Defamation League (Schreckinger, 2017).

Those wishing to motivate people to embrace conspiracy theories like election denialism—and perhaps even move them to action like those on January 6—are able to take the tools of fandom and apply them to standom— the exciting civic possibilities found in fandom can also be used for stans and the dark side. Like fans, stans are organized and motivated, they have deep emotional attachments to their fan-objects and create fanon lore that comes from bits and pieces of real life and feel as authentic as canon. Pizzagate is an example of this, where the conspiracy that Hilary Clinton and other leaders in the Democratic Party were running a pedophilia ring out of the back of a pizza shop went from fanon to canon. This conspiracy theory became so convincing, that a man showed up at the pizza shop with a gun, ready to free the children from the clutches of the perverted. We can see that stans understand the participatory cultures of fandom that have taught them how to connect with other like-minded people, how to persuade folks of their vision for the fandom, and how to use the language of fandom to weaponize their fandom communities. The behavior exhibited by fans serves as a foundation of known and accepted behavior that can translate to unacceptable behavior without the participant fully aware of the consequences. In essence, "practices that fans are engaged with are adapted into other cultural spheres" (Petersen et al., 2023, p. 5). During the January 6 riots many participants were engaged in classical fan behavior; people were dressed in costume, posing for selfies or filming themselves for social media content. Anthony Dannar and

CarrieLynn Reinhard go so far as to suggest the riots "looked like a fan convention ... [with a] carnivalesque nature ...[and a] festival-like atmosphere" (Petersen et al., 2023, pp. 4–5). As fan behavior becomes more mainstream and the practices of fandom become foundational tools for civic engagement, we must be aware that not all fandom is good fandom. Jenkins (2018) warns that alongside our enthusiasm for fandom's ability to reenergize democratic participation, "we are also seeing these same mechanisms allowing more reactionary fans to organize backlashes against those whom they see as threatening traditional forms of privilege" (p. 24). The fannish "ideals of relatability, authenticity, and accountability" and persuasive to audiences and can be just as easily used for evil as for good (Stanfill, 2020, p. 130).

Conclusion

Fandom is without a doubt a growing and powerful mode of political engagement in the modern political landscape. However, the citizen-fan is but one aspect of that political landscape. In 2016 Donald Trump would not have won without his fans—and his stans. The effort of his online keyboard warriors changed the tone and the tactics of elections not only in America but around the world and "their efforts have profound implications for the future of politics" (Schreckinger, 2017, para. 10). In 2020 though, MAGA fans were not enough to win a second term for Trump, and the winner in contrast had many supporters but very few fans. Though Joe Biden and his camp have worked to tap into the fan cultures exhibited for his opponents in 2020 he has had comparatively little success. The "Dark Brandon" meme has been the most visible fan content produced, but even that has limited circulation. Instead, Biden was able to win in 2020 through traditional political communication strategies, where the other participants in the presidential race, despite their fandoms, failed. Despite this, the "blurring of boundaries between fandom and politics underscores the transformative impact that fan culture has on public online discourse" and fandom and fan behavior has become our "new normal" (Le Clue, 2023, p. 2–3).

By examining the 2020 election through the lens of fan studies, we can see the ways in which fandoms have grown around particularly popular political figures in the campaign based on these four criteria and, in some cases, elevate their behavior from one of a fan to one of a stan. Belonging to a fandom community can have a number of benefits for people (Gray et al., 2017; Hinck, 2019), and a political fandom community is no different. People can engage with other like-minded individuals across broad geographic spaces and gender or racial or class differences. With the Internet providing a low barrier to entry, information sharing is easier than ever and is no longer restricted to traditional news gatekeepers. But, of course, there can be a darker side to being a member of a devoted fandom, particularly when your favorite politician loses. For some, losing is not simply disappointing, it instead can pose a threat to their very identity and can cause deep psychological discomfort that leads to stress, depression, and a greater willingness to confront others (Wakefield & Wann, 2006). Likewise, if a favored politician is knocked out of the race—either in the primaries or after—how likely is a fan to change allegiances? To use an analogy, if you are a die-hard fan of the original Star Wars trilogy, how likely are you to love the new Star Wars characters? If you are a Bernie Bro or a member of the KHive or the Yang Gang or MAGA and your candidate loses—what then? We saw some of the consequences of citizen-stan behavior on January 6, 2021, but even before that, what percentage of fans did not vote after their candidate lost in the primaries? So too there is an argument to be made about the citizen-fan and their fan behavior as a contributing factor to political polarization. "Identity performance, entertainment, and affective investment" are all fan behaviors that can lead to deep polarization over politics (Barnes, 2022, p. 2). Polarization is not just a result of increased technological affordances and individual access to the public sphere, she argues, instead it must be understood as an "affective practice" that is learned and deeply entrenched in fan behavior (Barnes, 2022, p. 9).

Fan behavior is now a major factor in how citizens engage with politics, and it is vital we understand both how positive fan behavior will influence people as well as dive into the darker side of standom. As Reinhard et al. (2022) write, "Fan studies, with its focus on affect and communal identity, could help explain why one individual can become a fan of *The Punisher*, while another dons that character's logo while attempting to overthrow a democracy" (p. 1169).

References

Allen, P., & Moon, D. S., (2023). 'Huge fan of the drama': Politics as an object of fandom. *Convergence*, 29(6), 1502–1516. https://doi.org/10.1177/13548565231203979

alexgarcia55. (2016, March 1). What do you guys think of Trump as a business man? [Reddit Post]. *R/Entrepreneur*. www.reddit.com/r/Entrepreneur/comments/48gzfs/what_do_you_guys_think_of_trump_as_a_business_man/

AndrewyangUBI. (2019, July 24). IamA Andrew Yang, Candidate for President of the U.S. in 2020 on Universal Basic Income AMA! [Reddit Post]. *R/YangForPresidentHQ.* www.reddit.com/r/YangForPresidentHQ/comments/ch8gph/iama_andrew_yang_candidate_for_president_of_the/

Asen, R. (2004). A discourse theory of citizenship. *Quarterly Journal of Speech, 90*(2), 189–211. https://psycnet.apa.org/doi/10.1080/0033563042000227436

Aw, E. C.-X., & Chuah, S. H.-W. (2021). "Stop the unattainable ideal for an ordinary me!" fostering parasocial relationships with social media influencers: The role of self-discrepancy. *Journal of Business Research, 132,* 146–157. https://doi.org/10.1016/j.jbusres.2021.04.025

Barnes, R. (2022). *Fandom and polarization in online political discussion.* Palgrave Macmillan.

Bello, S. (2020, October 29). Do you think Donald Trump is a good father? [Answer to question]. *Quora.* https://www.quora.com/Do-you-think-that-Donald-Trump-is-a-good-father?no_redirect=1

Bengtson, E. (2019, November 8). *I don't know who needs to hear this but let's elect a woman president* [Tweet]. *Twitter.* https://twitter.com/EmmyA2/status/1192610591015391235

Bennett, J. (2011). Celebrity and politics. *Celebrity Studies, 2*(1), 86–87. https://doi.org/10.1080/19392397.2011.544167

Bern_2020. (2020, March 9). I'm done. I quit. These people are insane. [Reddit Post]. *R/Enough_Sanders_Spam.* www.reddit.com/r/Enough_Sanders_Spam/comments/ffr6hp/im_done_i_quit_these_people_are_insane/

Bernie-sanders. (2019, June 18). I am Senator Bernie Sanders. Ask me anything! [Reddit Post]. *R/SandersForPresident.* www.reddit.com/r/SandersForPresident/comments/c26oqw/i_am_senator_bernie_sanders_ask_me_anything/

Bierman, N. (2021, April 8). Politicians dread the sting of #KHive, the fervent online fans of Kamala Harris. *Los Angeles Times.* https://www.latimes.com/politics/story/2021-04-08/politicians-dread-sting-khive-fervent-online-fans-of-kamala-harris

Blake, D. H. (2016). *Liking Ike: Eisenhower, advertising, and the rise of celebrity politics.* Oxford University Press.

Blistein, J. (2019, April 24). Eminem-inspired use of "stan" added to Merriam-Webster's dictionary. *Rolling Stone.* https://www.rollingstone.com/music/music-news/eminem-stan-merriam-websters-dictionary-entry-826557/

Bodacious_Dad_Bod (2020). *Is / was Donald Trump really a good salesman or just good at branding himself as a "lifestyle".* [Reddit Post]. R/Sales. www.reddit.com/r/sales/comments/jb07d5/is_was_donald_trump_really_a_good_salesman_or/. Accessed February 18, 2022.

Booth, P. (2015). *Playing fans: Negotiating fandom and media in the digital age.* University of Iowa Press.

Boys, J. D. (2021). Grand strategy, grand rhetoric: The forgotten covenant of campaign 1992. *Politics, 41*(1), 80–94. https://doi.org/10.1177/0263395720935782

Brett, T. (2015). Autechre and electronic music fandom: Performing knowledge online through techno-geek discourses. *Popular Music & Society, 38*(1), 7–24. https://doi.org/10.1080/03007766.2014.973763

Brough, M. M., & Shresthova, S. (2012). Fandom meets activism: Rethinking civic and political participation. *Transformative Works and Cultures*, 10. https://doi.org/10.3983/twc.2012.0303

Cavicchi, D. (1998). *Tramps like us music & meaning among Springsteen fans*. Oxford University Press.

Chatterjee, P. (2004). *The politics of the governed: Reflections on popular politics in most of the world*. Columbia University Press.

Juhl, C. (Director). (2021, January 1). *My Yang Gang Diary*. https://www.myyanggangdiary.com/

Chung, S., & Cho, H. (2017). Fostering parasocial relationships with celebrities on social media: Implications for celebrity endorsement. *Psychology & Marketing*, 34(4), 481–495. https://doi.org/10.1002/mar.21001

CNN (Director). (2016, February 20). *Bernie Sanders' 1963 arrest photo surfaces*[Video]. YouTube. https://www.youtube.com/watch?v=mFkIILjflT8

CNN (Director). (2020, February 7). *What it's like to be swarmed by Sanders supporters*[Video]. YouTube. https://www.youtube.com/watch?v=hgGl-NEMYec

Cohen, C. J. (2010). *Democracy remixed*. Oxford University Press.

Cohen, K. (2016, February 7). Bernie Sanders on "Bernie bros": "We don't want that crap." *Washington Examiner*. https://www.washingtonexaminer.com/bernie-sanders-on-bernie-bros-we-dont-want-that-crap

Cooper, A. F. (2008). Beyond one image fits all: Bono and the complexity of celebrity diplomacy. *Global Governance*, 14(3), 265–272. https://doi.org/10.1163/19426720-01403002

Dean, J. (2017). Politicising fandom. *The British Journal of Politics and International Relations*, 19(2), 408–424. https://doi.org/10.1177/1369148117701754

Dean, J., & Andrews, P. (2021). Celebritization from below: celebrity, fandom, and anti-fandom in British politics. *New Political Science*, 43(3), 320–338. https://doi.org/10.1080/07393148.2021.1957602

Definition of STAN. (n.d.). https://www.merriam-webster.com/dictionary/stan

Donk, R. (2020, March 18). So apparently Bernie's grandson has a TikTok. *Twitter*. https://twitter.com/katocollier/status/1240302101575749632

doublecremeoreo (2020). *Is / was Donald Trump really a good salesman or just good at branding himself as a "lifestyle"* [Reddit Post]. R/Sales. www.reddit.com/r/sales/comments/jb07d5/is_was_donald_trump_really_a_good_salesman_or/. Accessed February 18, 2022.

Trump, D. J. [@realDonaldTrump]. (2021, January 8). January 7th [Tweet]. *Twitter*. https://twitter.com/realDonaldTrump/status/1347334804052844550

Duffett, M. (2013). *Understanding fandom: An introduction to the study of media fan culture*. Bloomsbury

Fanon. (n.d.). In *Fanlore*. https://fanlore.org/wiki/Fanon

Feiner, E., & Javers, L. (2020, February 20). Twitter knocks down Bernie Sanders' suggestion that Russian trolls are behind online attacks from his supporters. *CNBC*. https://www.cnbc.com/2020/02/20/twitter-knocks-down-sanders-suggestion-russian-trolls-behind-supporters.html

Fisher, A. L. (2020, February 7). From "Trump train" to "Yang Gang": Meet the conservatives and swing voters who have fallen hard for Andrew Yang. *Business Insider, US Edition*. https://www.proquest.com/docview/2394205991/citation/C2E8CDF2E3CF446BPQ/1

Fiske, J. (2002). The cultural economy of fandom. In L. A. Lewis (Ed.), *The adoring audience: Fan culture and popular media* (pp. 30–49). Routledge.

Fiske, J. (2010). *Understanding popular culture* (2nd ed.). Routledge.

Gontcharova, N. (2019, May 7). Inside The world of the #KHive, Kamala Harris' biggest fans. *Refinery29*. https://www.refinery29.com/en-us/2019/05/230521/how-kamala-harris-can-win-2020-election-khive-community

Gray, J. (2005). Antifandom and the moral text: Television without pity and textual dislike. *American Behavioral Scientist, 48*(7), 840–858. https://doi.org/10.1177/0002764204273171

Gray, J., Harrington, C. L., & Sandvoss, C. (2017). *Fandom: Identities and communities in a mediated world* (2nd ed.). New York University Press. https://doi.org/10.18574/9781479845453

Grossberg, L. (1992). Is there a fan in the house?: The affective sensibility of fandom. In L. A. Lewis (Ed.), *The adoring audience: Fan culture and popular media* (pp. 50–68). Routledge.

Hadas, L., & Shifman, L. (2013). Keeping the elite powerless: Fan-producer relations in the "nu who" (and new YOU) era. *Critical Studies in Media Communication, 30*(4), 275–291. https://doi.org/10.1080/15295036.2012.676193

Happy PerpWalk Day. (2019, November 8). @TheKHive The nation owes itself a shot of gender reparations. We have other injustices to correct too but after #metoo and stealing President Hillary's victory, gender justice is a deserved first step. Plus, @KamalaHarris is a twofer! [Tweet]. Twitter. https://twitter.com/OnePageWriter/status/1192818863274115077

Harley-Lewis, E. [@ErinnFHarley]. (2020, October 6). "Mom, let's play Vice President!" Grateful that my 11yr old sees herself represented on the political stage. @KamalaHarris #KamalaHarris #BidenHarris @JoeBiden https://t.co/SRJlJRmUKb [Tweet]. Twitter. https://twitter.com/ErinnFHarley/status/1313473405514125313

Hartley, J. (2019, November 28). @SenKamalaHarris #KamalaHarris2020 #Khive YES we need a woman to be elected for President in 2020 and her name is @KamalaHarris ♡ [Tweet]. Twitter. https://twitter.com/Jeannie_Hartley/status/1199939988684587008

Hess, A. (2019). How fan culture is swallowing democracy. *New York Times*. https://www.nytimes.com/interactive/2019/09/11/arts/how-fan-culture-is-swallowing-democracy.html

Hills, M. (2002). *Fan cultures*. Routledge. https://doi.org/10.4324/9780203361337

Hinck, A. (2019). *Politics for the love of fandom: Fan-based citizenship in a digital world*. Louisiana State University Press.

Holland, S. (@sofie.holland). (2021, January 9). *Bernie is an ANGEL OK*[Video]. TikTok. https://www.tiktok.com/@sofie.holland/video/6916002062081723654

Horton, D., & Wohl, R. (1956). Mass communication and para-social interaction. *Psychiatry, 19*(3), 215–229. https://doi.org/10.1080/00332747.1956.11023049

Jackson, J. (2016, November 22). Moderators of pro-Trump Reddit group linked to fake news crackdown on posts. *The Guardian*. https://www.theguardian.com/technology/2016/nov/22/moderators-trump-reddit-group-fake-news-crackdown

Jeffrey, J. M. (2019, April 18). U.S. church membership down sharply in past two decades. *Gallup.com*. https://news.gallup.com/poll/248837/church-membership-down-sharply-past-two-decades.aspx

Jenkins, H. (1992) *Textual poachers: Television fans & participatory culture*. Routledge.

Jenkins, H. (1992). 'Stranger no more, we sing': Filking and the social construction of the science fiction fan community. In L. A. Lewis (Ed.), *The adoring audience: Fan culture and popular media* (pp. 208–236). Routledge.

Jenkins, H. (2006). *Convergence culture where old and new media collide*. New York University Press. https://doi.org/10.18574/9780814743683

Jenkins, H. (2009). *Confronting the challenges of participatory culture media education for the 21st Century*. MIT Press.

Jenkins, H. (2018). Fandom, negotiation, and participatory culture. In P. Booth (Ed.), *A companion to fandom and fan studies* (pp. 13–26). Wiley-Blackwell.

Jenson, J. (1992). Fandom as pathology: the consequences of characterization. In L. A. Lewis (Ed.), *The adoring audience: Fan culture and popular media* (pp. 9–29). Routledge.

Johnson, M., O'Connor, M., Tanner, E., & Brooks, D. M. (2019, June 10). Random man runs for president: The odd saga of Andrew Yang, explained. *The Washington Post*. https://www.washingtonpost.com/news/magazine/wp/2019/06/10/feature/random-man-runs-for-president-the-odd-saga-of-andrew-yang-explained/

Kath Anne, @katoutboy. (2020, February 27). *hey tiktok! Enjoy me UGLY CRYING bc i met #berniesanders*[Video]. TikTok. https://www.tiktok.com/@katoutboy

Kroll, A. (2019, July 19). "I came from the Internet": Inside Andrew Yang's wild ride. *Rolling Stone*. https://www.rollingstone.com/politics/politics-features/andrew-yang-2020-presidential-candidate-internet-basic-income-858755/

Labrecque, L. I. (2014). Fostering consumer–brand relationships in social media environments: The role of parasocial interaction. *Journal of Interactive Marketing*, 28(2), 134–148. https://doi.org/10.1016/j.intmar.2013.12.003

Lamerichs, N. (2018). *Productive fandom: Intermediality and affective reception in fan cultures*. Amsterdam University Press. https://doi.org/10.1515/9789048528318

Le Clue, N. (2023). The new normal: Online political fandom and the co-opting of morals. *Convergence*, 30(1), https://doi.org/10.1177/13548565231190343

Levine, P. (2015). *The future of democracy: Developing the next generation of American citizens*. University Press of New England.

Lin, Z., & Zhao, Y. (2020). Beyond celebrity politics: Celebrity as governmentality in China. *SAGE Open*, 10(3). https://doi.org/10.1177/2158244020941862

Livingstone, S. (Ed.). (2005). *Audiences and publics: When cultural engagement matters for the public sphere*. Intellect Books.

Lopez, L. K. (2016). *Asian American media activism: Fighting for cultural citizenship*. New York University Press.

lotsofmoxiee. (2020, October 10). *"Mr. Vice President, I'm speaking ... I'm speaking." That's my future #VP* [Video]. TikTok. https://www.tiktok.com/@lotsofmoxiee/video/6882164645679926534

Marsh, D., Hart, P. 't, & Tindall, K. (2010). Celebrity politics: The politics of the late modernity? *Political Studies Review*, 8(3), 322–340. https://doi.org/10.1111/j.1478-9302.2010.00215.x

McKernan, B. (2011). Politics and celebrity: A sociological understanding. *Sociology Compass*, 5(3), 190–202. https://doi.org/10.1111/j.1751-9020.2011.00359.x

Meyer, R. (2015, October 17). Here Comes the Bernie bro. *The Atlantic*. https://www.theatlantic.com/politics/archive/2015/10/here-comes-the-berniebro-bernie-sanders/411070/

Moon, D. S. (2020). The role of cultural production in celebrity politics: Comparing the campaigns of Jesse "The Body" Ventura (1999) and Donald Trump (2016). *Politics*, 40(2), 139–153. https://doi.org/10.1177/0263395719862446

Mukherjee, J. (2004). Celebrity, media and politics: An Indian perspective. *Parliamentary Affairs*, 57(1), 80–92. https://doi.org/10.1093/pa/gsh007

Ohlheiser, A. (2016). 'We actually elected a meme as president': How 4chan celebrated Trump's victory. *The Washington Post*. https://www.washingtonpost.com/news/the-intersect/wp/2016/11/09/we-actually-elected-a-meme-as-president-how-4chan-celebrated-trumps-victory/

Petersen, L. N., Reinhard, C. D., Dannar, A., & Le Clue, N. (2023). New territories for fan studies: The insurrection, QAnon, Donald Trump and fandom. *Convergence*, 30(1). https://doi.org/10.1177/13548565231174587

Putnam, R. D. (2000). *Bowling alone: The collapse and revival of American community*. Simon & Schuster.

Queen.Kamala. (2020, December 4). Another cooking with Kamala. *TikTok*. https://www.tiktok.com/@queen.kamalaa/video/6902554735694433541

Reinhard, C. L., & Miller, J. (2020). Academic dialogue: Why study politics and fandom? *Transformative Works and Cultures*,32. https://doi.org/10.3983/twc.2020.1857

Reinhard, C. D., Stanley, D., & Howell, L. (2022). Fans of Q: The stakes of QAnon's functioning as political fandom. *American Behavioral Scientist*, 66(8), 1152–1172. https://doi.org/10.1177/00027642211042294

Romano, A. (2024). If you want to understand modern politics, you have to understand modern fandom. *Vox*. https://www.vox.com/culture/24043045/politics-fandom-trump-fans-toxic-stan-culture-conspiracies

Roose, K. (2019, March 20). In Andrew Yang, the Internet finds a meme-worthy candidate. *The New York Times*. https://www.nytimes.com/2019/03/20/technology/andrew-yang-internet-democratic-primary.html

Reuters (2021, January 8th). *Trump acknowledges new administration in address* [Video]. YouTube. https://www.youtube.com/watch?v=bmAHM21o0O8

Sandvoss, C. (2005). *Fans: The mirror of consumption*. Polity.

Sandvoss, C. (2012). Enthusiasm, trust and its erosion in mediated politics: On fans of Obama and the Liberal Democrats. *European Journal of Communication*, 27(1), 68–81. https://doi.org/10.1177/0267323111435296

Saxon, L. (2020, December 7). Do you think Donald Trump is a good father? [Answer to question]. In *Quora*. https://www.quora.com/Do-you-think-that-Donald-Trump-is-a-good-father?no_redirect=1

Schreckinger, B. (2017). World war meme. *Politico*. https://www.politico.com/magazine/story/2017/03/memes-4chan-trump-supporters-trolls-internet-214856/

Shastry, A. (2016, February 7). Sanders addresses 'Bernie Bros,' says he doesn't want support from sexists. *The Washington Times*. https://www.washingtontimes.com/news/2016/feb/7/sanders-addresses-bernie-bros-says-he-doesnt-want-/

Shelby (@berniebro69). (2020, February 26). *That's on the great state of Vermont* [Video]. TikTok. https://www.tiktok.com/@berniebro69

shiyinglu. (2020, December 30). *Guess who I randomly ran into yesterday in a parking lot!* [Reddit Post]. R/YangGang. www.reddit.com/r/YangGang/comments/kn61du/guess_who_i_randomly_ran_into_yesterday_in_a/

Smith, A. (2019, September 11). Is Andrew Yang ready for prime time? *NBC News*. https://www.nbcnews.com/politics/2020-election/andrew-yang-ready-prime-time-n1051336

Stanfill, M. (2020). Introduction: The reactionary in the fan and the fan in the reactionary. *Television & New Media*, 21(2), 123–134. https://doi.org/10.1177/1527476419879912

Stanley-Becker, I. (2019, October 14). Trump says 'treason.' His fans invoke violence. How attacks against Schiff are escalating online. *The Washington Post*. https://www.washingtonpost.com/politics/trump-says-treason-his-fans-invoke-violence-how-attacks-against-schiff-are-escalating-online/2019/10/14/9f613974-ec4c-11e9-9306-47cb0324fd44_story.html

Stein, A., & Rawnsley, S. (2020, February 21). Experts say there's 'no evidence' for Bernie's Russian bot claim. *The Daily Beast*. https://www.thedailybeast.com/experts-call-bs-on-bernies-russian-bot-theory

Stein, L. E., & Busse, K. (Eds.). (2012). *Sherlock and transmedia fandom: Essays on the BBC Series*. McFarland.

StepMom Marie ♡ [@mariebabyyyyy_]. (2019, October 12). *Guess who he is for Halloween?* 🇺🇸🇺🇸 https://t.co/UI808QsOTP [Tweet]. Twitter. https://twitter.com/mariebabyyyyy_/status/1182808871519145984

Stevens, M. (2019, November 11). Andrew Yang's campaign has a lot of money. Now what? *The New York Times*. https://www.nytimes.com/2019/11/11/us/politics/andrew-yang-campaign.html

Street, J. (2004). Celebrity politicians: Popular culture and political representation. *The British Journal of Politics and International Relations*, 6(4), 435–452. https://doi.org/10.1111/j.1467-856X.2004.00149.x

Street, J. (2019). What is Donald Trump? Forms of 'celebrity' in celebrity politics. *Political Studies Review*, 17(1), 3–13. https://doi.org/10.1177/1478929918772959

Syphilis Two (Director). (2016, July 3). *Make America Great Again—A Retrospective* [Video]. YouTube. https://www.youtube.com/watch?v=txM0isUb7Xw

The KHive. (2019, November 8). *I don't know who needs to hear this but let's elect Kamala Harris president* [Tweet]. Twitter. https://twitter.com/TheKHive/status/1192817169530261506

The Matt Skidmore Show (Director). (2021, January 2). *Andrew Yang's 2020 Presidential Campaign | The Official Yang Gang Documentary* [Video]. YouTube. https://www.youtube.com/watch?v=xZ7mUgeu4x4

Trainer_Red99. (2020, October 14). *Is/was Donald Trump really a good salesman or just good at branding himself as a "lifestyle"* [Reddit Post]. R/Sales. www.reddit.com/r/sales/comments/jb07d5/is_was_donald_trump_really_a_good_salesman_or/

Tumulty, K. (2017, January 18). How Donald Trump came up with 'Make America Great Again.' *The Washington Post*. https://www.washingtonpost.com/politics/how-donald-trump-came-up-with-make-america-great-again/2017/01/17/fb6acf5e-dbf7-11e6-ad42-f3375f271c9c_story.html

van Biezen, I., & Poguntke, T. (2014). The decline of membership-based politics. *Party Politics, 20*(2), 205–216. https://doi.org/10.1177/1354068813519969

van Zoonen, L. (2006). The personal, the political and the popular: A woman's guide to celebrity politics. *European Journal of Cultural Studies, 9*(3), 287–301. https://doi.org/10.1177/1367549406066074

veganhater2000. (2020, February 25). *History speaks for itself*. TikTok.

Verba, S., Schlozman, K. L., & Brady, H. E. (1995). *Voice and equality: Civic voluntarism in American politics*. Harvard University Press.

Wakefield, K. L., & Wann, D. L. (2006). An examination of dysfunctional sport fans: Method of classification and relationships with problem behaviors. *Journal of Leisure Research, 38*(2), 168–186. https://doi.org/10.1080/00222216.2006.11950074

West, D. M., & Orman, J. M. (2003). *Celebrity politics*. Prentice Hall.

Wheeler, M. (2012). The Democratic worth of celebrity politics in an era of late modernity. *The British Journal of Politics and International Relations, 14*(3), 407–422. https://doi.org/10.1111/j.1467-856X.2011.00487.x

Wood, M., Corbett, J., & Flinders, M. (2016). Just like us: Everyday celebrity politicians and the pursuit of popularity in an age of anti-politics. *British Journal of Politics & International Relations, 18*(3), 581–598. https://doi.org/10.1177/1369148116632182

Zhou, L. (2019, July 25). *The #KHive, Kamala Harris's most devoted online supporters, explained*. Vox. https://www.vox.com/policy-and-politics/2019/7/25/20697783/khive-twitter-kamala-harris-2020-candidate-doug-hive

Zwarun, L., & Torrey, A. (2011). Somebody versus nobody: An exploration of the role of celebrity status in an election. *The Social Science Journal, 48*(4), 672–680. https://doi.org/10.1016/j.soscij.2011.06.005

Section II
Political Misinformation and Disinformation

· 5 ·

KNOWLEDGE GAPS AND MISINFORMATION: SOCIAL MEDIA ENGAGEMENT, IDEOLOGY, AND ELECTIONS

Ben Wasike

In a nutshell, the knowledge gap hypotheses (KGH) posits that those of higher socioeconomic status such as income and educational attainment acquire more knowledge than those of lower status (Tichenor et al., 1970). Related to the KGH is the belief gap hypothesis (BGH). The BGH posits that knowledge acquisition is subject to one's ideological orientation especially with controversial topics such as climate change, healthcare reform, sex education, same-sex marriage, and immigration, among others (Gaziano, 2014; Hindman, 2009; Hindman & Yan 2015; Saldaña et al., 2021). Although most research examines these two as separate or even competing paradigms, this chapter uses both to examine the effect of knowledge on the likelihood to engage with elections-related misinformation, a controversial issue in present-day U.S. politics (Seitz-Wal & Allen, 2022; Ulloa, 2022). Therefore, the chapter examines how the KGH and the BGH affect how people engage with such misinformation via social media engagement (SME). This refers to how people interact with social media content by sharing, commenting, retweeting, and liking it, among similar activities (Cao et al., 2017; Piatak & Mikkelsen, 2021; Wasike, 2022a, 2022b). Because research shows that exposure to partisan media (Hindman & Yan, 2015; Saldaña et al., 2018; Lee, et al., 2022 and interpersonal discussion

(Ho, 2012; Kim et al. 2011) also affect how people understand controversial topics, the chapter also examines the role of these two variables.

Elections-related Misinformation

Elections-related misinformation on social media runs the gamut from simple falsities and twisted facts to viral conspiracies and organized campaigns by nation states. Viral posts falsely claiming widespread voter fraud in U.S. elections is an example of the former (Cassidy & Mulvihill, 2022; Levitt, 2007). The Russia-backed meddling in the 2016 U.S. presidential elections is an example of the latter (Allcott & Gentzkow, 2017; Gunther et al., 2019), as well as the propagation of the "Big Lie" by former president Donald Trump and some right-leaning media outlets (Waldman, 2022). The "Big Lie" refers to a persistent misinformation claim that the 2020 election was stolen from Trump by conspiratorial actors (Wolf, 2021). While such misinformation campaigns are not new and flourish during crises (van Prooijen & Douglas, 2017), the internet and social media provide the perfect conduit for the rapid spread and wide diffusion of such misinformation (IFCN, 2022; Pew Research Center, 2017).

Like other types of misinformation, elections-related misinformation is consequential. For one, over a year after the 2020 elections, 66% of Republicans still believed the "Big Lie" (PRRI, 2021b). Research shows that the China-backed fake news campaign during the 2018 Taiwan local elections affected how voters judged the news as well as how they voted. This effect was more pronounced among the young, the less educated, lower income groups, and heavy social media users (Wang, 2020). Even though research is inconclusive about the direct effect on voting outcomes during the 2016 presidential elections due to the Russia-backed fake news campaign (Allcott & Gentzkow, 2017; Gunther et al., 2019), data shows that the campaign reached millions of potential voters and may have influenced segments of the population. Over 126 million Facebook users received Russia-backed content (Lee & Kent, 2017). In the five months leading to the elections, over 7.5 million tweets contained a fake news article, potentially reaching 2.2 million Twitter users (Bovet & Makse, 2019). Other research shows that segments of the population likely to have been influenced by this fake news campaign included older voters, Conservative leaning voters, and those who consume political news frequently (Grinberg et al., 2019).

Knowledge Gaps and Online Media

Early studies of the KGH and the internet showed that education-driven digital divides affected knowledge acquisition. In a study of internet adoption in Switzerland, Bonfadelli (2002) found that that the regular use of the internet, which was tied to educational attainment, affected knowledge. Higher educated people, who also had more access to the internet, used it for educational and information-seeking purposes as opposed to using it for entertainment as the less educated people did. Additionally, these trends held over time. Likewise, Lee (2009) found that internet use increased the knowledge gap between low and high education subjects regarding health-related knowledge. Here too, internet use was higher among the higher educated subjects. Gibson and McAllister (2015) reached similar conclusions in a study of internet use, access, and political knowledge gaps in Australia. The internet-driven knowledge divides also echoed in Yang and Grabe's (2011) study comparing print and online news sources. High education subjects reported higher comprehension levels from online news sources than low education subjects even though both groups spend equal times reading print news.

Recent studies confirm the effect of online media on knowledge. For instance, Chang et al. (2018) reported that highly educated people, who were more likely to read online news and use social media more, were more knowledgeable about scientific facts. In a study of nanotechnology knowledge in the U.S. and Singapore, Ho et al. (2020) also found education-based knowledge gaps that were exacerbated by social media use among U.S. subjects. Scholars currently examining the KGH and COVID-19-related information have come to similar conclusions. Social media use widened the education-driven knowledge gap of COVID-19 safety protocols early in the pandemic. Furthermore, social media users were more likely to believe COVID-19-related falsities (Gerosa et al., 2021). Likewise, the increased use of the internet widened the gap between high and low educated groups regarding knowledge about the coronavirus (Wang et al., 2021). While some studies show a narrowing of knowledge gaps due to internet use (Goh, 2015; Tran, 2013), others show that social media use specifically increases the subjective interpretation and of facts (Lee et al., 2022), thus increasing susceptibility to misinformation.

Research also shows that the KGH and interpersonal discussion are related (Ho, 2012; Kim et al., 2011) as are interpersonal discussion and political knowledge (Moore & Coronel, 2022). This angle is important to this study given that the focus here is on knowledge about elections and how people engage with related misinformation. Political knowledge refers to "a citizen's ability to provide correct answers to a specific set of fact-based questions" (Boudreau & Lupia, p. 171). It is the "factual knowledge on such topics as the institutions and processes of government, current economic and social conditions, the major issues of the day, and the stands of political leaders on those issues" (Delli Carpini & Keeter, 1996, p. 1). Interpersonal discussion generally improves political knowledge, even though the frequency of such discussions and the diversity of the political views of the discussants are important (Amsalem & Nir, 2021).

Interpersonal discussion on social media also improves knowledge, although the effect is not universal. Some studies show that social media use marginally improves political knowledge and may or even negatively impact such knowledge (Lee & Xenos, 2019; Shehata & Strömbäck, 2021; van Erkel & Van Aelst, 2021). Other studies show that depending on the issue at hand, interpersonal discussion on social media may improve political knowledge (Vermeer et al., 2021). Additionally, online interactions generally improve political knowledge via SME with others and via interaction with political social media influencers (Abidin, 2021; Maly, 2020; Oeldorf-Hirsch, 2018). The intensity of the news coverage about an issue also affects how people discuss the issue and how accurately they understand the related information (Hardy & Scheufele, 2009). The last point is important to this study given the extensive coverage of elections and related issues in the U.S. media (Seitz-Wal & Allen, 2022; Ulloa, 2022).

The Belief Gap Hypothesis

A major criticism of the KGH was that it lacks context specificity, meaning that it does not explain gaps across all types of knowledge uniformly (Gaziano & Gaziano, 1999; Hindman, 2009). Case in point is research indicating that educational attainment, a key measure of the KGH, has a bigger effect on political knowledge than other types of knowledge (Hwang & Jeong, 2009). The same applies to a myriad topics such as climate change (Hindman, 2009, 2012), sex-education (Hindman & Yan, 2015), and immigration (Saldaña et al., 2021). These findings reflect the partisan divide in elections-related and COVID-19 knowledge, two of the most divisive topics currently in the U.S. Data shows that a partisan divide existed before the 2020 presidential elections, where 43% of Republican-leaning voters believed that mail-in balloting was ridden with fraud as compared to 11%

of Democrat-leaning voters (Mitchell et al., 2020, para. 4). Research shows that mail-in ballots are secure (Scala et al., 2022). Yet, this partisan divide persisted years after the 2020 elections with the promotion of the elections-related conspiracies among Conservative-leaning voters (Greenberg, 2022, para. 4).

As mentioned, partisan media exposure also plays a role in knowledge gap development. Here, research shows that the BGH as well as exposure to right-leaning media affects sex-education knowledge (Hindman & Yan, 2015; Veenstra et al., 2014) as well as knowledge about immigration and attitudes towards immigrants (Saldaña et al., 2018; Saldaña et al., 2021). At the time of writing, data shows the same regarding knowledge about elections integrity. Not only are right-leaning voters likely to believe falsities about elections integrity as mentioned earlier, but they also tend to get this misinformation from right-leaning sources (Jurkowitz, 2021, para. 7; PRRI, 2021a, paras. 115–116). This trend is not isolated to elections, but also emerges among related topics such as the identity of the January 6 insurrectionists (Lange, 2022, para. 5), news literacy (Fox, 2021, para. 12), and misperceptions about political censorship on social media platforms (Barrett & Sims, 2021; Novacic, 2020).

Research Questions

The literature discussed above suggests that the KGH, the BGH, partisan media use, and interpersonal discussion affect knowledge. As shown below, this study queries the same regarding the effects of these variables on elections-related knowledge, as well as their effect on SME with elections-related misinformation:

RQ1: Does socio-economic status and educational attainment affect knowledge about U.S. elections?
RQ2: Does ideological orientation affect knowledge about U.S. elections?
RQ3: Does interpersonal discussion affect knowledge about U.S. elections?
RQ4: Does partisan media use affect knowledge about U.S. elections?
RQ5: Does socio-economic status and educational attainment affect social media engagement with elections-related misinformation?
RQ6: Does ideological orientation affect social media engagement with elections-related misinformation?

RQ7: Does interpersonal discussion affect social media engagement with elections-related misinformation?

RQ8: Does partisan media use affect social media engagement with elections-related misinformation?

RQ9: Is there a correlation between elections-related knowledge and SME with misinformation?

Method

Sampling and Data Collection

A Qualtrics panel was used to randomly draw the sample and an online survey was used to collect the data (N = 840). Qualtrics and other survey research firms keep pools of pre-registered subjects collectively known as panels. These subjects reflect various demographics from which scholars can randomly select samples (Qualtrics. n.d.). Research shows that Qualtrics panels are valid and representative sources for sampling (Brandon et al., 2014; Gil de Zúñiga et al., 2017; Holt & Loraas, 2019). Additionally,

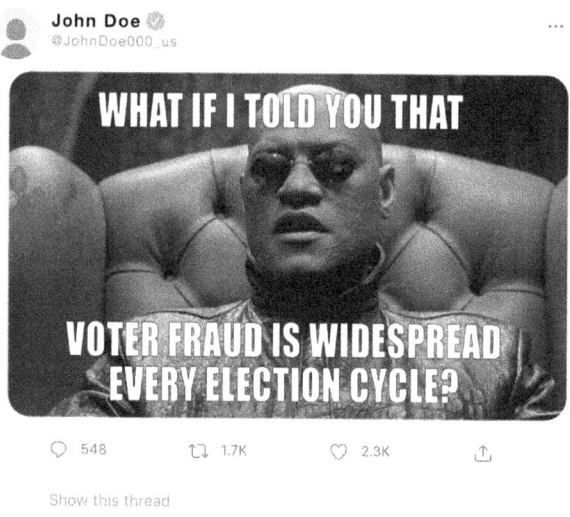

Figure 5.1: Twitter meme depicting elections-related misinformation
Source: Meme created by author to mimic popular "red pill vs blue pill" memes (see, https://imgflip.com/memetemplate/33301480/Matrix-Morpheus)

the sample reflected U.S. Census demographics such as age, income, gender, region, and ideological orientation. G*Power analysis also indicated that the sample was adequately powered regarding the effect size = 0.15; power = .80; and (two-tailed) alpha = .05 as suggested by Faul et al., 2007 (2007) and Faul et al. (2009). Data were collected between August 1–15, 2022, and the study was approved by the author's Institutional Research Board before data collection. After consenting to participate in the survey, subjects answered the demographics questions and were then tested about their knowledge of U.S. elections as described below. Subjects then viewed a meme portraying elections misinformation and were queried about their likelihood to share, like, retweet, and comment on the meme. The author created the meme from scratch using Adobe Photoshop, and they fashioned it after a series of popular "red pill vs blue pill" memes inspired by the film "The Matrix." This type of meme was used because it has lately been appropriated by conspiracy theorists as a means of spreading misinformation (Cunha, 2020). See Figure 5.1 for meme used in this study.

Variables

Elections-Related Knowledge

As mentioned, subjects were tested on their knowledge about U.S. elections. This knowledge test consisted of five questions based on information derived from a variety of sources, namely, the AARP (Bunis, 2020), the U.S. Citizenship and Immigration Services (n.d.), and the *Boston Herald* (Iafrato, 2020). Elections knowledge was measured on a 0–5 scale based on the total number of correct responses for the questions asked, as suggested by prior studies (Gerosa et al., 2021; Ho, 2012). See Figures 5.2 and 5.3.

The Knowledge Gap Hypothesis

To measure this variable, subjects were queried about their income and educational attainment. Income was measured as an ordinal variable based on categories of the annual household income in U.S. dollars (Ho et al., 2020). These were: Low income ($29,000 and less), lower middle income ($30,000–49,000), middle income ($50,000–89,000), and high income ($90,000 and above). Educational attainment was also measured as an ordinal variable: High school or less, some college, and college degree or higher (Gerosa et al., 2021).

1. The U.S. Congress mandated voting on the first Tuesday after the first Monday in November:
   1. To ensure the election occurs before Thanksgiving
   2. ***To ensure that farmers could vote conveniently***
   3. To ensure that voters can take their summer vacation
   4. To ensure that voters can take Christmas vacation

2. You can vote for president before Election Day.
   1. ***True***
   2. False

3. The U.S. House of Representatives has how many voting members?
   1. 100
   2. ***435***
   3. 325
   4. 200

4. This person was the first woman to be nominated as part of a major party presidential ticket.
   1. Kamala Harris
   2. Carly Fiorina
   3. ***Geraldine Ferraro***
   4. Sarah Palin

5. We elect a U.S. Senator for how many years?
   1. 2 years
   2. 5 years
   3. 4 years
   4. ***6 years***

Note: Correct answers shown in bold italics.

Figure 5.2: Elections information knowledge test

Ideological Orientation

To measure this variable, subjects were asked to indicate their ideological leanings (lean Republican, lean Independent, lean Democrat, or other) as done in prior studies (Hindman, 2009, 2012; Veenstra et al., 2014)

Interpersonal Discussion

This variable measured how often subjects engaged in conversations and discussions with others about politics. Subjects answered five questions whose responses were captured on a 1–10 (never to very often) scale as done in previous studies (Hindman & Yan, 2015; Ho, 2012; Ho et al., 2020; Kim et al., 2011). A composite score was then computed based on the average of the responses ($\alpha = .89$; items = 5).

> **Social Media Engagement Questions**
>
> *Answer the following questions on a scale of 1–10 where: 1 = not at all likely and 10 = very likely:*
>
> How likely are you to retweet the meme shown above?
> How likely are you to like the meme shown above?
> How likely are you to share the meme shown above?
> How likely are you to reply positively to the meme shown above?
>
> **Interpersonal Discussion Questions**
>
> *Answer the following questions on a scale of 1–10 where: 1 = Never and 10 = Very often:*
>
> How often do you engage in conversations and discussions with friends and family about politics?
>
> How often do you engage in conversations and discussions with your co-workers and acquaintances about politics?
>
> How often do you engage in conversations and discussions with strangers about politics?
>
> How often do you engage in conversations and discussions with people who agree with you about politics?
>
> How often do you engage in conversations and discussions with people who disagree with you about politics?

Figure 5.3: Social media engagement and interpersonal discussion questions

Partisan Media Use

This variable measured the extent to which subjects paid attention to partisan media sources. As suggested by previous studies (Saldaña et al., 2021; Veenstra et al., 2014), subjects were first asked how often they got news from right-leaning sources like Fox News, *Breitbart News Network*, and Conservative talk radio (right-leaning media). Subjects were then asked the same for left-leaning sources such as MSNBC, *HuffPost*, *Salon*, and liberal talk radio (left-leaning media). For each question, responses were measured on a 1–10 (never to very often) scale.

Social Media Engagement

SME was defined as how people interact with online content via sharing, commenting, retweeting, liking, etc. (Cao et al., 2017; Piatak & Mikkelsen, 2021; Wasike, 2022a, 2022b). Therefore, after viewing the meme with the false elections-related information, subjects answered a series of questions about their likelihood to share, like, retweet, and post a comment to the meme. Here, too, the subjects responded based on a 1–10 (not at all likely to very likely) scale. A composite SME score was then computed from the average of the responses (α = .95; items = 4).

Results

Overall, data showed that the socio-economic status, educational attainment, ideological orientation, partisan media use, and interpersonal discussion affected knowledge about elections. Income and educational attainment affected knowledge, therefore indicating the presence of the KGH as queried by RQ1. See Table 5.1 for KGH and SME means. As shown in Table 5.2, less education negatively impacted elections-related knowledge. Specifically, this effect was highest among those with a high school education or less (β = -.26, p < .001). This was also true for those with some college education, albeit with a smaller effect (β = -.13, p < .001). Income also inversely affected knowledge, more so among lower income subjects (β = -.15, p < .05). Even though income did not significantly affect knowledge among the lower middle-income subjects, the estimate (β = -.12) is noteworthy. Ideological orientation also affected elections-related knowledge (RQ2). Leaning Liberal positively affected knowledge (β = 23, p < .001) more than leaning Conservative leaning (β = .21, p < .001). Leaning Independent did not affect knowledge. Likewise, interpersonal discussion did not affect elections-related knowledge, thus answering RQ3, which queried about the association between interpersonal discussion and knowledge. The use of right-leaning media (RQ4) also reduced knowledge (β = -.10, p < .01), unlike left-leaning media use which had no effect on knowledge.

Data depicted in Table 5.3 shows similar results regarding the likelihood of SME with elections-related misinformation. The KGH partially predicted SME with elections-related misinformation, but this only occurred with income and not with education (RQ5). Those in the lower income (β = .19, p < .001) and lower middle-income groups (β = .15, p < .01) were significantly more likely to engage with misinformation. No significant results occurred with upper income subjects. Regarding the BGH (RQ6), leaning Liberal significantly reduced the likelihood of SME with elections-related misinformation (β = .12, p < .01). Leaning Independent or Conservative did have any significant effect. However, interpersonal discussion (RQ7) significantly

Table 5.1: Elections-related knowledge and social media engagement means

	Knowledge*	S.D.	SME**	S.D.
Liberal	2.84	1.48	3.00	2.99
Independent	2.22	1.37	3.69	2.72
Conservative	2.71	1.40	3.69	3.0
High school or less	1.85	1.22	3.83	2.90
Some college	2.38	1.35	3.35	2.75
College degree or more	2.95	1.44	3.27	2.93
Lower income	1.93	1.22	4.00	2.87
Lower middle income	2.16	1.27	3.67	2.82
Upper middle income	2.66	1.50	3.21	2.74
Upper income	2.83	1.42	3.23	2.97

Note: *Means for elections-related knowledge. **Means for the likelihood to engage in SME with elections-related misinformation.

Table 5.2: OLS regression predicting elections-related knowledge

	Estimate	S.E.	t	p	VIF
(Constant)		0.31	10.23	.001	
BGH measures					
Liberal	0.23	0.17	4.31	.001	2.80
Independent	0.07	0.16	1.44	0.152	2.55
Conservative	0.21	0.17	4.11	.001	2.72
KGH measures					
High school or less	-0.26	0.13	-6.57	.001	1.54
Some college	-0.13	0.12	-3.73	.001	1.30
Lower income	-0.15	0.27	-2.00	0.046	5.75
Lower middle income	-0.12	0.27	-1.82	0.069	4.63
Upper middle income	-0.08	0.23	-1.09	0.28	5.12
Upper income	-0.07	0.23	-0.87	0.39	6.47
Right-leaning media use	-0.10	0.02	-2.70	0.007	1.40
Left-leaning media use	-0.03	0.02	-0.74	0.46	1.58
Interpersonal communication	-0.07	0.02	-1.75	0.08	1.49
$R^2 = .17$; Adjusted $R^2 = .176$					

Note: Each category for ideology, education, and income were dummy coded. Also, the college or higher category was excluded from analysis due to collinearity.

increased the likelihood of SME with misinformation ($\beta = .34, p < .001$). Partisan media use increased the likelihood of SME with misinformation, with exposure to right-leaning media having a bigger effect ($\beta = .26, p < .001$) than exposure to left-leaning media ($\beta = .11, p < .001$). This answers RQ8. Lastly, political knowledge was negatively correlated with the likelihood of SME with misinformation ($r = -.28, p < .001$). This means that a person's elections-related knowledge increased, the less likely they were to engage in SME with related misinformation (RQ9).

Table 5.3: OLS regression predicting social media engagement with elections-related misinformation

	Estimate	S.E.	t	p	VIF
(Constant)		.56	-1.14	.25	
BGH measures					
Liberal	-.12	.30	-2.57	.01	2.80
Independent	.00	.29	.08	.94	2.55
Conservative	-.01	.30	-.13	.90	2.72
KGH measures					
High school or less	.05	.23	1.39	.164	1.54
Some college	.02	.21	.60	.55	1.30
Lower income	.19	.49	2.77	.006	5.75
Lower middle income	.15	.49	2.39	.017	4.63
Upper middle income	.08	.41	1.23	.22	5.12
Upper income	.09	.42	1.29	.20	6.47
Right-leaning media use	.26	.03	7.73	.001	1.40
Left-leaning media use	.11	.03	2.96	.003	1.58
Interpersonal communication	.34	.04	9.92	.001	1.49

$R^2 = .33$; Adjusted $R^2 = .32$

Note: Each category for ideology, education, and income were dummy coded. Also, the college or higher category was excluded from analysis due to collinearity.

Discussion

This study examined how social media users engage with elections-related misinformation and how knowledge gaps, partisan media use, and interpersonal discussion affect this process. Several important findings emerged. First, socio-economic factors and educational attainment affected elections-related knowledge and misinformation susceptibility. Belonging to the lower income groups decreased knowledge and increased SME with misinformation, while earning high income did not have any effects on knowledge or SME with misinformation. This aligns with pertinent studies (Gerosa et al., 2021; Ho et al., 2020; Wang et al., 2021). Additionally, interpersonal discussion played a role by increasing the likelihood of SME with misinformation, although it did not affect knowledge. That interpersonal discussion did not affect knowledge reflects the ambivalence of this variable. Research shows that interpersonal discussion generally improves political knowledge (Amsalem & Nir, 2021; Ho, 2012; Kim et al., 2011). However, there's less of this effect on social media (Lee & Xenos, 2019; Shehata & Strömbäck, 2021; van Erkel & Van Aelst, 2021) or the effect occurs only in certain circumstances (Abidin, 2021; Maly, 2020; Vermeer et al., 2021). The fact that this study specifically examined elections-related knowledge rather than general political knowledge may also explain some of this ambivalence, given the specificity of the approach.

Regarding the ideological orientation, data indicated that leaning Liberal or Conservative improved knowledge with Liberal ideology having a bigger effect on knowledge than Conservative ideology. This reflects prior research that showed similar effects of ideology on knowledge regarding divisive topics such as immigration, climate change, and healthcare reform (Hindman, 2009, 2012; Saldaña et al., 2021). Only leaning Liberal affect the likelihood of SME with information by reducing it while the other ideological orientations did not have any effects. However, exposure to right-leaning media reduced knowledge and increased the likelihood of SME with misinformation. This reflects research on the effect of right-leaning media exposure on knowledge and susceptibility to misinformation (Saldaña et al., 2018; Veenstra et al., 2014; Hindman & Yan, 2015).

Implications

As mentioned, most studies examine either the KGH or the BGH. By examining both, this study makes an important theoretical contribution. Examining these two theories regarding social media use and misinformation on one of the most important issues in present-day U.S. politics, i.e., elections-related misinformation, amplifies this contribution. Additionally, examining the role of knowledge in politics not only makes a theoretical contribution, but a practical one as well. The results pointed out variables that reduced elections-related knowledge and those that increased social media engagement with related misinformation. Stakeholders may use these results to guide initiatives aimed at improving civic knowledge and those aimed at combating misinformation. Given that the mean for elections knowledge for the entire sample was 2.5 (s.d. = 1.43) on a 0–5 scale and the average for the likelihood of SME with misinformation was 3.45 (s.d. = 2.88) on a 1–5 scale, targeting the knowledge gaps uncovered by the data is of paramount importance. Data indicated that the susceptible groups were those in the lower socioeconomic tiers, those who use right-leaning media, and those who engage in interpersonal discussions about politics and elections.

Limitations

The findings must be viewed within the lens of the study's limitations. For one, the self-reported responses used in the survey are prone to bias (Devaux & Sassi, 2016; Müller & Moshagen, 2019). Second, the sample consisted only of social media users and the findings may only be generalized within this cohort. Third, given that this study is cross-sectional, it captures dynamics at a specific point in time and does not reveal any changes over time. A longitudinal study examining dynamics before and after an election for instance, may reveal more nuance. Lastly, even though this study was not a full-fledged experiment, it used a meme as stimuli. This means that the effects reported here were based on a single stimulus. Additionally, the meme, although fashioned to resemble a real-life meme, was not presented to subjects in its natural milieu of a social media page.

References

Abidin, C. (2021). Minahs and minority celebrity: Parody YouTube influencers and minority politics in Singapore. *Celebrity studies*, *12*(4), 598–617. https://doi.org/10.1080/19392397.2019.1698816

Allcott, H., & Gentzkow, M. (2017). Social media and fake news in the 2016 election. *Journal of Economic Perspectives*, *31*(2), 211–236. https://doi.org/10.1257/jep.31.2.211

Amsalem, E., & Nir, L. (2021). Does interpersonal discussion increase political knowledge? A meta-analysis. *Communication Research*, *48*(5), 619–641. https://doi.org/10.1177/0093650219866357

Barrett, P. M., & Sims, J.G. (2021). False accusation: The unfounded claim that social media companies censor conservatives. *NYU STERN Center for Business and Human Rights*. https://static1.squarespace.com/static/5b6df958f8370af3217d4178/t/6011e68dec2c7013d3caf3cb/1611785871154/NYU+False+Accusation+report_FINAL.pdf

Bonfadelli, H. (2002). The internet and knowledge gaps: A theoretical and empirical investigation. *European Journal of Communication, 17*(1), 65–84. https://doi.org/10.1177/0267323102017001607

Boudreau, C., & Lupia, A. (2011). Political knowledge. In J. N. Druckman, D. P. Green, J. H. Kuklinski & A. Lupia (Eds.), *Cambridge handbook of experimental political science* (pp. 171–186). Cambridge University Press.

Bovet, A., & Makse, H. A. (2019). Influence of fake news in Twitter during the 2016 U.S. presidential election. *Nature Communications, 10*. https://doi.org/10.1038/s41467-018-07761-2

Brandon, D., Long, J., Loraas, T., Mueller-Phillips, J., & Vansant, B. (2014). Online instrument delivery and participant recruitment services: Emerging opportunities for behavioral accounting Research. *Behavioral Research in Accounting, 26*(1), 1–23. https://doi.org/10.2308/bria-50651

Bunis, D. (2020, August 24). What do you know about voting and the election? *AARP.* https://www.aarp.org/politics-society/government-elections/info-2018/election-quiz-trivia.html#quest1

Cao, B., Liu, C., Durvasula, M., Tang, W., Pan, S., Saffer, A. J., Wei, C., & Tucker, J. D. (2017). Social media engagement and HIV testing among men who have sex with men in China: A nationwide cross-sectional survey. *Journal of Medical Internet Research, 19*(7), https://doi.org/10.2196/jmir.7251

Cassidy, C. S., & Mulvihill, G. (2022). Minor poll problems twisted into false U.S. election claims. *The Associated Press.* https://apnews.com/article/2022-midterm-elections-voting-909279666c18777c44a9fad6754f3de7

Chang, J., Kim, S.-H., Kang, M.-H., Shim, J. C., & Ma, D. H. (2018). The gap in scientific knowledge and role of science communication in South Korea. *Public Understanding of Science, 27*(5), 578–593. https://doi.org/10.1177/0963662516685487

Cunha, D. (2020, September 6). Red pills and dog whistles: It is more than 'just the internet'. *Al Jazeera.* https://www.aljazeera.com/opinions/2020/9/6/red-pills-and-dog-whistles-it-is-more-than-just-the-internet

Delli Carpini, M. X., & Keeter, S. (1996). *What Americans know about politics and why it matters.* Yale University Press. https://doi.org/10.12987/9780300194319-002

Devaux, M., & Sassi, F. (2016). Social disparities in hazardous alcohol use: Self-report bias may lead to incorrect estimates. *European Journal of Public Health, 26*(1), 129–134. https://doi.org/10.1093/eurpub/ckv190

Faul, F., Erdfelder, E., Buchner, A., & Lang, A.-G. (2009). Statistical power analyses using G*Power 3.1: Tests for correlation and regression analyses. *Behavior Research Methods, 41*(4), 1149–1160. https://doi.org/10.3758/BRM.41.4.1149

Faul, F., Erdfelder, E., Lang, A.-G., & Buchner, A. (2007). G*Power 3: A flexible statistical power analysis program for the social, behavioral, and biomedical sciences. *Behavior Research Methods, 39*(2), 175–191. https://doi.org/10.3758/BF03193146

Fox, M. (2021). Conservatives more likely to believe false news, new study finds. *CNN.* https://www.cnn.com/2021/06/02/health/conservatives-false-news-study/index.html

Gaziano, C. (2014). Components of the belief gap: Ideology and education. *SAGE Open, 4*(1). https://doi.org/10.1177/2158244013518052

Gaziano, E., & Gaziano, C. (1999). Social control, social change, and the knowledge gap hypothesis. In D. Demers & K. Viswanath (Eds.), *Mass media, social control, and social change: A macrosocial perspective* (pp. 117–136). Iowa State University Press.

Gerosa, T., Gui, M., Hargittai, E., & Nguyen, M. H. (2021). (Mis)informed during COVID-19: How education level and information sources contribute to knowledge gaps. *International Journal of Communication, 15*, 2196–2217. https://ijoc.org/index.php/ijoc/article/view/16438

Gibson, R. K., & McAllister, I. (2015). New media, elections and the political knowledge gap in Australia. *Journal of Sociology, 51*(2), 337–353. https://doi.org/10.1177/1440783314532173

Gil de Zúñiga, H., Barnidge, M., & Scherman, A. (2017). Social media social capital, offline social capital, and citizenship: Exploring asymmetrical social capital effects. *Political Communication, 34*(1), 44–68. https://doi.org/10.1080/10584609.2016.1227000

Goh, D. (2015). Narrowing the knowledge gap: The role of alternative online media in an authoritarian press system. *Journalism & Mass Communication Quarterly, 92*(4), 877–897. https://doi.org/10.1177/1077699015596336

Greenberg, J. (2022). Most Republicans still falsely believe Trump's stolen election claims. Here are some reasons why. *Poynter.* https://www.poynter.org/fact-checking/2022/70-percent-republicans-falsely-believe-stolen-election-trump/

Grinberg, N., Joseph, K., Friedland, L., Swire-Thompson, B., & Lazer, D. (2019). Fake news on Twitter during the 2016 U.S. presidential election. *Science, 363*(6425), 374–378. https://doi.org/10.1126/science.aau2706

Gunther, R., Beck, P. A., & Nisbet, E. C. (2019). "Fake news" and the defection of 2012 Obama voters in the 2016 presidential election. *Electoral Studies, 61*. https://doi.org/10.1016/j.electstud.2019.03.006

Hardy, B. W., & Scheufele, D. A. (2009). Presidential campaign dynamics and the ebb and flow of talk as a moderator: Media exposure, knowledge, and political discussion. *Communication Theory, 19*(1), 89–101. https://doi.org/10.1111/j.1468-2885.2008.01334.x

Hindman, D. B. (2009). Mass media flow and differential distribution of politically disputed beliefs: The belief gap hypothesis. *Journalism & Mass Communication Quarterly, 86*(4), 790–808. https://doi.org/10.1177/107769900908600405

Hindman, D. B., & Yan, C. (2015). The knowledge gap versus the belief gap and abstinence-only sex education. *Journal of Health Communication, 20*(8), 949–957. https://doi.org/10.1080/10810730.2015.1018571

Hindman, D. B. (2012). Knowledge gaps, belief gaps, and public opinion about health care reform. *Journalism & Mass Communication Quarterly, 89*(4), 585–605. https://doi.org/10.1177/1077699012456021

Ho, S. S. (2012). The knowledge gap hypothesis in Singapore: The roles of socioeconomic status, mass media, and interpersonal discussion on public knowledge of the H1N1 Flu Pandemic. *Mass Communication & Society, 15*(5), 695–717. https://doi.org/10.1080/15205436.2011.616275

Ho, S. S., Looi, J., Leung, Y. W., Bekalu, M. A., & Viswanath, K. (2020). Comparing the knowledge gap hypothesis in the United States and Singapore: The case of nanotechnology.

Public Understanding of Science, 29(8), 835–854. https://doi.org/10.1177/0963662520952547

Holt, T., & Loraas, T. (2019). Using Qualtrics panels to source external auditors: A replication study. *The Journal of Information Systems,* 33(1), 29–41. https://doi.org/10.2308/isys-51986

Hwang, Y., & Jeong, S.-H. (2009). Revisiting the knowledge gap hypothesis: A meta-analysis of thirty-five years of research. *Journalism & Mass Communication Quarterly,* 86(3), 513–532. https://doi.org/10.1177/107769900908600304

Iafrato, A. (2020). Presidential election trivia quiz: How well do you know the process and its history? *Boston Herald.* https://www.bostonherald.com/2020/10/19/presidential-election-trivia-quiz-how-well-do-you-know-the-process-and-its-history/

IFCN. (2022). An open letter to YouTube's CEO from the world's fact-checkers. *Poynter.* https://www.poynter.org/fact-checking/2022/an-open-letter-to-youtubes-ceo-from-the-worlds-fact-checkers/

Jurkowitz, M. (2021). Republicans who relied on Trump for news more concerned than other Republicans about election fraud. *Pew Research Center.* https://www.pewresearch.org/fact-tank/2021/01/11/republicans-who-relied-on-trump-for-news-more-concerned-than-other-republicans-about-election-fraud/

Kim, Y., Moran, M. B., Wilkin, H. A., & Ball-Rokeach, S. J. (2011). Integrated connection to neighborhood storytelling network, education, and chronic disease knowledge among African Americans and Latinos in Los Angeles. *Journal of Health Communication,* 16(4), 393–415. https://doi.org/10.1080/10810730.2010.546483

Lange, J. (2022). Half of U.S. Republicans believe the left led Jan. 6 violence: Reuters/Ipsos poll. *Reuters.* https://www.reuters.com/world/us/half-us-republicans-believe-left-led-jan-6-violence-reutersipsos-2022-06-09/

Lee, C. (2009). The role of internet engagement in the health-knowledge gap. *Journal of Broadcasting & Electronic Media,* 53(3), 365–382. https://doi.org/10.1080/08838150903102758

Lee, C. E., & Kent, J. J. (2017). Facebook says Russian-backed election content reached 126 million Americans. *NBC News.* https://www.nbcnews.com/news/us-news/russian-backed-election-content-reached-126-million-americans-facebook-says-n815791

Lee, S., & Xenos, M. (2019). Social distraction? Social media use and political knowledge in two U.S. Presidential elections. *Computers in Human Behavior,* 90, 18–25. https://doi.org/10.1016/j.chb.2018.08.006

Lee, S., Yamamoto, M., & Tandoc, E. C. (2022). Why people who know less think they know about COVID-19: Evidence from U.S. and Singapore. *Journalism & Mass Communication Quarterly,* 99(1), 44–68. https://doi.org/10.1177/10776990211049460

Levitt, J. (2007). The truth about voter fraud. *Brennan Center for Justice.* https://www.brennancenter.org/our-work/research-reports/truth-about-voter-fraud

Maly, I. (2020). Metapolitical New right influencers: The case of Brittany Pettibone. *Social Sciences,* 9(7). https://doi.org/10.3390/socsci9070113

Mitchell, A., Jurkowitz, M., Oliphant, B., & Shearer, E. (2020). Political divides, conspiracy theories and divergent news sources heading into 2020 election. *Pew Research Center.*

https://www.pewresearch.org/journalism/2020/09/16/political-divides-conspiracy-theories-and-divergent-news-sources-heading-into-2020-election/\

Moore, R.C., & Coronel, J. C. (2022). Interpersonal discussion and political knowledge: Unpacking the black box via a combined experimental and content-analytic approach. *Human Communication Research, 48*(2), 230–264. https://doi.org/10.1093/hcr/hqac002

Müller, S., & Moshagen, M. (2019). Controlling for response bias in self-ratings of personality: A comparison of impression management scales and the overclaiming technique. *Journal of Personality Assessment, 101*(3), 229–236. https://doi.org/10.1080/00223891.2018.1451870

Novacic, I. (2020). Censorship on social media? It's not what you think. *CBS News.* https://www.cbsnews.com/news/censorship-social-media-conservative-liberal-cbsn-originals/

Oeldorf-Hirsch, A. (2018). The role of engagement in learning from active and incidental news exposure on social media. *Mass Communication & Society, 21*(2), 225–247. https://doi.org/10.1080/15205436.2017.1384022

Pew Research Center. (2017). *The future of truth and misinformation online.* https://www.pewresearch.org/internet/2017/10/19/the-future-of-truth-and-misinformation-online/

Piatak, J., & Mikkelsen, I. (2021). Does social media engagement translate to civic engagement offline? *Nonprofit and Voluntary Sector Quarterly, 50*(5), 1079–1101. https://doi.org/10.1177/0899764021999444

PRRI. (2021a, November 1). *Competing visions of America: An evolving identity or a culture under attack? Findings from the 2021 American Values Survey.* https://www.prri.org/research/competing-visions-of-america-an-evolving-identity-or-a-culture-under-attack/

PRRI. (2021b, May 12). *The "big lie": Most Republicans believe the 2020 election was stolen.* https://www.prri.org/spotlight/the-big-lie-most-republicans-believe-the-2020-election-was-stolen/

Qualtrics. (n.d.). *What is a research panel (and should we have one)?* https://www.qualtrics.com/experience-management/research/research-panels-samples/

Saldaña, M., Chacon, L. M. C., & Garcia-Perdomo, V. (2018). When gaps become huuuuge: Donald Trump and beliefs about immigration. *Mass Communication & Society, 21*(6), 785–813. https://doi.org/10.1080/15205436.2018.1504304

Saldaña, M., McGregor, S., & Johnson, T. (2021). Mind the gap! The role of political identity and attitudes in the emergence of belief gaps. *International Journal of Public Opinion Research, 33*(3), 607–625. https://doi.org/10.1093/ijpor/edab006

Scala, N. M., Goethals, P. L., Dehlinger, J., Mezgebe, Y., Jilcha, B., & Bloomquist, I. (2022). Evaluating mail-based security for electoral processes using attack trees. *Risk Analysis, 42*(10), 2327–2343. https://doi.org/10.1111/risa.13876

Seitz-Wald, A., & Allen, J. (2022). A spiral of violence and fear is creating angst for many voters ahead of the midterm elections. *NBC News.* https://www.nbcnews.com/politics/2022-election/spiral-violence-fear-creating-angst-many-voters-ahead-midterm-election-rcna55740

Shehata, A., & Strömbäck, J. (2021). Learning political news from social media: Network media logic and current affairs news learning in a high-choice media Environment. *Communication research, 48*(1), 125–147. https://doi.org/10.1177/0093650217749354

Tichenor, P. J., Donohue, G. A., & Olien, C. N. (1970). Mass media flow and differential growth in knowledge. *Public Opinion Quarterly, 34*(2), 159–170. https://doi.org/10.1086/267786

Tran, H. (2013). Does exposure to online media matter? The knowledge gap and the mediating role of news use. *International Journal of Communication, 7*, 831–852. https://ijoc.org/index.php/ijoc/article/view/1550/886

U.S. Citizenship and Immigration Services. (n.d.). *Civics (history and government) questions for the naturalization test.* https://www.uscis.gov/sites/default/files/document/questions-and-answers/100q.pdf

Ulloa, J. (2022). Obama casts Arizona's midterm election as a fight to preserve democracy. *The New York Times.* https://www.nytimes.com/live/2022/11/02/us/elections-midterms#obama-arizona-heckler

van Erkel, P. F. A., & Van Aelst, P. (2021). Why don't we learn from social media? Studying effects of and mechanisms behind social media news use on general surveillance political knowledge. *Political Communication, 38*(4), 407–425. https://doi.org/10.1080/10584609.2020.1784328

van Prooijen, J., & Douglas, K. M. (2017). Conspiracy theories as part of history: The role of societal crisis situations. *Memory Studies, 10*(3), 323–333. https://doi.org/10.1177/1750698017701615

Veenstra, A. S., Hossain, M. D., & Lyons, B. A. (2014). Partisan media and discussion as enhancers of the belief gap. *Mass Communication & Society, 17*(6), 874–897. https://doi.org/10.1080/15205436.2013.855791

Vermeer, S. A. M., Kruikemeier, S., Trilling, D., & de Vreese, C. H. (2021). WhatsApp with politics?!: Examining the effects of interpersonal political discussion in instant messaging apps. *The International Journal of Press/politics, 26*(2), 410–437. https://doi.org/10.1177/1940161220925020

Waldman, M. (2022, June 14). Focus on the big lie, not the big liar. *Brennan Center for Justice.* https://www.brennancenter.org/our-work/analysis-opinion/focus-big-lie-not-big-liar

Wang, H., Li, L., Wu, J., & Gao, H. (2021). Factors influencing COVID-19 knowledge-gap: A cross-sectional study in China. *BMC Public Health, 21*(1826). https://doi.org/10.1186/s12889-021-11856-9

Wang, T. (2020). Does fake news matter to election outcomes? The case study of Taiwan's 2018 local elections. *Asian Journal for Public Opinion Research, 8*(2), 67–104. https://doi.org/10.15206/ajpor.2020.8.2.67

Wasike, B. (2022a). Memes, memes, everywhere, nor any meme to trust: Examining the credibility and persuasiveness of COVID-19-related memes. *Journal of Computer-Mediated Communication, 27*(2), https://doi.org/10.1093/jcmc/zmab024

Wasike, B. (2022b). When the influencer says jump! How influencer signaling affects engagement with COVID-19 misinformation. *Social Science & Medicine, 315.* Advance online publication. https://doi.org/10.1016/j.socscimed.2022.115497

Wolf, Z. B. (2021, May 19). The 5 key elements of Trump's Big Lie and how it came to be. *CNN*. https://www.cnn.com/2021/05/19/politics/donald-trump-big-lie-explainer/
Yang, J., & Grabe, M. E. (2011). Knowledge acquisition gaps: A comparison of print versus online news sources. *New Media & Society*, *13*(8), 1211–1227. https://doi.org/10.1177/1461444811401708

· 6 ·

SOWING SEEDS OF DISTRUST: INVESTIGATING THE SPREAD OF MIS- AND DISINFORMATION BY EXPLORING THE PATHWAYS FOR RURAL AMERICANS TO NEWS

Todd R. Vogts and Jacob Groshek

Armed with bear spray, guns, and more (Dreisbach & Mak, 2021), they converged on the United States Capitol on January 6, 2021. Estimates suggest 10,000 people arrived before the violence ensued, which resulted in 2,000 individuals breaching security and storming the halls of American democracy, leaving five people dead and more than 700 charged with crimes related to the event (Rubin et al., 2022). Interestingly, a majority of the insurrectionists were not from areas considered to be Republican strongholds on the political map because "of those arrested for their role in the Capitol riot, more than half came from counties that Biden won; one-sixth came from counties that Trump won with less than 60 percent of the vote" (Pape & Ruby, 2021, para. 11).

The attack featured individuals from every state and Washington, D.C. (NPR Staff, 2021), and it sought to prevent the transfer of power from former President Donald Trump to President Joe Biden because of the belief that the election had been stolen (Whitehurst, 2022). Such an idea grew out of the political polarization dividing the country (Darr et al., 2018, 2021; Padgett et al., 2019). It was fertilized by President Donald Trump's conspiratorial and baseless assertions that 2020 elections were stolen, which is a falsehood that became known as the "big lie" and harkened back to Adolf Hitler and Nazi Germany (Block, 2021).

Despite clear evidence that the election was not stolen or rife with fraud, Republicans remain aligned with the sentiment of Trump's claims. Polls show that nearly 70% of Republicans don't believe President Joe Biden was legitimately elected (Greenberg, 2022). Conservatives in general seem to agree with this line of thinking. Pape (2021) argued that 21 million American adults believe the election was stolen and that force would be justified to keep Trump in office. What's more, such viewpoints continued to prevail into the 2022 midterm elections. Adopting such beliefs can be described as embracing the herd mentality (Barbaro, 2022; Tarm & Billeaud, 2021), which develops from a distrust of the news that is cultivated by mis- and disinformation spread by partisan media outlets.

For individuals believing that Biden is not the legitimate president, their preferred news sources are conservative, such as Fox News, Newsmax, and One America News Network (Ismail, 2022). According to Pape (2022), "Mainstream news media is more important than social media within the insurrectionist movement" (p. 36). Clearly, media influences are at play, cultivating particular political ideologies. Media consumption has been shown to impact political activity and belief (Johnson & Kaye, 2013), so it makes sense that this contributes to polarization and the entrenchment of political views (Iyengar et al., 2019). Bail et al. (2018) agreed as they found exposure to opposing views on social media can increase polarization. This can be attributed to the incivility that is generally associated with partisan news and information. However, research found that this incivility can actually decrease polarization if the emotional outbursts come from party-aligned sources, such as Fox News for Republicans or MSNBC for Democrats (Druckman et al., 2019).

To that end, partisan media provides fertile ground for mis- and disinformation to spread, fueling polarization and incivility. Social media makes it even easier for this false and unreliable information to reach the masses (Gaultney et al., 2022), but mis- and disinformation travel via all media channels. One goal of this communication is to achieve political goals or promote commercial interests through false or misleading statements designed to be believed by audiences and disseminators alike (de Ridder, 2021). Another goal is to evoke an emotional and visceral response (Han & Federico, 2018) and both liberal and conservative media do this. However, research shows conservative media creates more emotional responses by leveraging outrage (Sobieraj & Berry, 2011). Conservatives have dedicated cable television networks, and most AM radio stations also focus on conservative ideals, meaning conservatives have ample opportunity to have their beliefs affirmed (Frank, 2004).

Altogether various forms of both mis- and disinformation can fertilize citizen distrust in news (Kalogeropoulos et al., 2019; Karlsen & Aalberg, 2023; Swart & Broersma, 2021), which not only allows but also cultivates democracy-damaging polarization to grow within the United States. This polarization takes root due to the erosion of reliable information brought on by confirmation bias that constructs filter bubbles and echo chambers (Flaxman et al., 2016; Lee et al., 2021; Nechushtai & Lewis, 2019; Pearson & Knobloch-Westerwick, 2019).

In many cases, politically motivated individuals and media outlets plant these seeds of mis- and disinformation, leaving members of society to consume corrupted content. If this news diet lacks nutrients that serve the public good, this information constructs a skewed perception of society, weakening the social capital bonds that create a functioning democracy (Belair-Gagnon et al., 2019; Lewis et al., 2014; Putnam, 2001). In order to minimize mis- and disinformation from the public discourse of democracy and restore trust in journalism, the pathways to news that individuals take must be better considered and modeled.

This risk is particularly important as it relates to the news consumption habits of rural Americans, who largely live and work in agrarian communities and exist as an important voting block within democratic politics as was evident in the 2016 election of President Donald Trump and the controversy surrounding the outcome of the 2020 election. Yet despite its demonstrated importance to electoral outcomes, current research largely ignores this swath of the United States population.

As such, with the purpose of filling this gap in the literature, this study investigated the pathways to news for individuals living and working in rural areas of the country as a way to explore how individuals come to believe in and further spread mis- and disinformation, specifically looking at content produced by partisan media outlets that include, but are not limited to, talk radio, cable television, and social media. Specifically, this study focused on Kansas because, as a historically red state (Wenzel, 2020), it made national headlines when in 2022 residents of this reliably conservative territory shot down a proposed state Constitutional amendment seeking to outlaw abortions following the overturning of *Roe v. Wade* (Smith & Glueck, 2022). Such a divergence from electoral expectations positions Kansas as unique case study to investigate the implications of news consumption and misinformation exposure on rural citizens.

Through the implementation of semi-structured, in-depth interviews that collected data from these individuals, this study adds to the debate on how individuals access and use news in ways that stimulate political division and polarization to flourish (Bail et al., 2018; Darr et al., 2021; Gaultney et al., 2022; Talisse, 2021). In filling a vital gap in the existing literature, this study engaged both Cultivation Theory (CT) and Uses and Gratifications Theory (U&G) to examine the pervasive and spreading problem of mis- and disinformation among rural Americans.

Literature Review

In 1964, media theorist Marshall McLuhan pointed out that society "lives in a world of information overload" (McLuhan, 2003, p. 52). What one pays attention to is considered to be context-dependent based on what the individual is thinking, feeling, and experiencing (Stephens, 2013). Crary (2001) suggested, "Attention as a process of selection necessarily meant that perception was an activity of exclusion, of rendering parts of a perceptual field unperceived" (pp. 24–25). Therefore, keeping issues of attention in mind as they relate to media serves an important purpose. The news and information ecosystem is fragmented (Searles & Smith, 2016), so understanding how people find and use news helps shed light on how the belief in and spreading of mis- and disinformation occurs.

According to Newman et al. (2021), 66% of Americans got news via online channels in 2021, while 52% used television and 16% used print as their sources for news. Similarly, Shearer (2021) also reported that 52% of Americans preferred digital platforms for their news but found 35% prefer television. Furthermore, 84% of United States adults get their news on digital devices, compared to 67% for television, 50% for radio, and 34% for print publications (Matsa & Naseer, 2021). The dominance of digital platforms, which include social media, should come as no surprise. Such tools provide users the ability to tailor their news exposure to fit within ideological, interest-driven, or any other type of categorization (Batsell, 2015; Briggs, 2020).

Within an online environment, information presentation is more dynamic than in static mediums such as print or television. Users are accustomed to a level of interactivity (Allam, 2019; Belair-Gagnon et al., 2017; Briggs, 2007). For example, links to other pieces of content are an important way people use a news outlet's website (Collier et al., 2021) and being able to comment on a story provides users a way to interact with the news (Liu & McLeod, 2021). Of course, that presumes an individual is actively seeking news and information. In some cases, a person can "bump into" news online. Wieland and Kleinen-von Königslöw (2020) referred to this as "incidental news exposure," which is when an individual unintentionally comes across news and subsequently consumes it to the point that knowledge is gained. This inadvertent news exposure can cause the consumer to develop an inflated sense of being informed (Song et al., 2020). As Dahlgren (2018) suggested, perceived knowledge impacts participation in public discourse, especially online.

Obviously, other mediums also provide pathways to news. Shearer (2021) highlighted that 22% of United States adults get news from podcasts either often or sometimes. Newsletters also provide an entry point to news consumption (Henneman et al., 2015; Newman, 2020; Tornoe, 2017). Still, as has been highlighted, television remains an important way for individuals to get news (Newman et al., 2021). According to the Pew Research Center (2019), 86% of Americans get local news from television. For all news, 68% of Americans use the television (Matsa & Naseer, 2021; Shearer, 2021). Furthermore, television journalism exists as a key source of political knowledge creation among viewers (Gutsche, 2019; Ksiazek et al., 2019; Yamamoto et al., 2021). This resulted in the first research question:

RQ1: What are the news consumption habits of rural residents in Kansas?

Thanks to cable television, consumers have a plethora of channels they can turn to that provide news. The big three options are CNN, the Fox News Channel, and MSNBC. Despite being news-oriented, each of these channels is broadcasting 24 hours per day and actively seeks profit, which influences the types of programming they produce (Jones, 2012). To fill the timeslots, the channels produce a large quantity of commentary and opinion programming, which they were able to do thanks to Reagan-era deregulation that resulted in the repeal of the Fairness Doctrine's requirement of "equal time" being given to competing political voices (Vaughn, 2008; Young, 2021).

These networks capitalize on confirmation bias, or the tendency of a person to focus on messages that confirm their beliefs and opinions while avoiding messages that conflict with their beliefs and opinions (Lee et al., 2021; Pearson & Knobloch-Westerwick, 2019). This means individuals tend to only expose themselves to media messages from cable news networks that support their political ideologies (Knobloch-Westerwick et al., 2015). Doing so allows them to avoid uncomfortable cognitive dissonance, which is when recently received information that conflicts with previously held information or knowledge (Festinger, 1962; Hameleers & van der Meer, 2020). This resulted in the first hypothesis:

> H1: Rural residents in Kansas get most of their news via national outlets and social media platforms that focus on opinion-oriented content.

As such, partisan cable news channels become a haven for political ideologues. The opposing political party is presented as the enemy and in constant conflict with the other end of the political spectrum, which increases polarization (Han & Federico, 2017). Cable television news does this by relying on outrage, which fires up and exploits the emotions of individuals with certain political beliefs to maintain viewership and increase profitability (Young, 2021). As Sobieraj and Berry (2011) explained, leveraging outrage eliminates nuanced discussions of politics "in favor of melodrama, misrepresentative exaggeration, mockery, and improbable forecasts of impending doom" that becomes a rhetorical contest rather than a coherent discussion of the issues at hand aimed at scoring points with audiences and politicians alike (p. 20).

Radio also leverages outrage and drama, and the use of the medium has remained steady for more than a decade (Pew Research Center, 2021). Though music became a focus of radio, especially with the development of the FM band and the Top 40 and other radio programming formats (Campbell et al., 2019), news radio broadcasting continues. As was the case in the early days of radio, news, commentary, and political talk shows continue to remain popular (Horten, 2002). Specifically, talk radio consists of opinion-based programming, and it is often cited as the most popular format on the radio (Campbell et al., 2019). Since American adults spend almost 12 hours per week listening to traditional radio (Nielsen, 2019), the likelihood that individuals are spending at least some of that time listening to news or talk radio seems high. Of course, talk radio in its current form would not exist if it weren't for Reagan-era deregulation that resulted in the repeal of the Fairness Doctrine's requirement of "equal time" being given to competing political voices (Vaughn, 2008; Young, 2021). This rule revocation allowed radio stations to produce and broadcast on-sided programming, and by the end of the 1980s, conservative talk shows filled the airwaves (Vaughn, 2008).

The reason conservative talk radio found success is that the partisan messages clearly struck a nerve. By tuning in to conservative talk radio, listeners "could quickly and easily get detailed, informed assessments from someone they generally agreed with, a fellow conservative—a charming, articulate, well-informed one" (Jones, 1998, p. 370). This again feeds into the idea of filter bubbles and echo chambers that serve as vehicles to reinforce previously held beliefs and opinions (Flaxman et al., 2016; Geiß et al., 2021; Torres-Lugo et al., 2020). Also, the messages are delivered with emotion and energy, which pulls listeners in and excites them. As such, this type of content breeds incivility—understood to be disrespectful and hyperbolic claims toward a target that are delivered in a purposeful and confrontational manner—within society's political discourse by using emotional appeals that activate negative political beliefs and opinions (Gervais, 2014). Research from Conway and Stryker (2021) found people from all political beliefs recognized the incivility, especially when it came from talk radio show hosts or other broadcast political pundits, but Republicans seemed to be unfazed by the hostility and outrage while Democrats demonstrated more concern about the language being used.

Therefore, conservative talk radio can fuel polarization and division. It accomplishes this by exaggerating fringe opinions to motivate those who have low trust in the government to engage with politics (Hollander, 1997; Johnson & Kaye, 2013). Again, relying on outrage (Shrader, 2013; Sobieraj & Berry, 2011; Young, 2021), partisan pundits pontificating over the airwaves broadcast messaging designed to rally the like-minded listener and shore up the conservative ideals being put forth. For the diehard, these political messages confirm previously held beliefs. They can spur action that can be dangerous, such as the January 6, 2021, insurrection at the Capitol. However, the larger concern, as Hofstetter and Gianos (1997) suggested, is when the talk show hosts leverage passions, such as religion, to convince vulnerable people to view the world from their perspectives. This deepens division and cultivates mistrust of the other side. Even though talk radio is more about entertainment than news (Bennett, 2002), listeners often internalize the messaging differently.

Trust can be understood as a relationship between social actors that involves an orientation toward the future, includes risk due to unknown futures, and works to reduce the complexity found in social interactions (Prochazka & Schweiger, 2019). Specific to the news media, Strömbäck et al. (2020) suggested a viable conceptualization of trust as a concept, which was adopted for this study and is articulated as follows:

> [A]t the broadest conceptual level, there is significant consensus that news media trust refers to the relationship between citizens (the trustors) and the news media (the trustees) where citizens, however tacit or habitual, in situations of uncertainty

expect that interactions with the news media will lead to gains rather than losses. (p. 142)

To that end, Usher (2018) described trust as a constructed object within journalism and communication more broadly because it must be negotiated by all social actors, which includes journalists, audiences, and sources. Without this construct, the informed citizenry necessary for democracy fails to come to fruition thanks to choosing partisan sources of information that align with their predetermined beliefs. "When people do not trust news, they are more likely to choose nonmainstream, alternative news sources," which leads them "to rely on their political predispositions" more heavily (Kalogeropoulos et al., 2019, pp. 3672–3673). This results in the second research hypothesis:

> H2: Rural residents in Kansas distrust the news due to a belief that media outlets are not telling the truth about what is really going on in the world.

By leaning on politically charged content, polarization occurs due to a void of reliable information, which increases the lack of trust that cultivates an atmosphere of fertile ground for mis- and disinformation to grow and flourish. Darr et al. (2018) found loss of local newspapers increased community division as evident by down-ballot voting patterns. People become less knowledgeable about politics if no journalists are covering local politics. Disinformation and misinformation fill these voids. Maresh-Fuehrer and Gurney (2021) defined disinformation as false information created and shared intentionally with the goal of harm, and misinformation was defined as unintentionally spreading false information. Such messages often take root because of confirmation bias (Lee et al., 2021; Pearson & Knobloch-Westerwick, 2019). This can be done through traditional media outlets (e.g., Bauer et al., 2022; Hemmer, 2016; Tsfati et al., 2020), and it is easy to do on social media (e.g., Nissen et al., 2022; Pasquetto et al., 2020; Xiao, 2021). This resulted in the second research question:

> RQ2: Why do rural residents in Kansas believe and spread mis- and disinformation they encounter?

As such, this study's utilization of Cultivation Theory (CT) and Uses and Gratifications Theory (U&G) fits well. CT focuses on television and how that medium shapes and distorts viewers' perceptions of reality (Rubin & Haridakis, 2001). As primary developers of CT, Gerbner and Gross (1976) argued that the "substance of the consciousness cultivated by TV is not so much specific attitudes and opinions as more basic assumptions about the 'facts' of life and standards of judgment on which conclusions are based" (p. 175). This social construction of reality is a complex process that requires more than just a viewer or just a content producer who exercises some form of power or overt influence over the other.

Perhaps the most notable use of CT, though, concerns how depictions of violence on television shape viewers' beliefs about their safety in society. Gerbner et al. (1986) referred to this as the "mean world" syndrome and suggested that "television may cultivate exaggerated notions of the prevalence of violence and risk out in the world" (p. 29), which means that "one lesson viewers derive from heavy exposure to the violence-saturated world of television is that in such a mean and dangerous world, most people 'cannot be trusted' and that most people are 'just looking out for themselves'" (p. 28).

Due to CT's view that media shapes reality by affecting attitudes and beliefs, the theory provides an important lens for looking at trust or mistrust of the media. Shrum (2017) highlighted how television viewing cultivated interpersonal mistrust. Earlier research also found a correlation between television viewing and a lack of trust (Gerbner & Gross, 1976; Jin & Kim, 2014). As such, the cultivation ability of mass media discourses becomes evident. Discourse consists of the language, words, images, symbols, and other artifacts being used to create knowledge and reality (Fairclough, 2010; Gee, 2015; White, 2004).

Of course, CT shows up in non-television-related research too. This includes newspapers (Lubbers et al., 2000), video games (Scharrer & Warren, 2022; Williams, 2006), social media and user-generated content (Nevzat, 2018), and social media networks and hate groups (Eddington, 2018). With such examples in mind, digital technologies and social media provide fertile ground for CT research as well. After all, at its core, CT is used "to determine what, if anything, viewers absorb from living in the world of television" (Gerbner & Gross, 1976, p. 182), but society is saturated with media.

Therefore, CT is applicable to all forms of communication because people can absorb messaging via all media platforms. As such, CT's applicability as a way to make sense of the effects of various media types presents an important way to look at the news usage and opinion construction this study investigates. Along with such considerations, though, one must also understand how and why individuals access news, information, entertainment, and other forms of media content. After all, individuals will engage only if their use provides them with gratification, which is why U&G provides a useful approach to this study because it places an emphasis on the agency of the audience, which CT overlooks.

U&G attempts to understand the "how" and "why" people actively choose certain media to satisfy their needs (Valkenburg et al., 2016). Communication and media scholars Elihu Katz, Jay G. Blumler, and Michael Gurevitch developed U&G into its current form (Severin & Tankard, 2000). In their review of the state of gratification research, Katz et al. (1973) laid the groundwork for the full development of U&G by arguing that media research needed to explore the extent to which media content addressed human needs and interests by looking at what individuals seek from the media.

However, prior to this work, McQuail et al. (1972) outlined four categories of media use, which included the following: Diversion, which includes an escape from routine or problems and serves as an emotional release; Personal Relationships, which considers the media as a substitute for companionship as well as a social utility; Personal Identity, which looks at self-reference, reality exploration and reinforcement of values; and Surveillance, which entails information seeking. These categories allowed Katz et al. (1973) to propose five assumptions regarding the relationship between media and audience, and these include the idea that the audience is conceived as active, linking gratification and media choice lies with the audience, the media and other sources of satisfaction compete with one another, the goals of mass media use can be determined through research that utilizes data coming from individual audience members, and judgments regarding the cultural significance of media should be separated from audience orientations toward the media. This led to the suggestion that media goals can be grouped into uses such as informing or educating, identifying with characters, entertainment, enhancing social interactions, and escapism to avoid daily life stress (McQuail, 2010).

Outside of entertainment (Barton, 2013; Billings et al., 2019; Brown et al., 2012), U&G also applies to a variety of news and information content (e.g., Sherry, 2006; Towers, 1985; Wei, 2009). "Specifically, attitudes such as news affinity, perceived news realism, and informational viewing motivations" have been the focus of this type of research (Haridakis & Whitmore, 2006, p. 770), which positions U&G as a valuable lens for investigating the spread of mis- and disinformation and how partisan media plays a role.

Of course, U&G kept up with the evolution of technology as well, furthering its utility in the world of communication and media research. This is thanks to the recognition of the important role of Computer-Mediated

Communication (CMC) (Ruggiero, 2000), which considers the process of communication creation and exchange using networked computers and digital media such as email, social media, video conferencing, and other internet-facilitated forms of discourse (Kiesler et al., 1984; Luppicini, 2007; Romiszowski & Mason, 2013). Therefore, U&G can be used to examine how the use of social media impacts the frequency of political discussion among people within the same political party (in-group members) and people from different political parties (out-group members) related to motives for using traditional and social media for political information (Ponder & Haridakis, 2015), which is important for understanding "political socialization" (Haridakis & Whitmore, 2006, p. 770).

As such, it becomes clear why U&G is an influential theory for looking at audiences and media effects of a variety of communication platforms and methods (Weiyan, 2015; Wimmer & Dominick, 2014). This stems from the theory's focus on individual differences that drive media use behaviors (Haridakis & Whitmore, 2006). To that end, this theory provides important support for investigating mis- and disinformation spread and its impacts because it seeks an understanding of why a person uses certain media, such as partisan news outlets, social media, or conservative talk radio. The methods for accomplishing this investigation are explained in the following section.

Methods

Rural areas make up a small portion of the country's population, but they represent much of the country's land mass (Ratcliffe et al., 2016). Due to the lack of residents, rural areas in the United States often get ignored, yet people living rural America exist as an important voting block within democratic politics. This was made evident in the 2016 election of President Donald Trump and the controversy surrounding the outcome of the 2020 election. Therefore, in order to investigate the pathways to news for individuals living and working in rural areas of the country as a way to explore how individuals come to believe in and further spread misinformation and disinformation promulgated by partisan media outlets that include, but are not limited to, talk radio, cable television, and social media, a qualitative approach was used. This consisted of a series of qualitative interviews that provided more depth and context to the investigation. By gathering interview data, this research reveals the nuances of rural living. Through the words of the interviewees, the lived experiences of the respondents provide contextual information regarding how rural citizens receive and use the news, which includes encountering and spreading misinformation and disinformation. Such detailed understanding would not be achievable through simple surveys. To participate, all respondents signed off on the necessary informed consent documentation as stipulated by the Institutional Review Board (IRB).

For this study, interview participants were recruited through two methods. In some cases, participants were recruited using direct contact in the form of phone calls and emails to individuals known to the researchers that fit the ideal parameters of the study, which is living or working in rural Kansas. In other cases, individuals volunteered to be interviewed by completing a form that indicated their willingness to be part of the research. This form, created using Google Forms, was made available via recruitment messaging disseminated via social media and agriculture-related organizations, such as Kansas Farm Bureau, as a way to reach people throughout the state. This purposive sample targeted anyone who is an adult and lives in rural Kansas. The goal was to collect a broad cross-section of people representing various viewpoints and news consumption habits. No one was turned away for age, gender, political beliefs, employment status, or any other reason other than not having lived in Kansas. Though people working in any industry were welcomed, the research specifically targeted famers because Kansas as the nation's number one wheat and sorghum producer and as the number three cattle producer and beef processor in the U.S., which highlights the importance of agriculture-related industries to the state's economy (Kansas Commerce, 2021). Respondents were interviewed via a time and method (e.g., in-person, video conferencing, phone call) agreed upon by all parties.

The study included twenty-one interview participants from across Kansas, which served as a convenience sample aimed at helping to understand the phenomenon in question rather than achieve generalizability (McCracken, 1988). Through these twenty-one interviews, this research achieved saturation as the last few individuals shared no new information and the same themes appeared in their comments, which indicated it was time to stop the data collection process (Glaser & Strauss, 1967; Guest et al., 2020; Sebele-Mpofu, 2020). All interviewed participants were identified by an assigned alias, title, general organizational affiliation, and other demographic information as applicable. Participants were asked a series of questions during a 30-to-90-minute session or series of sessions with the researchers. These questions, asked in a semi-structured format, sought information regarding how individuals accessed news, their thoughts regarding misinformation and disinformation, their civic engagement activities, and their political and religious beliefs, among other topics. No one was directly paid for participating, and the researcher explained that the information collected might be used for future research without additional informed consent.

The interviews were recorded using video and/or audio recording devices. The recordings were used to develop transcripts of the interviews that were coded and analyzed, but the raw recordings are not being made public. The coding and analyzing of the transcripts used the method of thematic analysis (TA). Thematic analysis, according to Terry and Hayfield (2021), "is a flexible analytical method that enables the researcher to construct themes—meaning-based patterns—to report their interpretation of a qualitative data set" (p. 3). Codes were developed inductively, using the aforementioned research questions as a guide (Saldaña, 2021). This entailed multiple reading and coding sessions to identify and refine themes while organizing and describing the data (Braun & Clarke, 2006, 2021; Connaughton et al., 2017; Nowell et al., 2017). As such, a combination of open and axial coding was used (Pentina & Tarafdar, 2014), which helped determine selective codes that developed into the themes (Boczkowski et al., 2018; Matthews, 2022). Through this, saturation was achieved.

Of course, it must be recognized that this study does have some limitations. The relatively small sample size confined to Kansas residents only allowed for an exploration of general themes relating to this topic, so it is acknowledged that a wider array of individuals might uncover more nuanced interactions with news and mis- and disinformation in rural America. However, these results do illuminate how rural citizens encounter and use the news in ways that can cultivate polarization and division, which are unpacked in more detail in the results of this study, which are presented in the following section.

Results

The twenty-one individuals interviewed for this study represented various demographic aspects of the state. Five of the interviewees were female, and the remaining 16 were male. They ranged in age from 31 to 76, averaging 47.86 years old. Of the 21, 12 worked in agriculture-related fields, such as farming and ranching or agriculture-focused financial industries. The remaining respondents worked in areas such as education, manufacturing, and the service industry (see Table 6.1). They hailed from across the state, representing four of the five conservation district areas that divide Kansas (Kansas Department of Agriculture, 2023), with the exception being the region representing the northeast corner of Kansas. In total, the interviews resulted in 30.75 hours of recorded conversation and 216,264 transcribed words to be analyzed.

Through the analysis, several commonalities came to light. For instance, the majority of the people interviewed (n = 13) aligned with conservative politics and reported they were registered as Republicans, which aligns with Kansas typically being depicted as a conservative state when discussing electoral politics. Similarly, 18 respondents indicated a strong alignment with religion, specifically Christianity. This aligns with prior research highlighting the importance of religion in rural areas (e.g., Wuthnow, 2012). Though connections exist between such demographic markers and the focus of this study, three categorical themes emerged as most salient to this research. These themes include the following: Rural Residents Incessantly Ingest News,

Table 6.1: Interview participants

Assigned Alias	Age	Gender	Professional Industry	Education Level	Political Party Affiliation
Arthur	52	Male	Agriculture	High School	Republican
Cyril	34	Male	Finance	Bachelor's	Unaffiliated
Barry	37	Male	Education	Master's	Unaffiliated
Len	37	Male	Manufacture	Bachelor's	Republican
Algernon	37	Male	Agriculture	Bachelor's	Republican
Tony	43	Male	Agriculture	Bachelor's	Republican
Cheryl	44	Female	Education	Bachelor's	Democrat
Randy	39	Male	Construction	Bachelor's	Republican
Lucas	76	Male	Agriculture	Doctorate	Republican
Conway	39	Male	Agriculture	Bachelor's	Republican
Raymond	75	Male	Agriculture	MFA	Democrat
Lana	31	Female	Agriculture	Doctorate	Unaffiliated
Sterling	35	Male	Service	Bachelor's	Unaffiliated
Fabian	40	Male	Education	Doctorate	Independent
Cecil	46	Male	Agriculture	Bachelor's	Republican
Torvald	69	Male	Agriculture	High School	Republican
Ramon	55	Male	Manufacture	High School	Republican
Malory	64	Female	Agriculture	High School	Republican
Lemuel	73	Male	Agriculture	High School	Democrat
Zara	37	Female	Education	Bachelor's	Republican
Pam	42	Female	Marketing	Bachelor's	Republican

National Outlets Plant Media Distrust, and Disinformation Contaminates Media Ecosystems.

Rural Residents Incessantly Ingest News

The first research question (RQ1) asked what the news consumption habits of rural residents in Kansas are considering the unfettered access to content afforded by digital technologies. Based on the interviews conducted for this study, it is clear that news consumption plays an important role in the everyday lives of the individuals interviewed for this study. All but one person reported consuming news daily, and most respondents indicated they do so multiple times per day or even hourly. A 75-year-old male who owns cropland and pastures, who was assigned the alias of Raymond, described his consumption as high, indicating he subscribes to *The New York Times*.

As part of this consumption, certain types of news were frequently mentioned. The two most cited types of news were politics and local. Each was mentioned by 11 respondents. A 37-year-old female teacher assigned the alias of Zara explained the appeal of local news as being important for sharing information about a community that highlights the positives and brings awareness to the negatives. Likewise, sports and weather were each driving factors of news consumption for nine people. World and national news were also cited, being mentioned seven and five times respectively.

Though Raymond was one of only two respondents who mentioned *The New York Times* specifically, all individuals described diverse pathways to the news they take in. For most, this included four primary avenues—radio, television, print, and online. Thirteen respondents highlighted radio as an important vehicle for news reception. For the majority, their radio listening consisted of either conservative talk radio or NPR. A 40-year-old male educator assigned the alias of Fabian and a 37-year-old male farmer assigned the alias of Algernon were outliers in that they reported listening to both conservative talk radio and NPR; however, most individuals listened to one or the other. Lucas, a 76-year-old rancher, said he listened to conservative talk radio because it's the only content he can tune into while driving through his pastures. Arthur, a 52-year-old male working in the agriculture industry, also indicated conservative talk radio's accessibility is part of its appeal. However, both also indicated they agreed with most of the content, which was a consistent reason for listening among respondents. Arthur summed it up by explaining that talk radio "validates your thoughts."

In general, radio news consumption was popular among respondents due to them being able to listen while driving or operating farming machinery. In most cases, these individuals explained they listened to a commercial AM station broadcasting from central Kansas or the NPR station out of Wichita, Kansas. For those not interested in any form of news or talk radio, the dial was typically tuned to country music, though classical music and oldies were also mentioned. Still, radio wasn't the only broadcast medium that was popular. Television also provided a dominant pathway to news.

Only six respondents indicated they didn't use television to keep up with the news. For example, a 44-year-old female educator assigned the alias of Cheryl explained she only used the television to watch DVDs she borrowed from her local library. As an avenue to news, television was fairly popular, though. Only five respondents indicated they don't watch any television for informational programming, and Malory, a 64-year-old farmer and rancher, said she didn't like to watch television. However, she explained the television is on a lot in her home because her husband likes to watch it, and his preferred channel is Fox News. Of the national cable news outlets cited by individuals in this study's population, Fox News was mentioned most frequently. For four of the interviews, Fox News served as a primary news source, and those individuals discussed watching it often and for long periods of time. When Fox News was mentioned by others, it was within the context of believing the content was biased and untrustworthy. CNN, MSNBC, and Newsmax TV also were discussed with various interviewees, but those outlets were often mentioned only in passing, if at all. Instead, most respondents suggested they consume more localized television news. Specifically, most individuals said they watched the CBS affiliate in Wichita, Kansas. The ABC and NBC affiliates also had viewers.

When it comes to local news, the interviewees also discussed weekly newspapers as a source of news. Nine people indicated they read their local papers in order to stay informed about what was happening locally. That number increased to 12 when including people who read the paper periodically at work, at the doctor's office, or at the grocery store. As a 42-year-old marketing professional assigned the alias of Pam explained, the weekly newspaper is appealing because it is entirely focused on local news, leading her to read it immediately after it is published.

To that end, a driving factor of local news consumption was proximity, as many respondents expressed that they found local news more applicable to them and their lives because they were living it, which is in line with national findings showing that local media is viewed as more trustworthy than national outlets (Lakshmanan, 2018; Nyhan, 2019). Still, online avenues also provided rural residents with access to news. This included social media and websites. In terms of social media, Facebook was the most popular platform among respondents as 17 of the 21 said they had an account. However, the majority said they only received the news via this pathway if one of their connections shared something. Of course, a few of the individuals said they followed local news outlets on Facebook, so they ended up getting a fair amount of news that way. Several respondents also highlighted Twitter as an important news pathway, especially for headlines. Overall, though, only two respondents indicated social media was their primary news conduit.

While on various social media platforms, interviewees said the news they encountered usually led them to click on links and visit the websites of news outlets. For 10 of the respondents, this meant navigating to local news sites. However, 12 interviewees indicated the links in their social media feeds led them to national or international outlets. The most popular outlets among the respondents were Fox News, *The Wall Street Journal*, the BBC, CNN, Reuters, and *Yahoo! News*. A 39-year-old male construction worker assigned the alias of Randy said that in addition to Fox News, he also looked at *Breitbart News*, *The Epoch Times*, and *The Gateway Pundit*, which he referred to as "independent media" outlets. Similarly, a 39-year-old male farmer assigned the alias of Conway said he reads CNN, Fox News, *Newsmax*, and *One America News*. Outlets such as *Breitbart News*, *The Gateway Pundit, and Newsmax* regularly create partisan content aligning with conservatism, and they have been found to spread misinformation (Stocking et al., 2022).

The first hypothesis (H1) suggested that rural residents in Kansas get most of their news via national outlets and social media platforms that focus on opinion-oriented content. The results of this study partially confirm this. The interviews highlighted that a majority of the respondents do receive news from national outlets and social media platforms. However, the bulk of that news does not necessarily seem to be opinion-oriented content. Though nine of the twenty-one interviewees consumed news from objectively partisan outlets (Ad Fontes Media, 2023; Jurkowitz et al., 2020) that tend to rely on commentary for content, it is a stretch to suggest rural residents get most of their news in this fashion. This can be attributed to a pervasive lack of trust in the media expressed by the respondents.

National Outlets Plant Media Distrust

Out of the twenty-one individuals interviewed for this study, only three described their trust in the news as more than "half," "average," or "medium," and only one of those people described their trust as "high." Arthur succinctly summed up his views by suggesting the news lies. A 43-year-old male dairy farmer assigned the alias of Tony went a step further. He said he had zero trust in the news. He said he believes media outlets are propaganda tools for their corporate owners and "the deep state cabal."

The feelings of distrust pervaded the opinions of all respondents, regardless of their political alignment or preferred news outlets. Individuals representing both sides of politics ideologically speaking expressed such sentiments, and some directed their criticism toward outlets they viewed as representing political views that were opposite their own. For example, Cecil, a 46-year-old dairy farmer, suggested that Fox News was akin to the propaganda machine of Nazi Germany. Others described the issue more generally as not being tied to politics. Barry, a 37-year-old male educator, suggested he doesn't feel like he always gets the full story. A 73-year-old male farmer assigned the alias of Lemuel agreed, suggesting it is difficult to get clear and reliable information because too much of the information being presented is conflicting. Cyril, a 34-year-old male financial professional, viewed the media's focus on being first instead of right as a major factor in cultivating distrust. These various perspectives combine to demonstrate the confusion rural citizens face when trying to navigate the news landscape, leading to the pervasive feelings of media distrust.

For a majority of the respondents, though, the level of trust in the media could be broken down between national and local outlets. Fourteen of the 21 interviewees suggested they trust their local outlets more than national outlets, even if the difference was marginal. In many instances, this stemmed from views that national outlets were more focused on entertainment, political alignments, and ratings as they tried to persuade audiences, while local outlets avoided political partisanship and focus on news that has a more direct impact on the lives of interviewees. This seemed to fertilize trust because, as Algernon explained, it's easier to believe local reporting because he can witness the events for himself since he is in the same place as the reporters. Torvald and Zara expressed similar views.

Overall, individuals viewed the news as more trustworthy when looked at only through their preferred news outlets. Raymond described these sources as "legitimate media," while several others suggested their levels of trust increased if the outlet was "recognizable" and "reputable." Also, seeing the same story being reported by multiple outlets increased trust for the respondents. Still, Cecil cautioned that even an individual's preferred or "trusted" source needed to be viewed critically, paying attention to whether or not the language being used is slanted, biased, or otherwise polarized.

Despite the lack of trust described by the interviewees, 13 believed the news is largely accurate. According to Zara, the accuracy comes from the access reporters have since they can go places citizens can't or don't want to go. Overall, though, the view on the news being accurate or not broke on lines of local versus national organizations and outlet preferences. A 37-year-old male manufacturing worker assigned the alias of Len expressed the opinion that the information within news content is accurate but that the outlets present it in a way that attempts to persuade or convince the audience. Sterling, a 35-year-old service worker, agreed. He suggested the information being reported is accurate, but it changes when the focus shifts away from just reporting the news and starts to become more opinion oriented.

The second hypothesis (H2) suggested that rural residents in Kansas distrust the news due to a belief that the media outlets are not telling the truth about what is really going on in the world. This hypothesis is supported. The perceived amount of opinion and bias caused respondents to believe the news is inaccurate. Though there may be kernels of truth presented in reports, Lucas said, "They're clearly quite colored with the particular author's viewpoints." Barry agreed, arguing that what is being reported doesn't align with what is actually happening. Likewise, Pam believed the news "is too skewed," and several respondents discussed how they believed the media exaggerates or sensationalizes the news. For Conway, the concept of accuracy doesn't factor into his trust in the media because the coverage might be the same, but the way it is presented is different, often skewing the information to support a particular political viewpoint. To that end, several interviewees mentioned they do their own research, which often entailed looking at multiple news sources and using Internet searches in an attempt to determine the truth. Lemuel alluded to this as well, expressing that he seeks out all perspectives of a given story.

The quest for truth was another commonality among the respondents. "I'm after truth," Randy explained. Conway agreed. "I'm looking for the truth. It isn't readily available," he said. For some, such as Cheryl, truth is information that is "fact-based and you can verify it." However, for others, true news is determined by the source. Torvald explained that if he sees it on TV, he feels he must trust it. In short, the truth seems to be in the eye of the beholder. This cultivates fertile ground for mis- and disinformation to take root.

Disinformation Contaminates Media Ecosystems

All respondents indicated they believe mis- or disinformation exist. However, not all of them agreed that it was a problem for society. Four of the 21 interviews suggested it either isn't a problem or isn't a full-blown problem yet. Both Torvald and Conway explained it isn't a problem because inaccurate information and politically motivated news have always existed. Conway cited the examples of World War II propaganda and the newspaper wars of yellow journalism between William Randolph Hearst and Joseph Pulitzer. From her perspective, Zara believed it is sometimes a problem because of social media, which allows anyone to share anything just because they want to regardless of its accuracy. Lemuel, on the other hand, struck a more optimistic tone. He suggested mis- or disinformation is just starting to become a problem in society and that it hasn't always been an issue.

In contrast, the 17 other respondents all agreed that mis- or disinformation is a problem for society. A 31-year-old female veterinarian assigned the alias of Lana argued that its existence damages communities and social ties, especially when a person pushes back against inaccurate information. She explained that constantly refuting what others have to say makes it more difficult to cultivate trust because any interaction starts from a place of skepticism. According to the respondents, a lack of trust can lead to division and polarization. Raymond said he believes this is the cause for division within the United States, and he sees with fissure widening. In terms of politics, this was a common refrain from the interviewees. For example, Pam suggested each political "side" has its own media, which causes people to view each other as enemies.

Similarly, many respondents suggested it makes it difficult to know what is true or what can be trusted. Cyril pointed out that this causes a snowball effect, leading to multiple issues. One such issue is apathy, and that leads members of society to simply stop paying attention to the news, according to Lucas. Cheryl also pointed out that democratic decision-making suffers if mis- or disinformation flourishes: She said that if those decisions are made based on faulty information, the enacted policies can damage society. Such a sentiment was of key concern to Ramon, a 55-year-old male who works in the manufacturing industry. He expressed the view that mis- or disinformation inhibits an individual's ability to make their own decisions, which stems from the power of media to manipulate and shape people's opinions.

To that end, the second research question (RQ2) asked why rural residents in Kansas believe and spread mis- and disinformation they encounter. A primary reason cited by interviewees was politics. Cecil argued that politics "clouded the judgement" of individuals. From Arthur's perspective, mis- or disinformation spreads because people are too gullible. Such a statement aligned with the general consensus of the interviewees that social media and national news outlets are leading spreaders of this faulty information. Lana pointed at talk radio as a vocal part of the problem. According to Raymond, outlets like Fox News, *Newsmax*, and *One America News* are prime examples of the issue as well. He argued those outlets are the epitome of mis- and disinformation spreaders. Algernon agreed, adding CNN to the list of perpetrators. Conway also laid the blame at the feet of cable news, but he had a different perspective. He suggested the political left dominates TV and the political right dominates talk radio, but he argued that TV carries more influence.

Outside of television, respondents cited social media often when discussing how mis- or disinformation spreads. Several of them pointed out that because anyone can post, the content is often more inflammatory and one-sided. This leaves a void of honest and reputable sources of information, according to Sterling, because opinions are more prevalent than actual news. From Fabian's perspective, this results in a domino effect that perpetuates mis- or disinformation and causes more of it to spread: "I think that's sad because I think people just see that information right away and they believe it."

The sentiment of education levels being related to believing and spreading mis- or disinformation came up with a few different respondents. Lana suggested less educated, lower socioeconomic individuals, who she believes are typically white males, are some of the worst offenders. Raymond and Cecil agreed and suggested religious beliefs can play a role because Christianity has become synonymous with conservatism. Fabian agreed with. Similarly, several interviewees argued rural, small-town citizens spread mis- or disinformation more than their urban or suburban counterparts due to the aforementioned education and socioeconomic concerns, as well as a narrower worldview stemming from less exposure to a diversity of thoughts and opinions.

Additionally, perceptions of money and power influenced respondents' views of how mis- or disinformation spreads. For example, Ramon explained that those with the most wealth and influence get to dictate what is reported, whether it is accurate or not. Randy, as well as several others, related this idea of money and power to ratings, which they acknowledged news outlets needed to make money and stay in business. Barry took this a step further. He suggested news outlets twist facts in an attempt to make stories "juicier" and more interesting, which increases audience attention and results in more profitability. As Pam argued, "They know who their viewers are, and they know what sells."

Discussion

As Raymond said, misinformation divides people, leading to a fractured society. Without taking steps to stem the flow, such a prediction undoubtedly will come true. However, effectively combatting dis- or misinformation may not be easy. Considering the microcosm of rural Kansans and their news consumption habits, several hurdles to combating faulty and inaccurate information become evident. Though respondents in this study indicated they consume news at high rates, the pathways they use seem problematic. A large portion relies on partisan and biased news outlets to become informed about what is going on in the country and the world. Individuals are cultivated to view the world through the lens constructed by the reporting of these outlets (Jin & Kim, 2014; Shrum, 2017). As such, dis- and misinformation taints their media diets, which causes distrust to grow.

Some might believe this doesn't affect them. In fact, Arthur claimed as much. However, nearly all interviewees admitted the news they consume impacts their views on society in some fashion, which highlights the power of the media to cultivate beliefs (Gerbner & Gross, 1976). For example, Lucas, who explained he believes abortion is morally and biblically wrong, said his perspective has changed slightly to the point where now he is more comfortable with allowing abortions up to 15 weeks of pregnancy if such an option has to be pursued. Previously, he thought four weeks was the maximum window during which the procedure should be allowed. He attributed this change in views to some of the news he consumed. Also, Pam described the impact news consumption has on her by explaining that she had to stop watching the news each night because it was impacting her mental health.

Her sentiments speak to a larger feeling of helplessness some respondents expressed. Both Zara and Malory didn't see how worrying about the news could matter because they couldn't do anything to change what was occurring, though Zara said she prays about those issues. Similarly, Barry suggested what he consumes stays in his mind, which would undoubtedly affect his thought processes. Torvald agreed, and he also brought up that where he lives plays a role in how the news impacts him. He highlighted the fact that decisions made in Washington D.C. have little influence on his day-to-day life.

No matter the rationalization, these impacts stem from the type of news these individuals consume. As the interviewees revealed, this consists of a fair amount of biased and partisan media outlets. A few individuals even pointed this out. They discussed how the news they trust and distrust are guided by their political beliefs. As Randy said, people only want to hear information that makes them feel good. This speaks directly to the root of this study and demonstrates how media choices are made, which means people pick the news to consume based on its usefulness to them and the feels it elicits (Katz et al., 1973). For example, a farmer might choose to listen to conservative talk radio because it is the only station he can get on his tractor's radio while tilling his fields, and the steady stream of politically charged content emanating from the speakers affirms his beliefs, leaving him feeling vindicated in his thoughts.

This is how and why mis- and disinformation is believed and spread in rural Kansas. It is about selective exposure and confirmation bias (Hameleers & van der Meer, 2020; Knobloch-Westerwick et al., 2015; Lee et al., 2021; Pearson & Knobloch-Westerwick, 2019). Every person interviewed shared certain news outlets they trusted more than others. For many, it was the difference between local and national. However, a majority of the individuals also said they trusted, at least to some degree, specific national news organizations. In nearly every instance, these outlets are known to have a political bias (Ad Fontes Media, 2023; Jurkowitz et al., 2020). Therefore, if those are considered to be trusted news outlets by the rural residents, they will continue to consume the content those organizations produce. The result is the construction of an echo chamber where individuals are only being exposed to messages that agree with their pre-existing beliefs and opinions. To borrow from Cyril, this creates a snowball effect. Political beliefs influence the media being consumed. Then the media being consumed reaffirms political beliefs (Haridakis & Whitmore, 2006; McQuail et al., 1972; Ponder & Haridakis, 2015) and cultivates views of the world (Gerbner & Gross, 1976). It becomes a perpetual motion machine that results in distrust of news and information that doesn't come from the selected outlets, and that breeds dis- and misinformation.

Of course, interviewees seemed to understand how this works, but they also considered themselves immune to the effects. This is the essence of the third-person effect, which states that individuals believe others to be more susceptible to persuasive messages than they are (Banning, 2006; Davison, 1983). Several made it a point to suggest they see others being influenced in this way, but they believed they weren't impacted. For example, though he said he only trusts certain people he follows on Facebook, Tony's entire perspective on the world was changed during the COVID-19 pandemic when he watched the "26-minute video called 'Plandemic,' a slickly produced narration that wrongly claimed a shadowy cabal of elites was using the virus and a potential vaccine to profit and gain power" (Frenkel et al., 2020, para. 3). Tony repeatedly expressed the belief that he didn't blame others for not being better informed because he had been misled before too, but he said people needed to educate themselves and see the truth.

Such a statement speaks to the idea of media literacy, or being able to understand and analyze media messages (Gaultney et al., 2022; Matthews, 2022; Potter, 2016). Several interviewees also mentioned this idea. Generally, it came up in the context of looking at multiple sources and doing the "research" necessary to verify the information. Algernon and Fabian even explained that they intentionally listen to outlets from both sides of the political spectrum in order to compile a more complete picture of what is happening in the world. However, that wasn't the norm for most interviewees. Instead, they tended to rely on partisan news outlets or local.

The fact that local news was viewed as being more reliable and trustworthy can be attributed to the perception that those outlets and their journalists understand rural residents more. Pam expressed her belief that rural areas were often ignored in media coverage. A component of this is that local news organizations represent the values of their audience. This representation also applies to national outlets, though. If Fox News or MSNBC aligns with an individual's beliefs and values, that person feels seen. That cultivates a sense of belonging and affiliation (Eddington, 2018). As Cramer (2016) argued, people who feel misunderstood or misrepresented tend to retreat back into their comfort zones because they believe they are being ignored or not taken seriously. That sows the seeds of distrust that are fertilized by the mis- and disinformation spread by partisan media outlets as they plow through the fields of the media ecosystem available to rural Kansans.

Conclusion

In conclusion, this study sheds important light on how rural Kansans receive news. By understanding that many rural Americans are heavily influenced by their chosen media outlets, we can better approach concepts of media literacy and how to more effectively combat dis- and misinformation. An important aspect of this is media representation. When consumers feel vindicated in their opinions and beliefs because the media they consume gratifies them, stronger and more entrenched views are cultivated, producing polarization and division. Even reasonable individuals, such as the ones interviewed for this study, can be misled by the news if their media diets consist of unhealthy content that lacks nutritious information.

Though this study might be limited by the relatively small sample size that was confined to Kansas residents only, it opens an important line of inquiry that sets the stage for future research. Even though rural areas contain only about 20% of the country's population, they make up nearly 97% of the land mass (Ratcliffe et al., 2016). That is a large amount of the United States that often gets ignored, yet people living in those areas exist as an important voting block within democratic politics as was evident in the 2016 election of President Donald Trump and the controversy surrounding the outcome of the 2020 election.

Therefore, in order to better understand the country and its media consumption as it relates to polarization and division cultivated by mis- and disinformation, one must understand the rural citizens of the United States. By zooming in on rural Kansas, this study highlights how rural citizens encounter and use the news in ways that can cultivate polarization and division. This foundational study prepares this otherwise fertile ground for future academic study.

References

Ad Fontes Media. (2023). *Interactive Media Bias Chart*. https://adfontesmedia.com/interactive-media-bias-chart/

Allam, R. (2019). Constructive journalism in Arab transitional democracies: Perceptions, attitudes and performance. *Journalism Practice*, 13(10), 1273–1293. https://doi.org/10.1080/17512786.2019.1588145

Bail, C. A., Argyle, L. P., Brown, T. W., Bumpus, J. P., Chen, H., Hunzaker, M. B. F., Lee, J., Mann, M., Merhout, F., & Volfovsky, A. (2018). Exposure to opposing views on social media can increase political polarization. *Proceedings of the National Academy of Sciences*, 115(37), 9216–9221. https://doi.org/doi:10.1073/pnas.1804840115

Banning, S. A. (2006). Third-person effects on political participation. *Journalism & Mass Communication Quarterly*, 83(4), 785–800.

Barbaro, M. (2022). Jan. 6, Part 1: 'The Herd Mentality'—Inside an F.B.I. interview with one of the Capitol rioters. In *The Daily*. The New York Times. https://www.nytimes.com/2022/01/05/podcasts/the-daily/january-6-capitol-riots-anniversary.html

Barton, K. M. (2013). Why we watch them sing and dance: The uses and gratifications of talent-based reality television. *Communication Quarterly*, 61(2), 217–235. https://doi.org/10.1080/01463373.2012.751437

Batsell, J. (2015). *Engaged journalism: Connecting with digitally empowered news audiences*. Columbia University Press.

Bauer, A. J., Nadler, A., & Nelson, J. L. (2022). What is Fox News? Partisan journalism, misinformation, and the problem of classification. *Electronic News*, 16(1), 18–29. https://doi.org/10.1177/19312431211060426

Belair-Gagnon, V., Agur, C., & Frisch, N. (2017). The changing physical and social environment of newsgathering: A case study of foreign correspondents using chat apps during unrest. *Social Media + Society*, 3(1). https://doi.org/10.1177/2056305117701163

Belair-Gagnon, V., Nelson, J. L., & Lewis, S. C. (2019). Audience engagement, reciprocity, and the pursuit of community connectedness in public media journalism. *Journalism Practice*, 13(5), 558–575. https://doi.org/10.1080/17512786.2018.1542975

Bennett, S. E. (2002). Americans' exposure to political talk radio and their knowledge of public affairs. *Journal Of Broadcasting & Electronic Media*, 46(1), 74–86. https://doi.org/10.1207/s15506878jobem4601_5

Billings, A., Brown-Devlin, N., Brown, K., & Devlin, M. B. (2019). When 18 days of television coverage is not enough: A six-nation composite of motivations for mobile device use in 2018 winter Olympic games. *Mass Communication & Society*, 22(4), 535–557. https://doi.org/10.1080/15205436.2019.1587781

Block, M. (2021, January 16). *Can the forces unleashed by Trump's big election lie be undone?* NPR. https://www.npr.org/2021/01/16/957291939/can-the-forces-unleashed-by-trumps-big-election-lie-be-undone

Boczkowski, P. J., Mitchelstein, E., & Matassi, M. (2018). "News comes across when I'm in a moment of leisure": Understanding the practices of incidental news consumption on social media. *New Media & Society*, 20(10), 3523–3539. https://doi.org/10.1177/1461444817750396

Braun, V., & Clarke, V. (2006). Using thematic analysis in psychology. *Qualitative Research in Psychology*, 3(2), 77–101. https://doi.org/10.1191/1478088706qp063oa

Braun, V., & Clarke, V. (2021). *Thematic Analysis: A Practical Guide*. SAGE.

Briggs, M. (2007). *Journalism 2.0: How to survive and thrive*. The Institute for Interactive Journalism.

Briggs, M. (2020). *Journalism next: A practical guide to digital reporting and publishing* (4th ed.). SAGE.

Brown, D., Lauricella, S., Douai, A., & Zaidi, A. (2012). Consuming television crime drama: A uses and gratifications approach. *American Communication Journal*, 14(1), 47–61.

Campbell, R., Martin, C. R., & Fabos, B. (2019). *Media & culture: Mass communication in a digital age* (12th ed.). Bedford/St. Martin's.

Collier, J. R., Dunaway, J., & Stroud, N. J. (2021). Pathways to deeper news engagement: Factors influencing click behaviors on news sites. *Journal of Computer-Mediated Communication*, 26(5), 265–283. https://doi.org/10.1093/jcmc/zmab009

Connaughton, S. L., Linabary, J. R., Krishna, A., Kuang, K., Anaele, A., Vibber, K. S., Yakova, L., & Jones, C. (2017). Explicating the relationally attentive approach to conducting engaged communication scholarship. *Journal of Applied Communication Research*, 45(5), 517–536. https://doi.org/10.1080/00909882.2017.1382707

Conway, B. A., & Stryker, R. (2021). Does a speaker's (in)formal role in news media shape perceptions of political incivility? *Journal of Broadcasting & Electronic Media*, 65(1), 24–45. https://doi.org/10.1080/08838151.2021.1897819

Cramer, K. J. (2016). *The politics of resentment: Rural consciousness in Wisconsin and the rise of Scott Walker*. University of Chicago Press.

Crary, J. (2001). *Suspensions of perception: Attention, spectacle, and modern culture*. MIT Press.

Dahlgren, P. (2018). Public sphere participation online: The ambiguities of affect. *International Journal of Communication*, 12, 2052–2070.

Darr, J. P., Hitt, M. P., & Dunaway, J. L. (2018). Newspaper closures polarize voting behavior. *Journal of Communication*, 68(6), 1007–1028. https://doi.org/10.1093/joc/jqy051

Darr, J. P., Hitt, M. P., & Dunaway, J. L. (2021). *Home style opinion: How local newspapers can slow polarization*. Cambridge University Press. https://doi.org/10.1017/9781108950930

Davison, W. P. (1983). The third-person effect in communication. *The Public Opinion Quarterly*, 47(1), 1–15. http://www.jstor.org/stable/2748702

de Ridder, J. (2021). What's so bad about misinformation? *Inquiry*, 1–23. https://doi.org/10.1080/0020174X.2021.2002187

Dreisbach, T., & Mak, T. (2021, March 19). *Yes, Capitol rioters were armed. Here are the weapons prosecutors say they used*. NPR. https://www.npr.org/2021/03/19/977879589/yes-capitol-rioters-were-armed-here-are-the-weapons-prosecutors-say-they-used

Druckman, J. N., Gubitz, S. R., Lloyd, A. M., & Levendusky, M. S. (2019). How incivility on partisan media (de)polarizes the electorate. *Journal of Politics*, 81(1), 291–295. https://doi.org/10.1086/699912

Eddington, S. M. (2018). The communicative constitution of hate organizations online: A semantic network analysis of "Make America Great Again". *Social Media + Society*, 4(3). https://doi.org/10.1177/2056305118790763

Fairclough, N. (2010). *Analysing discourse: Textual analysis for social research*. Routledge.

Festinger, L. (1962). Cognitive dissonance. *Scientific American*, 207(4), 93–106. http://www.jstor.org/stable/24936719

Flaxman, S., Goel, S., & Rao, J. M. (2016). Filter bubbles, echo chambers, and online news consumption. *Public Opinion Quarterly*, 80(S1), 298–320. https://doi.org/10.1093/poq/nfw006

Frank, T. (2004). *What's the matter with Kansas?: How conservatives won the heart of America*. Metropolitan Books.

Frenkel, S., Decker, B., & Alba, D. (2020, May 20). How the 'Plandemic' movie and its falsehoods spread widely online. *The New York Times*. https://www.nytimes.com/2020/05/20/technology/plandemic-movie-youtube-facebook-coronavirus.html

Gaultney, I. B., Sherron, T., & Boden, C. (2022). Political polarization, misinformation, and media literacy. *Journal of Media Literacy Education*, *14*(1), 59–81. https://doi.org/10.23860/JMLE-2022-14-1-5

Gee, J. P. (2015). Discourse, small d, big d. In K. Tracy (Ed.), *The international encyclopedia of language and social interaction*. John Wiley & Sons.

Geiß, S., Magin, M., Jürgens, P., & Stark, B. (2021). Loopholes in the echo chambers: How the echo chamber metaphor oversimplifies the effects of information gateways on opinion expression. *Digital Journalism*, *9*(5), 660–686. https://doi.org/10.1080/21670811.2021.1873811

Gerbner, G., & Gross, L. (1976). Living with television: The violence profile. *Journal of Communication*, *26*(2), 172–199. https://doi.org/10.1111/j.1460-2466.1976.tb01397.x

Gerbner, G., Gross, L., Morgan, M., & Signorielli, N. (1986). Living with television: The dynamics of the cultivation process. In J. Bryant & D. Zillmann (Eds.), *Perspectives on media effects* (pp. 17–40). Lawrence Erlbaum Associates.

Gervais, B. T. (2014). Following the news? Reception of uncivil partisan media and the use of incivility in political expression. *Political Communication*, *31*(4), 564–583. https://doi.org/10.1080/10584609.2013.852640

Glaser, B. G., & Strauss, A. L. (1967). *The discovery of grounded theory: Strategies for qualitative research*. Routledge. https://doi.org/10.4324/9780203793206

Greenberg, J. (2022, June 16). Most Republicans still falsely believe Trump's stolen election claims. Here are some reasons why. *Poynter*. https://www.poynter.org/fact-checking/2022/70-percent-republicans-falsely-believe-stolen-election-trump/

Guest, G., Namey, E., & Chen, M. (2020). A simple method to assess and report thematic saturation in qualitative research. *PLOS ONE*, *15*(5), e0232076. https://doi.org/10.1371/journal.pone.0232076

Gutsche, R. E. (2019). The state and future of television news studies: Theoretical perspectives, methodological problems, and practice. *Journalism Practice*, *13*(9), 1034–1041. https://doi.org/10.1080/17512786.2019.1644965

Hameleers, M., & van der Meer, T. (2020). Fight or flight? Attributing responsibility in response to mixed congruent and incongruent partisan news in selective exposure media environments. *Information, Communication & Society*, *23*(9), 1327–1352. https://doi.org/10.1080/1369118X.2019.1566394

Han, J., & Federico, C. M. (2017). Conflict-framed news, self-categorization, and partisan polarization. *Mass Communication & Society*, *20*(4), 455–480. https://doi.org/10.1080/15205436.2017.1292530

Han, J., & Federico, C. M. (2018). The polarizing effect of news framing: Comparing the mediating roles of motivated reasoning, self-stereotyping, and intergroup animus. *Journal of Communication*, *68*(4), 685–711. https://doi.org/10.1093/joc/jqy025

Haridakis, P. M., & Whitmore, E. H. (2006). Understanding electronic media audiences: The pioneering research of Alan M. Rubin. *Journal of Broadcasting & Electronic Media*, *50*(4), 766–774. https://doi.org/10.1207/s15506878jobem5004_13

Hemmer, N. (2016). *Messengers of the right: Conservative media and the transformation of American politics*. University of Pennsylvania Press.

Henneman, A., Franzen-Castle, L., Colgrove, K., & Wells, C. (2015). Who says online newsletters are a dying breed? How an email newsletter can grow your nutrition education outreach. *Journal of Nutrition Education & Behavior, 47*, 20. https://doi.org/10.1016/j.jneb.2015.04.053

Hofstetter, C. R., & Gianos, C. L. (1997). Political talk radio: Actions speak louder than words. *Journal of Broadcasting & Electronic Media, 41*(4), 501–515. https://doi.org/10.1080/08838159709364423

Hollander, B. A. (1997). Fuel to the fire: Talk radio and the Gamson hypothesis. *Political Communication, 14*(3), 355–369. https://doi.org/10.1080/105846097199371

Horten, G. (2002). *Radio goes to war: The cultural politics of propaganda during World War II.* University of California Press.

Ismail, A. (2022, January 4). *We know exactly who the Capitol rioters were: A year later, a fuller picture of who really drove the riot is clear. The lessons for 2022 and beyond are sobering.* Slate. https://slate.com/news-and-politics/2022/01/january-6-capitol-riot-arrests-research-profile.html

Iyengar, S., Lelkes, Y., Levendusky, M., Malhotra, N., & Westwood, S. J. (2019). The origins and consequences of affective polarization in the United States. *Annual Review of Political Science, 22*(1), 129–146. https://doi.org/10.1146/annurev-polisci-051117-073034

Jin, B., & Kim, S. (2014). Telethon viewing, social capital, and community participation in South Korea. *Communication Quarterly, 62*(3), 253–268. https://doi.org/10.1080/01463373.2014.911762

Johnson, T., & Kaye, B. (2013). Putting out fire with gasoline: Testing the Gamson hypothesis on media reliance and political activity. *Journal of Broadcasting & Electronic Media, 57*(4), 456–481. https://doi.org/10.1080/08838151.2013.845825

Jones, D. A. (1998). Political talk radio: The Limbaugh Effect on primary voters. *Political Communication, 15*(3), 367–381. https://doi.org/10.1080/105846098198948

Jones, J. P. (2012). The 'new' news as no 'news': U.S. cable news channels as branded political entertainment television. *Media International Australia, 144*(1), 146–155. https://doi.org/10.1177/1329878X1214400119

Jurkowitz, M., Mitchell, A., Shearer, E., & Walker, M. (2020). *U.S. media polarization and the 2020 election: A nation divided.* Pew Research Center. https://www.pewresearch.org/journalism/wp-content/uploads/sites/8/2020/01/PJ_2020.01.24_Media-Polarization_FINAL.pdf

Kalogeropoulos, A., Suiter, J., Udris, L., & Eisenegger, M. (2019). News media trust and news consumption: Factors related to trust in news in 35 countries. *International Journal of Communication, 13*, 3672–3693.

Kansas Commerce. (2021). *Grown from the middle: Agriculture in Kansas.* Kansas Department of Commerce. https://www.kansascommerce.gov/industry/agriculture/

Kansas Department of Agriculture. (2023). *Division of Conservation (DOC).* State of Kansas. https://agriculture.ks.gov/divisions-programs/division-of-conservation

Karlsen, R., & Aalberg, T. (2023). Social media and trust in news: An experimental study of the effect of Facebook on news story credibility. *Digital Journalism, 11*(1), 144–160. https://doi.org/10.1080/21670811.2021.1945938

Katz, E., Blumler, J. G., & Gurevitch, M. (1973). Uses and gratifications research. *Public Opinion Quarterly, 37*(4), 509–523. https://doi.org/10.1086/268109

Kiesler, S., Siegel, J., & McGuire, T. W. (1984). Social psychological aspects of computer-mediated communication. *American Psychologist, 39*(10), 1123–1134.

Knobloch-Westerwick, S., Mothes, C., Johnson, B. K., Westerwick, A., & Donsbach, W. (2015). Political online information searching in Germany and the United States: Confirmation bias, source credibility, and attitude impacts. *Journal of Communication, 65*(3), 489–511. https://doi.org/10.1111/jcom.12154

Ksiazek, T. B., Kim, S. J., & Malthouse, E. C. (2019). Television news repertoires, exposure diversity, and voting behavior in the 2016 U.S. election. *Journalism & Mass Communication Quarterly, 96*(4), 1120–1144. https://doi.org/10.1177/1077699018815892

Lakshmanan, I. A. R. (2018, August 22). *Finally some good news: Trust in news is up, especially for local media.* Poynter. https://www.poynter.org/ethics-trust/2018/finally-some-good-news-trust-in-news-is-up-especially-for-local-media/

Lee, J., Ott, T., & Deavours, D. (2021). Combating misinformation in risk: Emotional appeal in false beliefs. In R. Luttrell, L. Xiao, & J. Glass (Eds.), *Democracy in the disinformation Age: Influence and activism in American politics* (pp. 165–181). Routledge.

Lewis, S. C., Holton, A. E., & Coddington, M. (2014). Reciprocal journalism: A concept of mutual exchange between journalists and audiences. *Journalism Practice, 8*(2), 1–13. https://doi.org/10.1080/17512786.2013.859840

Liu, J., & McLeod, D. M. (2021). Pathways to news commenting and the removal of the comment system on news websites. *Journalism, 22*(4), 867–881. https://doi.org/10.1177/1464884919849954

Lubbers, M., Scheepers, P., & Vergeer, M. (2000). Exposure to newspapers and attitudes toward ethnic minorities: A longitudinal analysis. *Howard Journal of Communications, 11*(2), 127–143. https://doi.org/10.1080/106461700246661

Luppicini, R. (2007). Review of computer mediated communication research for education. *Instructional Science, 35*(2), 141–185. https://doi.org/10.1007/s11251-006-9001-6

Maresh-Fuehrer, M. M., & Gurney, D. (2021). Infowars and the crisis of political disinformation on social media. In R. Luttrell, L. Xiao, & J. Glass (Eds.), *Democracy in the disinformation age: Influence and activism in American politics* (pp. 147–164). Routledge.

Matsa, K. E., & Naseer, S. (2021, November 8). *News platform fact sheet.* Pew Research Center. https://www.pewresearch.org/journalism/fact-sheet/news-platform-fact-sheet/

Matthews, J. C. (2022). College students' perspectives of bias in their news consumption habits. *Journal of Media Literacy Education, 14*(3), 39–52. https://doi.org/10.23860/JMLE-2022-14-3-4

McCracken, G. (1988). *The Long Interview* (Vol. 13). SAGE.

McLuhan, M. (2003). *Understanding me: Lectures and interviews* (S. McLuhan & D. Staines, Eds.). MIT Press.

McQuail, D. (2010). *McQuail's mass communication theory* (6th ed.). SAGE.

McQuail, D., Blumler, J. G., & Brown, J. R. (1972). The television audience: A revised perspective. In D. McQuail (Ed.), *Sociology of mass communications: Selected readings* (pp. 135–165). Penguin.

Nechushtai, E., & Lewis, S. C. (2019). What kind of news gatekeepers do we want machines to be? Filter bubbles, fragmentation, and the normative dimensions of algorithmic recommendations. *Computers in Human Behavior*, 90, 298–307. https://doi.org/10.1016/j.chb.2018.07.043

Nevzat, R. (2018). *Reviving cultivation theory for social media*. The Asian Conference on Media, Communication & Film, Tokyo, Japan. http://papers.iafor.org/wp-content/uploads/papers/mediasia2018/MediAsia2018_42554.pdf

Newman, N. (2020). The resurgence and importance of email newsletters. *Reuters Institute Digital News Report*. Reuters Institute for the Study of Journalism.

Newman, N., Fletcher, R., Schulz, A., Andi, S., Robertson, C. T., & Nielsen, R. K. (2021). *Reuters Institute Digital News Report*. Reuters Institute for the Study of Journalism. https://reutersinstitute.politics.ox.ac.uk/sites/default/files/2021-06/Digital_News_Report_2021_FINAL.pdf

Nielsen. (2019). *Tops of 2019: Radio*. The Nielsen Company. https://www.nielsen.com/insights/2019/tops-of-2019-radio/

Nissen, I. A., Walter, J. G., Charquero-Ballester, M., & Bechmann, A. (2022). Digital infrastructures of COVID-19 misinformation: A new conceptual and analytical perspective on fact-checking. *Digital Journalism*, 10(5), 738–760. https://doi.org/10.1080/21670811.2022.2026795

Nowell, L. S., Norris, J. M., White, D. E., & Moules, N. J. (2017). Thematic analysis: Striving to meet the trustworthiness criteria. *International Journal of Qualitative Methods*, 16(1). https://doi.org/10.1177/1609406917733847

NPR Staff. (2021, February 9). *The Jan. 6 attack: The cases behind the biggest criminal investigation in U.S. history*. National Public Radio. https://www.npr.org/2021/02/09/965472049/the-capitol-siege-the-arrested-and-their-stories

Nyhan, B. (2019, October 31). *Americans trust local news. That belief is being exploited*. The New York Times. https://www.nytimes.com/2019/10/31/upshot/fake-local-news.html

Padgett, J., Dunaway, J. L., & Darr, J. P. (2019). As seen on TV? How gatekeeping makes the U.S. House seem more extreme. *Journal of Communication*, 69(6), 696–719. https://doi.org/10.1093/joc/jqz039

Pape, R. A. (2021). *Why we cannot afford to ignore the American insurrectionist movement*. Chicago Project of Security & Threats at The University of Chicago. https://cpost.uchicago.edu/publications/why_we_cannot_afford_to_ignore_the_american_insurrectionist_movement/

Pape, R. A. (2022). *Deep, divisive, disturbing and continuing: New survey shows mainstream community support for violence to restore Trump remains strong*. Chicago Project of Security & Threats at The University of Chicago. https://d3qi0qp55mx5f5.cloudfront.net/cpost/i/docs/Pape_AmericanInsurrectionistMovement_2022-01-02.pdf?mtime=1641247259

Pape, R. A., & Ruby, K. (2021, February 2). *The Capitol rioters aren't like other extremists*. The Atlantic. https://www.theatlantic.com/ideas/archive/2021/02/the-capitol-rioters-arent-like-other-extremists/617895/

Pasquetto, I. V., Swire-Thompson, B., Amazeen, M. A., Benevenuto, F., Brashier, N. M., Bond, R. M., Bozarth, L. C., Budak, C., Ecker, U. K. H., Fazio, L. K., Ferrara, E., Flanagin, A. J.,

Flammini, A., Freelon, D., Grinberg, N., Hertwig, R., Jamieson, K. H., Joseph, K., Jones, J. J., ... Yan, K.-C. (2020). Tackling misinformation: What researchers could do with social media data. *Harvard Kennedy School (HKS) Misinformation Review, 1*(8). https://doi.org/10.37016/mr-2020-49

Pearson, G. D. H., & Knobloch-Westerwick, S. (2019). Is the confirmation bias bubble larger online? Pre-election confirmation bias in selective exposure to online versus print political information. *Mass Communication & Society, 22*(4), 466–486. https://doi.org/10.1080/15205436.2019.1599956

Pentina, I., & Tarafdar, M. (2014). From "information" to "knowing": Exploring the role of social media in contemporary news consumption. *Computers in Human Behavior, 35,* 211–223. https://doi.org/https://doi.org/10.1016/j.chb.2014.02.045

Pew Research Center. (2019). *For local news, Americans embrace digital but still want strong community connection.* https://www.pewresearch.org/journalism/wp-content/uploads/sites/8/2019/03/PJ_2019.03.26_Local-News_FINAL.pdf

Pew Research Center. (2021). *Audio and podcasting fact sheet.* The Pew Charitable Trusts. https://www.pewresearch.org/journalism/fact-sheet/audio-and-podcasting/

Ponder, J. D., & Haridakis, P. (2015). Selectively social politics: The differing roles of media use on political discussion. *Mass Communication & Society, 18*(3), 281–302. https://doi.org/10.1080/15205436.2014.940977

Potter, W. J. (2016). *Media literacy* (8th ed.). SAGE.

Prochazka, F., & Schweiger, W. (2019). How to measure generalized trust in news media? An adaptation and test of scales. *Communication Methods & Measures, 13*(1), 26–42. https://doi.org/10.1080/19312458.2018.1506021

Putnam, R. D. (2001). *Bowling alone: The collapse and revival of American community.* Simon & Schuster.

Ratcliffe, M., Burd, C., Holder, K., & Fields, A. (2016). *Defining rural at the U.S. census bureau: American community survey and geography brief.* U.S. Census Bureau. https://www.census.gov/content/dam/Census/library/publications/2016/acs/acsgeo-1.pdf

Romiszowski, A., & Mason, R. (2013). Computer-mediated communication. In D. H. Jonassen (Ed.), *Handbook of research on educational communications and technology* (pp. 402–436). Routledge.

Rubin, A. M., & Haridakis, P. M. (2001). Mass communication research at the dawn of the 21st century. *Annals of the International Communication Association, 24*(1), 73–98.

Rubin, O., Mallin, A., & Steakin, W. (2022). *By the numbers: How the Jan. 6 investigation is shaping up 1 year later.* ABC News. https://abcnews.go.com/US/numbers-jan-investigation-shaping-year/story?id=82057743

Ruggiero, T. E. (2000). Uses and gratifications theory in the 21st century. *Mass Communication and Society, 3*(1), 3–37. https://doi.org/10.1207/S15327825MCS0301_02

Saldaña, J. (2021). *The coding manual for qualitative researchers* (4th ed.). SAGE.

Scharrer, E., & Warren, S. (2022). Adolescents' modern media use and beliefs about masculine gender roles and norms. *Journalism & Mass Communication Quarterly, 99*(1), 289–315. https://doi.org/10.1177/10776990211035453

Searles, K., & Smith, G. (2016). Who's the boss? Setting the agenda in a fragmented media environment. *International Journal of Communication, 10*, 2074–2095.

Sebele-Mpofu, F. Y. (2020). Saturation controversy in qualitative research: Complexities and underlying assumptions. A literature review. *Cogent Social Sciences, 6*(1), 1838706. https://doi.org/10.1080/23311886.2020.1838706

Severin, W. J., & Tankard, J. W. (2000). *Communication theories: Origins, methods, and uses in the mass media* (5th ed.). Pearson College Division.

Shearer, E. (2021, January 12). *More than eight-in-ten Americans get news from digital devices*. Pew Research Center. https://www.pewresearch.org/fact-tank/2021/01/12/more-than-eight-in-ten-americans-get-news-from-digital-devices/

Sherry, J. L. (2006). Flow and media enjoyment. *Communication Theory, 14*(4), 328–347. https://doi.org/10.1111/j.1468-2885.2004.tb00318.x

Shrader, J. (2013). Folly of outrage: Talk radio's unethical and damaging business model. *Journal of Mass Media Ethics, 28*(4), 289–292. https://doi.org/10.1080/08900523.2013.837291

Shrum, L. J. (2017). Cultivation theory: Effects and underlying processes. In P. Rössler (Ed.), *The international encyclopedia of media effects*. John Wiley & Sons.

Smith, M., & Glueck, K. (2022, August 2). *Kansas votes to preserve abortion rights protections in its constitution*. The New York Times. https://www.nytimes.com/2022/08/02/us/kansas-abortion-rights-vote.html

Sobieraj, S., & Berry, J. (2011). From incivility to outrage: Political discourse in blogs, talk radio, and cable news. *Political Communication, 28*(1), 19–41. https://doi.org/10.1080/10584609.2010.542360

Song, H., Gil de Zúñiga, H., & Boomgaarden, H. G. (2020). Social media news use and political cynicism: Differential pathways through "news finds me" perception. *Mass Communication and Society, 23*(1), 47–70. https://doi.org/10.1080/15205436.2019.1651867

Stephens, P. (2013). "Reading at it": Gertrude Stein, information overload, and the makings of Americanitis. *Twentieth Century Literature, 59*(1), 126–156. http://www.jstor.org/stable/24247113

Stocking, G., Mitchell, A., Matsa, K. E., Widjaya, R., Jurkowitz, M., Ghosh, S., Smith, A., Naseer, S., & St. Aubin, C. (2022). *The role of alternative social media in the news and information environment*. Pew Research Center. https://www.pewresearch.org/journalism/2022/10/06/the-role-of-alternative-social-media-in-the-news-and-information-environment/

Strömbäck, J., Tsfati, Y., Boomgaarden, H., Damstra, A., Lindgren, E., Vliegenthart, R., & Lindholm, T. (2020). News media trust and its impact on media use: Toward a framework for future research. *Annals of the International Communication Association, 44*(2), 139–156. https://doi.org/10.1080/23808985.2020.1755338

Swart, J., & Broersma, M. (2021). The trust gap: Young people's tactics for assessing the reliability of political news. *The International Journal of Press/Politics, 27*(2), 396–416. https://doi.org/10.1177/19401612211006696

Talisse, R. B. (2021). *Sustaining democracy: What we owe to the other side*. Oxford University Press.

Tarm, M., & Billeaud, J. (2021, May 23). *The mob made me do it: U.S. Capitol rioters claim Jan. 6 crowd at fault*. The Denver Post. https://www.denverpost.com/2021/05/23/us-capitol-rioters-defense/

Terry, G., & Hayfield, N. (2021). Conceptual foundations of thematic analysis. In G. Terry & N. Hayfield (Eds.), *Essentials of thematic analysis* (pp. 3–14). American Psychological Association. https://doi.org/10.1037/0000238-001

Tornoe, R. (2017). Creating a "customer-engagement funnel": Why email newsletters continue to succeed for newspapers. *Editor & Publisher, 150*(11), 24–25.

Torres-Lugo, C., Yang, K.-C., & Menczer, F. (2020). The manufacture of partisan echo chambers by follow train abuse on Twitter. *Proceedings of the International AAAI Conference on Web and Social Media, 16*(1), 1017–1028. https://doi.org/10.1609/icwsm.v16i1.19354

Towers, W. M. (1985). Weekday and Sunday readership seen through uses and gratifications. *Newspaper Research Journal, 6*(3), 20–32. https://doi.org/10.1177/073953298500600303

Tsfati, Y., Boomgaarden, H. G., Strömbäck, J., Vliegenthart, R., Damstra, A., & Lindgren, E. (2020). Causes and consequences of mainstream media dissemination of fake news: Literature review and synthesis. *Annals of the International Communication Association, 44*(2), 157–173. https://doi.org/10.1080/23808985.2020.1759443

Usher, N. (2018). Re-thinking trust in the news: A material approach through "Objects of Journalism". *Journalism Studies, 19*(4), 564–578. https://doi.org/10.1080/1461670X.2017.1375391

Valkenburg, P. M., Peter, J., & Walther, J. B. (2016). Media effects: Theory and research. *Annual Review of Psychology, 67*(1), 315–338. https://doi.org/10.1146/annurev-psych-122414-033608

Vaughn, S. L. (Ed.). (2008). *Encyclopedia of American Journalism*. Routledge.

Wei, F.-Y. (2009). Birthdays then and now: Applying uses and gratifications theory to analyze the media progression cycle. *Communication Teacher, 23*(1), 23–27. https://doi.org/10.1080/17404620802592940

Weiyan, L. (2015). A historical overview of uses and gratifications theory. *Cross-Cultural Communication, 11*(9), 71–78. http://cscanada.net/index.php/ccc/article/view/7415

Wenzel, A. (2020). Red state, purple town: Polarized communities and local journalism in rural and small-town Kentucky. *Journalism, 21*(4), 557–573. https://doi.org/10.1177/1464884918783949

White, R. (2004). Discourse analysis and social constructionism. *Nurse researcher, 12*(2), 7–16. https://doi.org/10.7748/nr.12.2.7.s3

Whitehurst, L. (2022, October 12). *Oath Keepers jury hears about massive weapon cache on Jan. 6*. The Associated Press. https://apnews.com/article/capitol-siege-florida-virginia-conspiracy-government-and-politics-6ac80882e8cf61af36be6c46252ac24c

Wieland, M., & Kleinen-von Königslöw, K. (2020). Conceptualizing different forms of news processing following incidental news contact: A triple-path model. *Journalism, 21*(8), 1049–1066. https://doi.org/10.1177/1464884920915353

Williams, D. (2006). Virtual cultivation: Online worlds, offline perceptions. *Journal of Communication, 56*(1), 69–87. https://doi.org/10.1111/j.1460-2466.2006.00004.x

Wimmer, R. D., & Dominick, J. R. (2014). *Mass media research: An introduction* (10th ed.). Wadsworth Cengage Learning.

Wuthnow, R. (2012). *Red state religion: Faith and politics in America's heartland*. Princeton University Press.

Xiao, L. (2021). Fighting disinformation in social media: An online persuasion perspective. In R. Luttrell, L. Xiao, & J. Glass (Eds.), *Democracy in the Disinformation Age: Influence and Activism in American Politics* (pp. 201–220). Routledge.

Yamamoto, M., Ran, W., & Xu, S. (2021). How you watch television news matters: A panel analysis of second screening and political learning from the news. *Journal of Broadcasting & Electronic Media, 65*(3), 377–396. https://doi.org/10.1080/08838151.2021.1957894

Young, D. G. (2021). *Irony and outrage: The polarized landscape of rage, fear, and laughter in the United States*. Oxford University Press.

· 7 ·

THEDONALD.WIN: ELECTORAL FRAUD AND A NATION IN CRISIS

Tyler Martinez and Majia Nadesan

The January 6, 2021, assault against the U.S. Capitol building following the 2020 election shocked the nation. Images of the invasion by President Donald Trump's supporters in the halls and galleys were as bewildering as they were astonishing. What forces drove his following to such an assault? Experienced and/or perceived political marginalization, growing social polarization, and the economic dislocations of the crumbling apparatus of neoliberal capitalism have been offered as explanations for the rise of right-wing populism (Ron & Nadesan, 2020). However, although contextual and institutional drivers should not be ignored, this study focuses on the accounts provided by avowed Trump supporters to understand their stated perceptions and intentions as expressed in comments posted at the online fandom site "theDonald.win" during the 2020 election run-up, capturing an important period of online political activity among Trump's fandom. "theDonald.win" was an online forum website supporting his 2020 election bid. theDonald.win site allowed community users to post screenshots, images, videos, or links to other websites. These posts were rated by users through upvotes and downvotes. The images and discursive realities articulated and shared on theDonald.win arguably played an important role in assembling audiences for Donald Trump and for empowering narratives of existential peril conductive to uncivil demonstrations. The Wayback Machine recorded the first capture of this site on August 11, 2018.

Cyber Dreams of Digital Commons and Dystopic Political Polarizations

The Internet was an alleged political game-changer, moving from "periphery to the mainstream in American politics," as it was recast from an "oddity" in 1994 into a core and "mainstream tool for candidacy and issue campaigns in 2000" (Van Slambrouck, 1999). Persily and Tucker (2020) described early optimism about the Internet's potential as a democracy-promoting free-speech zone as encoding a theory of the Internet as "liberational technology," facilitating "unimpeded transnational communication that would disrupt authoritarian regimes and promote freedom around the world" (p. 1; see also Nothhaft, 2015). The Internet's capacities to enable small donor fundraising and online community building, coupled with its "subversive" uses in protests and campaigns, were believed to empower democratic forces, especially against authoritarian governments (Persily & Tucker, 2020, p. 1). Nelson et al., (2017) suggested the Internet compensated for declines in more traditional forms of political participation, while Gerbaudo (2014) opined that social media activism's anti-establishment and anti-institutional rhetoric invigorated direct democracy, tailored to the interactive and open dynamics of the Web 2.0 architecture.

However, Internet optimism met considerable criticism from the start. In 1995, *Information Week* ran an article complaining of the "Internet Democracy Hoax" as "Internet-enabled political change" was "peddled as a cure for all our civic ills" (Stahlman, 1995). Hindman and Cukier (2004) challenged the Internet's alleged decentralizing tendencies, pointing out that Google and Yahoo were responsible for 95 percent of all Web searches in the U.S. in 2004, demonstrating a "worrisome ... trend toward consolidation." In addition to the problems of centralized ownership of electronic platforms and search engines, critics questioned the promise that online discourse would promote reasoned, democracy-building exchanges. For instance, Carlin et al. (2005) observed adversarial online discussion of the 2004 Presidential debates and a failure to honor diversity and equality of ideas in the absence of active moderation.

Ambivalence about the Internet's democracy-delivering potential was amplified by the events of January 6, 2021, tempering optimism about the prospects of digital democracy. Social media platforms, such as Parler (a social media website positioned as a conservative alternative), circulated allegations of election fraud and enabled coordination among those who invaded the Capitol Building (Ng et al., 2021). The more general role of social media in promoting content coded as mis- and dis-information has emerged as a key research arena (e.g., see Wittenberg & Berinsky, 2020). Moreover, contemporary consumption patterns may increase audience susceptibility to polarizing messages, especially "filter bubbles," which are identified as a key problem leading to siloed information consumption (Spohr, 2017). Although empirical evidence for cultivation of polarization is conflicted (see Guess et al., 2018), divisive and "fake" news stories are framed as a "viral" contagion afflicting those among whom it circulates (e.g., see Mukerjee, 2017). Fake news accounts allegedly threaten democracy by promoting discontent in social media "echo chamber" feeds and platforms wherein individuals are siloed and susceptible to group pressures to conform to the dominant narrative in a media spiral of silence (e.g., see Guess et al., 2018; Spohr, 2017).

Research studies addressing the qualitative features of online discussion have produced mixed results. Findings in the 2010s suggested anger was the emotion most likely to spread across social media platforms, with dissemination measured by the extent of forwarding messages to others (Guadagno et al., 2013). The emotive nature of online discussion was documented by Wilhelm (1998), who concluded that online political discussion analyzed lacked sustained community deliberation. However, Nadesan's (2017) analysis of online discussion forums addressing the Fukushima nuclear crisis found the opposite, with reasoned debate and sharing of educational links regarding the disaster and its politics. Kushin and Kitchener (2009) also noted a general lack of "flaming" or inflammatory responses in their analysis of a Facebook political discussion forum despite only a minority of respondents opposing the majority supported viewpoints. Gervais (2015) experimentally manipulated online discussants exposure to uncivil political talk, finding that exposure generates anger and aversion but also amplifies uncivil behavior when the incivility is like-minded. The potential for amplification of incivility among the like-minded is reinforced by other studies that have found indignation to be exacerbated by in-group reinforcement, leading to charged encounters in other social media or "real world" contexts (Hissu & Beck, 2018; Kakutani, 2018). The emotional forces that lead to charged encounters between groups simultaneously promote internal cohesion within groups.

Political Fandom

Research on fandom provides insight into the socially cohesive power of shared narratives, especially threat narratives, in assembling and mobilizing online audiences (Sandvoss, 2013). Of particular relevance is Erikson's (2008) findings that social media was changing electoral politics, encouraging candidates to cultivate "political fandom" as a "model for doing politics" (p. 6). Fans studied by Erikson took it upon themselves to establish unofficial fan sites within MySpace where information about their candidate, Hillary Clinton, was shared montage-like. Erikson observed that a personal politics of relationship prevailed, replacing a public-sector politics of value and policy debates. Politics become highly personalized and emotionally organized around protection of elevated political figures. Rodriguez and Goretti (2022) found emotional camaraderie in Alexandria Ocasio-Cortez fans Twitter feeds, indicating that political fandom can deliver authentically experienced communities organized around narratives of resistance. However, some of AOC's fans' intense identification led to charged encounters with her critics not conducive to civil dialogue. Romano (2024) argued that Donald Trump's fandom functioned akin to a conduit, whereupon followers transferred highly politicized emotional investments directly to his personhood, reinforcing a highly charged emotive politics. These findings suggest that political fandom across the political spectrum often entails deep and defensive emotional identifications built through shared narratives, which have the potential to undermine civil dialogue.

Political Narratives Binding Fandoms

The narratives shared by political fandoms vary significantly across established political parties, as well as within them. However, Solomon (2014) reported that discourses that encode anxiety, fear, desire and/or hope promote audience identification regardless of political persuasion. This constellation of emotions was previously found to characterize Donald Trump's political rhetoric during the 2016 election campaign. Wells et al. (2020) explained how Donald Trump optimized his audience assemblage with his 2015–2016 Twitter campaigning, which enabled unfiltered communication with followers and engendered news amplification. Trump supporters' distrust of legacy media encouraged their mobilization using non-traditional media platforms such as Twitter, Reddit, and Parler to disseminate his rhetorical vision, recruit fans, and attack enemies.

Donald Trump's rhetorical vision countered progressive optimism regarding America's national standing and cultural integrity. Homolar and Scholz (2019) described Trump's rhetoric as encoding divisive crisis narratives painting a picture of American decline, while promising to lead the country back to greatness (see also, Skonieczny, 2018). The truth value of Trump's claims mattered less than the emotional economy of the crisis narratives and his ethos as a leader promising to restore lost greatness by battling nefarious forces. In this regard, Trump's narrative vision aligned with traditional populist rhetoric on the right emphasizing nationalism, immigration, and openness to alternative accounts of historical events and contemporary processes delivered by hidden hands of power (see Speakman & Funk, 2020). The so-called "conspiratorial" view of history was labeled "paranoid rhetoric" by Hofstadter (1964), who disdained theories of history that centered powerful hidden actors, including C. Wright Mills' (1956/1999) power elite. In the contemporary era, conspiracy theories exist as a category of disqualification argued Jack Bratich (2008), othering narratives through epistemic disqualification (p. 3). Yet, globalization, the expansion of the billionaire class, and growing inequality have renewed populist interest in elite theories of power across the political spectrum (see Ron & Nadesan, 2020).

Post-Truth Digital Commons

Communication scholar Jayson Harsin (2018) used the phrase "post-truth" to describe contemporary public communications. According to Harsin, post-truth does not imply a simple dualism between truth and ideology, but rather encapsulates the public's loss in institutional trust, resulting in increased public confusion and suspicion. According to Harsin, post-truth addresses "discord, confusion, polarized views, and understanding, well-and-misinformed convictions, and elite attempts to produce and manage these 'truth markets' or competitions" (p. 3). Loss of institutional power over meaning production enables the proliferation of significations and narratives whose affective modes of authentication seem unmoored from neoclassical logics of empirical verification and structured argumentation, described, for example, by Stephen Edelson Toulmin (1969) in *The Uses of Argumentation*.

The reality principle, the Enlightenment faith in the capacity for certain forms of human reasoning, is losing a privileged epistemological stance.

Jean Baudrillard (1994) denoted modern communications as "hyperreal" due to their increasing detachment from the reality principle and their tendency toward self-referentiality. According to Baudrillard, early twentieth century advertising practices encouraged these characteristics of modern signification, elevating the pleasure principle over the reality one, and thereby facilitating the institutionalization and cultural dispersion of hyperreality, a mode of meaning production trading in signs without concrete referents, denoted in the final stage of the modernist sign:

> it is the reflection of a profound reality;
> it masks and denatures a profound reality;
> it masks the absence of a profound reality;
> it has no relation to any reality whatsoever;
> it is its own pure simulacrum. (Baudrillard, 1994, p. 6)

The first order or stage is where an image "is the reflection of a profound reality" (Baudrillard, 1994, p. 6). For example, when introducing the first order of simulation, Baudrillard referenced a model of a map created by cartographers of an empire that was "so detailed that it ... cover[ed] the territory exactly" (p. 6). He abstractly alluded to this model as representational in the sense that it seeks to re-present key features of the territory it maps. According to Baudrillard, "representation stems from the principle of the equivalence of the sign and of the real (even if this equivalence is Utopian, it is a fundamental axiom)" (p. 6). The point Baudrillard is making here is that in past history meaning production was understood publicly as a reflection of some profound reality, regardless of whether that reality was coded as a transcendent truth, or a contingently determined one. Over time, the modernist epistemological paradigm of truth production was loosened as self-referential significations, detached from the reality principle, grew in circulation and influence. Consequently, the affective flows of the pleasure principle and its inversion in the form of thanatos, or the principle of death and destruction (Mender, 2019), overshadowed the disciplining logics of the reality principle in dictating cultural significations.

Following Baudrillard's insights about the ascendancy of the simulacrum at the end of the twentieth-century, Brett Nicholls (2016) observes that the contemporary "post-truth situation" privileges resonate feelings, beliefs and personal opinions over "objectivity" understood as empirically verifiable facts (p. 7). It is important to note here that Nichols does not invoke a binary between the real and the floating simulacrum in his reading of Baudrillard.

Nicholls explains: "There is no external objective reality in a formal antagonistic relationship to the abstract terrain of commodity exchange" (p. 10). Simulacra are "productive" entities (p. 16) and the "hyperreal is a representational logic in which the real emerges as excess, or more real than the real" (p. 18). The referential outside of signification is "folded back into representation itself" as the reality principle disappears, its erasure effaced (p. 19).

The concept of hyperreality is helpful for understanding the excess and self-referentiality of the Internet. Significations proliferate unmoored from the demands of the Enlightenment reality principle. Traditional forms of argumentation and verification circulate still, but have lost influence to affective resonances, both pleasurable and disturbed. Digitally mediated fandoms and other social media communities are characteristically hyperreal, proliferating self-referential significations and affective modes of relating to, and authenticating, shared narratives. Donald Trump's emotive rhetoric (Homolar & Scholz, 2019) would predictably encourage highly charged meaning productions among his digital fans. James Morris (2021) points out Trump's rhetorical promise to "Make America Great Again" circulated nostalgically among fans without measured consideration of "any truth about whether America was great in the first place or whether Trump will be able to re-establish this even if it was" (p. 327). The reality principle is irrelevant, not simply for Trump rhetoric, but also for contemporary fandoms and hyperreal communities more generally, where attentional economies vie for engagement via emotive appeals.

Political Fandom in the 2020 Election: theDonald.win

The emotionally charged 2020 Presidential election (see Balsamo, 2020) offered an opportunity to examine online communities in a particularly fraught political context. In the months leading up to the election, then President Trump warned fans his victory would be stolen, engendering vigorous efforts after his defeat by supporters to challenge results with more than two dozen lawsuits (Vasilogambros, 2020). These allegations of election fraud encouraged GOP voters to believe results were "neither free nor fair," further reducing institutional trust (Vasilogambros, 2020). In order to understand the shared significations uniting Trump's fandom, this study focused on the discursive communications posted on the (unofficial) theDonald.win site, which was first established as a Reddit online platform discussion forum titled, r/theDonald. Reddit placed a "quarantine" on the forum in response to allegations that its comments violated Reddit's content policy, including strict rules against the use of harassment, bullying, and violence (Reddit, n.d.b). This quarantine meant that users would have to "opt-in" to access content, would not be able to profit from advertising, and would essentially be removed from Reddit's recommendation algorithms, i.e., the removal of the forum from the "popular" page and the removal of the forum from the "recommendations" in the search bar (Reddit, n.d.a). In response, a new domain site, theDonald.win was registered and went live, mimicking the previous Reddit forum (Emerson, 2020). The Wayback Machine records the first capture of this site on August 11, 2018.

According to the traffic analysis company, Alexa, theDonald.win was at one point the 1,207th ranked website in the United States (Emerson, 2020). The site's standing and audience traffic support its importance for assembling a highly sympathetic political audience for the Trump campaign. The stated purpose of the site was as follows:

> Welcome to the forum of choice for The President of The United States, Donald Trump! Be advised this forum is for serious supporters of President Trump. We have discussions, memes, AMAs, and more. We are not politically correct.

The rules for engagement included:

> Trump Supporters. Our community is a high-energy rally for supporters of President Trump.
> High Energy. No forum sliding, consensus cracking, topic dilution, etc.
> No Racism. No racism, including slurs, non-factual content, and general unfounded bigotry.
> No Doxing. No doxxing of yourself or others, including revealing PII of non-public figures, as well as addresses, phone numbers, etc. of public figures.
> Follow the Law. No posts or comments that violate laws in your jurisdiction or the United States.

This Trump fandom site was significant for articulating interests and concerns of Trump fandom while also delivering an accessible and receptive audience to the Trump campaign.

The data represented and analyzed in this chapter were first collected by Tyler Martinez (2021) as part of his master's thesis. The thesis aimed to represent and understand Trump supporters' stated perceptions and intentions as expressed in comments posted at the online fandom site "theDonald.win" during the 2020 election cycle. This chapter focuses on the emergent themes that were constituted from the online discussions, with the research objective of understanding how conversational concerns may have contributed to the uncivil Capitol assault.

Methodology

theDonald.win site allowed users of the community to post screenshots, images, or links to other websites. There were three sets of data collected from theDonald.win website in 2020. The data collections took place on August 31, October 31, and the day after the election, November 4, 2020. This timing guaranteed the data contained content that captured that month's highest-rated posts approaching the election and the immediate reaction to its results. Totaled, the data included 75 discussion posts and 750 comments, which were manually collected using copy and paste for textual content and screenshots using Encapture to preserve the sequence and visual appearance of comments *in situ*. Google spreadsheets and Google docs were used as a way to link and keep track of each post and its comments.

The discussion posts and comments were selected for data collection using the following process. First, the word "election" was searched on August 30–31 and October 30–31 using the "top" rated filter to produce results. Data collected on November 4, 2020, varied slightly as no filters beyond upvotes were used to search for posts. The top 25 most upvoted posts were selected from the filtered results. User comments found in the discussion threads were then drawn from these posts. The comments in the threads often diverged in conversational topics from the theme of the post. Comments that strayed from the topic of elections were de-selected for data collection as the top ten topical comments focusing on the election were selected based on upvotes.

Data collected from the forums were analyzed using grounded thematic analysis because it emphasizes inductive pattern recognition in textual data. Thematic analysis is a form of qualitative analysis that taps into the human "propensity for pattern making" and the capacity for researchers to identify and interpret these patterns (Saldana et al., 2011, p. 91). At its most basic level, the approach requires researchers to construct inductive categories in a process described by Saldana, Leavy and Beretvas (2011) as "clustering the most seemingly alike things into the most seemingly appropriate groups" (pp. 90–91). In this study, thematic clustering followed the approach outlined by Ryan and Bernard (2003), who emphasize repetitions and analogic regularities of symbolic content in the form and meaning of discourse. This "in vivo" coding requires researchers' categories to be derived directly from symbols found in the discourse being analyzed after multiple passes through the data. Although it does not aim to document frequency of particular expressions, thematic analysis does work effectively to categorically identify dominant and contested thematic values, beliefs, and worldviews in the language used by participants.

Findings

The categories that emerged from the emergent thematic analysis included characterizations of protagonists (Trump fans) and antagonists (the Democrats), the bias and problematic influence of "Big Tech," and threats to election integrity. These themes are summarized in Table 1.1. Themes shifted over the 3 periods of data collection as representations became increasingly emotionally charged, especially in the final data collection the day after the election. Findings from the emergent thematic analysis are summarized in Table 7.1. The specific comments cited below to illustrate the thematic categories all ranked among the topmost upvoted for each post selected for data collection.

August 31, 2020, Emergent Themes

Emergent themes identified in the three data sets evolved across time. In the first data set, "Democrats as Cheaters" and "Big Tech" were the most prominent and re-occurring themes and both categories of antagonists were represented as antithetical to the health of the nation. The most commonly advocated responses to these posited threats to democracy were "voting" and "taking action."

Table 7.1: Emergent themes on theDonald.win

Date of Data Collection	Themes	Themes	Themes
August 31, 2020	Democrats as Cheaters	Big Tech	Voting
October 31, 2020	Democrats' Leadership	Mail-in Voting Fraud	Fraudulent Ballots
November 4, 2020	Stolen Election	Incorrigible Democrats	Civil War

Democrats as Cheaters

"Democrats" had two main identifiers: "Democrat" and "the left," defined as socialists, communists, and Marxists. These identifiers were used synonymously within the forum so they were regarded as interchangeable, although the former was mentioned far more often than the latter. Another term used by commentators to describe their alleged nemesis was the more ambiguous term "they." In some contexts, "Big Tech" and the Democrats seemed to be collapsed into a homogeneous "they," whereas in other contexts the terms referred more concretely to their direct referents, such as Democratic voters or politicians and the CEOs of Big Tech companies.

Democrats were typically signified as "cheaters," "liars," "communists," and "extremely anti-Trump" with his elimination often identified as the Democrat's endgame. For example, one post read: "True. Make NO mistake. This has ALWAYS been about taking out Trump." This comment implied that the Democrats were both the antithesis and negation of Trump, whose thematic meanings tended to be implied enthymematically, rather than directly articulated. Relatedly, one user suggested that the Democrats would go as far as sabotaging their own country to see Trump fail: "No, when Trump wins they will push the virus twice as hard to wreck his economy for the midterm elections." Cheating was signaled as the Democrats' most likely strategy to defeat Trump. For example, a number of top-rated comments cast suspicion on fraud in balloting, both in the collection and reading of voter selections, as illustrated in this comment emphasizing Democrat's duplicity:

> This time they are planning for more contingencies. If they don't out right steal the Election with stuffed ballot boxes and "finding" extra mail in ballots for weeks after the election, they are going to use the D governors of some swing states to issue EO at the last minute that will stop those states from sending electors. I think they might target NV, MI, NC, PA, and WI. If they can get one or more of those D governors to hold electors hostage, then maybe this 12th amendment hell breaks loose. Whatever the case they are telling us now that they do not plan on accepting the results of the election, and have even "War gamed" what generals to involve. The Democrats are taking this country to a very dark place. Be ready. Food, Liquor, Bullets.

The comment's description of the breakdown of electoral integrity was echoed in comments that detailed Democrat's alleged cheating methods, such as "ballot harvesting." Ballot harvesting was offered as one likely tactic for altering election outcomes, as illustrated in this comment that describes how Democrats would enable this practice despite state laws that prohibit this practice:

> In several states "ballot harvesting" is illegal under state law. How are the Democrats confronting this issue? One of the terms they are demanding in the COVID-19 relief package is a federal law prohibiting states from banning "ballot harvesting."

Ballot harvesting, whereupon political operatives collect ballots from voters' homes and drop them off at a polling location, was called out as threatening election integrity by the Republican-led Committee on House Administration in the U.S. House of Representatives (Christie, 2022). The committee decried "unlimited" ballot harvesting due to the pandemic, articulating Republican concerns about election fraud, with widespread suspicion fueled by a prominent case of illegal ballot harvesting by Democrats in Arizona in the 2020 primaries (Christie, 2022).

Big Tech

As mentioned above, "Big Tech" and the Democrats seemed to be categorically collapsed into a homogeneous and communist "they," threatening media integrity and democracy more generally. The comment below inflects this generalized categorization of antagonism as qualitatively "communist":

> The truth is our media is controlled by communist infiltrators. The truth is a lot of our politicians are controlled by communist infiltrators. The truth is our schools are run by communist movement infiltrators. Our process of democracy itself is of course under attack by communist infiltrators.

Criticism of a corrupted Big Tech most commonly referenced four major players: Facebook, Google, Amazon, and Apple. Twitter and YouTube featured less predominately, but were also invoked, as Twitter was described as a social media platform rather than a Big Tech giant. YouTube is owned by Google, and there were a couple of instances where YouTube was mentioned as merely it's extension. Users were quick to point out that Big Tech was responsible for censorship, a problem that was represented as particularly significant and pernicious in comments. Trump's supporters were cast as censored victims. Examples of censorship were specific and included the alleged removal by YouTube of "dislike" votes from Biden videos and the removal of "like" votes from Trump videos. Facebook and Instagram were also accused of censorship by blocking URLs and redirecting their links. These activities were construed as representing election interference, as illustrated in this allegation that, "We constantly see election meddling, censoring and people being banned." Legacy news was also implicated in censoring content to promote the Democrats, as illustrated in this comment: "They are literally stealing the election right in front of our eyes by limiting NEWS that's not favorable to Biden in real time." Another upvoted comment echoed this theme: "They are blatantly protecting Biden from any negative stories, it's amazing and infuriating."

Responses to Threats: Voting

Voting and increased political participation were early themes articulated as necessary to "defend" the country from the posited evil forces promoting its dissolution. Comments about voting were most optimistically framed in the first data set with some users expressing hope for enhanced voter participation: "I hope this very real fear of election fraud drives republicans to vote like never before. Hoping we turnout in record numbers." Other commentators reinforced the personal importance of voting: "I didn't vote for him in 2016, but even though I live in the bluest area in the country and my vote literally will not matter, I am still taking time out of my day to vote." Voting is represented as a patriotic act in comments such as: "America needs YOU" and "Voted. The Silent Majority in WA is waking up!" There was a sense of optimism surrounding the action of voting and a sense of duty as commentators identify as believers in American values.

Concerns that the "cheating" Democrats might manipulate election results emerge in this first data set, accompanied by pledges to defend American democracy: "I'm a grown man and this is the first election I have felt was worth me fighting for," read one post. Another said, "Most other elections I was ambivalent about but I won't stand for my country being torn apart by the left." Civil war was not a dominant theme, but did emerge as a distinct possibility in some commentators' remarks, as illustrated here:

> Civil war is ONLY possible if the left controls the federal government. The right can successfully stage an uprising because we have the guns, the vets, law enforcement, and men who can actually fight. If we control the federal government / the military as well, there is no path forward for blue states to stage a rebellion.

A few commentators expressed their readiness and called on the Democrats to "Bring it on." The readiness for conflict was not a dominant theme but was expressed occasionally, as illustrated in the comment above.

October 31, 2020, Emergent Themes

The second data set took place the last week of October, approximately one week before the election. The theme of Democrats as cheater's was amplified across the top 25 comments selected for analysis. Comments focused also on Democrats' insufficient leadership, their alleged incapacities to lead and instill confidence. Democrats were cast as weak, duplicitous cheaters. Additionally, comments addressing the theme of mail-in voting fraud were specific and narrowly focused, framed declaratively as factual. Although Big Tech still appeared in comments, it was replaced in prominence by references to mail-in voting as the key component of the Democrat's plot against the conservative right.

The Democrats' Flailing Leadership

Although Nancy Pelosi was referenced a few times in user comments, it was Joe Biden who received the most attention. Biden was represented as weak and as lacking the confidence of his party, such as in this post:

> Gee, I guess their vote by mail scams aren't working out so well for them since now they are trying to remove Trump before the election. Someone ask Joe how it feels to know his party has no confidence in him.

The alleged weakness of leadership fed into user comments that the party was flailing, but desperate, in its efforts to wrestle back leadership.

Mail-in Voting Fraud

The theme of mail-in voting producing a fraudulent election emerged as the clear talking point for the entire forum site the week before the election. Mishandling of ballots was a commonly expressed concern: "Too many ballots can get 'lost' with early voting. That being said. I will wait till the last days of early voting to vote. I'm not taking too many chances." Another comment emphasized alleged Democratic "harvesting":

> That is EXACTLY what the Democrats are doing. There is a huge scandal in Houston where poll workers associated with the Biden campaign are harvesting fake IDs and casting votes for Democrats. A witness was subject of an assassination attempt. This story was on TD.win for all of 5 mins.

The alleged use of fake IDs to produce fraudulent votes reinforced the theme found previously of Democrats as cheaters, as illustrated here:

> Make no mistake, the democrats are cheating ... as they always have. VOTE and report anything suspicious. A friend voted early, his vote for Trump kept changing to Biden. Thankfully he caught it during the Review option. After 3 failed attempts before finalizing he called a worker over. She looked at what was happening, without surprise, made a change on the machine, and it was corrected.

Concerns about electronic voting machines susceptibility to hacking and other fraud are not new (see *Associated Press*, 2006) but historically the Republicans were less likely to raise this concern than Democrats.

Other comments alleged that the COVID-19 pandemic was weaponized by Democrats to increase their opportunities for electoral fraud, as illustrated in this quote:

> And they're trying like mad to suppress that in-person vote by pushing the "second wave" of Covid narrative. I'm sure you've all heard about your local spikes delivered by breathless news readers. The left wants us to: 1. Vote by mail by promoting fear of contracting covid, even less serious (and more manageable) in its subsequent "waves." 2. Vote by mail by letting you think that in-person voting might not be allowed on Election Day (it MUST be) and polling places might be closed (they WON'T be) due to hysteria over "spikes." LOL of course, they're real dream is that we don't vote by mail ... then aren't allowed to vote in person due to a coronavirus threat.

This comment suggested the COVID-19 narrative was exploited to encourage mail-in voting, thereby facilitating Democrats' fraudulent ballot harvesting.

November 4 Emergent Themes

The final data set was collected on November 4, 2020, one day after the election. When the data were collected, Nevada, Arizona, Pennsylvania, North Carolina, and Georgia had yet to be called. President Trump had declared victory on the night of November 3. While the narratives surrounding the election in the first two data sets focused on mishandling of mail-in ballots, the third data set contained allegations of "evidence" of other types of fraudulent tactics. Comments also validated previously expressed concerns regarding the Democrats' cheating and duplicity.

Stolen Election

Themes identified in earlier data collections, such as Democrats as Cheaters and Election Fraud were crystalized into a narrative of a stolen election in the final set of comments collected.

Multiple users claimed that Trump had won regardless of results, such as this user:

> We already won. The rest is political theatre to see if they can use the media to convince us Biden won. Don't even give it the light of day. Election is over. Trump is our president for 4 more years.

Many comments reinforced this narrative of a stolen election, amplifying the previously expressed allegations of inevitable election fraud. For instance, one user asserted:

> President Trump, as well as anyone with a brain, knew that the Democrats would pull this shit from day one. After their push for mail in ballots, the die was set. If anyone is surprised by this, then you are naive or stupid. WE WILL WIN THIS, ONE WAY OR THE OTHER. MAGA.

There were multiple posts where users compiled "evidence" of voter fraud and instructed others on how to document and report any election irregularities:

> Go to the locations where they are counting votes and take cameras. Report any suspicious activity such as truckloads of ballots being brought in, boxes of ballots being thrown out, or people moving ballots around. Also, record anything overheard that hints at voter fraud. If you can't make it out to those places, do online searches for voter fraud such as people who are no longer registered, moved away, are deceased, or are incarcerated, but had a vote cast for them anyway. Share with Veritas, Judicial Watch, on here, to Trump himself and his campaign, as well as on social media and via text and email to everyone you know to help get the information out there.

Comments from this final round of data collection reinforced Democrats' perceived malfeasance within an escalated rhetoric of violence:

> Worst case is they actually cheat Joe in, covering up Trumps historical victory the likes of which no one has ever seen and cheats it with mass votes showing up. Miscounts. And by the end of the week we're opening fire on communists who are trying to throw us into the furnaces for not voting for their retard pedophile monster. If they cheat joe in and steal trumps record braking landslide that we all knew he got but the dems will never admit because they're thieves and 70% of their voters are braindead, assbackwards retarded to ever think outside of their box they're told they

can't think outside of, so they'll never question voter legitimacy when their guy is finally cheating to win. Only when they're losing do they do that. I have no problem killing all of these people and starting over even if I have to die to help ensure it gets done. They stopped being Americans to me the second they called us a democracy.

The perceived failure of "voting" as a solution to the Democrats and the expressed certainty of fraud likely contributed to the call for violence expressed above. Calls for violence were uncommon in comments collected previously, but the alleged "silencing" of fraud was represented as an exigency demanding an immediate response, as illustrated in this comment:

We all knew the Dems were going to cheat, and the Fake News media (including Fox, never watching them again) is helping them by silencing stories of voter fraud. The President needs your help now. They will not steal Arizona, they will not steal this election. Get the word out!

The election is articulated in these comments as ultimately a "psyop" and readers are encouraged to challenge results:

They know if we keep the pressure on their fraud will be found out This is a full scale psyop underway, do not fall victim to it. After all the shit they pulled to try to stop Trump over the last 4 years, practically committing treason/crimes out in the open, do you really think they were just going to let an election determine their fate?

The Democrats and other conspirators' alleged treason and crimes signify they are incorrigible and previously expressed faith in voting represented as inadequate to counter Democrats' alleged cheating and capacities of media censorship.

Discussion

The themes reported in the results represent Democrats as elite outsiders desperate to regain power and willing to deploy fraud and other criminal activity, especially through manipulation of mail-in voting. Unlike Hofstadter's paranoid rhetoric, these thematic elements did not emphasize a hidden hand of power directly, but rather highlighted alleged illicit actions by duplicitous Democrats and deliberate and politically biased censorship by Big Tech. The distrust expressed by political fandoms reinforces concerns that political legitimacy has been significantly eroded and that public epistemology is irrevocably shattered in the form of incommensurable narratives of truth. Belief in widespread censorship by technology companies (e.g., see Al Khatib & Dia, 2019; Cutter, 2018; Shellenberger, 2023), especially the growing use of algorithmic censorship, contributes to communities' perceptions of political marginalization and fuels "outrage" based fandoms. The reality principle loses its grip as a mechanism for adjudicating truth when information is believed to be weaponized, a finding that has relevance across the political spectrum: for example see Munro's (2017) findings regarding the malleability and mobilization of truth games in the WikiLeaks case.

The lack in faith in democratic institutions amplified across time in these data is inescapably exacerbated by the "hyperreal" characteristics of contemporary mediated communications. In an important sense, the election itself can be construed as a sign of first order signification as described by Baudrillard (1994). Elections are commonly perceived as the fundamental representation of the "will of the people," the primal energizing force of the demos and democracy itself. Yet, although the election promises to reflect the profound reality of the will of the people, it operates also as a sign that masks and "denatures" a profound reality. Just as Baudrillard's map anachronistically denotes lands as prosperous components of a long-gone empire, the election masks the impossibility of representation of the will of the people. The representational limits of the will of the people introduces a certain juridical undecidability about their power as political subjects. Canovan (2002) suggests this undecidability about the power of "the people" in fact represents a democratic paradox because democratic processes of *"bringing the people into politics"* impinge on understanding how power operates because its dispersions and circulations are not transparent. The opaque circulations of decentered power work against coherent conceptualizations of agency, leaving "the people feeling" disempowered (p. 26). Populist mobilizations feed on this paradox of democracy and tend to attribute perceived ruptures in collective sovereignty to the effects of elite forces/groups working against idealized community and/or national norms.

The populist worldview found on theDonald.win fandom is nostalgic, describing a debased capitalism requiring reforms aimed at reinstating morality, market disciplines, and entrepreneurialism. This worldview presupposes that America once represented a more democratic "producers republic," characterized by small and medium sized enterprise in the context of a disciplining market (see Nadesan, 2013). This is a Jacksonian, aspirational ideal for contemporary capitalists unhappy with the reign of large, transnational corporations without national allegiances. This nostalgic yearning for a producers' republic doesn't simply inform economic criticism, but also has shaped critiques of a wide range of American social institutions, including baseball. Nick Trujillo's (1992) description of "romantic" critiques of baseball revealed nostalgic yearnings for a purer and more communal America. Yet, the America that is nostalgically constructed through its absence masks the reality that this America never existed as imagined, and of course was characterized in actuality by deep and rigid inequalities (see Nadesan, 2013).

Finally, with hyperreality, "simulation envelops the whole edifice of representation itself as a simulacrum" (Baudrillard, 1994, p. 6). Simulation essentially swallows up the original representation and offers a new image in place of the original, thus creating a new reality in which the new sign/image, with no origin, is represented as primal. Despite failures to find widespread voter fraud, U.S. Attorney General, William Barr, insisted "the U.S. Justice Department has uncovered no evidence of widespread voter fraud that could change the outcome of the 2020 election" (Balsamo, 2020, para. 1). There was no original act of deception according to election inspectors, yet each comment on theDonald.win articulated the process of election fraud anew with details of tactics such as harvesting IDs and voting dumps. The passion of Trump's fans, the malleability of the stolen election narrative and the lack of internal consistency in explanatory accounts across discussion forums impinged against verification. The continuous renewal of alleged fraud effaced past allegations with little symbolic "deaths." theDonald.win was essentially hyperreal, disconnected from the demands of the reality principle and post-truth in the sense described by Harsin (2018), encapsulating loss in institutional trust and burgeoning suspicion. Disconnected from the demands of verification, the defensive and highly affective flows of political fandoms can increase likelihood of charged encounters in real world contexts (Hissu & Beck, 2018; Kakutani, 2018) and, in this case, may have played a role in prompting the Capitol invasion.

Some observers of social media content contend that this hyperreal virtual reality requires heightened surveillance and algorithms of control to select against misinformation, which is represented as directly causing civil conflict. Allegations of ubiquitous censorship by Trump fans received empirical support with the release of the "Twitter files" by Elon Musk in 2020 after his acquisition of that social media platform (The Wall Street Journal Editorial Board, 2022). The files indicated extensive and deeply political censorship of user generated content, reinforcing censorship concerns. In contrast to this new paradigm of information control, this chapter follows Maxime Polleri

(2022) in recommending online narratives be framed as signals of "broader social and epistemological crises" that ought to prompt further analyses aimed at understanding the "causes of mistrust in experts' organizations, the frustrations of specific communities in post-crisis situations and the formation of new modes of public participation in the digital sphere" (p. 18). Moreover, in addition to helping map and understand public epistemologies, communication research can contribute to efforts to re-establish the reality principle by revisiting in scholarship, pedagogy, and service well-established canons of argumentation and evidence, while simultaneously working to recognize and promote dialogue across the inevitably disparate and conflicted narratives of self-and-political understanding defining pluralistic societies. Democratic flourishing will not be achieved by censoring and/or stigmatizing difference, but rather by promoting civil and deliberative norms of political participation (see, for example, Waisanen, 2014).

This study offers a limited slice in time representation of Trump's fandom in 2020. Comments were drawn from a single site and do not necessarily reflect the beliefs and attitudes of his many constituents. The 2024 election cycle offers a promising opportunity for additional research to evaluate the scope of appeal and durability of the themes identified in this analysis. The highly charged emotive convictions that Democrats are cheaters casts doubt on the electoral process and contributes to the erosion of legitimacy of U.S. democratic institutions. It will be important to understand whether and to what extent political fandoms' emotive communities shape political speech and opportunities for civil debate and dialogue.

Conclusion

The election of Joe Biden represented a foregone conclusion for the supporters of the theDonald.win. Their lack of faith in automatic election technology introduced the impossible task of re-presenting each and every vote introduced an endless set of uncertainties associated with voting and democracy more generally. The existential threat of an exogenous communist take-over and flailing Democrat leadership articulated across sites such as Parler and theDonald.win gave form to a public epistemology of a nation in crisis. Narratives of crisis can be found across the political spectrum as globalization and automation have de-territorialized power and produced a growing sense of cultural malaise and nostalgic yearning for an imagined lost America. For everyday supporters of the Capitol assault, this sense of crisis was given intelligibility by narratives of electoral fraud and media censorship documented in this analysis. Voting had failed and civil war was inevitable. Further research could explore how other, highly polarized fandoms articulate exogeneous and endogenous threats and pathways to change.

References

Al Khatib, H., & Kayyali, D. (2019, October 23). YouTube is erasing history. *The New York Times.* https://www.nytimes.com/2019/10/23/opinion/syria-youtube-content-moderation.html

The Associated Press. (2006, September 13). Princeton prof hacks e-vote machine. *NBC News.* https://www.nbcnews.com/id/wbna14825465

Balsamo, M. (2020, December 1). Disputing Trump, Barr says no widespread election fraud. *The Associated Press.* https://apnews.com/article/barr-no-widespread-election-fraud-b1f1488796c9a98c4b1a9061a6c7f49d

Baudrillard, J. (1994). *Simulacra and simulation.* University of Michigan Press.

Bratich, J. (February 7, 2008). *Conspiracy panics: Political rationality and popular culture.* SUNY Press.

Canovan, M. (2002). Taking politics to the people: Populism as the ideology of democracy. In Y. Mény & Y. Surel (Eds.), *Democracies and the populist challenge* (pp. 25–42). Palgrave Macmillan.

Carlin, D.B., Schill, D., Lavesseur, D.G., & A.S. King (2005). The post-9/11 public sphere: Citizen talk about the 2004 presidential debates. *Rhetoric and Public Affairs, 8*(4), 617–638. https://doi.org/10.1353/rap.2006.0005

Christie, B. (2022, June 1). Records show coordinated Arizona ballot collection scheme. *The Associated Press.* https://apnews.com/article/arizona-presidential-elections-conspiracy-election-2020government-and-politics-65a3f0f130905dd7151e5189e7242784

Cutter, J. (2018, January 24). Facebook, Twitter and Google censor alternative media – was Telesur targeted? *Liberation: Newspaper of the Party for Socialism and Liberation.* https://www.liberationnews.org/facebook-twitter-google-target-alternative-media-telesur-english-targeted/

Emerson, S. (2020, July 2). Months before Reddit purge, The_Donald users created a new home. *Medium.* https://onezero.medium.com/monthsbefore-reddit-purge-the-donald-users-created-a-ne-home-a732f79e4f04

Erikson E. (2008). "Hillary is my friend": MySpace and political fandom. *Rocky Mountain Communication Review, 5*(1), 3–16.

Gerbaudo, P. (2014). "Populism 2:" Social media activism, the generic Internet user and interactive direct democracy. In D. Trottier & C. Fuchus (Eds.), *Social media, politics and the state: Protests, revolutions, riots, crime and policing in the age of Facebook, Twitter and YouTube* (pp. 67–87). Routledge.

Gervais, B. T. (2015). Incivility online: Affective and behavioral reactions to uncivil political posts in a web-based experiment. *Journal of Information Technology & Politics, 12*(2), 167–185. https://doi.10.1080/19331681.2014.997416

Guadagno, R., Rempala, D., Murphy, S., & Okdie, B. (2013). What makes a video go viral? An analysis of emotional contagion and Internet memes. *Computers in Human Behavior, 29*(6), 2312–2319. https://doi.org/10.1016/j.chb.2013.04.016

Guess, A., Nyhan, B., & Reifler, J. (2018). Selective exposure to misinformation: Evidence from the consumption of fake news during the 2016 U.S. presidential campaign. *Askforce.* http://www.ask-force.org/web/Fundamentalists/Guess-Selective-Exposure-to-Misinformation-Evidence-Presidential-Campaign-2018.pdf

Harsin, J. (2018, December 20). Post-truth and critical communication studies. *Oxford Research Encyclopedia of Communication.* https://doi.org/10.1093/acrefore/9780190228613.013.757

Hindman, M., & Cukier, K.N. (2004, August 23). More is not necessarily better. *The New York Times.* https://www.nytimes.com/2004/08/23/opinion/more-is-not-necessarily-better.html

Hissu, H., & Beck, R. (2018). Emotions trump facts: The role of emotions in social media—a literature review. *Proceedings of the 51st Hawaii International Conference on System Sciences,* 1797–1806. https://doi.org/10.24251/HICSS.2018.226

Hofstadter, R. (1964). *The paranoid style in American politics.* Harvard University Press.

Homolar, A., & Scholz, R. (2019). The power of Trump-speak: Populist crisis narratives and ontological security. *Cambridge Review of International Affairs, 32*(3), 344–364. https://doi.org/10.1080/09557571.2019.1575796

Kakutani, M. (2018). *The death of truth: Notes on falsehood in the age of Trump.* Tim Duggan Books.

Kushin, M. J., & Kitchener, K. (2009). Getting political on social network sites: Exploring online political discourse on Facebook. *First Monday, 14*(11). https://doi.org/10.5210/fm.v14i11.2645

Martinez, T. (2021). *Conspiracy talk among fan groups: Narratives contributing to a hyperreality* (Master's thesis, Arizona State University). ProQuest.

Mender, D. (2019). The cunning of thanatos: An archeology of consumerism beyond the pleasure principle. *The Journal of Psychohistory, 47*(2), 144–153. ISSN 0145-3378

Mills, C. W. (1956/1999). *The power elite.* Oxford University Press.

Morris, J. (2021). Simulacra in the age of social media: Baudrillard as the prophet of fake news. *Journal of Communication Inquiry, 45*(4), 319–336. https://doi.org/10.1177/0196859920977154

Mukerjee, M. (July 14, 2017). How fake news goes viral—Here's the math. *Scientific American.* https://www.scientificamerican.com/article/how-fake-news-goes-viral-mdash-heres-the-math/

Munro, I. (2017). Whistle-blowing and the politics of truth: Mobilizing 'truth games' in the WikiLeaks case. *Human Relations, 70*(5), 519–543. https://doi.org/10.1177/0018726716672721

Nadesan, M. (2017). Catastrophe, transparency and social responsibility on online platforms: Contesting cold shutdown at the Fukushima Nuclear Plant. In A. Lindgreen, J. Vanhamme, F, Maon, & R. Watkins (Eds.), *Communicating corporate social responsibility in the digital era.* (pp. 291–302). Routledge.

Nadesan, M. (2013). Neofeudalism and the financial crisis: Implications for OWS. In R. Heath, C. Fletcher, & R. Munoz (Eds.), *Understanding occupy from Wall Street to Portland* (pp. 35–52). Lexington Books.

Nelson, J., Lewis, D., & Lei, R. (2017). Digital democracy in America: A look at civic engagement in an internet age. *Journalism & Mass Communication Quarterly, 94*(1), 318–334. https://doi.org/10.1177/1077699016681969

Ng, L. H. X., Cruickshank, I., & Carley, K. M. (2021). Coordinating narratives and the capitol riots on Parler. *arXiv:2109.00945v1.* https://doi.org/10.48550/ARXIV.2109.00945

Nicholls, B. (2016). Baudrillard in a 'post-truth' world: Groundwork for a critique of the rise of Trump. *MEDIANZ, 16*(2), 7–30. https://doi.org/10.11157/medianz-vol16iss2id206

Nothhaft, H. (2015). The dream of enlightenment within digital reach? In W. Coombs, J. Falkheimer, M. Heide, & P. Young (Eds.), *Strategic communication, social media and democracy: The challenge of the digital naturals* (pp. 65–82). Routledge.

Persily, N., & Tucker, J.A. (2020). Introduction. In N. Persily & J.A. Tucker (Eds.), *Social media and democracy* (pp. 1–9). Cambridge University Press.

Polleri, M. (2022). Towards an anthropology of misinformation. *Anthropology Today, 38*(5), 17–20. https://doi.org/10.1111/1467-8322.12754

Reddit. (n.d.a). *Quarantined subreddits.* https://www.reddithelp.com/hc/en-us/articles/360043069012-Quarantined-Subreddits

Reddit. (n.d.b). *Reddit content policy.* https://www.redditinc.com/policies/content-policy

Rodriguez, N. S., & Goretti, N. (2022). From hoops to hope: Alexandria Ocasio-Cortez and political fandom on Twitter. *International Journal of Communication, 16,* 65–84. https://doi.org/1932-8036/20220005

Romano, A. (2024, January 18). If you want to understand modern politics, you have to understand modern fandom. *Vox.* https://www.vox.com/culture/24043045/politics-fandom-trump-fans-toxic-stan-culture-conspiracies

Ron, A., & Nadesan, M. (Eds.). (2020). *New directions in the study of populism.* Routledge.

Ryan, G. W., & Bernard, H. R. (2003). Techniques to identify themes. *Field Methods, 15*(1), 85–109. https://doi.org/10.1177/1525822x02239569

Saldana, J., Patricia Leavy, P., & Beretvas, N. (2011). *Fundamentals of qualitative research.* Oxford University Press.

Sandvoss, C. (2013). Toward an understanding of political enthusiasm as media fandom: Blogging, fan productivity and affect in American politics. *Participations, 10*(1), 252–296.

Shellenberger, M. (2023, March 9). *The Censorship Industrial Complex: U.S. Government Support for Domestic Censorship and Disinformation Campaigns, 2016—2022.* Testimony to the United States House Select Subcommittee on the Weaponization of the Federal Government. https://judiciary.house.gov/sites/evo-subsites/republicans-judiciary.house.gov/files/evo-media-document/shellenberger-testimony.pdf

Skonieczny, A. (2018). Emotions and political narratives: Populism, Trump and trade. *Interdisciplinary Approaches to Studying Emotions within Politics and International Relations, 6*(4), 62–72. https://doi.org/10.17645/pag.v6i4.1574

Solomon, T. (2014). The affective underpinnings of soft power. *European Journal of International Relations, 20*(3), 720–41. https://doi.org/10.1177/135406611350347

Speakman, B., & Funk, M. (2020). News, nationalism, and hegemony: The formation of consistent issue framing throughout the U.S. political right. *Mass Communication and Society, 23*(5), 656–681. https://doi.org/10.1080/15205436.2020.1764973

Spohr, D. (2017). Fake news and ideological polarization: Filter bubbles and selective exposure on social media. *Business Information Review, 34*(3), 150–160. https://doi.org/10.1177/026638211772244

Stahlman, M. (1995, December 25). Internet democracy hoax -- Internet-enabled political change is peddled as a cure for all our civic ills. *InformationWeek*, 90.

The Wall Street Journal Editorial Board. (2022, December 4). The Twitter censorship files. *The Wall Street Journal*. https://www.wsj.com/articles/the-twitter-censorship-files-intelligence-spooks-russia-new-york-post-laptop-taibbi-11670189776

Toulmin, S.E. (1969). *The uses of argument*. Cambridge University Press.

Trujillo, N. (1992). Interpreting (the work and the talk of) baseball: Perspectives on ballpark culture. *Western Journal of Communication, 56*(4), 350–371. https://doi.org/10.1080/10570319209374423

Van Slambrouck, P. (1999, March 18). In the Internet age, politics rallies to a new tool. *The Christian Science Monitor*, 2.

Vasilogambros, M. (2020, November 20). Election disinformation fears came true for state officials. *The Pew Charitable Trusts*. https://www.pewtrusts.org/en/research-andanalysis/blogs/stateline/2020/11/20/election-disinformation-fears-came-true-for-state-officials

Waisanen, D. (2014). Toward robust public engagement: The value of deliberative discourse for civil communication. *Rhetoric & Public Affairs, 17*(2), 287–322.

Wells, C., Zhang, Y., Lukito, J., & Pevehouse, J.C.W. (2020). Modeling the formation of attentive publics in social media: The case of Donald Trump. *Mass Communication & Society, 23*(2), 181–205. https://doi.org/10.1080/15205436.2019.1690664

Wilhelm, A. G. (1998). Virtual sounding boards: How deliberative is on-line political discussion? *Information, Communication & Society, 1*(3), 313–338. https://doi.org/10.1080/13691189809358972

Wittenberg, C., & Berinisky, A. J. (2020). Misinformation and its correction. In N. Persily & J. A. Tucker (Eds.), *Social media and democracy* (pp. 163–199). Cambridge University Press.

Section III
Political Partisanship and Polarization

· 8 ·

STREAMING ENTERTAINMENT INTO POLITICAL PANDEMONIUM: EXAMINING (EVEN MORE) PARTISANSHIP AND POLARIZATION IN THE 2020 CAMPAIGN

Sarah Krongard and Jacob Groshek

This study explores the social and civic dimensions of popular culture, shedding light on the ways in which viewers make meaning from popular culture. More specifically, it investigates the civic implications of today's on-demand television ecosystem, propelled by algorithmically- informed streaming platforms known as over-the-top (OTT) TV. In 2016, Groshek and Krongard unearthed a positive relationship between time spent binge-watching streamed television, which has been defined as consuming three or more episodes of one specific series in a sitting (TiVo Research Group, 2015), and both political participation and political talk, suggesting a pro-social dimension of a practice often linked with negative consequences, such as chronic illness (Keadle et al., 2015) and depression (Sung et al., 2015). OTT TV consumption requires engagement and deliberate choice on the part of the consumer (Lotz, 2014), resulting in opportunities for carefully curated TV experiences,

---

* The research presented in this chapter was originally published in Krongard, Sarah Lorraine. *The civic and social implications of over-the-top television* [Doctoral dissertation: Boston University]. Boston University Theses & Dissertations. https://open.bu.edu/handle/2144/39280.

challenging the "couch potato" stereotype often associated with viewers of the past (Matrix, 2014). Perhaps lean-forward, active TV habits extend beyond our media lives and into civic worlds (Groshek & Krongard, 2016).

The present study re-examines the relationship between political participation and streaming television consumption in-depth and explores potential theoretical underpinnings for the phenomenon. First, this research retests the association between time spent binge-watching and political engagement to determine whether this phenomenon persists and, second, delves into the civic and social elements of TV consumption in the digital media ecosystem, examining the relationships among binge-watching, empathy, and political engagement.

Literature Review

At the core of this study is the philosophy that media users are active agents for creativity and decision-making in their relationships with technology, consistent with the foundational elements of Apparatgeist Theory (Katz & Aakhus, 2002). As Apparatgeist Theory suggests, technology emerges in response to, rather than dictating, human needs, and simultaneously, the capabilities of specific technologies offer unique affordances and constraints which then interact with social processes, empowering a particular set of behaviors among technology users (Katz & Aakhus, 2002). The affordances and constraints of streaming television interact with human needs, manifesting in a set of cultural norms that inform and are informed by the technology.

Past studies have investigated binge-watchers, their motivations, and their behaviors. Binge-watching television is a common practice that is continuously evolving in today's media landscape. In 2018, Deloitte research found that 91% of Generation Z, 86% of millennials, and 80% of Generation X reported binge-watching ("Meet the MilleXZials," 2018). However, more recent studies suggest that Generation Z and millennials express frustration with subscription streaming services due to high, and often increasing, costs ("2023 Digital Trends," 2023). Motivations for binge-watching have been examined from various perspectives, particularly through the theoretical lens of Uses and Gratifications theory (Katz et al., 1973). Binge-watching fulfills human needs ranging from coping with mental health challenges (Gadino et al., 2023) and vying cultural inclusion (Steiner & Xu, 2018) to seeking entertainment or escapism (Rubenking et al., 2018) and building social capital (Jenner, 2019).

This study also builds upon the Theory of Networked Publics (boyd, 2010), considering the ways in which civic life, and particularly civic discourse, is activated in today's technological ecosystem. According to boyd (2010), networked publics are "simultaneously (1) the space constructed through networked technologies; and (2) the imagined collective that emerges as a result of the intersection of people, technology, and practice" (p. 39). This study examines OTT TV as a connected space that deserves unique attention through the lens of the public sphere.

Looking at the content of discourse that arises within networked public spheres, this study analyzes the role of informal conversation stimulated by TV texts. In his seminal work, Habermas' (1962/1989) emphasis on the importance of rationality within the public sphere has been challenged by scholars who have highlighted the need for additional emotions, such as humor (Benacka, 2016), gossip (Frost, 2011; Temple, 2012), and storytelling (Dahlberg, 2005). Lyotard (1984) cited the importance of strong emotions and individuality which can make powerful social change, as in the example of anarchist movements. Papacharissi (2015) similarly highlighted the importance of strong emotion in her work on affective publics, which builds upon boyd's (2010) Theory of Networked Publics and suggests that social media has provided opportunities for online solidarity to build from shared emotions (Papacharissi, 2015).

Turning specifically to television, Graham and Harju (2011) and Graham (2012) suggest that engaging in online discourse about reality television, which has been deemed detrimental to political engagement (Shah, 1998), can serve as a trigger for political talk. In content analyses of reality TV discussion boards, Graham and Harju (2011) and Graham (2012) found that discussions of social behaviors and lifestyles, prompted by conversation about the TV program, led to civic discourse, which demonstrated the civic power of seemingly frivolous content.

The term "civic engagement" serves as a broad umbrella concept capturing all activity where citizens engage with their society and government (Adler & Goggin, 2005). The term "political participation" more directly examines actions related to influencing the government (Ekman & Amnå, 2012). Political discourse is a form of civic engagement that helps cultivate civic identity (Walsh, 2004) and is critical to the health and wellbeing of a thriving, active democracy (McCoy & Scully, 2002). Several studies suggest that information-seeking behaviors via TV, such as news viewership, relates positively to political participation, while TV for entertainment and escape relates negatively (Norris, 1996; Shah et al., 2001). Similarly, social media used for news consumption and information seeking has also been linked positively with civic engagement (Gil de Zúñiga et al., 2012; Shah et al., 2001). Studies on entertainment content suggest that this positive relationship is not limited to news consumption. Shah (1998) found that viewership of upbeat sitcoms relates positively to social trust, perhaps due to the time spent with kind, close-knit friend groups represented on screen, while dramas related positively with civic participation, perhaps encouraging viewers to consider social issues.

To be civically engaged is to think and act in support of the well-being of society, considering the experiences, lives, and needs of the individuals who make up the community rather than focusing on oneself; these are the foundational elements embedded within other-oriented dimensions of empathy. Therefore, this study integrates and contributes to the theory of narrative empathy which originated within the field of fictional literature (Keen, 2006) and asserts that fictional narratives can serve as a social simulation that fosters empathy.

From a social-neuroscience perspective, "empathy" is composed of three major components (Decety & Jackson, 2006): "(a) an affective response to another person, which often, but not always, entails sharing that person's emotional state; (b) a cognitive capacity to take the perspective of the other person; and (c) emotion regulation" (p. 54). The affective response speaks to the commonly held idea of empathy as emotional contagion, where an individual demonstrates the ability to feel what another person feels, while perspective-taking is a more complex cognitive process where individuals adopt, synthesize, and coordinate perspectives of others (Decety & Jackson, 2006; Selman, 2003; Kim et al., 2018; Shamay-Tsoory et al., 2009). Other-oriented dimensions of empathy are linked to prosocial attitudes and behaviors, such as the reduction of stereotyping (Galinsky & Moskowitz, 2000), decreased bullying (Ang & Goh, 2010), reduction of prejudice (Doyle & Aboud, 1995), decreased in-group bias (Galinsky & Moskowitz, 2000), and increased altruism (Oswald, 1996). Further, the personality trait of empathic concern has been positively related to civic participation (Bekkers, 2005; Penner, 2002; Penner & Finkelstein, 1998).

Reflective of Keen's (2006) theory of narrative empathy, Mar et al. (2006) found that those who engaged more with fictional text predicted measures of social ability, while nonfiction print text exposure was a negative predictor. Relatedly, Mar et al. (2006) found that the tendency to become absorbed in a story predicted empathy scores above participants. Kidd & Castano (2013) determined that readers of literary fiction, as opposed to nonfiction and popular fiction, also performed better on affective empathy tasks.

Turning to TV, Nathanson et al. (2013) found that preschoolers who consumed television content and then subsequently discussed the TV program with parents demonstrated enhanced cognitive perspective-taking; children who used TV as background noise performed worse on perspective-taking evaluations (Nathanson et al., 2013). Here, a distinction between active engagement with television texts and passive consumption emerges. Black and Barnes (2015) found that adult viewers of critically acclaimed dramas demonstrated higher levels of cognitive perspective-taking than those who consumed documentaries, suggesting the importance of genre.

Research Questions and Hypotheses

Building upon the past work described above, this study investigates political participation and binge-watching television to understand the dynamics in greater depth.

> RQ1: What is the frequency of binge-watching among respondents?
> H1: Increased time binge-watching television will be positively related to both a) online and b) offline political participation.
> H2: Increased time binge-watching television will be positively related to a) online and b) offline political talk.

Due to the limited investigation of genre in earlier research (Groshek & Krongard, 2016), this study aims to investigate the differences among TV genre as exploratory research questions:

> RQ2: How does the genre of programs binged relate with both a) online and b) offline political participation?
> RQ3: How does the genre of programs binged relate with time spent engaging in political talk a) online and b) offline?
> RQ4: How does binge-watching relate with operational dimensions of a) perspective-taking and b) empathic concern?

Finally, building upon prior work regarding civic discourse and television, this study aims to understand the ways in which discussion relates to streaming TV:

> RQ5: To what extent do viewers discuss the TV programs they binge?

RQ6: In what ways does talking about binge-watched television relate with political participation, a) online and b) offline?

RQ7: In what ways does talking about binge-watched television relate with political talk, a) online and b) offline?

Method

Data were collected over the period of April 8, 2019, through April 23, 2019, with 526 respondents via an opt-in survey panel accessed via Qualtrics, a survey and research company. Participants were required to be 18-years-old or older and live within the U.S. Collaborating with Qualtrics offers access to samples of participants that are reflective of the general U.S. population, which is beneficial for statistical analysis. While there are limitations regarding generalizability using an opt-in panel, similar samples are being used within the field and apply inferential statistics (Baker et al., 2010; Bouillanne, 2015; Peifer & Garrett, 2014).

Demographics

In terms of gender, there were 111 male respondents (21.3%) and 409 female respondents (78.6%). The median age was 42 years old ($M = 42.67$, $SD = 16.18$). Regarding annual income, 24% earned $24,999 or less, 33.6% between $25,000 and $49,999, 30.2% between $50,000 and $99,999, 10.1% between $100,000 to $199,999, .8% between $200,000 and $299,999, and finally, 1.3% of $300,000 and above. Turning to race and ethnicity, 62% identified as White/Caucasian, 12.4% African American, 16.8% Hispanic / Latinx, 5.3% Asian, .6% Native American, .2% Pacific Islander, and 2.7% Other. While this sample offers insights into the U.S. population, it is not perfectly generalizable due to its size and skewed gender distribution.

Political Antecedents

Consistent with the conventions for studies within the field of political communication, this survey examined the political affiliation, political ideology, and political knowledge of respondents through self-reports. Here, 23% identified as Republican, 45.4% Democrat, 26% Independent, 1% Other, and 4% reported Don't Know. This survey measured political ideology using a scale from 1 (*very liberal*) to 7 (*very conservative*) ($M = 4.04$, $SD = 2.12$). Through a series of seven multiple choice questions, such as the number of Supreme

Court Justices, this survey measured general political knowledge (M = 4.31, SD = 1.94): 18.7% of respondents answered all questions correctly, and 14.1% and 13.9% answered six and five questions correctly, respectively. Fifteen and a half percent (15.5%) answered four questions correctly, while 17.0% and 12.6% answered three and two questions correctly respectively. Just over seven percent (7.3%) answered one correct answer while 1% answered all questions incorrectly.

Political Participation

Online political participation (Cronbach's alpha [α] = .91) and offline political participation (α = .92) were measured through a series of seven items that have been validated in past political communication research (Gil de Zúñiga et al., 2014). Participants were asked to share how often in the past twelve months they have engaged in specific activities on a scale from 0 (*never*) to 4 (*always*). For online political participation (M = .92, SD = .78), items included activities such as posting comments about politics to social media or creating posts for a blog about current events. Similar items measured offline political participation (M =. 59, SD = .80) but referred to offline activities that are not easily replicated online, such as attending a political rally or voting in a local or state election.

This study also examined the use of social media for political participation through a nine-item scale where respondents indicated the extent to which they agreed that certain statements about social media use sounded like them on a scale from 1 (*strongly disagree*) to 5 (*strongly agree*) (α = .91). It is important to note the correlational overlap with the political participation questions; for online political participation, the correlation was statistically significant and positive but somewhat weak (r = .336, p < .001). Offline political participation suggested a weaker but statistically significant, positive correlation (r = .272, p < .001).

Talking Politics

Offline and online political talk was measured on two eight-item scales which asked respondents to share on a scale of 1 (*never*) to 5 (*always*) how frequently they engaged in discourse about politics with family, people they know well, people from different social classes, and strangers. For offline (α = .93), the average was 2.36 (SD = .93), and online (α = .961) the average was 2.11 (SD = 1.01). These variables were strongly correlated with one another (r = .809, p < .001); those who talk politics seemed to do so both on- and offline.

Media Use

Respondents identified the time in hours spent per day using the social media where they have a profile (M = 4.61, SD = 4.25). They reported the number of hours per day they spent watching TV via: smartphones (M = 3.23, SD = 4.39), tablet (M = 1.62, SD = 3.01), laptop (M = 2.05, SD = 3.44), desktop computer (M = 1.88, SD = 3.57), TV through online streaming (M = 3.34, SD = 4.19), and traditional TV (broadcast, cable, or satellite) (M = 4.03, SD = 4.32). A new variable was computed combining the number of hours spent watching TV on all devices (M = 16.20, SD = 17.27). Another captured nontraditional TV, combining hours spent watching TV via smartphones, tablets, laptops, desktops, and streaming (M = 12.16, SD = 14.87).

Binge-Watching

Respondents shared how many television programs they have binge-watched in the month prior to completing the survey (M = 1.75, SD = 1.95). Here, binge-watching was defined within the question as watching three or more episodes of one specific TV program in a sitting. Next, participants were asked to share how frequently they view specific genres when they binge-watch. Respondents indicated how frequently they consumed each genre when binge-watching using a sliding scale from zero (*never*) to five (*sometimes*) to ten (*always*). Participants shared the frequency with which they binged irreverent comedies such as *Arrested Development* (M = 3.03, SD = 3.07), political dramas such as *House of Cards* (M = 2.53, SD = 2.94), historical dramas such as *Marco Polo* (M = 2.34, SD = 2.78), superhero dramas such as *Supergirl* (M = 2.73, SD = 3.12), crime dramas such as *Better Call Saul* (M = 3.81, SD = 3.36), dramatic comedies such as *This Is Us* (M = 3.81, SD = 3.41), dramas such as *Mad Men* (M = 2.97, SD = 3.20), action and adventure such as *24* (M = 3.26, SD = 3.13), science-fiction such as *Stranger Things* (M = 3.38, SD = 3.35), horror such as *American Horror Story* (M = 3.51, SD = 3.50), thrillers such as *Dexter* (M = 3.26, SD = 3.32), news and informational programs such as documentaries or political talk shows (M = 2.80, SD = 3.18), sports including games and commentaries (M = 2.33, SD = 3.10), reality programs such as *Keeping Up with the Kardashians* (M = 3.24, SD = 3.39), and other (M = 1.53, SD = 2.60).

Respondents shared the extent to which they discuss the shows they binge-watch, measured through three items; respondents indicated the frequency with which they talk about the shows on a scale from 1 (*never*) to 5 (*always*) (α = .78). Questions inquired how often respondents talked with people they knew well, like friends and family (M = 3.11, SD = 1.09), people they do not know very well such as acquaintances (M = 2.28, SD = 1.16), and strangers or people only met online (M = 2.09, SD = 1.22). A total talking television variable was created, combining the frequency of the three items (M = 2.50, SD = 1.09).

Empathy

This study employed the Interpersonal Reactivity Index (IRI) (Davis, 1983) as the instrument for measurement of empathy. This instrument uses four seven-item subscales to assess four dimensions of empathy. Respondents indicated the extent to which certain statements describe them, ranging from 1 (*does not describe me at all*) to 5 (*describes me very well*). The Interpersonal Reactivity Index provides four scales that are considered relatively independent; combining the final score does not provide an ultimate empathy score for the respondent (Davis, 1983). Rather, the four subscales are used independently to measure the specific dimensions that comprise the construct. This study focuses on the other-oriented dimensions of empathy due to their theoretical alignment with civic engagement.

The perspective-taking (PT) subscale (M = 3.52, SD = .60) speaks to the ability to adopt the cognitive position of others, measured by statements such as, "I sometimes try to understand my friends better by imagining how things look from their perspective." The empathic concern (EC) subscale (M = 3.72, SD = .67) measures affective empathy, or the ability to feel compassion and sympathy for others, measured through items such as, "I often have tender, concerned feelings for people less fortunate than me."

Results

Binge-Watching and Political Participation

With regard to RQ1, 27.9% of respondents reported never having binge-watched. Similarly, 23.3% reported binge-watching one program in the month prior to taking this survey, and 23.5% reported binge-watching two programs during this time. Fewer said they binge-watched three programs, resulting in 13.5%. The highest amount of binge-watching was practiced by the smallest number of respondents, where 6% binge-watched four programs and 2% binge-watched five shows. Eight percent (8%) reported bingeing six or more programs during this time period.

H1a–b asserted that more time binge-watching television will be positively related to online and offline political participation. A bivariate correlation matrix of all relevant variables illustrated the relationships between binge-watching television and political participation. Findings offered support for these hypotheses, suggesting that there are statistically significant but relatively modest positive relationships among the number of programs binge-watched and both online ($r = .327, p < .001$) and offline ($r = .279, p < .001$) political participation.

A series of hierarchical linear regression models illuminated the relationships among the pertinent independent variables investigated, beginning with online and offline political participation. Each model was built with five blocks, controlling for the following variables. Block one comprised demographics (gender, age, and income). Block two included variables related to politics (political ideology and political knowledge). Block three comprised empathy dimensions (empathic concern, perspective-taking, fantasy, and personal distress). Block four included general media use (traditional TV consumption, social media use, and non-traditional TV consumption). Finally, block five consisted of binge behavior (number of programs binged; frequency of bingeing genres: comedy, political drama, historical drama, superhero drama, crime drama, dramatic comedy, general drama, action and adventure, science fiction, horror, thriller, news and informational, sports, reality, and other; and frequency of talking about binged TV). Political engagement was not included in the model to avoid redundancy.

First, online political participation was set as the dependent variable. The hierarchical linear regression suggesting that the number of programs binged within the past month proved to be a statistically significant predictor of online political participation ($B = .058$, $SE = .024$, $p < .05$), with a relatively modest effect on the model when comparing standardized Beta values ($\beta = .129$) offering additional support for H1a. This finding suggested that with each additional program binged, there was a .058 increase in engaging in political activities online ($p < .05$).

Turning to genre and RQ2a, the frequency of binge-watching news and informational programming proved to be a statistically significant predictor of online political participation ($B = .083$, $SE = .017$, $p < .001$) with the most substantial effect on the model ($\beta = .309$). Considering RQ6a, this model indicating that the frequency of discussing the programs binged proved to be a statistically significant (B = .196, SE =.051, p < .001) predictor for online political participation with relatively strong effect on the full model (β = .220). With every one increase in the frequency level of discussing binged TV programs, there was a robust .196 increase in online political participation (p < .001). Overall, the binge-behavior block resulted in a statistically significant R-square change (ΔR^2 = .139, p < .001), and the full model explained 39.3% of the variance, according to the adjusted R^2. Results are detailed in Table 8.1.

In the second model, offline political participation was set as the dependent variable. Similar to the model for online political participation, this hierarchical linear regression suggesting that the number of programs binged within the past month proved to be a statistically significant predictor of offline political participation (B = .050, SE = .024, p < .05), although with a relatively modest effect on the model (β = .114), offering additional support for H1b. Turning to genre (RQ2b), the frequency of binge-watching news and information proved to be a statistically significant predictor of offline political engagement (B = .079, SE = .016, p < .001), serving as the variable with the largest effect on the model when comparing standardized Betas (β = .303).

With regard to talking about binge-watched programs (RQ6b), the frequency of discussing the programs binged also proved statistically significant (B = .194, SE = .050, p < .001) with relatively substantial effect on the full model (β = .225). Unlike in the first model, this regression model revealed that the perspective-taking dimension of empathy served as a statistically significant predictor of offline political participation (B = .185, SE = .081, p < .05) with relatively moderate effect on the full model (β = .135). The binge-behavior block resulted in a statistically significant R-square change (ΔR^2 = .144, p < .001), and the full model explained 32.3% of the variance, according to the adjusted R^2. Results are detailed in Table 8.2.

Binge-Watching and Political Talk

Analyses continued with hierarchical linear regression models for both online and offline political talk, examining the role of pertinent independent variables. Again, each model was built with five blocks, controlling for the same variables as the prior models. Block one included demographic variables. Block two comprised variables related to politics, and block three consisted of empathy dimensions and block four addressed general media use. Block five

Table 8.1: Hierarchical linear regression of online political participation

	Coefficient (B)	Standard Error	Beta (β)
Step 1: Demographics			
Gender (being female)	.020	.104	.010
Age	-.004	.003	-.067
Income	.006	.041	.007
ΔR² .041**			
Step 2: Politics			
Political Ideology Scale (v. liberal - v. conservative)	-.090***	.022	-.201
Political Knowledge	.031	.025	.067
ΔR² .044***			
Step 3: Empathy Dimensions			
Empathic Concern Scale	-.122	.082	-.096
Perspective-Taking Scale	.144	.083	.101
Fantasy Scale	.073	.073	.055
Personal Distress Scale	-.040	.057	-.035
ΔR² .028*			
Step 4: General Media Use			
Traditional TV Consumption	.027*	.010	.140
Social Media Use	.003	.012	.017
Nontraditional TV Consumption	.006	.004	.117
ΔR² .141***			
Step 5: Binge Behavior			
Programs Binged in Past Month	.058*	.024	.129
Frequency of Bingeing Comedy	-.013	.016	-.045
Frequency of Bingeing Political Drama	.018	.020	.061
Frequency of Bingeing Historical Drama	.012	.022	.037
Frequency of Bingeing Superhero Drama	-.001	.017	-.003
Frequency of Bingeing Crime Drama	-.010	.016	-.038
Frequency of Bingeing Dramatic Comedy	-.013	.016	-.052
Frequency of Bingeing General Drama	-.015	.016	-.055
Frequency of Bingeing Action - Adventure	.006	.019	.024
Frequency of Bingeing Sci-Fi	-.009	.017	-.033
Frequency of Bingeing Horror	-.019	.015	-.078
Frequency of Bingeing Thriller	.010	.017	.038
Frequency of Bingeing News	.083***	.017	.309
Frequency of Bingeing Sports	-.015	.015	-.055
Frequency of Bingeing Reality	-.009	.015	-.036
Frequency of Bingeing Other	.012	.016	.036
Frequency of Talking about Binged TV	.196***	.051	.220
ΔR² .139***			

Note: N = 340, listwise deletion; overall Adjusted R^2 = .393; * $p < 0.05$; ** $p < 0.10$; *** $p < 0.001$.

Table 8.2: Hierarchical linear regression of offline political participation

	Coefficient (B)	Standard Error	Beta (β)
Step 1: Demographics			
Gender (being female)	.051	.102	.025
Age	-.001	.003	-.020
Income	.074	.040	.091
ΔR^2 .052***			
Step 2: Politics			
Political Ideology Scale (v. liberal–v. conservative)	-.094***	.021	-.216
Political Knowledge	.013	.025	.029
ΔR^2 .047***			
Step 3: Empathy Dimensions			
Empathic Concern Scale	-.088	.080	-.071
Perspective-Taking Scale	.185*	.081	.135
Fantasy Scale	.054	.072	.041
Personal Distress Scale	-.083	.056	-.074
ΔR^2 .031*			
Step 4: General Media Use			
Traditional TV Consumption	.017	.010	.090
Social Media Use	-.005	-.012	-.026
Nontraditional TV Consumption	.007	.004	.132
ΔR^2 .108***			
Step 5: Binge Behavior			
Programs Binged in the Past Month	.050*	.024	.114
Frequency of Bingeing Comedy	-.010	.016	-.038
Frequency of Bingeing Political Drama	.016	.020	.057
Frequency of Bingeing Historical Drama	.025	.021	.082
Frequency of Bingeing Superhero Drama	.004	.017	.017
Frequency of Bingeing Crime Drama	-.009	.016	-.034
Frequency of Bingeing Dramatic Comedy	.006	.016	.024
Frequency of Bingeing General Drama	-.025	.016	-.097
Frequency of Bingeing Action - Adventure	.017	.019	.063
Frequency of Bingeing Sci-Fi	-.020	.016	-.079
Frequency of Bingeing Horror	-.018	.015	-.074
Frequency of Bingeing Thriller	.001	.017	.006
Frequency of Bingeing News	.079***	.016	.303
Frequency of Bingeing Sports	-.015	.017	-.057
Frequency of Bingeing Reality	-.013	.014	-.054
Frequency of Bingeing Other	.006	.016	.018
Frequency of Talking about Binged TV	.194***	.050	.225
ΔR^2 .144***			

Note: $N = 340$, listwise deletion; overall Adjusted $R^2 = .323$; * $p < 0.05$; ** $p < 0.10$; *** $p < 0.001$.

included the elements of binge behavior. Political engagement variables were not included.

In examining the variable of talking politics online as the dependent variable, the model did not suggest support for H2a; the number of programs binged was not a statistically significant predictor of online political talk. However, compelling results emerged regarding genre, considering RQ3a. The model suggests that dramatic comedy ($B = -.040$, $SE = .020$, $p < .05$), horror ($B = .049$, $SE = .019$, $p < .01$), and news and informational ($B = .062$, $SE = .020$, $p < .01$) genres each are statistically significant predictors of participating in civic discourse online. Each genre had a similar moderate effect on the model when comparing standardized Betas: dramatic comedy ($\beta = -.125$), horror ($\beta = .160$), and news and informational ($\beta = .184$). Curiously, dramatic comedy had a negative impact, suggesting that for every one frequency level of bingeing dramatic comedy, online political talk decreased by .040 ($p < .05$), while horror and news and information both were positively related. For every one frequency level of bingeing horror, online political talk increased by .049 ($p < .01$), and for every one frequency level of bingeing news and information programming, online political talk increased by .062 ($p < .01$).

Again, the variable of talking about the TV binged proved to be a statistically significant ($B = .393$, $SE = .061$, $p < .001$) predictor of talking politics online, with the strongest effect on the full model when comparing standardized betas ($\beta = .437$). The variable of social media use was a statistically significant ($B = .020$, $SE = .015$, $p < .05$) predictor of talking politics online, and when comparing standardized Betas, revealed a relatively moderate effect on the full model ($\beta = .124$). Ultimately, the binge-behavior block resulted in a statistically significant R-square change ($\Delta R^2 = .253$, $p < .001$), and the full model explained 47.5% of the variance, according to the adjusted R^2. Results are in Table 8.5.

The next hierarchical linear regression model examined the dependent variable of talking politics offline. Like the previous regression, this model does not suggest support for H2b; the quantity of programs binge-watched did not serve as a statistically significant predictor of talking politics offline. Turning to genre (RQ3b), a similar pattern as the political participation variables emerged. The model suggests that the frequency of bingeing news and informational programming ($B = .050$, $SE = .017$, $p < .01$) was a statistically significant predictor of participating in civic discourse online. This genre had a relatively moderate effect when comparing standardized Betas: ($\beta = .171$). Again, the variable of talking TV binged proved to be a statistically significant

Table 8.3: Hierarchical linear regression of online political talk

	Coefficient (B)	Standard Error	Beta (β)
Step 1: Demographics			
Gender (being female)	-.125	.126	-.048
Age	.001	.004	.020
Income	-.016	.048	-.015
ΔR^2 .048**			
Step 2: Politics			
Political Ideology Scale (v. liberal - v. conservative)	-.068**	.026	-.121
Political Knowledge	.036	.030	.061
ΔR^2 .031**			
Step 3: Empathy Dimensions			
Empathic Concern Scale	-.032	.099	-.020
Perspective-Taking Scale	.126	.098	.070
Fantasy Scale	.073	.087	.043
Personal Distress Scale	.010	.069	.007
ΔR^2 .044**			
Step 4: General Media Use			
Traditional TV Consumption	-.001	.012	-.005
Social Media Use	.020*	.015	.124
Nontraditional TV Consumption	.000	.005	.002
ΔR^2 .100***			
Step 5: Binge Behavior			
Programs Binged in the Past Month	.036	.030	.059
Frequency of Bingeing Comedy	-.023	.019	-.065
Frequency of Bingeing Political Drama	.017	.024	.048
Frequency of Bingeing Historical Drama	-.001	.026	-.001
Frequency of Bingeing Superhero Drama	-.004	.021	-.010
Frequency of Bingeing Crime Drama	.009	.019	.027
Frequency of Bingeing Dramatic Comedy	-.040*	.020	-.125
Frequency of Bingeing General Drama	-.018	.019	-.054
Frequency of Bingeing Action - Adventure	.012	.023	.034
Frequency of Bingeing Sci-Fi	.007	.020	.021
Frequency of Bingeing Horror	.049**	.019	.160
Frequency of Bingeing Thriller	-.023	.01821	-.069
Frequency of Bingeing News	.062**	.020	.184
Frequency of Bingeing Sports	.004	.021	.013
Frequency of Bingeing Reality	-.007	.018	-.022
Frequency of Bingeing Other	.023	.019	.056
Frequency of Talking about Binged TV	.393***	.061	.437
ΔR^2 .253***			

Note: N = 329, listwise deletion; overall Adjusted R^2 = .475; * $p < 0.05$; ** $p < 0.10$; *** $p < 0.001$.

(B = .399, SE =.053, p < .001) predictor of talking politics offline, with the strongest effect on the full model (β = .410). The binge-behavior block resulted in a statistically significant R-square change (ΔR^2 = .220, p < .001), and the full model explained 39.6% of the variance, according to the adjusted R^2. Results are summarized in Table 8.3.

Dimensions of Empathy

Analyses continued with another series of hierarchical linear regression models to better understand the relationships among binge-watching television and the various dimensions of empathy, again considering the germane independent variables. A regression model was both built with three blocks, controlling for the following variables: block one included demographics, while block two consisted of general media use and block three comprised binge behavior.

First, the dimension of perspective-taking was examined as the dependent variable (RQ4a). The regression model suggested that while the number of programs binged did not serve as a statistically significant predictor of perspective-taking, more compelling findings emerged when considering genre. The frequency of bingeing action and adventure programming (B = -.057, SE = .016, p < .001) was a statistically significant predictor of perspective taking. This genre had a moderate, negative effect when comparing standardized Betas: (β = -.292). The variable of talking about television binged served as a statistically significant predictor (B = .102, SE = .041, p < .05), with a somewhat moderate effect on the full model (β = .162). The binge-behavior block resulted in a statistically significant R-square change (ΔR^2 = .088, p < .05), and the full model explained 17.7% of the variance. Details are within Table 8.4.

Next, the dimension of empathic concern was examined as the dependent variable, turning to RQ4b. The regression model suggested that the same variables served as statistically significant predictors for empathy as for perspective-taking. The frequency of bingeing action and adventure (B = -.055, SE = .016, p < .01) was a statistically significant predictor of empathic concern, and again, this genre had a moderate-to-strong and negative effect when comparing standardized Betas: (β = -.254). With every increased step in the frequency of bingeing action and adventure TV, the level of empathic concern decreases .055, similar to perspective-taking.

Table 8.4: Hierarchical linear regression of perspective-taking

	Coefficient (B)	Standard Error	Beta (β)
Step 1: Demographics			
Gender (being female)	-.010	.084	-.007
Age	.008**	.003	.195
Income	.039	.033	.065
Political Ideology Scale (v. liberal - v. conservative)	.029	.018	.092
ΔR² .034*			
Step 2: General Media Use			
Traditional TV Consumption	-.017	.009	-.126
Social Media Use	.003	.010	.018
Nontraditional TV Consumption	-.002	.020	-.031
ΔR² .012			
Step 3: Binge Behavior			
Programs Binged in the Past Month	-.010	.020	-.031
Frequency of Bingeing Comedy	-.009	.013	-.048
Frequency of Bingeing Political Drama	.005	.017	.023
Frequency of Bingeing Historical Drama	-.007	.018	-.031
Frequency of Bingeing Superhero Drama	-.006	.014	-.030
Frequency of Bingeing Crime Drama	.020	.013	.111
Frequency of Bingeing Dramatic Comedy	.024	.014	.136
Frequency of Bingeing General Drama	.007	.014	.035
Frequency of Bingeing Action - Adventure	-.057***	.016	-.292
Frequency of Bingeing Sci-Fi	.008	.014	.046
Frequency of Bingeing Horror	.004	.013	.026
Frequency of Bingeing Thriller	-.008	.014	-.042
Frequency of Bingeing News	.014	.014	.072
Frequency of Bingeing Sports	.004	.015	.022
Frequency of Bingeing Reality	.008	.012	.044
Frequency of Bingeing Other	-.006	.014	-.024
Frequency of Talking about Binged TV	.102*	.041	.162
ΔR² .088*			

Note: $N = 340$, listwise deletion; overall Adjusted $R^2 = .177$; * $p < 0.05$; ** $p < 0.10$; *** $p < 0.001$.

Table 8.5: Hierarchical linear regression of empathic concern

	Coefficient (B)	Standard Error	Beta (β)
Step 1: Demographics			
Gender (being female)	.114	.088	.070
Age	.014***	.003	.310
Income	.055	.035	.083
Political Ideology Scale (v. liberal - v. conservative)	.005	.019	.013
ΔR^2 .117***			
Step 2: General Media Use			
Traditional TV Consumption	-.013	.009	-.084
Social Media Use	.000	.011	.002
Nontraditional TV Consumption	-.003	.004	-.073
ΔR^2 .026*			
Step 3: Binge Behavior			
Programs Binged in the Past Month	-.011	.021	-.030
Frequency of Bingeing Comedy	.005	.014	.021
Frequency of Bingeing Political Drama	.016	.018	.071
Frequency of Bingeing Historical Drama	-.036	.019	-.148
Frequency of Bingeing Superhero Drama	-.021	.015	-.096
Frequency of Bingeing Crime Drama	.033*	.014	.166
Frequency of Bingeing Dramatic Comedy	.010	.014	.049
Frequency of Bingeing General Drama	-.005	.014	-.026
Frequency of Bingeing Action - Adventure	-.055**	.016	-.254
Frequency of Bingeing Sci-Fi	.011	.014	.053
Frequency of Bingeing Horror	.002	.013	.011
Frequency of Bingeing Thriller	-.013	.015	-.063
Frequency of Bingeing News	.020	.014	.096
Frequency of Bingeing Sports	-.006	.015	-.030
Frequency of Bingeing Reality	.012	.013	.062
Frequency of Bingeing Other	-.009	.014	-.034
Frequency of Talking about Binged TV	.088*	.043	.126
ΔR^2 .093**			

Note: $N = 340$, listwise deletion; overall Adjusted $R^2 = .177$; * $p < 0.05$; ** $p < 0.10$; *** $p < 0.001$

In contrast with perspective-taking, binge-watching the genre of crime drama ($B = .033$, $SE = .014$, $p < .05$) served as a statistically significant predictor of empathic concern, although the effect on the full model was limited ($\beta = .166$). Unlike action and adventure, crime drama was related positively.

The binge-behavior block produced a statistically significant R-square change ($\Delta R^2 = .093$, $p < .05$), and the full model explained another low 17.7% of the variance, according to the adjusted R^2. Table 8.5 summarizes the model.

Talking About Binge-Watched Television

Respondents shared the frequency with which they talk about binged TV (RQ5) to people they know well (never: 6.5%, rarely: 11.5%, sometimes: 28.8%, most of the time: 16.6%, and always: 8.0%.), acquaintances (never: 24.2%, rarely: 16.8%, sometimes: 20.0%, most of the time: 8.0%, and always: 2.9%.), and strangers / people who have only met online (never: 32.8%, rarely: 12.8%, sometimes: 16.6%, most of the time: 5.7%, and always: 3.8%.).

RQ6a–b and RQ7a–b examined the ways in which talking about binge-watched television relates with online and offline political talk. The previously described hierarchical linear regressions demonstrate the ways in which talking about binged TV serves as a statistically significant predictor for online and offline political participation, as well as online and offline political talk. More specifically, for both online and offline political engagement, comparing standardized Betas demonstrated that the talking about binged TV variables had the second strongest effects on the full models. More strikingly, for both online and offline political talk, the talking about television variable had the strongest effects on the full models when comparing standardized Betas.

Discussion

Findings reinforce the positive relationships between streaming TV and political engagement, as well as political talk (Groshek & Krongard, 2016). Results offered support for H1a–b, suggesting that the more binge-watching, the more political participation among respondents. For both online and offline political participation, the amount of binge-watching remained a statistically significant predictor of participation when included within the final block of the hierarchical linear regression. Binge-watching did not serve as a statistically significant predictor of political discourse, failing to offer sustained support for H2a–b. Results suggest that engaging in the rituals of binge-watching and discussing TV may be intricately linked with political engagement, particularly through the process of discourse. Individuals are activated through persistent engagement with cultural texts, bridging entertainment and civic worlds.

Findings demonstrate that binge-watching news and informational content remained a statistically significant predictor when included within the last block of the model, in alignment with prior research (Gil de Zúñiga et al., 2012; Norris, 1996, Shah et al., 2001). Binge-watching specific genres did, indeed, prove to be critical and serve as statistically significant predictors of political discourse. Looking first at online political talk, consuming news and informational programming remained statistically significant, unsurprisingly; the more unexpected genre that proved statistically significant was horror, which may be due to the ways in which horror is often used to explore social and political issues through metaphorical representation. Often, the horror genre employs terror situations that symbolically speak to the experiences of underrepresented or historically oppressed groups (Schneider, 1999). The frequency of bingeing dramatic comedies was statistically significant and, importantly, negative in its relationship with online political talk.

This study initially posited that the connection between binge-watching TV and political participation may be empathy; however, findings suggest that the quantity of binge-watching does not encourage or even relate positively with development of other-oriented dimensions of empathy, namely perspective-taking and empathic concern. Rather, findings suggest the opposite phenomenon; the quantity of binge-watching did not sustain significance as a predictor of any of the empathy dimensions. Compelling results emerged regarding genre; the genre of action and adventure remained a statistically significant and *negative* predictor of perspective-taking while crime dramas proved to be a statistically significant and *positive* predictor of empathic concern.

Talking about binged TV proved to be a statistically significant predictor of online and offline political participation, speaking to RQ6, as well as online and offline political talk, when included within the final block of each regression model. Further, talking about the programs binge-watched served as a positive and statistically significant predictor for perspective-taking and empathic concern. Therefore, talking about television ought to be further investigated to better understand how to best harness the prosocial potential of this practice.

From a theoretical perspective, findings suggest perhaps support the idea of "perpetual content" which extends the original notion of Apparatgeist Theory's "perpetual contact" (Katz & Aakhus, 2002) as applied to the always-on culture of OTT TV. "Perpetual content" refers to the social norms and behaviors associated with contemporary TV; individuals can be constantly connected with content through personal communication technologies and streaming television applications, with TV permeating all aspects of life on and offline.

Findings extend the Theory of Networked Publics (boyd, 2010) by considering its application to OTT television. While OTT television is not precisely a social network, it is, indeed, a connected virtual space that integrates social media logic (Van Dijck & Poell, 2013) and demonstrates the elements of a networked publics. Streaming platforms, such as Netflix and Hulu, use all expressions of preference to inform suggestions. Users actively choose, curate, and indicate programming preferences, and data can be shared with a wider audience, such as advertisers. Content can be searched and accessed through the sites themselves. Most importantly, the content available on these sites, once delivered to a passive audience through mass media, is now manipulated and controlled by the users. Thus, the functionality of the network itself is empowering users, fostering the general habit of active participation (Groshek & Krongard, 2016). Blending the perspectives of Apparatgeist Theory (Katz & Aakhus, 2002) and the Theory of Networked Publics (boyd, 2010) suggests that the intermingling of technology, social desires, and individual needs has resulted in a culturally activated, connected public.

Limitations and Future Work

The oversampling of females and overall small size of the sample limits the generalizability of these findings. Additionally, this questionnaire relied on self-report data, which are inherently biased and ought to be triangulated with additional methods. As suggested in the Methods, some respondents shared that they spent more than 24 hours per day consuming television. This may be due to second-screening or media multi-tasking; alternatively, these reports may be more reflective of how respondents experienced their viewership. Therefore, such self-reported data might be more aligned with perceived reality as opposed to factual experience. Finally, this is a cross-sectional study, suggesting that the data can suggest relationships but not causality; future studies could employ deliberate mediation analysis. A qualitative perspective could offer further nuance to better understand the contexts that support thoughtful discourse on binged TV.

References

2023 Digital media trends: Immersed and connected. (2023, April 14). *Deloitte Insights.* https://www2.deloitte.com/us/en/insights/industry/technology/digital-media-trends-consumption-habits-survey/2023.html#read-the-digital-media-trends

Adler, R. P., & Goggin, J. (2005). What do we mean by "civic engagement"? *Journal of Transformative Education, 3*(3), 236–253. https://doi.org/10.1007/s10578-010-0176-3

Ang, R. P., & Goh, D. H. (2010). Cyberbullying among adolescents: The role of affective and cognitive empathy, and gender. *Child Psychiatry & Human Development, 41*(4), 387–397. https://doi.org/10.1007/s10578-010-0176-3

Baker, R., Blumberg, S., Brick, J., Couper, M., Courtright, M., Dennis, M., Dillman, D., Frankel, M., Garland, P., & Groves, R. (2010). AAPOR report on online panels. *Public Opinion Quarterly, 74*(4), 711–781. https://doi.org/10.1093/poq/nfq048

Bekkers, R. (2005). Participation in voluntary associations: Relations with resources, personality, and political values. *Political Psychology, 26*(3), 439–454. https://doi.org/10.1111/j.1467-9221.2005.00425.x

Benacka, E. (2016). *Rhetoric, humor, and the public sphere: From Socrates to Stephen Colbert.* Rowman & Littlefield.

Black, J., & Barnes, J. (2015). Fiction and social cognition: The effect of viewing award-winning television dramas on theory of mind. *Psychology of Aesthetics, Creativity, and the Arts, 9*(4), 423–429. https://doi.org/10.1037/aca0000031

Boulianne, S. (2015). Social media use and participation: A meta-analysis of current research. *Information, Communication & Society, 18*(5), 524–538. https://doi.org/10.1080/1369118X.2015.1008542

boyd, d. (2010). Social network sites as networked publics: Affordances, dynamics, and implications. In Z. Papacharissi (Ed.), *Networked self: Identity, community, and culture on social network sites* (pp. 39–58). Routledge.

Dahlberg, L. (2005). The Habermasian public sphere: Taking difference seriously? *Theory and Society, 34*(2), 111–136. https://doi.org/10.1007/s11186-005-0155-z

Davis, M. H. (1983). Measuring individual differences in empathy: Evidence for a multidimensional approach. *Journal of Personality and Social Psychology, 44*(1), 113–126. https://doi.org/10.1037/0022-3514.44.1.113

Decety, J., & Jackson, P. L. (2006). A social-neuroscience perspective on empathy. *Current Directions in Psychological Science, 15*(2), 54–58. https://doi.org/10.1111/j.0963-7214.2006.00406.x

Doyle, A. B., & Aboud, F. E. (1995). A longitudinal study of White children's racial prejudice as a social-cognitive development. *Merrill-Palmer Quarterly,* 209–228. http://www.jstor.org/stable/23090532

Ekman, J., & Amnå, E. (2012). Political participation and civic engagement: Towards new typology. *Human Affairs, 22*(3), 283–300. https://doi.org/10.2478/s13374-012-0024-1

Frost, J. (2011). Hollywood gossip as public sphere: Hedda Hopper, reader-respondents, and the red scare, 1947–1965. *Cinema Journal, 52*(2), 84–103. https://www.jstor.org/stable/41240695

Gadino, N., Ellithorpe, M. E., Ulusoy, E., Wirz, D. S., & Eden, A. (2023). Binge-watching to feel better: Mental health gratifications sought and obtained through binge watching. *Psychology of Popular Media*. Advance online publication. https://doi.org/10.1037/ppm0000485

Galinsky, A. D., & Moskowitz, G. B. (2000). Perspective-taking: Decreasing stereotype expression, stereotype accessibility, and in-group favoritism. *Journal of Personality and Social Psychology, 78*(4), 708–724. https://doi.org/10.1037/0022-3514.78.4.708

Gil de Zúñiga, H., Jung, N., & Valenzuela, S. (2012). Social media use for news and individuals' social capital, civic engagement and political participation. *Journal of Computer Mediated Communication, 17*(3), 319–336. https://doi.org/10.1111/j.1083-6101.2012.01574.x

Gil de Zúñiga, H., Molyneux, L., & Zheng, P. (2014). Social media, political expression, and political participation: Panel analysis of lagged and concurrent relationships. *Journal of Communication, 64*(4), 612–634. https://doi.org/10.1111/jcom.12103

Graham, T. (2012). Beyond "political" communicative spaces: Talking politics on the Wife Swap discussion forum. *Journal of Information Technology & Politics, 9*(1), 31–45. https://doi.org/10.1080/19331681.2012.635961

Graham, T., & Harju, A. (2011). Reality TV as a trigger of everyday political talk in the net basedpublic sphere. *European Journal of Communication, 26*(1), 18–32. https://doi.org/10.1177/0267323110394858

Groshek, J., & Krongard, S. (2016). Netflix and engage? Implications for streaming television onpolitical participation during the 2016 U.S. presidential campaign. *Social Sciences, 5*(4). https://doi.org/10.3390/socsci5040065

Habermas, J. (1989). *The structural transformation of the public sphere*. (T. Burger, Trans.). Cambridge: MIT Press, 85, 85–92. (Original work published 1962).

Jenner, M. (2019). Control issues: Binge-watching, channel-surfing and cultural value. *Participations: Journal of Audience & Reception Studies, 16*(2), 298–317. https://www.participations.org/16-02-15-jenner.pdf

Katz, E., Blumler, J. G., & Gurevitch, M. (1973). Uses and gratifications research. *The Public Opinion Quarterly, 37*(4), 509–523. https://www.jstor.org/stable/2747854

Katz, J. E., & Aakhus, M. (Eds.). (2002). *Perpetual contact: Mobile communication, private talk, public performance*. Cambridge University Press.

Keadle, S. K., Arem, H., Moore, S. C., Sampson, J. N., & Matthews, C. E. (2015). Impact of changes in television viewing time and physical activity on longevity: A prospective cohort study. *International Journal of Behavioral Nutrition and Physical Activity, 12*(1), 156. https://doi.org/10.1186/s12966-015-0315-0

Keen, S. (2006). A theory of narrative empathy. *Narrative, 14*(3), 207–236. https://www.jstor.org/stable/20107388

Kidd, D. C., & Castano, E. (2013). Reading literary fiction improves theory of mind. *Science, 342*(6156), 377–380. https://doi.org/10.1126/science.1239918

Kim, H. Y., LaRusso, M. D., Hsin, L. B., Harbaugh, A. G., Selman, R. L., & Snow, C. E. (2018). Social perspective-taking performance: Construct, measurement, and relations with academic performance and engagement. *Journal of Applied Developmental Psychology, 57*, 24–41. https://doi.org/10.1016/j.appdev.2018.05.005

Lotz, A. (2014). *The TV will be revolutionized*. New York University Press.

Lyotard, J. F. (1984). *The postmodern condition: A report on knowledge*. University of Minnesota Press.

Mar, R. A., Oatley, K., Hirsh, J., Paz, J., & Peterson, J. B. (2006). Bookworms versus nerds: Exposure to fiction versus non-fiction, divergent associations with social ability, and the simulation of fictional social worlds. *Journal of Research in Personality, 40*(5), 694–712. https://doi.org/10.1016/j.jrp.2005.08.002

Matrix, S. (2014). The Netflix effect: Teens, binge watching, and on-demand digital media trends. *Jeunesse: Young People, Texts, Cultures, 6*(1), 119–138. https://doi.org/10.3138/jeunesse.6.1.119

McCoy, M. L., & Scully, P. L. (2002). Deliberative dialogue to expand civic engagement: What kind of talk does democracy need? *National Civic Review, 91*(2), 117–135. https://doi.org/10.1002/ncr.91202

Meet the MilleXZials: Generational lines blur as media consumption for Gen X, Millennials and Gen Z converge. (2018, March 20). *Deloitte Insights*. https://www2.deloitte.com/us/en/insights/industry/technology/digital-media-trends-consumption-habits-survey.html?id=us:2el:3pr:4di4479:5awa:6di:032018:&pkid=1005131

Nathanson, A. I., Sharp, M. L., Aladé, F., Rasmussen, E. E., & Christy, K. (2013). The relation between television exposure and theory of mind among preschoolers. *Journal of Communication, 63*(6), 1088–1108. https://doi.org/10.1111/jcom.12062

Norris, P. (1996). Does television erode social capital? A reply to Putnam. *PS: Political Science & Politics, 29*(3), 474–480. https://doi.org/10.2307/420827

Oswald, P. A. (1996). The effects of cognitive and affective perspective taking on empathic concern and altruistic helping. *The Journal of Social Psychology, 136*(5), 613–623. https://doi.org/10.1080/00224545.1996.9714045

Papacharissi, Z. (2015). *Affective publics: Sentiment, technology, and politics*. Oxford University Press.

Penner, L. (2002). Dispositional and organizational influences on sustained volunteerism: An interactionist perspective. *Journal of Social Issues, 58*(3), 447–467. https://doi.org/10.1111/1540-4560.00270

Penner, L., & Finkelstein, M. (1998). Dispositional and structural determinants of volunteerism. *Journal of Personality and Social Psychology, 74*(2), 525. https://doi.org/10.1037/0022-3514.74.2.525

Peifer, J., & Garrett, K. (2014). *Best practices for working with opt-in online panels*. Ohio State University.

Rubenking, B., Bracken, C. C., Sandoval, J., & Rister, A. (2018). Defining new viewing behaviours: What makes and motivates TV binge-watching? *International Journal of Digital Television*, 9(1), 69–85. https://doi.org/10.1386/jdtv.9.1.69_1

Schneider, S. (1999). Monsters as (uncanny) metaphors: Freud, Lakoff, and the representation of monstrosity in cinematic horror. *Other Voices*, 1(3), 167–191.

Selman, R. L. (2003). *Promotion of social awareness: Powerful lessons for the partnership of developmental theory and classroom practice*. Russell Sage Foundation.

Shah, D.V., McLeod, J. M., & Yoon, S. H. (2001). Communication, context, and community: An exploration of print, broadcast, and Internet influences. *Communication Research*, 28(4), 464–506. https://doi.org/10.1177/009365001028004005

Shah, D. (1998). Civic engagement, interpersonal trust, and television use: An individual-level assessment of social capital. *Political Psychology*, 19(3), 469–496. https://doi.org/10.1111/0162-895X.00114.

Shamay-Tsoory, S. G., Aharon-Peretz, J., & Perry, D. (2009). Two systems for empathy: A dissociation between emotional and cognitive empathy in inferior frontal gyrus versus ventromedial prefrontal lesions. *Brain*, 132(3), 617–627. https://doi.org/10.1093/brain/awn279

Steiner, E., & Xu, K. (2020). Binge-watching motivates change: Uses and gratifications of streaming video viewers challenge traditional TV research. *Convergence*, 26(1), 82-101.

Sung, Y. H., Kang, E. Y., & Lee, W. N. (2015, May). A bad habit for your health? An exploration of psychological factors for binge-watching behavior. In *65th Annual International Communication Association Conference*, San Juan, Puerto Rico (pp. 21–25).

Temple, K. (2012). Gossip and the public sphere. *The Eighteenth Century*, 53(4), 509–512. https://www.jstor.org/stable/23365046.

TiVo Research Group. (2015). *Binge-viewing*. TiVo, Inc.

Van Dijck, J., & Poell, T. (2013). Understanding social media logic. *Media and Communication*, 1(1), 2–14. https://doi.org/10.17645/mac.v1i1.70

Walsh, K. C. (2004). *Talking about politics: Informal groups and social identity in American life*. University of Chicago Press.

· 9 ·

THE INFLUENCE OF PARTISAN CUES ON SOCIAL MEDIA: ACCEPTANCE OF THE 2020 PRESIDENTIAL ELECTION RESULTS

Madeleine Montgomery, Freddie J. Jennings, Kathleen Coyle, Ariana Aquino, and Malloree Murdock

In 2020, Americans were faced with the COVID-19 pandemic, the rise of protest concerning racial inequality, and political polarization resulting in the largest voter turnout in U.S. politics to date (Balz, 2020). All of these pivotal events culminated into a polarized American political arena and led to a violent riot on the steps of the United States Capitol on January 6, 2021. Political rhetoric, including that from President Donald Trump, encouraged American citizens to become more polarized in their political values (Filindra, 2021). This polarization of American politics that persisted during his presidency led to a highly passionate 2020 election. The country was highly divided on the choice for president, and when Joe Biden was announced as the winner, Republican voters across the country were outraged and many demanded a rejection of the electoral results.

On the day that the Electoral College votes were to be certified by Congress, voters who believed Donald Trump had won the election rioted in protest on the steps and inside of the United States Capitol building. Perspectives of the January 6 events varied greatly depending on the political biases of the media sources that one consumed (Bauder, 2021). Many citizens sympathized with the rioters who pushed their way into the U.S. Capitol while most citizens condemned the rioters and demanded consequences for their actions (Kleinfeld, 2021). Emotional claims about the events from both sides were shown in the media. Because of the potential democratic effects on our political system and the extensive media coverage, the issue was of great salience for the American people and strong opinions were formed.

According to the Elaboration Likelihood Model, information is processed, and attitudes are influenced through either the central route, utilizing cognitive analysis of an argument, or a peripheral route, relying on heuristic cues or mental shortcuts; increased issue salience is one factor that predicts a person utilizing the central route to process information (Petty & Cacioppo, 1986). Viewers of political messages may rely on partisan cues within the message without engaging in critical cognitive attention to evaluate the complexities and implications of the message (Dancey & Sheagley, 2013; Jennings, 2019), taking a peripheral approach to cognition. While many partisans rely on peripheral cues from prototypical leaders of their social group to position themselves on an issue (Greene, 2004), increased elaboration would minimize the influence of such partisan heuristics. However, the Theory of Identity-Motivated Elaboration (TIME) argues that partisan cues do not always limit cognition; in fact, sometimes partisan cues may actually motivate greater elaboration in order to defend their party's position on an issue (Jennings, 2019). The current study is a test of the TIME model, in a new context of high knowledge and salience, to better understand how partisan social identities guide the elaborative and political attitudinal attitude formation processes.

This study seeks to explore the effects of partisan cues in the media on Americans' political beliefs and attitudes. Through an experimental design, we examined participants' reactions to messages about the January 6 riots at the United States Capitol. By asking our participants questions related to the events that took place on January 6, we were able to further understand the attitudinal effects of valenced elaboration. The current study extends and builds on the TIME model of political attitudes formation, as well as other related theories: the theory of motivated reasoning (Kunda, 1990), social identity theory (Tajfel & Turner, 1979), and the elaboration likelihood model (Petty & Cacioppo, 1986) Accordingly, we examine this theoretical literature in the following section of the paper. After proposing and theoretically justifying five hypotheses, the experimental method of addressing these hypotheses is detailed. Following, the results are presented, before concluding by discussing the theoretical and practical implications of the findings.

Political Parties, Elaboration, and Attitude Formation

Social Identity Theory

Social identity theory (Tajfel, 1978; Tajfel & Turner, 1979) explains the attitudinal and behavioral influence of belonging to a social group. The partisan social identity hypothesis posits that political parties operate as social identities and the expectations of the social identity theory (SIT) can therefore be applied to the American political system (Green et al., 2002; Iyengar et al., 2012; Mason, 2014). American individuals tend to make decisions about which political party to align with based on the lessons of their parents, teachers, and life experiences. Beginning at a young age, individuals are socialized into one group as they are taught a party's values and belief systems (Warren & Wicks, 2011). As a person continues to age those values then become instilled within them, shaping their identities (Greene, 2004). Our current study will expand on the concept of partisanship as an aspect of socially constructed individual identity.

Social identity theory further posits that people seek to maximize their perceived positive differences between characteristics of people in the in-group and minimize perceived differences between characteristics of people in the out-group. Tajfel (1978) defines social identity as "part of an individual's self concept which derives from his knowledge of his membership of a group (or groups) together with the value and emotional significance attached to the membership" (p. 63). This is significant because as an individual's social identity to a political party grows stronger, so do their perceived differences between their self-identified in-group and out-group. This idea can be connected to Turner et al. (1987) self-categorization theory that explains how as individuals form unified groups, they develop shared behaviors and beliefs that become central to their shared identities. The increased perception of differences between groups is also attributed to a decrease in the likelihood of an individual withdrawing from their in-group or political party (Greene, 2004). As individuals develop a social identity around a particular party, they also develop stereotypes of what opposite parties represent and the people that belong in them. These beliefs are formed based on common themes held by their identifying party (Rau, 2021).

As individuals sort social and political information containing partisan social cues, they fit the information into their constructed mental schemas.

This helps them form beliefs and attitudes about both political parties and the values they each represent. Once an individual has identified as a member of a specific political party, social identity perspective explains that members will actively work to maintain a positive view and standing of that identity to diminish possible cognitive dissonance that may occur (Rees et al., 2015). A central element of SIT is that a person's social identity is a leading force in their actions and decision-making processes. As individuals connect larger portions of their identities to a political party, their decisions and actions will be more similar to those of their identifying party (Pauls et al., 2015).

Moreover, in-group favoritism and out-group derogation function in unison to strengthen an individual's social identity. In-group favoritism occurs when an individual mentally exaggerates positive characteristics of in-group members (Smith, 1999). Out-group derogation occurs when an individual mentally exaggerates the negative characteristics of out-group members. These processes lead to enhanced group differentiation (Greene, 2004). Positive in-group bias develops due to the individual's personal identification with the group. Because the individual's ego is involved in cognitions about the group, their ideas will serve to uplift attributes of group members (Rau, 2021). Strong identification with a political party could cause someone to have stronger emotions surrounding their political identity and political ideas. Emphasizing the negative attributes of members of the out-group or opposing political party can lead to stereotyping. As the authors of SIT stated, "In order for the members of an ingroup to be able to hate or dislike an outgroup, or to discriminate against it, they must first have acquired a sense of belonging to a group which is clearly distinct from the one they hate, dislike or discriminate against" (Tajfel, 1978, p. 66). Our study on partisanship identification will exemplify this social identification phenomenon. As a result of in-group favoritism and out-group denigration we propose the following two hypotheses:

> H1: a) Viewers affiliated with the same party as a speaker will have more congruent attitudes with the message and b) viewers of the opposing party as a speaker will have less congruent attitudes than when the speaker has no party identification.

Motivated Reasoning

Motivated reasoning is the process in which citizens view new information through a lens that favors their prior beliefs and values, resulting in lower critical analysis rates and higher acceptance rates of messages that align with those of their party identification (Kahne & Bowyer, 2017). This theory works to explain how individuals defend their current existing beliefs through a process of rationalization, particularly those concerning political issues or events. Kunda (1990) explains that people can process new information with accuracy or directional goals. People have an accuracy goal when they process information in an unbiased, objective manner. However, directional goals are used through a cognitively biased lens to defend pre-existing opinions deemed to be correct (Slothuus & Vreese, 2010). Motivated reasoning also occurs due to people feeling the need to protect or defend ideas that are central to a person's social identity when they perceive it as being under attack (Bolsen et al., 2014). In other words, people favor and form evaluative opinions that are positive more readily for arguments that parallel pre-existing beliefs and values and ignore information that contradicts these ideas to minimize the distance between their perceived in-groups and themselves. Motivated reasoning has a critical influence on a person's political attitudes. As individuals engage in directional processing, they consume media that confirms preexisting beliefs and reject those that contain counter arguments or opinions (Bolsen et al., 2014). As a result, information that supports preexisting opinions is often accepted, while counter-attitudinal information is rejected (Kunda, 1990). Accepting messages that only align with a party's current values and beliefs hinder individuals' ability to discover and educate themselves about diverse perspectives (Peterson & Iyengar, 2021). This is a result of limiting exposure to information that opposes preexisting beliefs and maximizing distance between current values held and those of perceived out-groups (Kahne & Bowyer, 2017).

When a partisan receives a political message, they may understand messages that oppose their political party's ideologies as a threat to their identity and stand more firmly within their own political identity (Aghakhani et al., 2021; Colvin et al., 2020). Partisan motivated reasoning, a cognitive tool utilized to protect the part of an individual's identity that is tied to a political party, can limit a partisan from becoming educated on a polarizing political topic (Jennings, 2019). Bolsen and colleagues (2014) argue that partisan motivated reasoning "is likely to occur when one is primed to pay particular attention in being consistent with his/her partisan identity" (p. 237). When a person is informed of a message's political affiliation before they begin to engage in the decision-making process, it will affect the way citizens will receive and evaluate that information. A person's identity and desire to be loyal to their party identification will lead to acceptance of messages that align with party identification and rejection of information that is from opposing parties without sufficient evaluation (Bolsen et al., 2014; Robison, 2021). Partisan motivated reasoning influences individuals to search more consistently for information that is affiliated with pre-existing values and judge consonant messages less critically than those with opposing arguments (Kahne & Bowyer, 2017). Partisan motivated reasoning not only will influence individuals to use selective exposure for information that aligns with their identifying party beliefs but will also result in altering facts and information they consume to align with their party affiliation. When partisan cues are present, individuals will use selective parts of messages that support beliefs and values that align with their party identification and reject others to maximize distance from perceived out-groups. Peterson and Iyengar (2021) state that selective exposure and individuals' readiness to reject ideas contradictory to party identification without adequate evaluation increases acceptance and integration of misinformation into political decisions.

Theory of Identity-Motivated Elaboration

An informed electorate and educated political decision-making are essential for a well-functioning deliberative democracy (Dahl, 1956; Habermas, 1962; Jennings et al., 2020). Individuals gather information through exposure to political messages (Bolsen et al., 2014; Huddy et al., 2015) and in turn construct their attitudes about policies that matter to them. As discussed, individuals rely on partisan cues in messages to reaffirm their beliefs and social identities. These partisan cues promote identity-motivated elaboration to defend one's partisan social identity. Extending assumptions of the social identity theory and the theory of motivated reasoning, TIME incorporates how partisan social identity influences the valence of elaboration and subsequent knowledge acquisition and attitude formation (Jennings, 2019). As previously explained, political elites function as prototypical leaders, who often utilize mass media to send partisan cues in order to direct 'correct' political opinions (Greene, 2004). As partisans receive social cues from the political elite, they engage in biased, valenced elaboration to support the position of their partisan social identity (Jennings et al., 2020). The partisan divide in the U.S. is an affective, not simply ideological, divide (Iyengar et al., 2012) laden with emotion that factors into political deliberation.

As a social identity, party affiliation may present bias in evaluations and attitudes (Bolsen et al., 2014). As one's political social identity affects the way one thinks about, evaluates, and forms opinions, consumers of political media rely on partisan cues in a message as they accept and rationalize a party's stance (Lodge & Taber, 2013). As individuals view a political message, they adhere more strongly to their political identities (Colvin et al., 2020). Thus, a strong partisan social identity would result in greater identity-consistent elaboration (Jennings et al., 2020). The affective connection a partisan has with their political party may not negate issue-relevant elaboration but instead motivate identity-defensive cognition. Thus, we predict:

H2: A shared partisan identity with the speaker will a) increase message-consistent elaboration and b) decrease message-inconsistent elaboration.

H3: An opposing partisan identity with a speaker will a) decrease message-consistent elaboration and b) increase message-inconsistent elaboration.

Elaboration and Elaboration Valence

Elaboration is understood as thinking about issue-relevant arguments in a message (Petty & Cacioppo, 1986) and is a well-developed method of persuasion. Like all methods of persuasion, the desired outcome is a change in attitude. On any given day, individuals will encounter an abundance of persuasive messages ranging from commercials about a specific brand of dog food to political ads urging them to support a certain candidate. According to the elaboration likelihood model, individuals process these stimuli differently depending on the extent to which they are willing and able to scrutinize a message. In instances where an individual is exerting high levels of cognition, they are said to be engaging in high elaboration and processing messages through the central route to persuasion. This act allows for a deeper understanding of the message being presented. High levels of elaboration can be seen in various ways:

> People are likely to attend to the appeal; attempt to access relevant associations, images, and experiences from memory; scrutinize and elaborate upon the externally provided message arguments in light of the associations available from memory; draw inferences about the merits of the arguments for a recommendation based upon their

analyses; and consequently, derive an overall evaluation of, or attitude toward, the recommendation. (Petty & Cacioppo, 1986, p. 128)

In other words, messages that are processed through the central route are more heavily scrutinized and are less likely to be swayed by counter attitudinal messages. However, a number of variables can determine one's level of elaboration to a given stimulus.

Of these variables are peripheral cues, like one's partisanship. Partisan cues afford individuals a shortcut in decision making regarding politics (Bullock, 2011), lowering their levels of elaboration and engagement with a message or argument. In other words, when presented with a message from someone within one's political party or ideology, the individual will align themselves with that message because their "political leader" aligned with it. On the other hand, some scholars believe that one's partisanship encourages them to engage in central route processing, ignoring the schemas that their partisanship affords them (Bolsen et al., 2014). Instead, they will be motivated to engage with the message and preserve their image within that party (Peterson et al., 2021). Individuals will engage with a message more deeply and interpret a message in a way that aligns with the party's ideologies.

Though the amount of elaboration is often the focus of academic studies, the direction of elaboration can be influential. Elaboration can be either positively valenced, where people consider the perspective of the message sender, or negatively valenced, where people develop counterarguments for the message (O'Keefe, 2012). In a study on partisan motivated reasoning and identity-motivated elaboration, Jennings (2019) found "that partisans engaged in positively valenced elaboration if the article was presented in a gain frame that benefited their political party. Conversely, a loss frame containing cues indicating that the policy was supported by and would benefit the out-party resulted in an increase in negative elaboration" (p. 541). In sum, elaboration consistent with the message would be considered positively valenced and enhances persuasion, while elaboration inconsistent with the message would be considered negatively valenced and hinders persuasion.

> H4: a) Message-consistent elaboration will foster greater attitudinal congruency with the message, and b) message -inconsistent elaboration will decrease attitudinal congruency.

The first four hypotheses construct a hypothesized model (See Figure 9.1) that illustrates the way a congruent or incongruent partisan identity with a speaker

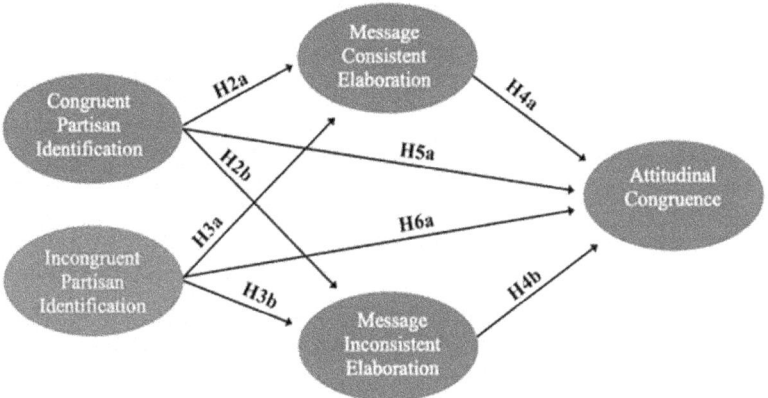

Figure 9.1: Hypothesized model of the direct and indirect influence of partisan identification and attitudinal congruence.
Source: The authors.

can dramatically alter the effect of the message by changing the way a person thinks about the argument. The valence of a person's elaboration can change the effect a message has on that individual's attitude toward the topic. This mediated effect of partisan identification on attitude through elaboration, as well as the direct effect, is articulated in the final two hypotheses:

- H5: A shared partisan identity with the speaker will positively predict attitudinal congruence both a) directly and b) indirectly through valenced elaboration.
- H6: An opposing partisan identity with the speaker will negatively predict attitudinal congruence both a) directly and b) indirectly through valenced elaboration.

Method

Participants

A total of 400 students at an accredited Southern university completed an online experiment concerning their beliefs and attitudes surrounding the January 6 riots at the U.S. Capitol. After failing one of two manipulation checks, 23 participants were removed from data analysis. Of the remaining 377 participants, 190 identified as female (50.4%) and 187 identified as male

(49.6%). Participants were asked to respond to all race/ethnicities in which they identify: The majority of respondents identified as White (n = 329; 87.3%); 18 identified as Black/African American (4.8%); 13 identified as Asian (3.4%); 29 identified as Hispanic (7.7%); eight identified as Native American (2.1%); three identified as Pacific Islander (0.8%); and seven (1.9%) selected "other race/ethnicity." The average age of respondents was 19.73 (SD = 1.10).

Participants were asked to self-report partisanship measured through the survey by presenting the question, "to what extent do you consider yourself a Democrat or Republican." Participants were able to identify as strong, moderate, or leaning Republicans or Democrats; also, a "no preference" option was available. The breakdown of respondent identities follows as such: Strong Democrat (n = 9, 2.4%), Democrat (n = 38, 10.1%), Lean Democrat (n = 42, 11.1%), No Preference (n = 60, 15.9%), Lean Republican (n = 90, 23.9%), Republican (n = 94, 24.9%), and Strong Republican (n = 44, 11.7%). Respondents who selected "no preference" were directed to the following question: "I know you don't have a preference between the two parties, but say you had to vote for a generic candidate from one of the two. In this case, who would you be more likely to vote for?" Each participant was then categorized as either a Republican or Democrat. In summation, there was a conservative skew with 111 respondents who identified as a Democrat (29.4%) and 266 respondents who identified as Republican (70.6%).

Procedure and Design

Qualtrics online software was utilized to create and distribute the experiment. After collecting demographic information, the posttest only design was executed. All participants watched a brief clip (1:21) of a U.S. Congressman, identified as Jeff Baker (the clip was actually Congressman Jamie Raskin). Participants who had correctly identified Rep. Raskin in the pre-test (n = 4) were removed from data collection. Before the video was shown, the manipulation was given: "REPUBLICAN [DEMOCRAT or no partisanship revealed] Congressman Jeff Baker Addresses Congress about January 6." Following the video, participants were asked to identify the party of Jeff Baker (Republican, Democrat, or "It did not say") to ensure the manipulation was successfully received; 19 participants answered incorrectly and were removed from data analysis. By identifying Jeff Baker as a Republican/Democrat or not providing his partisanship, three conditions were created: (1) Partisan

Identity Congruent (Republican viewer watching a Republican politician or a Democratic viewer watching a Democratic politician; $n = 127$, 33.7%); (2) Partisan Identity Incongruent (Republican viewer watching a Democratic politician or a Democratic viewer watching a Republican politician, $n = 130$, 34.5%); and (3) Nonpartisan (the party of the politician not indicated, $n = 120$, 31.8%). In the video, the politician addresses Congress to condemn the "bloodthirsty mob" that invaded the Capitol on January 6 and call for punishment for the rioters. To maintain Raksin's anonymity in the stimulus video, the video was edited to remove any mention of his name, position, or partisan identity. Following the video, cognitive and attitudinal measures were given in the posttest.

Measures

Message-Consistent/Inconsistent Elaboration

Consistent with other studies (e.g., Krosnick & Petty, 1995; LaMarre & Walther, 2013), elaboration was measured through thought-listing prompts. Respondents were asked "Why might a person think that the actions of the January 6 protestors were wrong?" and "Why might a person defend the actions of protestors on January 6?" They were asked to "list as many reasons as you can think of." Message-consistent elaboration was operationalized by tallying the reasons given for the first question ($M = 3.58$, $SD = 1.37$), and message-inconsistent elaboration was operationalized using the second question ($M = 2.03$, $SD = 1.25$).

Attitudinal Congruence

Participants were asked their level of agreement using a seven-point, Likert-type scale (1 = *strongly disagree*; 7 = *strongly agree*) with three statements. Each statement (i.e., "There should be consequences for participants of January 6 attacks," "The citizens that overtook the Capitol acted inappropriately," and "The rioters are traitors") was reflective of the opinion of the speaker in the video ($M = 4.99$, $SD = 1.07$, $\alpha = .88$).

Results

The first hypothesis predicted that partisan identification would influence attitudes on a political issue. H1a predicted that a shared identity with a politician would lead to greater attitudinal congruence compared to when the partisanship of the politician was not revealed, while H1b predicted a competing partisan identity would decrease attitudinal congruence. There were significant differences between groups [$F(2, 376) = 15.10, p < .001$]. H1a was supported as those with congruent partisan identities ($M = 5.41$, $SD = 1.06$) agreed more strongly with the position being discussed than did those who did not know the partisanship of the speaker ($M = 4.76$, $SD = .89$, $p < .001$). However, the attitudinal difference between people watching a candidate of unknown partisanship and people watching a politician from the opposing party ($M = 4.83$, $SD = 1.13$, $p = .59$) was not significant. H1b was not supported. Thus, the results reveal partial support for the first hypothesis.

The next two hypotheses, making up the first level of the hypothesized model (See Figure 9.2 for the final model), examined the influence of partisanship on elaboration. There were significant group differences for both message-consistent [$F(2, 376) = 60.10, p < .001$] and message-inconsistent elaboration [$F(2, 376) = 66.87, p < .001$]. Post-hoc analysis revealed strong support for the second hypothesis, which examined the influence of in-party favoritism on cognition. If viewers were of the same party, they engaged in greater positive ($M = 4.28$, $SD = 1.18$) and reduced negative ($M = 1.20$, $SD = .88$) elaboration than if the partisanship of the politicians was unknown (Message-Consistent Elaboration: $M = 3.58$, $SD = 1.18$, $p < .001$; Message-Inconsistent Elaboration: $M = 2.11$, $SD = 1.05$, $p < .001$). H2 was fully and strongly supported, as a shared partisan identity biased elaboration.

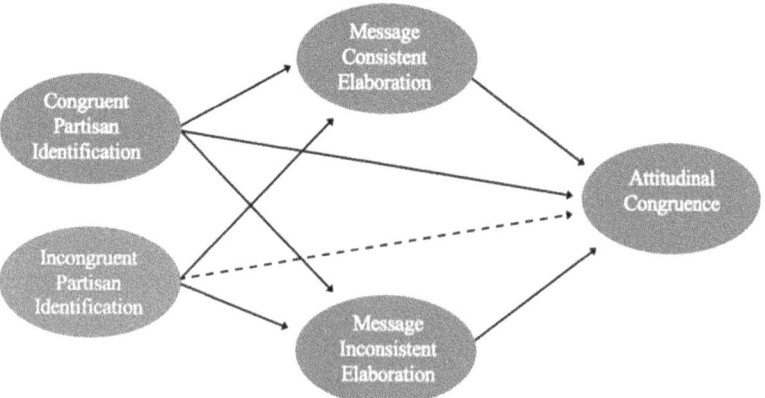

Figure 9.2: Final model of the direct and indirect influence of partisan identification and attitudinal congruence.
Source: The authors.

The third hypothesis predicted that a competing partisan identity would have the opposite effect: decrease positively valenced, message-consistent elaboration and increase negatively valenced, message-inconsistent elaboration. H3 was strongly supported, as a competing partisan identity hindered message-consistent elaboration ($M = 3.23$, $SD = .89$, $p < .001$) and fostered message-inconsistent elaboration ($M = 2.75$, $SD = 1.26$, $p < .001$). The data fully supported the third hypothesis, as a competing partisan social identity also biased elaboration.

The effect of valenced elaboration was examined in the fourth hypothesis. A linear regression revealed an influence of valence elaboration on attitudes [$F(2, 374) = 142.95$, $p < .001$]. In support of H4a, positively valenced, message-consistent elaboration led to increased attitudinal congruence with the position argued in the video ($B = .37$, $se = .04$, $\beta = .48$, $t = 10.56$, $p < .001$). Negatively valenced, message-inconsistent elaboration, conversely, decreased attitudinal congruence ($B = -23$, $se = .04$, $\beta = -.27$, $t = -5.85$, $p < .001$), supporting H4b. The fourth hypothesis was fully supported, as the valence of elaboration determined its influence on the attitudes of viewers. In sum, positively and negatively valenced elaboration explained over 40% of the variance in attitudes ($R^2 = .43$).

PROCESS analysis was used to test the fifth hypothesis examining the direct and indirect influences of a shared partisan identity on attitudes. The indirect effect of partisan identification on attitudinal congruence was mediated by positively valenced elaboration ($B = .33$, $se = .08$, $LLCI = .19$, $ULCI = .49$) and negatively valenced elaboration ($B = .30$, $se = .07$, $LLCI = 17$, $ULCI = .46$). After accounting for these indirect effects, a positive direct effect of a shared partisan identity on attitudinal congruence remained ($B = .32$, $se = .11$, $LLCI = .11$, $ULCI = .53$). Because there was a significant direct effect and two indirect effects, H5 was fully supported.

The direct and indirect influences of a competing partisan identity on attitudes were examined in H6 through PROCESS analysis. A competing partisan identity had an indirect negative influence on attitudinal influence through decreased message-consistent elaboration ($B = -.31$, $se = .08$, $LLCI = -.49$, $ULCI = -.15$) and increased message-inconsistent elaboration ($B = -.32$, $se = .09$, $LLCI = -.50$, $ULCI = -.16$). Interestingly, the remaining direct effect after considering the indirect effects was positive ($B = .39$, $se = .11$, $LLCI = .17$, $ULCI = .61$), explaining the null finding in H1b of the total (combined direct and indirect) effect of a competing identity on attitudes. Support for H6, then, was mixed.

Discussion

This study explored the effects of partisan cues in the media on Americans' political attitudes and the elaborative mechanism of influence. The results of the experiment revealed partisan motivated reasoning, as the presence of identity-congruent partisan cues, specifically about the party of the speaker, resulted in greater positively valenced elaboration and less negatively valenced elaboration. In other words, individuals of the same partisan affiliation as the speaker spent more time considering the merits of the argument and less time developing counterarguments. On the other hand, incongruent partisan indicators fostered message-inconsistent, negatively valenced elaboration while limiting message-consistent, positively valenced elaboration. The valenced elaboration had opposing effects on the persuasiveness of the message. Message-inconsistent, negatively valenced elaboration hindered persuasion, while message-consistent, positively valenced elaboration enhanced it. The hypothesized model was supported with one exception that has theoretical implications.

The findings support the theory of identity-motivated elaboration (TIME) and the related theories: motivated reasoning, social identity theory, and the elaboration likelihood model. As predicted by TIME, people were more persuaded, even with a highly salient issue, when the speaker was presumed to be of the same political party than when the party of the speaker was not disclosed. Likewise, viewers of the opposing party expressed less attitudinal congruence with the speaker. The foundational premise of TIME is that partisan social identities motivate identity-defensive cognition to defend the political position of one's party (Jennings, 2019). The current study extends TIME beyond knowledge acquisition to persuasion, as this biased elaboration can either enhance or hinder the persuasiveness of a message. Four indirect effects were observed: in-party indicators increased message-consistent elaboration and decreased message inconsistent elaboration and resultingly increased attitudinal congruence, while out-party indicators decreased message-consistent elaboration and increased message-inconsistent elaboration and resultingly decreased attitudinal congruence. In other words, if a person shared a party identity with the speaker, they were more likely, in comparison to someone that was of the opposing party, to consider the merits of the argument while spending less cognitive effort developing counterarguments. This difference in elaboration resulted in a partisan being more persuaded by a politician in their own party than by a politician of the opposing party. In sum, a shared partisan identity influenced attitudes by changing the valence or direction of a person's elaboration. The theory was further supported by the two direct effects from party indicators to attitude. The direct effect, after factoring in the indirect effects, of in-party cues (B = .32) and out-party cues (B = .39) was quite similar. However, the overall (direct + indirect) effects were in opposing directions. This indicates that the differing effects is fully explained by the biased elaboration predicted in TIME. Though partisan heuristics in political decision making have been shown to occur in regard to low-salience issues, when an issue is highly discussed, like the January 6 riots, partisan cues do not limit cognition but instead bias it.

The partisan social identity hypothesis argues that political parties operate as social groups (e.g., Greene, 2004; Huddy et al., 2015). As predicted by the social identity theory (Tajfel & Turner, 1979), members of the social group (i.e., political party) expressed ingroup favoritism and outgroup denigration, as partisans evaluated the arguments of a speaker presumed to be of the same party more favorably than the same arguments from a member of the political outgroup. Defending one's partisan social group provided viewers with a directional goal for processing the information. When processing information with a directional goal, the theory of motivated reasoning explains, people used biased cognition to come to a preferred attitudinal outcome (Kunda, 1990). The present study demonstrates that individuals go beyond just cognitively defending preexisting opinions by engaging in biased elaboration to defend one's partisan social group, even on a highly salient issue. This empirical study demonstrating the importance of differentiating positively and negatively valenced elaboration, which theoretically is discussed with the elaboration likelihood model (O'Keefe, 2012; Petty & Cacioppo, 1986) but often neglected in academic research in favor of total elaboration (e.g., Jennings et al., 2019), contributed to our understanding of elaboration and politics.

Additionally, the findings of this study aid in understanding the public's attitudes and the American political system. Partisan cues are frequently present in political messages consumed by individuals every day. The year of 2020 was polarized across the board as citizens maneuvered the COVID-19 pandemic, the rise of racial protests, and the presidential election. With the largest voter turnout in U.S. elections to date (Balz, 2020), the presence of partisan cues in messages is significant in understanding how individuals interact with political messages. How a citizen interacts with and is exposed to political messages impacts their attitude formation and subsequent behaviors.

These can include activities like voting, public discourse, and involvement in social movements (Simas & Ozer, 2021). The results of the study demonstrate the power of partisan cues, which could be abused. Out-party cues may hinder attitudinal congruence on an issue that may benefit society, while in-party cues could enhance the persuasiveness of a message advocating for a position that may not be in the best interest of society. As such, media outlets must be cognizant of the way partisan cues are presented in political stories. Addressing how the presence of partisan cues within political messages affect viewers furthers the ability of American citizens to become more informed and conscious of the messages they consume.

Limitations

Like all research, this study has its limitations. The lack of diversity in age, race/ethnicity, education level, and geography limit the generalizability of the findings. Additionally, the conservative skew of the sample must be considered. The January 6 riots was used as an issue because of the extensive media coverage on the event. However, the findings should be carefully generalized to other political issues. The high salience of the issue would predispose viewers to engage in greater central-route elaboration rather than partisan heuristics and peripheral processing. Future studies should utilize more representative samples on a variety of political issues of differing degrees of salience.

Conclusion

This experiment revealed that minimal partisan cues can influence cognition and attitudes on a highly salient political issue. Consistent with partisan motivated reasoning and identity-motivated elaboration theoretical expectations, partisan social identification prompted identity-defensive elaboration. Compared to a speech condemning the rioters that overtook the Capitol building from a politician with no partisan identifiers, the same speech from an in-party politician was related to more message-consistent and less message-inconsistent elaboration, which resultingly led to more attitudinal congruence with the speaker. Meanwhile, if the same message was from a member of the opposing party, the reverse effect was observed. The findings provide supporting evidence for the role of or partisan cues and valenced elaboration in the political attitude formation process.

References

Aghakhani, N., Onook, O., Dawn, G. G., & Karimi, J. (2021). Online review consistency matters: An elaboration likelihood model perspective. *Information Systems Frontiers, 23*(1), 1287–1301. https://doi.org/10.1007/s10796-020-10030-7

Balz, D. (2020, December 27). *After a year of pandemic and protest, and a big election, America is as divided as ever.* The Washington Post. https://www.washingtonpost.com/graphics/2020/politics/elections-reckoning/

Bauder, D. (2021). *Riot? Insurrection? Words matter in describing Capitol siege.* AP News. https://apnews.com/article/donald-trump-capitol-siege-riots-media-8000ce7db2b176c1be386d945be5fd6a

Bolsen, T., Druckman, N. J., & Cook, F. L. (2014). The Influence of Partisan Motivated Reasoning on Public Opinion. *Political Behavior, 36*(2), 235–262. https://doi.org/10.1007/s11109-013-9238-0

Bullock, J. G. (2011). Elite influence on public opinion in an informed electorate. *American Political Science Review, 105*, 496–515. https://doi.org/10.1017/S0003055411000165

Colvin, R. M., Witt, G. B., Lacey, J., & McCrea, R. (2020). The role of conflict framing and social identity in public opinion about land use change: An experimental test in the Australian context. *Environmental Policy and Governance, 30*(2), 84–98. https://doi.org/10.1002/eet.1879

Dahl, R. A. (1956). *A preface to democratic theory.* University of Chicago Press.

Dancey, L., & Sheagley, G. (2013). Heuristics behaving badly: Party cues and voter knowledge. *American Journal of Political Science, 57*(2), 312–325. https://doi.org/10.1111/j.1540-5907.2012.00621.x

Filindra, A. (2021). Who are we? How did we get here? And where are we going? New questions, new concepts, new ideas and the role of ascriptive categories in political life: A special edited collection of essays. *The Journal of Race, Ethnicity, and Politics, 6*(1), 1–2. https://doi.org/10.1017/rep.2021.1

Green, D., Palmquist, B., & Schickler, E. (2002). *Partisan hearts and minds: Political parties and the social identities of voters.* Yale University Press.

Greene, S. (2004). Social identity theory and party identification. *Social Science Quarterly, 85*(1), 136–153. https://doi:10.1111/j.0038-4941.2004.08501010.x

Habermas, J. (1962). *The structural transformation of the public sphere: An inquiry into a category of bourgeois society.* MIT Press.

Huddy, L., Mason, L., & Aarøe, L. (2015). Expressive partisanship: Campaign involvement, political emotion, and partisan identity. *American Political Science Review, 109*(1), 1–17. https://doi.org/10.1017/S0003055414000604

Iyengar, S., Sood, G., & Lelkes, Y. (2012). Affect, not ideology: A social identity perspective on polarization. *Public Opinion Quarterly. 76*, 405–431. https://doi.org/10.1093/poq/nfs038

Jennings, F. J. (2019). An uninformed electorate: Identity-motivated elaboration, partisan cues, and learning. *Journal of Applied Communication Research, 47*(5), 527–547. https://doi.org/10.1080/00909882.2019.1679385

Jennings, F. J., Bramlett, J. C., McKinney, M. S., & Hardy, M. M. (2020). Tweeting along partisan lines: Identity-motivated elaboration and presidential debates. *Social Media + Society*, 6(4). https://doi.org/10.1177/205630512096551

Jennings, F. J., Bramlett, J. C., & Warner, B. R. (2019). Comedic cognition: The impact of elaboration on political comedy effects. *Western Journal of Communication*, 83(3), 365–382. https://doi.org/10.1080/10570314.2018.1541476

Jennings, F. J., Warner, B. R., McKinney, M. S., Bird, C. C., Funk, M. E., & Bramlett, J. C. (2020). Watching televised presidential debates: Who learns the most and why. *Communication Studies*, 71(5), 896–910. https://doi.org/10.1080/10510974.2020.1807377

Kahne, J., & Bowyer, B. (2017). Educating for democracy in a partisan age: Confronting the challenges of motivated reasoning and misinformation. *American Educational Research Journal*, 54(1), 3–34. https://doi.org/10.3102/0002831216679817

Kleinfeld, R. (2021). The rise of political violence in the United States. *The Journal of Democracy*, 32(4), 160–176. https://doi.org/10.1353/jod.2021.0059

Krosnick, J., & Petty, R. (1995). Attitude strength: An overview. In R. Petty & J. Krosnick (Eds.), *Attitude strength: Antecedents and consequences* (pp. 1–24). Earlbaum.

Kunda, Z. (1990). The case for motivated reasoning. *Psychological Bulletin*, 108(3), 480–498. https://doi.org/10.1037/0033-2909.108.3.480

LaMarre, H. L., & Walther, W. (2013). Ability matters: Testing the differential effects of political news and late-night comedy on cognitive responses and the role of ability in micro-level opinion formation. *International Journal of Public Opinion Research*, 25(3), 303–322. https://doi.org/10.1093/ijpor/edt008

Lodge, M., & Taber, C. S. (2013). *The rationalizing voter*. Cambridge University Press. https://doi.org/10.1017/CBO9781139032490

Mason, L. (2014). "I disrespectfully agree": The differential effects of partisan sorting on social and issue polarization. *American Journal of Political Science*, 59(1), 128–145. https://doi.org/10.1111/ajps.12089

O'Keefe, D. J. (2012). The elaboration likelihood model. In J. P. Dillard & L. Shen (Eds.), The SAGE handbook of persuasion: Developments in theory and practice (pp. 137–149). Sage.

Pauls, S. D., Leibon, G., & Rockmore, D. (2015). The social identity voting model: Ideology and community structures. *Research & Politics*, 2(2), 1–11. https://doi.org/10.1177/2053168015570415

Peterson, E., & Iyengar, S. (2021). Partisan gaps in political information and information-seeking behavior: Motivated reasoning or cheerleading? *American Journal of Political Science*, 65(1), 133–147. https://doi.org/10.1111/ajps.12535

Petty, R. E., & Cacioppo, J. T. (1986). The elaboration likelihood model of persuasion. In L. Berkowitz (Ed.), *Advances in experimental social psychology* (Vol. 19, pp. 123–205). Academic Press.

Rau, E. (2021). Partisanship as cause, not consequence, of participation. *Comparative Political Science*, 55(6), 1021–1058. https://doi.org/10.1177/00104140211047406

Rees, T., Haslam, S. A., Coffee, P., & Lavallee, D. (2015). A social identity approach to sport psychology: Principles, practice, and prospects. *Springer International Publishing*, 45(8), 1083–1096. https://doi.org/10.1007/s40279-015-0345-4

Reynolds, K. J., Turner, J. C., & Haslam, S. A. (2000). When are we better than them and they worse than us? A closer look at social discrimination in positive and negative domains. *Journal of Personality and Social Psychology*, 78(1), 64–80. https://doi.org/10.1037/0022-3514.78.1.64

Robison, J. (2021). What's the value of partisan loyalty? Partisan ambivalence, motivated reasoning, and correct voting in U.S. presidential elections. *Political Psychology*, 42(6), 977–993. https://doi.org/10.1111/pops.12729

Simas, E. N., & Ozer, A. L. (2021). Polarization, candidate positioning, and political participation in the US. *Electoral Studies*, 73. https://doi.org/10.1016/j.electstud.2021.102370

Slothuus, R., & de Vreese, H. C. (2010). Political parties, motivated reasoning, and issue framing effects. *The Journal of Politics*, 72(3), 630–645. https://www.jstor.org/stable/10.1017/s002238161000006x

Smith, E. R. (1999). Affective and cognitive implications of a group becoming part of the self: New models of prejudice and of the self-concept. In D. Abrams & M. A. Hogg (Eds.), *Social identity and social cognition* (pp. 183–196). Basil Blackwell.

Tajfel, H. (1978). Social categorization, social identity, and social comparisons. In H. Tajfel (Ed.), *Differentiation between social groups.* (pp. 61–76). Academic Press.

Tajfel, H., & Turner, J. C. (1979). An integrative theory of inter-group conflict. In W. G. Austin & S. Worchel (Eds.), *The social psychology of inter-group relations* (pp. 33–47). Brooks/Cole.

Turner, J. C., Hogg, M. A., Oakes, P. J., Reicher, S. D., & Wetherell, M. S. (1987) *Rediscovering the social group: A self-categorization theory*. Basil Blackwell.

Warren, R., & Wicks, R. H. (2011). Political socialization: Modeling teen political and civic engagement. *Journalism & Mass Communication Quarterly*, 88(1), 156–175. https://doi.org/10.1177/107769901108800109

· 10 ·

THE MODERATING EFFECT OF RACIAL RESENTMENT AND AMBIVALENT SEXISM ON PARTISANSHIP AND THOUGHT LISTING AFTER VIEWING THE 2020 VICE PRESIDENTIAL DEBATE

Xavier Scruggs and Benjamin R. Warner

Compared to presidential debates, vice presidential debates have garnered substantially less scholarly attention (McKinney et al., 2011; Wrasse et al., 2018). However, vice-presidential debates present unique opportunities to examine the interaction of candidate identities, voter perceptions, and communication because they increase the number and type of case-studies that can be examined in a context that is inherently limited (i.e., there are only two major party presidential candidates every four years). For example, in the more than two centuries of presidential elections, the United States has never elected a woman president, and only one woman (Hillary Clinton in 2016, who lost) has run with a nomination from one of the two major parties. Similarly, all but one of the 46 people to win the presidency have been White. The vice-presidency has been similarly homogenous. Every vice-presidential candidate for a major party prior to 2016 has been White, and only twice before has a woman received the major party nomination (Congresswoman Geraldine Ferraro in 1984 and Governor Sarah Palin in 2008, both of whom lost).

The 2020 election was thus historic when, in August 2020, then-Presidential candidate Joe Biden nominated the first African American and

South Asian woman, Kamala Harris, to be his vice president. Thus, the victory of the Biden/Harris ticket made history. Harris's place on the ballot created a unique opportunity to consider the role of race and gender as it pertains to perceptions of campaign communication. Specifically, did the racial and gender attitudes of viewers influence perceptions of Harris's performance in her vice-presidential debate? This study answers this question by probing the moderating impact of ambivalent sexism and racial resentment on perceptions of Harris's performance.

This study also utilizes the social function of video-conferencing technology to assess the influence of communication environment on these processes. Specifically, we consider whether viewing the debate in a digital environment with homogenous chat (i.e., chatting with people of the same party) influences perceptions of debate participants compared to viewing the debate in an environment with mixed (bipartisan) chat or with no chat. We consider the moderating influence of racial resentment and hostile sexism on these digital media effects as well.

The Influence of Attitudes about Race and Gender

Viewer response to a candidate's performance in a debate may be, in part, a function of the racial and gender attitudes of the viewers. This is especially likely for a debate in which, for the first time in American history, a woman of color was present on the debate stage (Banwart, 2010; Huddy & Terkildsen, 1993). Specifically, racial resentment and hostile sexism are two well-studied attitudes that are likely to influence the way people process Harris's debate performance. We review each in turn.

Kinder and Sears (1981) forwarded the concept of *racial resentment* in the 1960s in reaction to race riots, which were occurring all over the United States as African Americans demanded the same rights and privileges as their White counterparts. Racial resentment is conceptually defined as the belief that African Americans are demanding, undeserving, and should not have access to governmental aid (Henry & Sears, 2002; Kinder & Sears, 1981). Voters higher in racial resentment tend to not support Black candidates and are less likely to vote for Democrats because Democrats are seen as supporting an agenda closely aligned to the interest of people from historically oppressed races, such as civil rights (Luttig & Motta, 2017; Tesler, 2012; Tesler & Sears, 2010). Yet, recent research found that Black Republicans still can garner support among voters that are high in racial resentment (Karpowitz et al., 2021). This is likely because Black Republicans discuss race and racism much differently in their party (or do not discuss their race or racism at all).

Filindra & Fagan (2022) also found that the selection of then-Senator Kamala Harris may have pushed more White people, especially those higher in racial resentment, to vote for Donald Trump. In 2016, scholars found that racial resentment was a key predictor of White people voting for Donald Trump, and that Trump capitalized on white racial animus (Banda & Cassese, 2022; Schaffner et al., 2018). Given this, participants that have higher degrees of racial resentment might provide less positive evaluations about Kamala Harris. Furthermore, there is some evidence that racial resentment influences how voters react to the identity of candidates. For example, the presidency of Barack Obama caused many White voters high in racial resentment to shift support away from Democrats and toward the Republican party (Tesler & Sears, 2010).

Given this, we expect that viewer reactions to Harris's debate performance will be influenced by their racial attitudes. Specifically:

H1: Racial resentment will be associated with more negative reactions to Harris's debate performance.

Similarly, we expect people's attitudes about gender to influence evaluations of Harris. A woman has never occupied the office of the presidency, and before 2020 had not occupied the office of vice president. This is likely, in part, due to the patriarchal structures that make it difficult for women to run and obtain political office. Scholars have identified two prominent concepts, hostile and benevolent sexism, that form the construct of ambivalent sexism (Glick & Fiske, 1996). Hostile sexism, in particular, has emerged as an important construct in the contemporary political moment (Schaffner et al., 2018). Hostile sexism views any power gained by a woman being at the man's expense (Cassese & Holman, 2018). For example, a hostile sexist would rather support unqualified men instead of qualified women (Christopher & Mull, 2006). Moreover, hostile sexists also condone violence and aggression toward women. Notably, hostile sexists were more likely to support Donald Trump in the 2016 election (Back et al., 2017; Begany & Milburn, 2002; Masser et al., 2006; Valentino et al., 2018). Given that the offices of president and vice president have traditionally been held by men, one would assume that the first woman of color vice presidential nominee would likely not only experience racism, but also sexism in evaluation of her performance. Given this research, we posit:

> H2: Hostile sexism will be associated with more negative reactions to Harris's debate performance.

Though hostile sexism and racial resentment have often been studied independently, people's attitudes about race and gender are often related. The discrimination people experience based on their multiple identities is not additive but rather interlocking, and it is important to consider the statistical interaction of identities (and prejudice) when seeking to understand the role of racism, sexism, and other oppressive systems (Bowleg, 2008). Thus, we expect racial resentment and hostile sexism to interact such that the combination of the two will most influence evaluations of Harris's debate performance:

> H3: The interaction of racial resentment and hostile sexism will influence evaluations of Harris's debate performance such that people high in each attitude will have the most negative response.

The Influence of Communication Environment

Scholars have also found that communication environments can influence the processing of political information. Specifically, homogeneous communication environments often present unbalanced information (i.e., only presenting one side of the argument) and therefore contribute to more polarized attitudes (Pariser, 2011; Putnam, 2000; Sunstein, 2009). Because these homogeneous communication environments can ossify one's prior beliefs and attitudes, they have direct implications for how someone might evaluate or make sense of political candidates' messages (Wojcieszak, 2010). These homogeneous communication environments, within the context of social watching, can contribute to one having more extreme positions and evaluations of candidates (Kim et al., 2021). Homogenous media environments can exacerbate attitude polarization when viewing a campaign debate because people are exposed to unbalanced information favoring one side over the other, because people are not encouraged to scrutinize the arguments advanced by the candidate they are supporting, because people receive social cues that reward outgroup denigration and punish statements that diminish the ingroup, and because people may have group-favorable events highlighted or recontextualized by members of their social watching community (Kim et al., 2021).

Recently, Kim et al (2021) found that individuals in homogeneous communication environments were more likely to have negative debate evaluations of the outgroup; interestingly participants within this group were not more likely to have positive evaluations of the ingroup candidates. To the contrary, heterogenous communication environments are more likely to provide balanced perspectives and has been shown to increase tolerance for outgroup candidates (Mutz, 2002, 2006). Homogeneous communication environments are more likely to foster more positive thoughts about the ingroup, while heterogeneous communication environments may foster less negative thoughts and more positive thoughts about the outgroup because of the outgroup exposure within the communication environment.

Homogenous communication environments naturally imply partisanship, since the homogeneity in question is ideological in nature. There is considerable evidence that partisans process political information in ways that are consistent with their partisan predilections (Bolsen et al, 2013; Taber & Lodge, 2006) and that this biased processing is evident in contexts of debates (Mullinix, 2015, though see Warner et al., 2020). Here, we are especially interested in the possibility that the homogenous group dynamic might further polarize evaluations of Harris among her partisan opponents, contributing to greater cross-partisan animosity. It is possible that group homogeneity will also benefit members of the in-group, such that Democrats will find Harris's performance especially strong if they are viewing among other Democrats, but our present theoretical focus is on the mechanisms that drive outgroup hostility. Thus, we hypothesize that homogeneity will influence evaluations of Harris specifically for Republicans:

> H4: Republicans in the homogeneous communication environment will provide more negative evaluations of Harris's debate performance.

Finally, as articulated above, we know viewers of debates are not unbiased. Instead, individuals view presidential debates as partisans, hoping to see their nominee outperform the opposition party in much the same way sports fans cheer on their team (Vancil & Pendell, 1984). Partisan identity thus influences how people perceive political events and behaviors (Huddy et al., 2015). Specifically, people engage in motivated reasoning such that they interpret favorable information in ways that affirm their existing beliefs and subject undesirable information to greater scrutiny (Bolsen et al., 2013;

Taber & Lodge, 2006). Regarding the experience of viewing a debate, there is considerable evidence that partisanship influences perceptions of candidate performance such that viewers tend to be more favorable to the ingroup candidate and more critical of the outgroup candidate (Cho & Ha, 2012; Mullinix, 2015). However, there is also evidence that viewers do not always exhibit partisan bias. Sometimes, viewers reward outgroup candidates for strong debate performances and punish ingroup candidates for weak ones (Schrott & Lanoue, 2013; Warner et al., 2020).

Beyond partisanship, we expect racial and gender attitudes to also filter the way viewers perceive Harris's debate performance in connection with the communication environment. Specifically, people process friendly information from ingroup cues with little scrutiny (Taber & Lodge, 2006). Thus, when those high in racial resentment and hostile sexism do chime in with prejudice-inflected commentary on Harris's performance, those who share these attitudes should be more receptive to their co-partisan's ideas. Thus:

> H5: The effect of communication environment on debate performance will be conditional on racial resentment and hostile sexism such that Republicans in the homogenous communication environment who are higher in racial resentment and hostile sexism will provide more negative evaluations of Harris's debate performance.

Method

Procedure

To test these predictions, we conducted an experiment in which people viewed the live 2020 Vice Presidential Debate between then-Senator Kamala Harris and then-Vice President Mike Pence. This debate occurred at the height of the COVID-19 pandemic, a time in which a traditional in-person debate watch would have been irresponsible. However, the rapid adoption of videoconferencing technology (e.g., Zoom) facilitated virtual debate watches and permitted the experimental manipulation of communication environments. This manipulation was achieved by controlling the partisan composition of Zoom room assignments and either enabling or restricting the chat function of the technology.

All chat conditions were monitored by a member of the research team. Each of these conditions included vibrant chat, though some members participated much more frequently than others, some were relatively silent, and it is possible that some participants ignored the chat altogether. Thus, these chat conditions represent intent-to-treat exposures, where we know the treatment (homogenous or mixed chat) was available to these participants, but we do not know the extent to which they engaged with the treatment. It is thus a conservative test of our hypotheses, though an externally valid test given people's agency to use or ignore social media in their natural environments.

Participants were contacted about the study the week of the vice-presidential debate and provided a link to a Qualtrics survey along with their invitation to participate. The link was activated approximately one hour prior to the live debate. Participants completed a pre-debate questionnaire and were then randomly assigned one of four Zoom links. Each Zoom link corresponded to one of four communication environments: no chat condition (control), mixed condition (Republicans and Democrats present), Republican only chat condition, and Democrat only chat condition. The Republican condition consisted of participants that identified as Republican or Republican leaning. Similarly, the Democratic condition consisted of participants that identified as Democratic or Democrat-leaning. The mixed condition consisted of both Republican and Democratic participants. Those who indicated no partisan preference were presented a follow-up question asking if they were forced to choose, whether they would prefer a Republican or Democrat to be president.

Participants were recruited from universities across the United States. Most were compensated for their participation by receiving course credit. Participants were able to take part in the experiment only after agreeing to the IRB consent form. This study was conducted following all specified procedures from the IRB at the lead institution.

Participants

In total, 221 people participated in the vice-presidential debate watch, a majority were White ($n = 171, 77\%$) and within 18–21 years of age ($M = 21.29$, $SD = 4.46$). Most were female ($n = 165, 75\%$). More participants identified as Democrat or leaning Democrat ($n = 137, 62\%$) compared to Republican ($n = 84, 38\%$). To account for the confounding role of partisanship, the mixed chat condition was split by partisanship. This resulted in five conditions: no chat control ($n = 55, 25\%$), homogenous chat Republican ($n = 44, 20\%$), homogenous chat Democrat ($n = 72, 33\%$), mixed chat Republican ($n = 13$,

6%), and mixed chat Democrat (*n* = 35, 16%). Though the mixed chat condition did not divide by Republican and Democrat, we split the conditions post-hoc because the outcome variables (various evaluations of Harris) are influenced by partisanship, so it was necessary to divide the mixed-chat participants into their partisan groups to generate apples-to-apples comparisons.

Measures

Racial Resentment

The measure of racial resentment was adapted from Kinder and Sanders' (1997) original scale. Historically, this measure focused on racial resentment toward African Americans, so Neville et al. (2000) created a measure that contained "colorblind" questions. This study used four items from the Kinder and Sanders' (1997) scale, e.g., "Over the past years, African Americans have gotten less than they deserve" (reversed) and two items from Neville's et al (2000) measure, e.g., "White people in the U.S. have certain advantages because of the color of their skin." (reversed). All items were measured on a 5-point scale with responses ranging from *Strongly disagree* (1) to *Strongly agree* (5). Higher scores were representative of more racial resentment ($M = 1.99$, $SD = 1.01$, $\alpha = 0.91$).

Hostile Sexism

Glick and Fiske's (1996) Ambivalent Sexism Inventory (ASI) was adapted to measure hostile sexism. The original ASI consisted of 22 items, however this study used six items to measure ambivalent sexism, three of which were adopted from the hostile sexism sub-factor, e.g., "Women seek to gain power by getting control over men." Responses ranged from *Strongly Disagree* (1) to *Strongly Agree* (5) ($M = 2.3$ $SD = 0.85$, $\alpha = 0.78$).

Harris Brand Image

Because campaign debates can be thought of as branding opportunities for candidates, a measure of candidate brand image has been developed for assessing debate performance (Bramlett, 2021). Following this procedure, participants were asked, "When thinking about the debate you just watched, what are ten things that come to mind first?" Participants would then write any ten thoughts that they had about the debate. For each thought, they were presented a follow-up question, "How would you rate that thought?" Responses to this question included, "Positive about Pence," "Negative about Pence," "Positive about Harris," "Negative about Harris," and "unrelated." This variable was recoded into two new variables, one which summed all of the thoughts that people rated as being positive about Kamala Harris ($M = 1.12$, $SD = 1.6$), and one which summed all of the thoughts people rated as being negative about Kamala Harris ($M = 0.7$, $SD = 1.23$).

Debate Performance

Participants were also asked, "thinking about the debate you just saw, please rate each candidate's performance," with Kamala Harris being evaluated on a scale from "Very Bad" = 1 to "Very Good" = 7 ($M = 5.29$, $SD = 1.61$).

Change in Feeling Toward Harris

Prior to and immediately after the debate, participants were presented with a traditional feeling thermometer question that asked them to rate Kamala Harris on a scale from 0–100 in which zero indicated that they very much disliked the person and 100 indicated that they very much liked the person ($M_{pre} = 52.08$, $SD_{pre} = 28.83$; $M_{post} = 62.04$, $SD_{post} = 32.47$).

Change in Image Perceptions of Harris

Finally, participants were presented a measure of candidate image adapted from Warner and Banwart (2016). They were asked to evaluate Harris as being: trustworthy, smart, a good leader, likable, and competent, as well as responding to the prompts "I believe Kamala Harris genuinely wants what is best for America," and "Kamala Harris understands the problems faced by people like me." Responses were recorded on a 7-point agreement scale in which 1 = "Strongly Disagree" and 7 = "Strongly Agree" ($M_{pre} = 4.78$, $SD_{pre} = 1.38$, $\alpha = 0.95$; $M_{post} = 5.15$, $SD_{post} = 1.44$, $\alpha = 0.96$).

Data Analysis

Data were analyzed in linear regression with evaluation of Harris's debate performance operationalized using (1) positive; (2) negative brand image; (3) debate performance; (4) change in feeling thermometer; and (5) change in image perceptions. Thus, each hypothesis was tested on a set of five models. The last two models were fit with pre-debate (4) feeling thermometer and (5) pre-debate image included as a statistical covariate so that theoretical variables would model variance in the post-debate score unaccounted for by pre-debate attitudes. Models were fit in five stages: first, a set of models with only partisanship was fit to establish a baseline. The second set of models added racial resentment and hostile sexism (H1 and H2). The third set of models added a product term (hostile sexism * racial resentment) to account for the interaction of these two attitudes (H3). The fourth set of models included dummy variables for the experimental conditions (H4) along with racial resentment and hostile sexism. The final set of models tested for the interaction of the homogenous Republican condition with racial resentment and hostile sexism (H5).

Results

The results of the tests for the first three hypothesis are presented in Table 10.1. There were no effects of racial resentment or hostile sexism on the brand image score (either positive or negative). At the same time, racial resentment was associated with more negative assessments of Harris's debate performance, a reduction in her feeling thermometer evaluations, and a reduction in perceptions of her image compared to pre-debate attitudes. This was true even after accounting for the influence of partisanship. The models incorporating partisanship, racial resentment, and hostile sexism accounted for 47% of variance in debate performance, an increase of 6% from the model with only partisanship. The feeling thermometer and image models improved by 3% and 1%, respectively. The estimated effect of racial resentment was larger than the effect of partisanship in all three models, suggesting that people's racial attitudes were slightly more influential in how they perceived Harris's debate performance compared to even their political party affiliation. These results generally support the first hypothesis.

The second hypothesis was not supported. After accounting for the role of partisanship and racial resentment, hostile sexism did not influence perceptions of Harris's debate performance. The third hypothesis predicted an interaction between racial resentment and hostile sexism. Figure 10.1 depicts the relationship between racial resentment and hostile sexism. As the figure illustrates, most participants in the study were on the low end of both attitudes, but there was a correlation such that those who were high in racial resentment were also more likely to be high in hostile sexism. Very few people were high in racial resentment but low in hostile sexism and, similarly, very few people were low in racial resentment but high in hostile sexism. In other words, hostile sexism and racial resentment were correlated attitudes.

Table 10.1: Effects of racial resentment and hostile sexism on evaluations of Harris's debate

	Positive Thoughts	Negative Thoughts	Performance	Feeling Thermometer	Image
Model 1: Partisanship Baseline					
Pre-Debate Score	—	—	—	0.62***	0.61***
				(0.06)	(0.05)
Partisanship	-0.32***	0.32***	-0.65***	-6.92***	-0.32***
(Republican)	(0.06)	(0.05)	(0.05)	(1.04)	(0.04)
Adjusted R^2	0.09	0.16	0.41	0.63	0.7
Model 2: Direct Effects Model					
Pre-Debate Score	—	—	—	0.57***	0.54***
				(0.06)	(0.05)
Partisanship	-0.28**	0.25***	-0.42***	-4.89***	-0.24***
(Republican)	(0.09)	(0.06)	(0.07)	(1.17)	(0.05)
Racial Resentment	-0.05	0.15	-0.64***	-5.59*	-0.27**
	(0.18)	(0.13)	(0.13)	(2.22)	(0.09)
Hostile Sexism	-0.06	0.07	-0.02	-2.35	-0.07
	(0.16)	(0.11)	(0.12)	(1.94)	(0.08)
Adjusted R^2	0.09	0.17	0.47	0.65	0.71
Model 3: Interaction Effects Model					
Pre-Debate Score	—	—	—	0.54***	0.52***
				(0.06)	(0.05)
Partisanship	-0.29***	0.25***	-0.42	-5.23***	-0.25***
(Republican)	(0.09)	(0.06)	(0.06)	(1.16)	(0.05)
Racial Resentment	0.49 (0.43)	-0.03	0.08	8.58	0.12
(RR)		(0.31)	(0.32)	(5.24)	(0.22)
Hostile Sexism (HS)	0.37 (0.34)	-0.07	0.55*	8.95*	0.24
		(0.25)	(0.26)	(4.25)	(0.18)
RR*HS	-0.22	0.07	-0.29*	-5.68**	-0.16*
	(0.15)	(0.11)	(0.12)	(1.91)	(0.08)
Adjusted R^2	0.09	0.17	0.48	0.67	0.72

Note: Regression coefficients are unstandardized with standard errors in parenthesis below. *$p<.05$, **$p<.01$, ***$p<.001$

As documented in Table 10.1 (Model 3), the data were consistent with our hypothesis that racial resentment and hostile sexism will interact to influence evaluations of Harris's debate performance. This was true for all three outcomes in which racial resentment was influential on perceptions of Harris's debate performance. The nature of the three interactions are illustrated in Figure 10.2

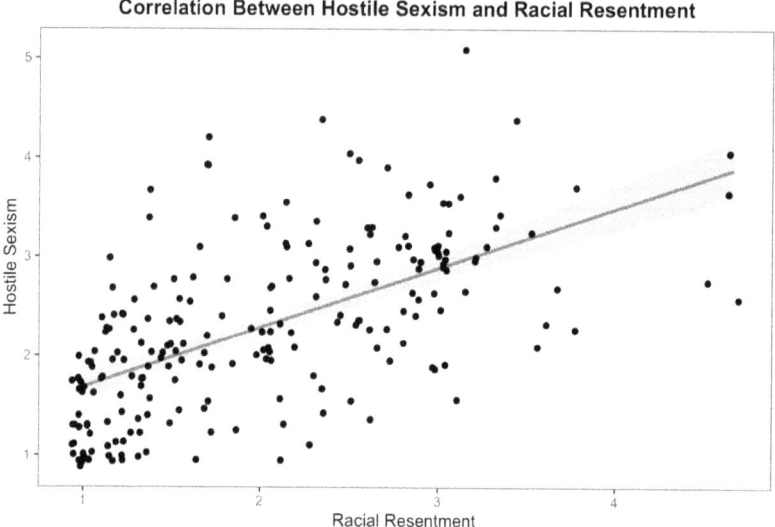

Figure 10.1: Correlation between hostile sexism and racial resentment.
Source: The authors.

(top panel). These illustrations show that racial resentment was more influential on negative perceptions of Harris's debate performance at higher levels of hostile sexism. In other words, the viewers who were high in both racial resentment and hostile sexism were most likely to say Harris did a poor job in the debate and reduce their feeling thermometer evaluations and image perceptions of her compared to their pre-debate evaluations. Conversely, racial resentment was relatively uninfluential for those low in hostile sexism.

The fourth and fifth hypothesis concerned the influence of communication environment on perceptions of Harris's debate performance and the possibility that the communication environment would interact with attitudes about racism and sexism. The direct effects model (Model 4) presented in Table 10.2 is generally consistent with the fourth hypothesis, that a homogenous communication environment would result in lower evaluations of Harris from Republicans. Republicans in this condition provided almost one additional negative thought about Harris, on average, compared to those in the control (no chat) condition. They provided one and one-quarter point lower performance evaluation of Harris's debate, and they reduced their feeling thermometer evaluations of her by more than ten points. Accounting for the experimental chat conditions increased the variance explained in feeling thermometer by 1%, in negative thoughts by 5%, and in debate performance by 11%.

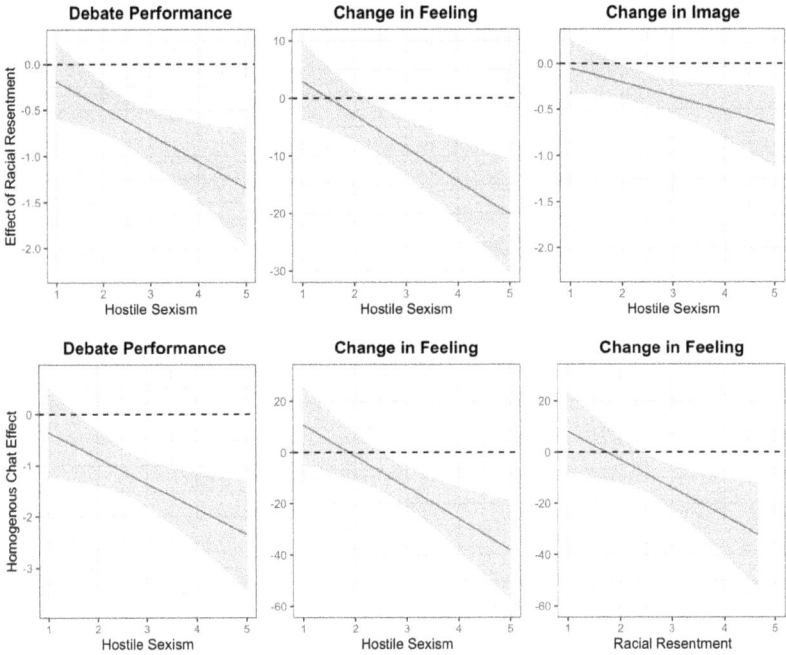

Figure 10.2: Interactions of racial resentment, hostile sexism, and digital communication environment on evaluations of Kamala Harris's debate performance.
Source: The authors.

The fifth hypothesis predicted that the influence of a homogenous chat condition on Republican evaluations of Harris would be stronger for those higher in racial resentment and hostile sexism. As reported in Table 10.2 (Models 5 and 6), there was some limited support for this hypothesis. Both racial resentment and hostile sexism exacerbated the effect of the homogenous chat condition on reductions in Harris's feeling thermometer, and hostile sexism also enhanced the effect of homogenous chat on evaluations of Harris's debate performance, though racial resentment did not. The nature of these interactions are illustrated in the bottom panel of Figure 10.2, which show that the homogenous chat condition had more negative effects on perceptions of Harris's debate performance for people higher in racial resentment and hostile sexism. Neither hostile sexism nor racial resentment moderated the influence of the homogenous chat condition on positive or negative thoughts about Harris's debate performance, nor did they influence the effect of homogenous chat on changes in Harris's image perceptions. Thus, results of the tests of H5 were mixed.

Table 8.2: Effects of communication environment on Harris's debate

	Positive Thoughts	Negative Thoughts	Performance	Feeling Thermometer	Image
Model 4: Direct Effects of Communication Environment					
Pre-Debate	—	—	—	0.55*** (0.06)	0.54*** (0.05)
Partisanship (Republican)	-0.24* (0.1)	0.14 (0.07)	-0.29*** (0.07)	-3.46* (1.34)	-0.19*** (0.05)
Racial Resentment (RR)	-0.04 (0.18)	0.06 (0.12)	-0.5*** (0.12)	-4.81* (2.25)	-0.23* (0.1)
Hostile Sexism (HS)	-0.06 (0.16)	0.08 (0.11)	-0.04 (0.11)	-2.49 (1.92)	-0.08 (0.08)
Republican Chat Condition	-0.19 (0.34)	0.83*** (0.23)	-1.23*** (0.23)	-10.2* (4.15)	-0.29 (0.17)
Democratic Chat Condition	0.16 (0.29)	-0.2 (0.21)	0.35 (0.2)	2.11 (3.62)	0.21 (0.15)
Republicans Mixed Chat	0.53 (0.5)	-0.16 (0.35)	0.82* (0.34)	-2.49 (6.14)	0.4 (0.25)
Democrats Mixed Chat	0.42 (0.35)	-0.13 (0.25)	0.12 (0.24)	2.85 (4.41)	0.21 (0.18)
Adjusted R^2	0.09	0.22	0.58	0.66	0.72
Model 5: Conditional Effects Model with Racial Resentment					
Republican Chat*RR	-0.25 (0.38)	0.27 (0.27)	-0.37 (0.26)	-10.91* (4.63)	-0.13 (0.19)
Adjusted R^2	0.09	0.22	0.58	0.67	0.72
Model 6: Conditional Effects Model with Hostile Sexism					
Republican Chat*HS	-0.13 (0.33)	0.32 (0.23)	-0.49* (0.22)	-12.12** (4.03)	-0.2 (0.17)
Adjusted R^2	0.08	0.23	0.59	0.67	0.73

Note: Model 5 and Model 6 include all elements from Model 4 but are omitted from this table for parsimony. Regression coefficients are unstandardized with standard errors in parenthesis below. *p<.05, **p<.01, ***p<.001

Discussion

This chapter sought to identify the role of racial resentment and hostile sexism in viewer evaluations of Harris's vice presidential debate performance. In doing so, it contributes to the scant literature on the effects of vice-presidential debates (McKinney et al., 2011; Wrasse et al., 2018) and answers recent calls to explicitly theorize the intersection of attitudes about race and gender in political communication (Coles & Lane, 2023; Freelon et al, 2023). We tested our hypotheses on five measures of Harris's debate performance: a performance evaluation question, change in feeling thermometer, change in image, and positive/negative thoughts generated. We found that, with regard to performance evaluation, feeling thermometer, and image, racial resentment profoundly influenced evaluations of Harris's debate performance—rivaling even partisanship for explaining variance in how viewers rated Harris's debate. Furthermore, racial resentment interacted with hostile sexism to generate this effect: those high in both racial resentment and hostile sexism were much more negative about Harris's debate compared to the (relatively few) viewers high in one attitude but not the other. Finally, the ideological composition of the debate-viewing environment functioned as an accelerant to these ideological biases. Republicans viewing the debate whilst chatting with other Republicans were much more negative about Harris, and those who were higher in racial resentment and hostile sexism were also more likely to be influenced by the ideological homogeneity of their chat environment.

The core finding of this analysis is that racial resentment and hostile sexism are attitudes that, like partisanship, bias the way communication is received. In this instance, the debate performance of the first Black, Asian American, woman vice president was rated more negatively by people higher in racial resentment even after accounting for partisanship. The effects of racial resentment and hostile sexism on candidate evaluations have been well-documented (Cassese & Holman, 2018; Schaffner et al., 2018). Recent experimental research has also documented that those higher in racial resentment were more likely to support Trump over Biden when Harris's name was included in the polling question (Filindra & Fagan, 2022), suggesting that racial resentment influenced how she was perceived. Our findings document that these attitudes not only influence how people feel about Harris, but also how they respond to communication from Harris. Thus, these attitudes are cognitive filters that should be accounted for when analyzing political communication. The impact of people's attitudes about race and gender is dynamic and unfolds over the course of a campaign as people's attitudes shift in reaction to campaign communication.

It is also significant that racial resentment and hostile sexism interact to produce this effect. The segmented view of identities, that is, that each identity has a discreate influence that can be quantified independent of the next, has been criticized for failing to understand the intersecting natures of power and identities (Bowleg, 2008). Our analysis further demonstrates the voracity of this critique. Examined independently, racial resentment was a powerful force in evolutions of Harris's debate performance, but hostile sexism contributed little to this picture. However, when the interaction of the two attitudes was considered, we found that negativity toward Harris's debate performance was concentrated amongst those high in both attitudes. We also found these attitudes to be highly correlated. Thus, it is no surprise that the role of hostile sexism was masked in the statistical analysis. Our findings here suggest that scholars should not endeavor to compare two forms of discrimination (i.e., is sexism or racism a more significant force in politics?) but rather to acknowledge that these attitudes typically align and collaborate to disadvantage both women and people from minoritized racial groups, and that this effect lands most starkly on those who hold multiple historically-oppressed identities. This finding also suggests that there may be a more fundamental ideology underlying both hostile sexism and racial resentment, perhaps something rooted in a dominant group's desire to maintain the power granted by occupying a privileged status (Cramer, 2019).

Our findings also extend work on the influence of the ideological composition of the communication environment (Hahn et al., 2018; Kim et al., 2021). Republicans who were chatting exclusively with other Republicans were more negative about Harris's debate performance by over a full point on the seven-point scale compared to Republicans in a mixed chat or control condition, they also reduced feeling thermometer evaluations of her by 10 points more than their mixed and no-chat counterparts, and they produced an additional negative thought compared to others. This corresponds to other research that finds ideologically homogenous communication environments can increase polarization (Hahn et al., 2018; Sunstein, 2009; Warner, 2017). Interestingly, the negative thoughts variable was not influenced by any of the attitudes under consideration here (beyond partisanship) but was influenced by the chat condition. This suggests that the ideologically homogenous chat may have worked, at least in part, by providing novel information to debate viewers. It is also notable that the effects of the homogenous chat were stronger for those higher in racial resentment and hostile sexism, though this effect was inconsistent. This seems to suggest that these attitudes not only influence how people receive communication, but the impact of communication environments on this information processing. However, given the inconsistency of the finding, more research is needed to confirm this possible effect.

As with any study, there are important limitations to acknowledge, each pointing the way toward future research. First, as with any campaign debate study, we are limited by the identities of our debate participants. However, attitudes about race and gender are not the only features of the contemporary political environment. Future research should pursue the interaction of various attitudes on evaluations of candidates from a variety of complex identities. Second, our manipulation of communication environment provides strong internal validity in that we were able to assign people to rooms based on their self-reported ideology and use the Zoom chat interface to monitor the conversation. However, we had no control over the content of the chat, the attention people paid to the chat, or the extent to which individuals contributed to the group discussion. Thus, our test is somewhat conservative—people were in homogenous chat environments, but was the chat homogenous? How many participants notice the chat? Our findings suggest that, at least to some extent, people were influenced by the content of the chat conditions. However, future research should probe the extent to which these communication environments are attended to by participants. Our chat conditions also raise questions about external validity. When people do second-screen debates, they tend to do so via Twitter, which has some important differences in terms of platform affordances compared to Zoom chat. Future research should pursue the various communication environments that comprise the contemporary debate viewing experience to determine how many people may be receiving additional co-partisan messaging. Finally, our convenience sample consisted largely of students. Though meta-analyses show that student and adult samples generate the same findings in debates research (Benoit et al., 2003), and though our objective is to make inference from theory to sample rather than from sample to population, thus obviating the need for a random sample (Mook, 1983), it is still possible that the effects we observed would be different in a larger and more demographically diverse sample. In particular, college students tend to be younger and in a more transient life-phase, both characteristics that may influence their cognitive engagement with politics.

Despite these limitations, our study makes important contributions to our understanding of political communication informed by the unique 2020 election. It occurred during a pandemic, which allowed for (or rather necessitated) widespread adoption of videoconferencing software. This allowed us to test the influence of digital chat on debate perceptions. Even more significantly for this study, Biden's decision to nominate Harris for vice president allowed us to test something hitherto impossible in presidential general election campaign debates—the interaction of attitudes about race and gender on candidate communication. We found that these attitudes collaborated to bias the reception of campaign messages sent by Harris. This suggests that attitudes about race and gender not only influence how candidates are perceived, but also how their communication is received.

References

Banda, K. K., & Cassese, E. C. (2022). Hostile sexism, racial resentment, and political mobilization. *Political Behavior, 44*, 1317–1335. https://doi.org/10.1007/s11109-020-09674-7

Back, H., Carroll, R., Hansen, M., & Back, E. (2017). *Chivalry or chauvinism? The impact of benevolent and hostile sexism in the 2016 U.S. presidential election.* Nordic Political Science Association.

Banwart, M. C. (2010). Gender and candidate communication: Effects of stereotypes in the 2008 election. *American Behavioral Scientist, 54*(3), 265–283. https://doi.org/10.1177/0002764210381702

Begany, J. J., & Milburn, M. A. (2002). Psychological predictors of sexual harassment: Authoritarianism, hostile sexism, and rape myths. *Psychology of Men & Masculinity, 3*(2), 119–126. https://psycnet.apa.org/doi/10.1037/1524-9220.3.2.119

Benoit, W. L., Hansen, G. J., & Verser, R. M. (2003). A meta-analysis of the effects of viewing U.S. presidential debates. *Communication Monographs, 70*(4), 335–350. https://doi.org/10.1080/0363775032000179133

Bolsen, T., Druckman, J. N., & Cook, F. L. (2013). The influence of partisan motivated reasoning on public opinion. *Political Behavior, 36*(2), 235–262. https://doi.org/10.1007/s11109-013-9238-0

Bowleg, L. (2008). When Black + lesbian + woman ≠ Black lesbian woman: The methodological challenges of qualitative and quantitative intersectionality research. *Sex Roles, 59*(5–6), 312–325. https://doi.org/10.1007/s11199-008-9400-z

Bramlett, J. C. (2021). Battles for branding: A political marketing approach to studying televised candidate debates. *Communication Quarterly, 69*(3), 280–300. https://doi.org/10.1080/01463373.2021.1944889

Cassese, E. C., & Holman, M. R. (2018). Playing the woman card: Ambivalent sexism in the 2016 U.S. Presidential race. *Political Psychology, 40*(1), 55–74. https://doi.org/10.1111/pops.12492

Christopher, A. N., & Mull, M. S. (2006). Conservative ideology and ambivalent sexism. *Psychology of Women Quarterly, 30*(2), 223–230. https://doi.org/10.1111/j.1471-6402.2006.00284.x

Cho, J., & Ha, Y. (2012). On the communicative underpinnings of campaign effects: Presidential debates, citizen communication, and polarization in evaluations of candidates. *Political Communication, 29*(2), 184–204. https://doi.org/10.1080/10584609.2012.671233

Coles, S. M., & Lane, D. (2023). Race and ethnicity as foundational forces in political communication. *Political Communication, 40*(4), 367–376. https://doi.org/10.1080/10584609.2023.2229780

Cramer, K. (2019). Understanding the role of racism in contemporary US public opinion. *Annual Review of Political Science*, 23(1), 1–17. https://doi.org/10.1146/annurev-polisci-060418-042842

Filindra, A., & Fagan, E. J. (2022). Black, immigrant, or woman? The implicit influence of Kamala Harris' vice presidential nomination on support for Biden in 2020. *Social Science Quarterly*, 103(4), 892–906. https://doi.org/10.1111/ssqu.13162

Freelon, D., Pruden, M. L., & Malmer, D. (2023). #politicalcommunicationsowhite: Race and politics in nine communication journals, 1991–2021. *Political Communication*, 40(4), 377–395. https://doi.org/10.1080/10584609.2023.2192187

Glick, P., & Fiske, S. (1996). The ambivalent sexism inventory: Differentiating hostile and benevolent sexism. *Journal of Personality and Social Psychology*, 70(3), 491–512. https://doi.org/10.1037/0022-3514.70.3.491

Hahn, K. S., Lee, H.-Y., Ha, S., Jang, S., & Lee, J. (2018). The influence of "social viewing" on televised debate viewers' political judgment. *Political Communication*, 35(2), 287–305. https://doi.org/10.1080/10584609.2017.1354947

Henry, P. J., & Sears, D. O. (2002). The symbolic racism scale. *Political Psychology*, 23(2), 253–283. https://doi.org/10.1111/0162-895x.00281

Huddy, L., Mason, L., & Aarøe, L. (2015). Expressive partisanship: Campaign involvement, political emotion, and partisan identity. *American Political Science Review*, 109(1), 1–17. https://doi.org/10.1017/s0003055414000604

Huddy, L., & Terkildsen, N. (1993). Gender stereotypes and the perception of male and female candidates. *American Journal of Political Science*, 37(1), 119–147. https://doi.org/https://doi.org/10.2307/2111526

Karpowitz, C. F., King-Meadows, T., Monson, J. Q., & Pope, J. C. (2021). What leads racially resentful voters to choose Black candidates? *The Journal of Politics*, 83(1), 103–121. https://doi.org/10.1086/708952

Kim, G., Warner, B., Kearney, C., Park, J., & Kearney, M. (2021). Social watching the 2020 presidential and vice presidential debates: The effect of ideological homogeneity and partisan identity strength. *Argumentation and Advocacy*, 57(3-4), 253–266. https://doi.org/10.1080/10511431.2021.1955446

Kinder, D. R., & Sanders, L. M. (1997). *Divided by color: Racial politics and democratic ideals*. University of Chicago Press.

Kinder, D. R., & Sears, D. O. (1981). Prejudice and politics: Symbolic racism versus racial threats to the good life. *Journal of Personality and Social Psychology*, 40(3), 414–431. https://doi.org/10.1037/0022-3514.40.3.414

Luttig, M., & Motta, M. (2017). President Obama on the ballot: Referendum voting and racial spillover in the 2014 midterm elections. *Electoral Studies*, 50, 80–90. https://doi.org/10.1016/j.electstud.2017.09.009

Masser, B., Viki, G. T., & Power, C. (2006). Hostile sexism and rape proclivity amongst men. *Sex Roles*, 54(7-8), 565–574. https://doi.org/10.1007/s11199-006-9022-2

McKinney, M. S., Rill, L. A., & Watson, R. G. (2011). Who framed Sarah Palin? Viewer reactions to the 2008 vice presidential debate. *American Behavioral Scientist*, 55(3), 212–231. https://doi.org/10.1177/0002764210392158

Mook, D. G. (1983). In defense of external invalidity. *American Psychologist, 38*(4), 379–387. https://doi.org/10.1037/0003-066x.38.4.379

Mullinix, K. J. (2015). Presidential debates, partisan motivations, and political interest. *Presidential Studies Quarterly, 45*(2), 270–288. https://onlinelibrary.wiley.com/doi/pdf/10.1111/psq.12187

Mutz, D. (2002). Cross cutting social networks: Testing democratic theory in practice. *American Political Science Review, 96*(1), 111–126. https://doi.org/10.1017/S0003055402004264

Mutz, D. (2006). *Hearing the other side: Deliberative versus participatory democracy*. Cambridge University Press.

Neville, H. A., Lilly, R., Duran, G., Lee, R., & Browne, L. (2000). Construction and initial validation of the color-blind racial attitudes scale (CoBRAS). *Journal of Counseling Psychology, 47*(1), 59–70. https://doi.org/10.1037/0022-0167.47.1.59

Pariser, E. (2011). *The filter bubble: What the internet is hiding from you*. Penguin.

Putnam, R. D. (2000). *Bowling alone: America's declining social capital*. Routledge.

Schaffner, B. F., MacWilliams, M., & Nteta, T. (2018). Understanding white polarization in the 2016 vote for president: The sobering role of racism and sexism. *Political Science Quarterly, 133*(1), 9–34. https://doi.org/10.1002/polq.12737

Schrott, P. R., & Lanoue, D. J. (2013). The power and limitations of televised presidential debates: Assessing the real impact of candidate performance on public opinion and vote choice. *Electoral Studies, 32*(4), 684–692. https://doi.org/10.1016/j.electstud.2013.03.006

Sunstein, C. R. (2009). *Going to extremes: How like minds united and divide*. Oxford University Press.

Taber, C. S., & Lodge, M. (2006). Motivated skepticism in the evaluation of political beliefs. *American Journal of Political Science, 3*(50), 775–769. https://doi.org/https://doi.org/10.1111/j.1540-5907.2006.00214.x

Tesler, M. (2012). The spillover of racialization into health care: How President Obama polarized public opinion by racial attitudes and race. *American Journal of Political Science, 56*(3), 690–704. https://doi.org/10.1111/j.1540-5907.2011.00577.x

Tesler, M., & Sears, D. O. (2010). *Obama's race: The 2008 election and the dream of a post-racial America*. University of Chicago Press.

Valentino, N. A., Wayne, C., & Oceno, M. (2018). Mobilizing sexism: The interaction of emotion and gender attitudes in the 2016 U.S. presidential election. *Public Opinion Quarterly, 82*(1), 213–235. https://doi.org/10.1093/poq/nfy003

Vancil, D., & Pendell, S. (1984). Winning presidential debates: An analysis of criteria influencing audience response. *Western Journal of Speech Communication, 48*(1), 62–74. https://doi.org/10.1080/10570318409374142

Warner, B. R. (2017). Modeling partisan media effects in the 2014 U.S. midterm elections. *Journalism & Mass Communication Quarterly, 11*(3), 647–669. https://doi.org/10.1177/1077699017712991

Warner, B. R., & Banwart, M. C. (2016). A multifactor approach to candidate image. *Communication Studies, 67*(3), 259–297. https://doi.org/10.1080/10510974.2016.1156005

Warner, B., McKinney, M., Bramlett, J., Jennings, F., Funk, M. (2020). Reconsidering partisanship as a constraint on the persuasive effects of debates. *Communication Monographs*, 87(2), 137–157. https://doi.org/10.1080/03637751.2019.1641731

Wrasse, J. W., Schill, D., & Kirk, R. (2018). Meeting the commander-in-waiting: Undecided voters and the 2016 vice-presidential debate. *Argumentation and Advocacy*, 54(1–2), 139–158. https://doi.org/10.1080/00028533.2018.1446871

Wojcieszak, M. (2010). 'Don't talk to me': Effects of ideologically homogeneous online groups and politically dissimilar offline ties on extremism. *New Media & Society*, 30(5), 316–327. https://doi.org/10.1177/0270467610380011

Section IV
POLITICAL COMMUNICATION STRATEGIES

· 11 ·

SHARED BLINDNESS IN FILTER BUBBLES: POLITICAL MESSAGES IN SOCIAL MEDIA

Yanjun Zhao

In the past decade, the growth of artificial intelligence (AI) has been exponential. AI is rapidly transforming numerous facets of daily life, including image recognition, medical diagnosis, voice recognition, music composition, business forecasting, and self-driving vehicles (Brockman, 2019). In many cases, AI is making business decisions more affordable in the same way computers have made mathematical calculations more economical (Agrawal et al., 2022).

AI techniques are powerful tools, but they can also be problematic and even hazardous (Cross, 2020). While many people are optimistic about the potential of data and AI, there are concerns regarding their potential dangers (Trammel & Cullen, 2021). For instance, Kissinger et al. (2021) argue that the distinctly different thinking of AI could lead to greater unpredictability and danger in the environment. With the phenomenal development of AI and its application in the media landscape, it is crucial to consider its social impacts (Broussard et al., 2019; Iliadis, 2018; McDowell, 2014).

The term "filter bubbles" describes a phenomenon in which individuals are constantly presented with information and opinions that align with their existing beliefs, thereby reinforcing those views (Pariser, 2011a). This is primarily due to social media platforms utilizing AI algorithms to tailor content for each user based on their previous behavior. This machine learning algorithm tracks users' history, location, and other factors to generate personalized environments for social media users (Southern, 2020). This practice has consequences for both what people see—and do not see—in their social media experience. The prevalence of these personalized information bubbles can lead to the spread of misinformation and further entrench people's pre-existing beliefs, rather than exposing them to diverse perspectives and information. Consequently, this can result in the creation of online communities that are isolated from opposing viewpoints, perpetuating false narratives and increasing divisive discourse.

This chapter is a call for a critical eye for AI ethical issues with a focus on the algorithms' impact on social media content. This chapter aims to answer three fundamental questions related to AI and its impact on society: (1) How does AI impact content environment?; (2) How does AI influence people?; and (3) What could help? Specifically, the first question will cover how AI works and its impact on messages. The second area will cover the algorithm's influence on people and its threat to democracy. The third topic will cover various proposals to address the issue.

How Does AI Control Content

The Function of Social Media AI

In today's highly competitive and dynamic market, media organizations must understand their customers to attract and retain them (Verma, 2022). To achieve this, many media platforms use AI technology to engage social media users. On platforms like Facebook and YouTube, AI algorithms are employed to analyze user data, identify patterns, and gain insights into social media behavior and usage patterns. Algorithms serve as a foundational element of AI, enabling it to process and analyze large amounts of data. However, AI goes beyond simple data analysis and is designed to make complex decisions to maximize market potential.

In this process, social media users are often passive and unaware of what is being filtered out. Holone (2016) introduced the concept of "Gravitational Black Holes of Information" to illustrate the challenges of escaping the influence of filters. As individuals are drawn closer to the gravitational center, their preexisting beliefs are further reinforced by the information that is presented to them, causing them to become increasingly trapped in a "black hole" of their perspectives.

A central promise of AI is its large-scale categorization and fast thinking speed, but AI needs human ethics (Penn, 2018). For example, Alphabet's YouTube uses AI to improve its service. Tech giants like YouTube have big advantages with vast amounts of data and leading computing power. Machines are trained with huge databases to recognize patterns. AI enables the company to predict people's preferences with data from past viewing history. In turn, YouTube can customize its offerings more precisely. For example, YouTube's recommendation system is among the most advanced in the industry, relying on Deep Neural Networks to suggest content that keeps viewers engaged (Covington et al., 2016; Lewis, 2018). The algorithm identifies the 20 most relevant videos for each user based on various criteria, such as their past viewing behavior, as well as factors like clicks, watch time, likes and dislikes, comments, freshness, and upload frequency. The "up next" feature, powered by AI, enables personalized and continuous viewing, making it easy for users to stay on the platform for extended periods. However, as with any technology, it is crucial to consider the potential ethical concerns and implications that may arise.

Although the specific algorithms used by YouTube to shape users' experiences are not transparent, studies suggest that the site's recommendation algorithm promotes divisive and conspiratorial content (Cosentino, 2020). Guillaume Chaslot, an engineer with experience working on the algorithm, has criticized the skewed priorities of YouTube's algorithms, with advertising revenue taking precedence over other considerations (Lewis, 2018). As a result, the algorithm has been updated to maximize users' engagement with the site, potentially at the expense of promoting credible and diverse content.

AI's Impact on Messages

Social media AI tends to create information bubbles, which feed people what they want, not necessarily what they need. This is akin to people eating treats such as candy or ice cream, which are tasty but do not provide nutrition. The same is true for people's information intake. Exposure to diverse perspectives would make them more informed citizens. It is needed because it is essential rather than just desirable. These algorithms have two potential impacts on the messages on social media: (1) the diversity of the content (in terms of the lack of diverse perspectives); and (2) the quality of the content (in terms of the potential for extremism and disinformation to be amplified).

Diversity of Perspectives

Social media AI algorithms cater to people's preferences, rather than presenting them with a diverse range of perspectives. The social media experience is analogous to a person joining Twitter and then following only those magazines or accounts that share their political views. As a result, they are likely to be bombarded with messages that reaffirm their preexisting worldview. It's like giving someone their favorite candy every day. While convenient and addictive, this approach provides a narrow range of nutrition and is unhealthy for a person's development. It makes them blind to other perspectives and limits their ability to see beyond their bubble.

In 2016, Holone suggested that the filter bubble can be thought of as an unseen in-car GPS that not only suggests the best route to take but also takes over the car's controls, leading the driver to their perceived destination. However, an automated system that doesn't give users the chance to pause and consider the implications of automation could result in misuse, annoyance, and even accidents.

The primary problem is the invisibility of the algorithms. Social media users are unaware of the content being concealed by social media. It is like the driver thought he is driving the car, but it is controlled by a hidden algorithm. Additionally, the impact of the algorithms on the quality of information on social media remains unknown to users. As noted by Pariser (*Time*, 2011), the fact that people do not even know what is being blocked will cloud people's ability to see the big picture and have an informed opinion.

Social media has increasingly become the information provider for news, opinions, and civic information (Bakshy et al., 2015). At the same time, it is increasingly challenging for people to get balanced exposure to information with social importance (Newton, 2016). Pariser (2011b) highlighted a critical difference between human editors and algorithms in terms of news coverage. For instance, stories about celebrities received more coverage than stories about the war in Afghanistan on social media platforms, although the latter is much more significant. While human editors understand the importance of this, algorithms struggle to discern social relevance. It is widely acknowledged the war that our soldiers are fighting on our behalf is more crucial than celebrity gossip.

Over time, the lack of exposure to diverse information can lead to the creation of "information cocoons" (Wu, 2021, p. 800). According to a recent study on college students' decision-making regarding their majors (Wu, 2021), many students are not aware of the filter bubbles that exist in their daily media consumption. The strength of these bubbles is related to their social connections, with those having fewer social relations experiencing more powerful cocoons. As a result, students may not receive the career information and advice they need, leading to uninformed major and career choices. The filter bubble, therefore, has a significant impact on students' academic and professional trajectories.

Similarly, social media algorithms block political information, especially for those who have few social relations. These algorithms have the power to control exactly how people get information, creating a different information environment for each person. For instance, a review of the empirical evidence about the impact of algorithms found that social media experience increased polarization in every age group (Van Bavel et al., 2021). Another interdisciplinary study by scholars from technology, business, and human rights analyzed evidence on social media's role in polarization and found the consequences of social media algorithms include less trust in fellow citizens, lack of respect for the presidential election, and political violence on January 6, 2021 (Barrett et al., 2021).

Facebook has come under fire for its role in political campaigns for failing to check disinformation and spread conspiracy theories from the extremist fringes (Lauer, 2021). Bradshaw and Howard's research (2019) on computational propaganda identified many disinformation campaigns on social media, and Facebook was the top platform.

With an unprecedented share of the world's media attention, Facebook has a responsibility to ensure that users who come to it for news are presented with truthful information (Newton, 2016). In response to this concern, Facebook changed its newsfeed algorithm in June 2016 to prioritize "meaningful" stories, which include posts from friends and family, as well as content that users frequently engage with (Sunstein, 2017).

Facebook has transcended beyond being just a social network. It has become the go-to platform for millions of people seeking to stay informed about current events. By taking proactive measures to mitigate political polarization, Facebook can foster greater trust among its users over the long term (Bleiberg & West, 2015).

Social media serves as a public forum for exchanging ideas, but even hashtags that aim to assist users in locating information on a specific subject can lead to distinct information bubbles. For instance, Democrats tend to use hashtags like "#ACA" and "#blacklivesmatter," while Republicans tend to use "#Obamacare" and "#alllivesmatter" (Sunstein, 2017). While social media platforms are effective at connecting people with similar beliefs, they fail to provide space for opposing opinions to engage in constructive debate (Newton, 2016). The filter bubble may shed light on the surprise at the outcome of the 2016 presidential election. Similarly, for the 2020 election, the filter bubbles explain the anger and even political violence in the 2020 election (Lauer, 2021). When social media encourages exaggerations and hate speech, Trump's Twitter account provided a feeling of belonging for the political extremists which resulted in the January 6 storming of the U.S. Capitol (Kirk & Schill, 2024).

Quality of Social Media Content: Polarization

The filter bubble is not just about restricting the exposure of media users to diverse perspectives. It also has a reinforcing effect on their beliefs and opinions. This reinforcing effect is commonly referred to as an "echo chamber" (Colleoni et al., 2014). Opinions get strengthened in the echo chamber because of two reasons. Firstly, when people are repeatedly exposed to information that supports their existing views, it reinforces those views and makes them appear to be the norm. Secondly, when people are shielded from opposing viewpoints, it can limit their critical thinking and lead them to believe that their opinions are the prevailing opinions in the political arena. As a result, the echo chamber can lead to an illusion of consensus among media users and make it challenging to consider alternative perspectives.

The proliferation of heavily biased news on social media has eroded the trust and credibility of news sources (Newton, 2016). The algorithms employed by social media platforms tend to reinforce users' pre-existing political biases, leading to a potential avoidance of exposure to opposing viewpoints. Research by the *Pew Research Center* (Gottfried, 2021) suggests that Republicans hold more negative attitudes toward journalists and the news media as a whole. Consequently, they are increasingly turning to non-mainstream outlets as their primary source of political news and information. For example, One America News Network (OAN), launched in 2013, saw a spike in viewership as it praised former President Donald Trump and spread his unfounded claims of election fraud (Shiffman, 2021). The OAN website garnered 8 million monthly visits from desktop and mobile users, peaking at 15 million from November to January. Similarly, the Gateway Pundit, the American far-right fake news website, attracted extremists with false claims about the 2020 election like the errors in the vote count and candidate scandals (Litke, 2020). This trend indicates a growing polarization in media consumption and highlights the need for more objective and trustworthy sources of information to bridge the ideological divide.

To capture and maintain the attention of their audience, social media platforms rely on AI algorithms that often prioritize infotainment, sensationalism, and political cynicism. However, these algorithms can be influenced by the biases of their designers and the data used to train them. Shockingly, research has revealed that AI systems can develop prejudices against certain groups, such as black people and women, simply by analyzing internet posts (Caliskan et al., 2017). This highlights the potential for these systems to perpetuate harmful biases and emphasizes the need for increased awareness and oversight to ensure that AI is employed in a just and ethical manner.

Research has shown that YouTube's AI algorithm is having a detrimental impact on the quality of content on the platform. For instance, a crowdsourced study (McCroskey & Geurkink, 2021) with more than 37,000 participants from 91 countries found that YouTube recommends content that is harmful, divisive, and baseless. This study gathered 3,362 reports from YouTube users who regretted viewing videos with terrible content recommended by the algorithm. A lot of the reports involved political extremism, hate speech, or conspiracy misinformation. For example, a person watching videos about the U.S. military was recommended a misogynistic video and a person who watched a video about software rights was recommended a video about gun rights.

Another criticism is that YouTube could force users to be exposed to unhealthy messages like hate speeches and explicit videos of children (Kiros, 2022). In fact, the *MIT Technology Review* concluded that YouTube's algorithm controls 70% of the messages people see. Even when users clicked the "dislike" button, a similar video would still be recommended for them.

According to an AI scientist with access to the algorithm, the system fails to prioritize truthful, balanced, or democratic content, instead favoring hate speech, political extremism, and conspiracy theories/disinformation (Lewis, 2018). These effects are particularly concerning, as they have negative consequences for individuals exposed to such content, including children who may be subjected to disturbing material.

In short, this section covers how AI algorithms shape social media content, examining their impact on both the diversity and quality of content in the 2020 election. The algorithms favor similarity over diversity and promote extreme and often harmful content filled with hatred, anger, and violence.

Algorithms' Impact on People

When social media algorithms cater to users' selective exposure, showing them only what reinforces their existing views, it creates a spiral of bias. It leads users toward a dead end of extreme perspectives. Such an information environment can result in a reduction of meaningful discussions among people with different viewpoints in the public forum.

This polarization of public opinion is more than just a division of viewpoints, but rather a significant polarization that can have far-reaching and negative effects on society as a whole. Therefore, it is crucial to ensure that AI is used ethically and transparently to encourage meaningful discussions across different viewpoints.

According to Bruns (2019), the consequences of the "filter bubble" are not as overt as being indoctrinated into a cult and losing touch with reality. Instead, individuals with the strongest attachment to extremist beliefs, ranging from anti-vaccine and anti-climate change activists to right-wing Trump supporters, remain active in mainstream media to at least know what their enemy says. In this situation, the filter bubble does not exist. Still, the filter bubble can affect those who are less invested in their beliefs. For example, people with personal experience of vaccine reactions might be different than those who did not have side effects. Consequently, individuals who have experienced vaccine-related complications might evaluate social media content about COVID-19 virus more carefully than those without.

People tend to gravitate toward people who share their beliefs and values, which can create an "echo chamber" effect (Nyhan, 2014). A *Pew* report (Michell et al., 2014) further confirms that people's preferred sources of news and political information are highly correlated with their political views. The data shows that half of the conservative respondents named Fox News as their primary source of news, while liberal respondents were more likely to name CNN (15%), NPR (13%), MSNBC (12%), and *The New York Times* (10%) as their main sources of information on politics and current events.

While the *Pew* study examines how people actively choose their preferred news sources, the dynamics of social media are different. Instead of making active choices, social media users are presented with content that is calculated and predicted by AI algorithms. These algorithms have the power to control what users see and effectively block out perspectives that do not align with their pre-existing beliefs. This results in a limitation of people's exposure to diverse perspectives, which is a disrespect to people's right to be well informed.

This lack of exposure to multiple perspectives can lead to a narrow-minded and biased view of the world. It can also cause further divisions and anger among individuals, as they are not provided with a well-rounded view of different opinions and experiences. This limitation of information can have serious negative consequences for individuals and society as a whole.

Nagal (2022) points out that discussions among individuals who hold opposing views can have a positive impact on the movement of opinions toward the middle ground. In contrast, discussions that take place within groups limited to one side of an issue often serve to reinforce and even increase the distance between groups. This group polarization is particularly prevalent in internet discussion groups where individuals with extreme views often congregate. Examples of such groups include those frequented by racists, gun fanatics, and suppliers of bomb recipes (Nagal, 2022).

Hundreds of years ago, access to information was difficult but selection was not an issue. Now, with the flood of information made available on the Internet, it is overwhelming to make a sensible choice of information to get a balanced view of the world. The public space where most people are well-informed about primary issues is shrinking, replaced by fragments of people with similar minds (Nagal, 2022). This trend is worrisome, as it can lead to individuals becoming isolated from diverse opinions and a narrowing of public discourse. In the 2020 election, Trump supporters predominantly followed conservative news outlets or influencers, while those who supported Joe Biden might have primarily engaged with liberal media sources. This narrow exposure reduces people's critical thinking and empathy. It also causes difficulty in understanding complex issues. For instance, topics such as healthcare, immigration, and racial justice were often framed in a binary manner, neglecting the nuances and complexities inherent in these issues.

Debate on AI's Impact

There are reasons to support algorithms in social media. In many cases, personalized content is beneficial (Holone, 2016). The algorithm helps to connect like-minded individuals and provides a sense of contentment. Social media

AI enhances users' overall satisfaction and comfort. However, the significance of technological advancements should not solely be measured by their ability to make people entertained. Instead, the value lies in the way these innovations enable people to have new experiences, ultimately enriching their lives (Nagal, 2022).

Another argument is that social media algorithms offer users the ability to select content that matches their interests and beliefs. However, this selective exposure is a significant factor contributing to the growing division among people (Self, 2016). The confirmation bias phenomenon, where individuals actively seek out and remember information that supports their existing opinions, is prevalent (American Psychology Association, 2018). When social media algorithms create information bubbles for users, it reinforces bias among like-minded individuals. Furthermore, repeatedly sharing biased content can lead to it being perceived as normal and justifiable. Even when exposed to diverse views, individuals may choose to gravitate towards content that confirms their existing beliefs, disregarding any information that challenges them.

While confirmation bias is a contributing factor to the polarization and division of society, social media algorithms also play a significant role in shaping individuals' information environments. A study conducted by Facebook revealed that the news feed algorithm reduces politically diverse content by 5% for conservatives and 8% for liberals (Bakshy et al., 2015). Newton (2016) argues that the algorithm's impact is just as significant as a user's personal choice of which links to click on their news feed. This finding is supported by Neely's (2021) study on Facebook during the 2020 presidential election, which showed a positive correlation between partisan intensity and politically motivated avoidance. Those individuals identifying as liberals or conservatives were notably more inclined to engage in politically motivated unfriending compared to moderates.

Impact on Political Discourse

The political conversations in recent years have highlighted a clear divide among people. Within society, various groups have developed distinct and contrasting interpretations of the same issue, such as "pro-life" and "pro-choice," each using positive terms to validate their stance, which makes discourse and deliberation arduous. This same logic applies to the terms "climate change" and "global warming." Social media often provides individuals with substantial support for their opinions without facing counterarguments, leading them to be less receptive to and appreciative of opposing viewpoints.

Evidence on political discourse shows how the algorithms divide people. According to the *Pew Research Center* (Anderson & Auxier, 2020), the percentage of social media users who find it stressful to discuss politics with those who hold opposing views has increased from 59% (2016) to 70% (2020). In addition, 55% of social media users in the U.S. feel exhausted by the number of political posts, a significant increase from 37% in 2016. The feeling of being "worn out" has increased more among Republicans, from 37% (2016) to 63% (2020). This shows the irony made by algorithms. People do not get diverse information, but they feel worn out by political posts.

The algorithm has the potential to amplify extreme content, hate speech, and misinformation, as evidenced by a 2019 *Pew Research Center* survey (Anderson & Auxier, 2019). The survey found that 85% of Americans believed that political discourse in the U.S. had become more negative, less respectful, less fact-based, and less issue focused. This has significantly impacted the nation's political discourse. Strikingly, the survey found that a majority of Americans expressed concerns (76%), confusion (70%), embarrassment (69%), and exhaustion (67%) due to Trump's comments.

The dangers of politicians using "heated or aggressive" language are widely recognized, as per *Pew's* survey in 2019. A significant majority (78%) believe that such language directed towards specific individuals or groups by elected officials increases the risk of violence against them. This belief is more prevalent among Democrats (and leaners) than Republicans (and leaners). In the 2020 election, hate speech and aggressive messages proliferated on social media platforms. When social media AI feeds these messages to far-right extremists, it creates an illusion for them that all these extreme opinions are mainstream opinions. The more messages they see on media, the more support they got. The result is the political violence in U.S. Capitol on January 6, 2021.

A closer look at the political discourse provides insights into political polarization. The tone of political debates in America is widely criticized (Anderson & Auxier, 2019). Certain language and tactics are considered undoubtedly unacceptable; a significant majority (81%) believe that it is never justifiable for politicians to intentionally mislead people about their opponent's record. Other tactics that are considered unacceptable include criticizing their opponent's physical appearance, talking over their opponent during a debate, ridiculing them, and using insulting terms such as "evil," "stupid," or "anti-American."

The division and polarization among people, formed by social media information cocoons, have an impact on the climate for discourse around the country. The *Pew* survey (Anderson & Auxier, 2019) presented participants with a scenario where they are attending a social gathering with individuals who hold varying viewpoints about Trump. Among those who approve of Trump's job performance, around 57% would express their views about Trump when conversing with people who do not like him. However, only 43% of those who disapprove of Trump would share their opinions when discussing with a group of Trump supporters. The division among people makes it harder to exchange opinions.

The same concern was also echoed in another poll by Public Agenda/ *USA Today* (Page, 2019). According to the poll, a majority of Americans believe that the country is heading in the wrong direction and that division is the cause of this anxiety and gridlock. Social media are exacerbating these divisions for their benefit, to the detriment of ordinary people. The negativity in media is more likely to sell than positive news. Overall, a large percentage of people think that political leaders, social media, and journalism are mostly destructive influences.

The majority of people believe that social media companies have an obligation to eliminate "offensive" content, with 66% agreeing and 32% disagreeing (Anderson & Auxier, 2019). However, the public does not trust social media companies to make judgments on which offensive content should be removed from their platforms. The 2020 election witnessed how hashtags came to life when online extremist fueled the Capitol Hill insurrection with posts containing false information about voting procedures, unsubstantiated claims of election fraud, and incitement to violence. As mentioned by Kirk and Schill (2024), hate was effectively employed during the 2020 election. A big portion of the public developed political avoidance of social media. This lack of trust in social media is rooted in the influence of these platforms on the democratic process. Algorithms could potentially shape public opinion, amplify polarization, and undermine the integrity of electoral processes.

Impact on Democracy

Democracy is facing a big challenge. Approximately 50% of American adults admit to no longer engaging in political or election-related conversations with someone (Jurkowitz & Mitchell, 2020). Democracy requires a cultural environment in which people actively engage with the viewpoints of their peers, and people must possess a comprehension of alternative perspectives (Sunstein, 2017). Social media has the potential to introduce individuals to novel and diverse perspectives that they might not have previously encountered.

The root of the issue with social media is that it is used for entertainment rather than enlightenment. Social media companies prioritize profits over being accountable. Their social algorithms enable users to have an enjoyable media experience, free from any unwanted or distracting content (Pariser, 2015).

In sum, social media algorithm makes people less informed, more biased, and less willing to participate in political discussions. AI algorithm contributes to the opinion divide and anger among people. The current social media ecosystem is not beneficial for democracy. In the worst scenario, AI could be a game-changer for humanity.

What Could Help?

AI-influenced social media creates an irony in communication: the more content available, the more divided people are. Developing media literacy in media users will provide people with a better insight into the information environment. To understand the impact of AI on the media landscape, the public shall be aware of how social media algorism is framing the information environment.

The task is two-fold. First, citizens shall develop critical thinking skills so they will not be victims of skewed media presentations due to social media AI. Second, strategies are necessary to tackle the problem and foster a more balanced media environment.

To develop critical thinking and media literacy, social institutions shall encourage the public to identify the information cocoons and recognize the potential for algorithms to intensify societal segmentation and polarization. Citizens need to get updates on ongoing efforts to combat fake news and increase the quality and diversity of media content. (Lewis, 2018). Without public awareness, the problem will continue to grow.

Calls for government regulation of social media have arrived. A survey by *USA Today* found that 74% of respondents believe that social media contributes to a destructive public discourse (Page, 2019). More than a third of the respondents expressed support for increased government regulation of social media to mitigate its negative impact.

Regulating social media poses a complicated challenge for governments. Predictive algorithms, which are used to customize the content, take advantage of the freedom of speech, and U.S. law has yet to determine how far the rights of speakers should extend in public forums. The Supreme Court has firmly rejected the attempt to force newspapers to carry diverse expressions of opinion. Nevertheless, it's better to be "Socrates dissatisfied than a pig satisfied" (Nagal, 2022). While social media algorithms provide the comfort of pleasant messages, life should encompass purpose, meaning, dignity, choice, critical thinking, open-mindedness, and freedom in decision-making. True happiness goes beyond merely seeking comfort in a bubble of familiarity.

It is still important to let social media companies be aware of their responsibility for democracy. If they take this responsibility seriously, they have the potential to develop algorithms that foster mutual understanding among people rather than further division.

Breaking information cocoons has been a topic of discussion, and one idea is to encourage access to divergent opinions. In his book "Public.com," Sunstein (2017) suggests listing links to opposing viewpoints on websites, particularly political sites with controversial topics (Nagal, 2022). For example, a website about gay rights groups could provide a link to a website of religious fundamentalists and vice versa. It might also be worthwhile to consider guidelines that ensure more links and hyperlinks, thus enabling people to achieve viewpoint-neutral media exposure.

Another way to break information cocoons is to reverse the steps. Piao et al. (2023) analyzed the mechanisms of the AI algorithms. Based on their empirical findings, they provided a suggestion to help individual users opt out of AI prediction control. If online users give the algorithm negative feedback on the recommended content, the algorithms will stop the perspective narrowing of the messages. Social media users can also escape from the cocoon by exploring other perspectives occasionally. This will limit the role algorithms play in predicting people's preferences.

There are other possible ways for media providers to create arenas for meaningful discourse, where the audience can hear from voices with various perspectives and engage in open discussions. Some newer platforms like TikTok and Snapchat could provide a "open mind" function to have the potential to provide a balanced viewpoint on any topic (although they also rely on algorithmic content recommendations). Additionally, formats like podcasts even generative AI can help diversity peoples' media diets and broaden their understanding of different viewpoints.

The future of the filter bubble issue depends on several factors. Social media users must be equipped with media literacy and skills to navigate and un-train the algorithms. Social media companies ought to take the responsibility to provide balanced information. And governments should take more measures to ensure that social media users are not simply hearing an echo of their voice (Sunstein, 2017). Exposing individuals to diverse perspectives can guard against fragmentation, polarization, and extremism. All these efforts will encourage meaningful discourse among people.

Conclusion

In summary, social media predictive AI reinforces biases, impacts message diversity and quality, decreases discourse quality, and is a threat to democracy, as shown in the 2020 presidential election.

This analysis of AI used by social media reveals three illusions: (1) media users may have the illusion of actively choosing messages, but in reality, their active choices are controlled by media technology; (2) media users may have the illusion of accessing a vast amount of information, but in fact, they only receive a narrow range of perspectives; and (3) media users may have the illusion of obtaining satisfactory information, but in reality, the algorithms hinder the development of an open mind.

Algorithms for predictive analysis pose a trap to netizens. When faced with a vast amount of information online, media users tend to choose only what they want to see. The algorithms will feed them with content that confirms their existing beliefs and opinions, narrowing their horizon. We can see from the 2020 election that many people are already cocooning themselves, with the illusion that they are active media users.

In 2020 election, social media algorithms failed to promote open-mindedness. It is time for media users to get out of their online cocoons and gain a better understanding of the world's reality. Technology shall not be the gatekeeper of the social media information environment, and human beings shall not let AI algorithms be a threat to democracy.

In conclusion, AI is a powerful tool that, if not controlled, could pose a danger to society. The filter bubble created by social media has the potential to further erode people's capacity for open-mindedness and empathy. The 2020 election has shown numerous cases where citizens became the victims of the algorithm. It is therefore urgent that people develop media literacy to safeguard future of elections. By gaining greater insight into how these algorithms operate and the consequences they produce, people will be better equipped to shape their information future.

References

Agrawal, A., Gans, J., & Goldfarb, A. (2022). *Prediction machines*. Harvard Business Review.
American Psychological Association (2018). Why we're susceptible to fake news – and how to defend against it. https://www.apa.org/news/press/releases/2018/08/fake-news
Anderson, M., & Auxier, B. (2019). Public highly critical of state of political discourse in the U.S. *Pew Research Center*. https://www.pewresearch.org/politics/2019/06/19/the-climate-for-discourse-around-the-country-on-campus-and-on-social-media/
Anderson, M., & Auxier, B. (2020). 55% of U.S. social media users say they are 'worn out' by political posts and discussions. *Pew Research Center*. https://www.pewresearch.org/fact-tank/2020/08/19/55-of-u-s-social-media-users-say-they-are-worn-out-by-political-posts-and-discussions/
Bakshy, E., Messing, S. & Lada, A. (2015). Exposure to ideologically diverse news and opinion on Facebook. *Science*, 348(6239) 1130–1132. https://doi.org/10.1126/science.aaa1160
Barrett, P, Hendrix, J., & Sims, G. (2021). *Fueling the fire: How social media intensifies U.S. political polarization*. NYU Stern Center for Business and Human Rights. https://bhr.stern.nyu.edu/polarization-report-page
Bleiberg, J., & West, D. (2015). *Political polarization on Facebook*. Brookings Institution. https://www.brookings.edu/blog/techtank/2015/05/13/political-polarization-on-facebook/
Bradshaw, S., & Howard, P.N. (2019). *The global disinformation disorder: 2019 global inventory of organized social media manipulation*. Project on Computational Propaganda. https://demtech.oii.ox.ac.uk/wp-content/uploads/sites/12/2019/09/CyberTroop-Report19.pdf
Brockman, J. (2019). *Possible minds: Twenty-five ways of looking at AI*. Penguin.
Broussard, M., Diakopoulos, N., Guzman, A. L., Abebe, R., Dupagne, M., & Chuan, C.-H. (2019). Artificial intelligence and journalism. *Journalism & Mass Communication Quarterly*, 96(3), 673–695. https://doi.org/10.1177/1077699019859901
Bruns, A. (2019). Filter bubble. *Internet Policy Review*, 8(4), 1–14. https://doi.org/10.14763/2019.4.1426
Caliskan, A., Bryson, J. & Narayanan, A. (2017, April 14). Semantics derived automatically from language corpora contain human-like biases. *Science*, 356(6334): 183–186. https://doi.org/10.1126/science.aal4230
Colleoni, E., Rozza, A., & Arvidsson, A. (2014). Echo chamber or public sphere? Predicting political orientation and measuring political homophily in Twitter using big data. *Journal of Communication*, 64(2): 317–332. https://doi.org/10.1111/jcom.12084
Cosentino, G. (2020). *Social media and the post-truth world order: The global dynamics of disinformation*. Palgrave Macmillan.

Covington, P., Adams, J., & Sargin, E. (2016, September). *Deep neural networks for YouTube recommendations*. Proceedings of the 10th ACM Conference on Recommender Systems, 191–198. https://doi.org/10.1145/2959100.2959190

Cross, T. (2020, June 11). *An understanding of AI's limitations is starting to sink in*. The Economist. https://www.economist.com/technology-quarterly/2020/06/11/an-understanding-of-ais-limitations-is-starting-to-sink-in

Gottfried, J. (2021). *Republicans less likely to trust their main news source if they see it as 'mainstream'; Democrats more likely*. Pew Research Center. https://pewrsr.ch/3jwf7lh

Holone, H. (2016). The filter bubble and its effect on online personal health information. *Croatian Medical Journal. 57*(3): 298–301. https://doi.org/10.3325%2Fcmj.2016.57.298

Iliadis, A. (2018). Algorithms, ontology, and social progress. *Global Media & Communication, 14*(2), 219–230. https://doi.org/10.1177/1742766518776688

Jurkowitz, M., & Mitchell, A. (2020). A sore subject: Almost half of Americans have stopped talking politics with someone. *Pew Research Center*. https://pewrsr.ch/37YU0PY

Kirk, R., & Schill, D. (2024). Sophisticated hate stratagems: Unpacking the era of distrust. *American Behavioral Scientist, 68*(1), 3–25. https://doi.org/10.1177/00027642211005002

Kiros, H. (2022). Hated that video? YouTube's algorithm might push your another just like it. *MIT Technology Review*. https://www.technologyreview.com/2022/09/20/1059709/youtube-algorithm-recommendations/

Kissinger, H., Schmidt, E., & Huttenlocher, D. (2021). *The age of AI*. Little, Brown and Company.

Lauer D. (2021). Facebook's ethical failures are not accidental; they are part of the business model. *AI and Ethics, 1*(4), 395–403. https://doi.org/10.1007/s43681-021-00068-x

Lewis, P. (2018, February 2). Fiction is outperforming reality: how YouTube's algorithm distorts the truth. *The Guardian*. https://www.theguardian.com/technology/2018/feb/02/how-youtubes-algorithm-distorts-truth

Litke, E. (2020, November 10). No, Rock County did not have a glitch that stole votes from Trump. *PolitiFact*. https://www.politifact.com/factchecks/2020/nov/10/eric-trump/no-rock-county-did-not-have-glitch-stole-votes-tru/

McDowell, Z. J. (2014). The machine question: Critical perspectives on AI, robots, and ethics. *New Media & Society, 16*(6), 1041–1043. https://doi.org/10.1177/1461444814535723d

Michell, A., Gottfried, J., Kiley, J., & Matsa, K. (2014). *Political polarization & media habits*. Pew Research Center. http://pewrsr.ch/1vZ9MnM

McCroskey, J., & Geurkink, B. (2021). *YouTube regrets: A crowdsourced investigation into YouTube's recommendation algorithm*. Mozilla Foundation. https://assets.mofoprod.net/network/documents/Mozilla_YouTube_Regrets_Report.pdf

Nagal, T. (2022). Information cocoons [Review of the book *Republic.com*, by Cass Sunstein]. *London Review of Books, 23*(13). https://www.lrb.co.uk/the-paper/v23/n13/thomas-nagel/information-cocoons

Neely, S. R. (2021). Politically motivated avoidance in social networks: A study of Facebook and the 2020 presidential election. *Social Media & Society, 7*(4). https://doi.org/10.1177/20563051211055438

Newton, C. (2016). *The author of The Filter Bubble on how fake news is eroding trust in journalism.* The Verge. https://www.theverge.com/2016/11/16/13653026/filter-bubble-facebook-election-eli-pariser-interview

Nyhan, B. (2014, October 25). Americans don't live in information cocoons. *The New York Times.* https://www.nytimes.com/2014/10/25/upshot/americans-dont-live-in-information-cocoons.html

Page, S. (2019, December 9). Divided we fall? Americans see our angry political debate as 'a big problem'. *USA Today.* https://www.usatoday.com/story/news/politics/elections/hiddencommonground/2019/12/05/hidden-common-ground-americans-divided-politics-seek-civility/4282301002/

Pariser, E. (2011a). *The filter bubble: What the internet is hiding from you.* Penguin Press.

Pariser, E. (2011b, May 26). Seven things human editors do that algorithms don't (yet). *Harvard Business Review.* https://hbr.org/2011/05/seven-things-human-editors-do

Pariser, E. (2015). Did Facebook's big study kill my filter bubble thesis? *Wired.* https://www.wired.com/2015/05/did-facebooks-big-study-kill-my-filter-bubble-thesis/

Penn, J. (2018, November 26). AI thinks like a corporation—and that's worrying. *The Economist.*

Piao, J., Liu, J., Zhang, F., Su, J. & Li, Y. (2023). Human–AI adaptive dynamics drives the emergence of information cocoons. *Nature Machine Intelligence, 5,* 1214–1224. https://doi.org/10.1038/s42256-023-00731-4

Self, W. (2016, November 28). Forget fake news on Facebook – the real filter bubble is you. *The New Statesman.* https://www.newstatesman.com/science-tech/2016/11/forget-fake-news-facebook-real-filter-bubble-you

Shiffman, J. (2021, October 6). A Reuters special report: How AT&T helped build far-right One America News. *Reuters.* https://www.reuters.com/investigates/special-report/usa-one-america-att/

Southern, M. (2020, November 9). YouTube reveals new details about its algorithm. *Search Engine Journal.* https://www.searchenginejournal.com/youtube-recommendation-algorithm/

Sunstein, C. (2017). *#Republic: Divided democracy in the age of social media.* Princeton University Press.

Time. (2011, May 16). 5 questions with Eli Pariser, author of "The Filter Bubble". https://techland.time.com/2011/05/16/5-questions-with-eli-pariser-author-of-the-filter-bubble/

Trammell, A., & Cullen, A. L. (2021). A cultural approach to algorithmic bias in games. *New Media & Society, 23*(1), 159–174. https://doi.org/10.1177/1461444819900508

Van Bavel, J. J., Rathje, S., Harris, E., Robertson, C., & Sternisko, A. (2021). How social media shapes polarization. *Trends in Cognitive Sciences, 25*(11), 913–916. https://doi-org.ezproxy.cameron.edu/10.1016/j.tics.2021.07.013

Verma, A. (2022). How AI is transforming the media and entertainment industry. https://www.wipro.com/holmes/how-ai-is-transforming-the-media-and-entertainment-industry/

Wu, X. (2021). The Influence of social network and information cocoon on major selection. *Proceedings of the 2021 International Conference on Social Development and Media Communication.* https://doi.org/10.1177/1461444819900508

· 1 2 ·

WHEN ELECTION LIES GO VIRAL: HOW SOCIAL MEDIA PLATFORMS AMPLIFIED CABLE NEWS NETWORKS' DEFAMATORY COMMENTS ABOUT DOMINION VOTING SYSTEMS AND SMARTMATIC CORPORATION

Juliet Dee

The focus of this chapter will be on the extent to which defamatory claims on Fox News, Newsmax, and One America News (OAN) were repeated and amplified on social media platforms. Two companies that make voting machines, Dominion Voting Systems and Smartmatic Corporation, filed defamation suits against Fox News, Herring Networks' One America News (OAN) and Newsmax Media, as well as Donald Trump allies Rudy Giuliani, Sidney Powell, Mike Lindell and Patrick Byrne after Fox News, Newsmax and OAN television hosts who accused Dominion and Smartmatic of programming their voting machines to "flip" votes from Donald Trump to Joe Biden during the 2020 Presidential election.

Although the trial of *Dominion v. Fox News* was scheduled to begin on April 18, 2023, at the last possible moment, Fox News agreed to pay $787.5 million to Dominion Voting Systems in order to settle the case out of court (Peters & Robertson, 2023b, A20). Although Fox News acknowledged that "certain claims" it had made about Dominion were false, the cable news network did not apologize. Fox News is still facing a $2.7 billion lawsuit from Smartmatic; the trial may take place in 2025, but no date has been set for the trial in this case.

In addition to Dominion and Smartmatic, former Dominion Director of Product Strategy & Security, Dr. Eric Coomer, has filed a defamation suit because he received so many death threats that he was forced to leave his home and go into hiding. Table 12.1 lists the defamation suits.

Dominion had sought $1.6 billion in damages from Fox News. Smartmatic is seeking $2.7 billion from Fox News. Dr. Eric Coomer is suing the Donald J. Trump for President campaign, OAN, and several other defendants.

The purpose of this research will be to analyze the extent to which social media platforms such as Facebook, Twitter, YouTube, Instagram, Parler, and Rumble amplified disinformation from Fox News, Newsmax, and OAN about Dominion Voting Systems, its employee Dr. Eric Coomer, and Smartmatic, leading Trump supporters to believe that the 2020 election had been "stolen" from Trump.

Attorneys for Dominion Voting Systems and Smartmatic have asked Facebook, Twitter, YouTube and Parler to preserve all Tweets and posts related

Table 12.1: Dominion and Smartmatic defamation suits related to the 2020 election

Plaintiff	Defendant	Year Complaint Filed
Eric Coomer v.	Donald J. Trump for President	(2022)
Smartmatic USA Corporation v.	Fox Corporation	(2022)
Smartmatic USA Corporation v.	Giuliani	(2021)
Smartmatic USA Corporation v.	Herring Networks	(2022)
Smartmatic USA Corporation v.	MyPillow, Inc. & Michael J. Lindell	(2022)
Smartmatic USA Corporation v.	Newsmax Media, Inc.	(2022)
Smartmatic USA Corporation v.	Powell	(2021)
US Dominion, Inc. v.	Byrne	(2022)
US Dominion, Inc. v.	Fox Corporation	(2021)
US Dominion, Inc. v.	Fox News Network	(2021)
US Dominion, Inc. v.	Giuliani	(2021)
US Dominion, Inc. v.	Herring Networks	(2022)
US Dominion, Inc. v.	MyPillow, Inc.	(2022)
US Dominion, Inc. v.	Newsmax Media, Inc.	(2022)
US Dominion, Inc. v.	Powell	(2021)

to the false accusations against Dominion. We will examine these Tweets and posts to determine how much influence Fox News, Newsmax and OAN had as agenda setters, and to determine the extent to which these false accusations "went viral" on social media platforms.

The theoretical foundation of this research will be that of media framing and agenda setting. In other words, the question is, after Fox News, Newsmax, and OAN "framed" the false accusations against Dominion, Dr. Eric Coomer, and Smartmatic as "objective reporting," to what extent did Trump supporters echo and recreate this frame on social media platforms?

Background

The presidential election took place on November 3, 2020, but it took four more days to count all mail-in ballots. Joe Biden was declared the winner on Saturday, November 7, 2020.

Unable to accept the fact that he had lost the 2020 election, former President Donald Trump sought numerous avenues by which to keep himself in power. For example, as he sought to discredit and overturn the results of the election in swing states, he and his attorneys Rudy Giuliani and Sidney Powell soon zeroed in on the Canadian company Dominion Voting Systems and the British company Smartmatic.

Both Dominion's and Smartmatic's voting systems are certified under U.S. Election Assistance Commission ("EAC") standards. In addition, both Dominion and Smartmatic design their voting systems to be auditable, with paper ballot backups to verify results. Despite Dominion's persistent efforts to get Fox News, Newsmax, and One America News (OAN) to set the record straight, the three cable networks quickly concluded that perpetrating "the big lie" that the election was stolen would win higher Nielsen ratings than acknowledging that Joe Biden had won the election.

As a result, "the big lie" soon drew academic researchers who analyzed the reach and impact of "the big lie." For example, Ian Kennedy and his team of researchers at the University of Washington analyzed 49 million tweets in a dataset termed *ElectionMisinfo2020* that the Election Integrity Partnership compiled (Kennedy et al., 2022, p. 4). They reported that:

> By far the largest story in our dataset, and indeed the largest misinformation story of the 2020 election, was the allegation that election software developed by Dominion Voting Systems had systematically changed votes from candidate Trump to candidate

Biden ... In 2020 this story spread almost exclusively from pro-Trump [Twitter] accounts. The narrative was picked up by then-President Trump, who used the term "Dominion" in 24 tweets, which garnered collectively a total of 849,000 retweets between November 6 and December 15, 2020. (Kennedy et al., 2022, pp. 30–33)

Kennedy et al. explained that then-President Donald Trump had zeroed in on the false narrative about Dominion; this false narrative was the most tweeted and re-tweeted in the researchers' data.

In November 2020, Dominion repeatedly e-mailed Fox News, Newsmax, and One America Network (OAN) its "Setting the Record Straight" document, in which it refuted point by point the lies that the television news hosts were disseminating. For example, in "Setting the Record Straight," Dominion pointed out that Donald Trump had clearly won the vote in 12 of the 14 Pennsylvania counties that used Dominion's voting machines, but none of the television news hosts for Fox News, Newsmax, or OAN bothered to acknowledge this (*US Dominion v. Fox Corporation*, Complaint, 2021, p. 55).

Following his 24 tweets in which he falsely accused Dominion of switching votes from him to Joe Biden, Donald Trump dispatched his attorneys Rudy Giuliani and Sidney Powell to wage a full-fledged assault against Dominion and Smartmatic. Giuliani and Powell found that certain television hosts on Fox News, Newsmax, and OAN were eager to air vicious lies about Dominion and Smartmatic with the purpose of increasing their Nielsen ratings.

For example, because Fox News was the first television network to call Arizona for Joe Biden, Donald Trump urged Fox News viewers to switch to Newsmax or One America News (OAN). When Fox News realized that it was losing viewers to Newsmax and OAN, it set out to lure them back "by falsely blaming Dominion for Trump's loss" with the accusation that Dominion had rigged the election (*US Dominion, Inc. v. Fox Corporation*, 2021, Complaint, pp. 1–2).

In 2020, Fox News Channel averaged more than 3.5 million viewers during its primetime evening news programming and nearly 2 million daytime viewers, while Fox News Digital reported that its "digital network earned 24 billion multiplatform views" and "54 billion total multiplatform minutes" (Business Wire, 2021, para. 2). Newsmax averaged 58,000 viewers each evening, but after its television hosts invited Sidney Powell and Rudy Giuliani on their shows to accuse Dominion and Smartmatic of siphoning off votes from Donald Trump to Joe Biden, Newsmax increased its viewership to 580,000 viewers each evening. Although few news consumers had ever heard of One

America Network (OAN) before the 2020 election, both Newsmax and OAN "won outsized attention as both covered and supported former President Trump's fight to contest his election loss" (Mastrangelo, 2022, para. 3).

U.S. Dominion, Inc., Dominion Voting Systems, Inc. and Dominion Voting Systems Corporation (hereinafter collectively referred to as "Dominion") filed suit against the Fox Corporation, Fox News, Newsmax, Herring Networks' OAN, Sidney Powell, Rudy Giuliani, Patrick Byrne, and My Pillow chief executive officer (CEO) Mike Lindell for defamation. Dominion's attorneys are charging that they repeated defamatory falsehoods about Dominion and then republished those falsehoods across their websites, social media accounts, and subscription service platforms. "Republication of these falsehoods through digital media, including social media platforms such as Twitter, Facebook, and Instagram reached hundreds of millions of viewers in addition to [the cable news networks'] television audience through followers of its social media accounts" (*US Dominion, Inc. v. Fox Corporation*, 2021, Complaint, p. 8). Former Dominion Director of Product Strategy and Security Dr. Eric Coomer sued the Donald J. Trump for President campaign for defamation. Although the Trump Campaign moved to dismiss, district court Judge Marie Moses ruled that the case could proceed to trial (*Coomer v. Donald J. Trump for President*, Order Regarding All Defendants' Special Motions to Dismiss, 2022, p. 136). The Donald J. Trump for President campaign appealed to the Colorado Court of Appeals, again asking that Coomer's case be dismissed. The Colorado Court of Appeals heard oral arguments on January 30, 2024; thus, the case is pending (Pampuro, 2024, para. 1).

Smartmatic USA Corporation (SUSA), Smartmatic International Holding B.V. (SIH) and SGO Corporation Limited (hereinafter collectively referred to as "Smartmatic") sued the Fox Corporation, Newsmax, Herring Networks' OAN, Sidney Powell, Rudy Giuliani, and My Pillow CEO Mike Lindell.

Fox News Hosts

In their lawsuits, both Dominion and Smartmatic focused on Fox News because it has a larger number of viewers than Newsmax and OAN. Specifically, the lawsuits zeroed in on the cable newscasts and social media posts of Fox News hosts Maria Bartiromo, Lou Dobbs, and Jeanine Pirro.

Maria Bartiromo

The day after Joe Biden was declared the winner on Sunday, November 8, Fox News host Maria Bartiromo invited Trump's attorney Sidney Powell to her *Sunday Morning Futures* program. In response to Bartiromo's question, Powell stated [falsely] that "[Dominion's software] is where the fraud took place, where they were flipping votes in the computer system or adding votes that did not exist . . . . That's when they had to stop the vote count and go in and replace votes for Biden and take away Trump votes" (*US Dominion v. Fox News Network*, 2021, p. 7).

Trump supporters tweeted and retweeted Powell's false claim that Dominion had stolen their votes to the point that nine days after the election, on November 12, 2020, "81% of Trump voters believed that fraud influenced the election outcome" (*US Dominion v. Fox News Network*, 2021, p. 16).

A week later on November 15, 2020, Bartiromo hosted Sidney Powell and Rudy Giuliani. Powell falsely accused Georgia's Republican Governor Brad Kemp and its Republican Secretary of State Gabriel Sterling of taking kickbacks from Dominion in exchange for its contract (*US Dominion, Inc. v. Fox Corporation*, 2021, Complaint, p. 41). Giuliani also falsely claimed that Dominion was using Smartmatic's software, which he said had been used to steal elections in other countries. Giuliani falsely claimed that the late Hugo Chavez had founded Smartmatic, and that Chavez's allies still owned Smartmatic. He stated falsely that Smartmatic had been banned in the United States, but had returned as a subcontractor to other companies, adding that Smartmatic "was a very dangerous foreign company with close ties to Venezuela and China." Bartiromo then falsely stated that Smartmatic's software had a "back door" used to determine how many votes needed to be switched to rig an election. Giuliani agreed and said that there was "'proof of some of the connections' to the back door" (*Smartmatic v. Fox Corporation*, 2022, para. 105). Further, Powell falsely claimed that Smartmatic software shifted millions of votes to Joe Biden; Powell said she had "sworn witness testimony" that the software was designed expressly for the purpose of rigging elections. Powell also falsely claimed that there was evidence that Smartmatic United States of America (SUSA) rigged votes in California in 2016 and that Smartmatic's own manual explained how votes could be "wiped away" (*Smartmatic v. Fox Corporation*, 2022, para. 105).

Bartiromo's program drew two million viewers on Fox News. Fox News had several Twitter accounts for Maria Bartiromo: @MorningsMaria, @

SundayFutures, @MariaBartiromo, @Fox Business, and @FoxNews. Fox News, using the @MariaBartiromo account, followed up with a Tweet that Bartiromo would "keep investigating," suggesting to viewers that "they would learn more about this false fraud narrative" if they kept watching her show (*US Dominion, Inc. v. Fox Corporation*, 2021, Complaint, p. 41).

Bartiromo, whose salary was $10 million per year, also hosted Donald Trump on *Sunday Morning Futures* on November 29, 2020, where she endorsed Trump's claim that Dominion had rigged the election, calling it "disgusting and corrupt" (*US Dominion v. Fox News Network*, 2021, p. 12). Fox News promoted the show via @MariaBartiromo and tagged @realdonaldtrump, sending the tweet to Trump's 88 million followers (*US Dominion, Inc. v. Fox Corporation*, 2021, Complaint, p. 56). After Bartiromo interviewed Trump, an angry viewer "Irish Girl @Twiggyoh" tweeted, "Voter fraud, #Dominion swing states with Trump winning … refused2report vote count in federal election to steal the votes" (*US Dominion, Inc. v. Fox Corporation*, 2021, Complaint, p. 104).

Lou Dobbs

Lou Dobbs hosted the program *Lou Dobbs Tonight*. On November 12, 2020, Dobbs invited Rudy Giuliani as a guest on his show. On the program, Giuliani falsely claimed that Dominion had sent its data to servers in Canada, Spain, and Germany to change votes from Trump to Biden. Dobbs tweeted: "Election Fraud: @RudyGiuliani says he has uncovered enough unlawful ballots in Pennsylvania and Michigan to turn the election in favor of @realDonaldTrump" (Dobbs, 2020a). Dobbs posted the same statement on Instagram.

Fox News viewers were outraged. One viewer posted to Instagram: "Bring in our military and lock them up" (bgolf45, 2020). This comment had 14,407 views. Another viewer tweeted:

> Our voting machines are owned by Canada, the Dominion Company. The servers are located in Canada, Spain and Germany. This is a total stolen election. Source: Rudy Giuliani on Lou Dobbs. Kim Melody, @u2cldknow (*US Dominion, Inc. v. Fox Corporation*, 2021, Complaint, p. 103)

Dobbs also invited Sidney Powell as a guest, where she repeated her lies about Dominion and Smartmatic. On November 14, 2020, he tweeted on the @loudobbs Twitter account:

Read all about the Dominion and Smartmatic voting companies and you'll soon understand how pervasive this Democrat electoral fraud is, and why there's no way in the world the 2020 Presidential election was either free or fair. #MAGA @realDonaldTrump #AmericaFirst #Dobbs (*US Dominion, Inc. v. Fox News, LLC*, 2021, p. 22; *Smartmatic v. Fox Corporation 2022*)

On November 16, Dobbs again invited Powell as a guest on his show where she again made false accusations about Dominion and Smartmatic. Dobbs then tweeted and posted to Facebook the following comment: "Electoral Fraud: Sidney Powell says she has first-hand evidence that Smartmatic voting software was designed in a way to change the vote of a voter without being detected" (Dobbs, 2020b). This tweet had 7,264 retweets. On November 18, Dobbs again invited Rudy Giuliani as a guest on his show, after which Dobbs tweeted: "@Rudy Giuliani says votes in 28 states were sent to Germany and Spain to be counted by Smartmatic" (*US Dominion, Inc. v. Fox Corporation*, 2021, Complaint, Exhibit 22). This tweet had 8,489 retweets.

Dobbs again invited Sidney Powell as a guest on his show on November 19, 2020, after which he tweeted: "Inextricably intertwined: @SidneyPowell1 has no doubt that Dominion voting machines run Smartmatic software which allows them to manipulate the votes" (Dobbs, 2020c). This tweet had 2,050 retweets. Dobbs posted the same information on Instagram, where it had 32,920 views. (Neither Powell nor Dobbs appeared to realize that Dominion and Smartmatic are competitors, and Dominion has never run Smartmatic software on its voting machines.)

Responding to Powell, Dobbs said: "It's stunning. And they're private firms and very little is known about their ownership, beyond what you're saying about Dominion." Dobbs added: "The states . . . have no ability to audit meaningfully the votes that are cast" (*US Dominion v. Fox News Network*, 2021, p. 9). Dobbs later hosted Powell again, and she falsely claimed that Smartmatic was created in Venezuela to rig elections for Hugo Chavez. Fox published those claims to its live audience and republished them on its websites and social media accounts (*US Dominion v. Fox News Network*, 2021, p. 10).

On November 30, 2020, after having Powell as a guest on his show, Dobbs tweeted and posted on Instagram: "Battle for the White House: @SidneyPowell1 celebrates a court victory for @realDonaldTrump in Georgia which stops Dominion voting machines in three counties from being wiped" (Dobbs, 2020d). This tweet had 3,367 retweets. In response, an irate viewer, @denise4re, tweeted: "Obvious fraud . . . tech experts testifying about corrupt

Dominion voting machines and Smartmatic software; the only thing transparent about this election is the fraud, to quote Lou Dobbs" (*US Dominion, Inc. v. Fox Corporation*, 2021, Complaint, p. 106). Another angry viewer, @RussG45523886, tweeted "Why counting stopped in middle of the night in battleground states and why Dominion deleted staff on web sites; talk to Lou Dobbs about evidence of massive election fraud" (*US Dominion, Inc. v. Fox Corporation*, 2021, Complaint, p. 106). One viewer posted a threat on Instagram: "Sydney and Lou, great interview … mass arrests are needed … Start charging them all with treason … execute a few" (danayelavich, 2020). This threat against Dominion employees had 88,108 views on Instagram. The First Amendment does not protect true threats. If prosecutors had perceived the post demanding that someone should "execute a few" [Dominion employees], they could have filed charges against the person who posted this threat if they had perceived it to be specific enough.

On December 4, Dobbs invited Colonel Phil Waldron as a guest on his program; to promote the show, Dobbs sent the following tweet: "Cybersecurity expert Colonel Phil Waldron explains how easily Dominion's voting machines can be manipulated to swing an election" (*US Dominion, Inc. v. Fox Corporation*, 2021, Complaint, Exhibit 12).

On December 10, 2020, Fox tweeted a promotion for *Lou Dobbs Tonight* stating: "The 2020 Election is a cyber Pearl Harbor: The leftwing establishment have aligned their forces to overthrow the United States government #MAGA #AmericaFirst #Dobbs." Fox also embedded a "typewritten document with no other markings or attributions" (*US Dominion v. Fox News Network, LLC*, 2021, p. 39) in the tweet claiming to prove that Dominion concealed a controller that manipulated the voting machines through the Internet. The embedded document charged that Dominion had colluded with the Democratic Party and China to commit voting fraud. The Lou Dobbs promotion tweet, including the two-page typewritten memorandum on machine-controlling devices, was published to more than 2 million Twitter followers.

The embedded document said:

> We have a warning to the mainstream media: you have purposely sided with the forces that are trying to overthrow the U.S. system. [This was] an electoral 9–11 against the United States, with the cooperation and collusion of the media and the Democrat Party …. It is a cyber Pearl Harbor. We have identities, roles, and background of Dominion and Smartmatic people. This will turn into a massive RICO filing. It is Smartmatic, Dominion Voting Systems …. We have technical presentations that prove there is an embedded controller in every Dominion machine …. We have the architecture and systems that show how the machines can be controlled

from external sources, via the Internet, in violation of voting standards, federal law, state laws, and contracts. (*US Dominion v. Fox News Network, LLC*, 2021, p. 39)

Fox News' attorneys never identified the source of the document, which was clearly a fake. But Fox News' viewers apparently accepted the false document along with the "big lie" that the election was stolen. Even in August 2023, 69% of Republicans still believed that Joe Biden had not legitimately won the November 2020 election (Agiesta & Edwards-Levy, 2023, para. 1); in other words, the "big lie" has done profound damage to our democracy.

Jeanine Pirro

Jeanine Pirro's program on Fox News was *Justice with Judge Jeanine*. She had the Twitter account @JudgeJeanine and the "Judge Jeanine Pirro" Facebook account. She invited Sidney Powell as a guest on her show on November 14, 2020. Powell falsely claimed that there was "massive" election fraud in the swing states, resulting from changing "millions of votes" by "different means of manipulating the Dominion and Smartmatic software." (*Smartmatic USA Corporation v. Fox Corporation*, 2022, para. 208). Powell further claimed that the money used to create Smartmatic came from Venezuela or Cuba for the express purpose of securing the re-election of Hugo Chavez and that Smartmatic was part of a "huge criminal conspiracy" which should be "investigated by military intelligence." (*Smartmatic USA Corporation v. Fox Corporation*, 2022, para. 102).

Pirro agreed and said she hoped the Department of Justice would investigate as well, allegedly implying that Smartmatic had engaged in a criminal conspiracy. Powell added that the Dominion machines and Smartmatic software "dumped" votes for President Trump and "flipped" those votes to President Biden. Powell also falsely claimed that there was "mathematical," "statistical," and "forensic" evidence, "as well as witnesses, to prove the vote manipulation" (*Smartmatic USA Corporation v. Fox Corporation*, 2022, para. 103).

After Pirro suggested that Dominion and Smartmatic had rigged the election for Biden, on November 16, 2020, @CliveLion tweeted, "... devilocrats and lucifers and dominion voter fraud will not see the light of day in Trump's White House" (*US Dominion, Inc. v. Fox Corporation*, Complaint, 2021, p. 103). Clive Lion's tweet received only two retweets and two "likes," but it indicates the depth of Fox News viewers' anger in their belief that Dominion and Smartmatic had rigged the election in Biden's favor.

Newsmax Media Hosts and Viewers' Tweets in Response

Christopher Ruddy is the chief executive officer (CEO) of Newsmax and is a close personal friend of Donald Trump. On November 7, 2020, most news networks, including Fox News, projected that Joe Biden had won the election. Newsmax refused to call the election for Biden, however, and boasted that it remained "the only major news network not to call the election" (*US Dominion v. Newsmax Media, Inc.*, 2022, p. 12). Newsmax hosts Greg Kelly (*Greg Kelly Reports*), Grant Stinchfield (*Stinchfield*), Emma Rechenberg (*National Report*), Joe diGenova, who appeared on the *Howie Carr Show*, White House correspondent Emerald Robinson, and Benny Johnson (*The Benny Report*) often invited Trump supporters Sidney Powell, Rudy Giuliani, MyPillow CEO Mike Lindell, and former CEO of Overstock.com Patrick Byrne to repeat the same lies about Dominion and Smartmatic that they had spewed on Fox News. On November 9, 2020, Newsmax's White House correspondent Emerald Robinson tweeted that "once the Trump campaign investigates Dominion Voting Systems, the whole thing is going to fall apart" (*US Dominion v. Newsmax Media, Inc.*, 2022, p. 13). Robinson retweeted the false claim that Smartmatic was synonymous with fraud and that Smartmatic was a subsidiary of Dominion. Robinson's tweet claimed: "All crooked roads lead to Dominion Voting Systems. Newsmax and its on-air talent sold to the American public the story that Dominion and Smartmatic "rigged the 2020 election and stole it from Trump" (*US Dominion v. Newsmax Media, Inc.*, 2022). Newsmax host Benny Johnson tweeted, "Ban mail-voting and Dominion voting machines and pass mandatory voter ID now!" (*US Dominion v. Newsmax Media, Inc.*, 2022, p. 15). The sad irony is that Fox News, Newsmax, and OAN were vying for higher Nielsen ratings with their "big lie" about the election being stolen. There was apparently no concern with responsible journalism or reporting the truth that Joe Biden had won the election, and the three networks were unconcerned about the very real harm they were causing to Dominion Voting Systems and its employees.

In response to a November 16, 2020, newscast, @ronnieverrut tweeted: "Breaking: U.S. Military raids company in Germany connected to Dominion Voting Systems. This is where the U.S. votes get electronically tabulated by Smartmatic! Howie Carr on Newsmax is talking with Lin Wood about this now!" (*Smartmatic v. Newsmax Media, Inc.* Complaint, 2021, p. 215).

On November 17, 2020, Newsmax television host Emerald Robinson tweeted, "Once you look at our election companies (Dominion … Smartmatic …) you realize they're just shell companies. They routinely get bought out by private equity firms after an election—when the cards must be shuffled. It's a trick" (*Smartmatic v. Newsmax Media, Inc.* Complaint, 2021, p. 217). In response, a Newsmax viewer, @Q90ceo tweeted: "Good point, just another shady irregularity in this election. This is consistent with criminal conduct seen in drug dealing, illegal gambling, et cetera" (*Smartmatic v. Newsmax Media, Inc.* Complaint, 2021, p. 217).

On November 20, 2020, Newsmax tweeted, "Sidney Powell says Trump team will prove case within two weeks." In response, Newsmax viewer AnaMaria @RomeroAmg tweeted:

> Smartmatic/Dominion owners are from Venezuela and live here in Florida. They sold out their own country with these machines to make sure [Hugo] Chavez won the last election. Meanwhile they are living here as billionaires and now selling these machines to Democrats to take our freedom! (*Smartmatic v. Newsmax Media, Inc.* Complaint, 2021, p. 213)

Also that day, Sir Maximus Derrida @Maximus_4EVR tweeted, "As I said yesterday (per Newsmax), Smartmatic server seized by United States. This is now confirmed by U.S. Army per @SidneyPowell1" (*Smartmatic v. Newsmax Media, Inc.* Complaint, 2021, p. 216).

On November 24, 2020, Newsmax television host Michelle Malkin (@michellemalkin) tweeted, "Glenn Chong explains how Smartmatic's digital line on ballots resulted in automated vote padding/shaving … Common denominator = Smartmatic & Dominion" (*Smartmatic v. Newsmax Media, Inc.* Complaint, 2021, p. 217). In response on November 25, 2020, Newsmax viewer Sergio Peter (@belovedpeter54) tweeted, "Yes, it looks like the Dominion and Smartmatic were forefront to criminal acts for wealthy politicians who were willing to spend money to ensure their election" (*Smartmatic v. Newsmax Media, Inc.* Complaint, 2021, p. 217). The responses from Newsmax viewers Glenn Chong and Sergio Peter suggest that they *believed* Michelle Malkin's false statement that the election was stolen; in other words, they accepted her accusations against Dominion and Smartmatic as true, and then expanded on explanations for "the big lie" in a way that made sense to them.

One America News Hosts

Robert and Chalres Herring of Herring Networks own One America News (OAN). Although Verizon and DirecTV had included OAN in their line-up, August 1, 2022, was OAN's final day on any major cable or satellite multi-system operators (MSOs). In November 2020, however, OAN's Chief White House correspondent Chanel Rion falsely reported that "the bottom line is votes were switched from President Trump to ... Joe Biden, and it happened in dozens of states, and it's a Dominion System software glitch that we are going to dig into" (*US Dominion, Inc. v. Herring Networks, Inc.*, 2022, 4–5). After November 12, 2020, when OAN began to highlight the "election fraud" story, Donald Trump tweeted @OAN to his 88 million followers more than 40 times. On December 1, 2020, Trump (@realDonaldTrump) tweeted, "Hope everybody is watching @OAN right now. Other media afraid to show" (*Smartmatic USA Corporation v. Herring Networks, Inc.* Complaint, 2021, p. 175).

OAN television hosted Alex Salvi (*After Hours with Alex Salvi*), Elma Aksalic (*Newsroom*), and Erik Bolling (*America This Week*) all hosted Sidney Powell and Rudy Giuliani. When Giuliani appeared on OAN, he falsely claimed that Dominion might be "getting paid millions to help Biden win" (*US Dominion, Inc. v. Herring Networks, Inc.*, 2022, p. 3). He also claimed that Dominion's voting machines were "programmed to give somewhere between a 2% to 5% advantage to Biden." Giuliani also said that "the Dominion voting machines ... were basically built to cheat" (*US Dominion, Inc. v. Herring Networks, Inc.*, 2022, p. 5). On November 14, 2020, Giuliani tweeted:

> Did you know a foreign company, Dominion, was counting our votes in Michigan, Arizona, Georgia and other states. But it was a front for Smartmatic, who was really doing the computing. Look up Smartmatic and tweet me what you think? It will all come out. (*Smartmatic USA Corporation v. Herring Networks, Inc.* Complaint, 2021, p. 36)

Whenever OAN television hosts invited Sidney Powell and Rudy Giuliani to spew lies about Dominion and Smartmatic, OAN would post videos from the newscasts with promotional tweets to its more than 1 million Twitter followers and to its more than 1.5 million followers on Facebook. OAN also posted videos of its broadcasts on OAN's YouTube web site with 1.4 million followers and 215 million views, and OAN's Rumble web site with 900,000 subscribers

(*Smartmatic USA Corporation v. Herring Networks, Inc.* Complaint, 2021, p. 77–78).

On November 18, 2020, OAN promoted its program *Tipping Point* with a Facebook post and a tweet announcing, "Dominion scandal goes worldwide with Michael Johns" (*Smartmatic USA Corporation v. Herring Networks, Inc.* Complaint, 2021, p. 76). On November 20, 2020, an OAN viewer (@Jaxm53) tweeted: "So the question is, why on earth would the United States allow [Smartmatic] to be used here?" (*Smartmatic USA Corporation v. Herring Networks, Inc.* Complaint, 2021, p. 179).

On November 21, 2020, OAN viewer (@Typhon 16424376) tweeted: "Smartmatic is the deep state obviously—just most desire to plead ignorance to what is obvious. These agencies need to be shattered in Donald Trump's second term" (*Smartmatic USA Corporation v. Herring Networks, Inc.* Complaint, 2021, p. 181). Although the OAN television hosts kept referring to Smartmatic as a Venezuelan company (or having ties to Venezuela), the headquarters of Smartmatic are actually in the United Kingdom. The OAN viewers such as Jaxm53 and Typhon had apparently bought the "big lie" and had then conveniently slotted Smartmatic into their conspiracy theories about the "deep state." Those who believe conspiracy theories also seem to assume that they are among a select few who know "the truth," whereas most of the general public are being hoodwinked (although the sad reality is that the opposite is true).

On November 25, 2020, OAN viewer (@JennJa8) watched OAN television host Pearson Sharp's program and then tweeted: "@PearsonSharp just ripped CNN and other news media concerned about voter fraud and Smartmatic, owned by Venezuela . . . Must watch @OAN for this story!" (*Smartmatic USA Corporation v. Herring Networks, Inc.* Complaint, 2021, p. 177). On November 30, 2020, OAN viewer Alicia Magee (@AliciaMagee6) tweeted: "On OAN now: Former military information warfare specialist: Dominion and Smartmatic totals can be made to jump from lower totals on election day to higher on recounts. Built-in algorithms or messages go into the computer to make the changes. Machines are connected to Internet" (*Smartmatic USA Corporation v. Herring Networks, Inc.* Complaint, 2021, p. 178).

Trump ally Mike Lindell made several documentaries, *Absolute Proof, Scientific Proof, Absolute Interference,* and *Absolutely 9-0,* which falsely accused Dominion and Smartmatic as having "switched votes" from Trump to Biden. OAN aired *Absolute Proof* 13 times and used OAN's official Twitter account to promote *Absolute Proof* with the tweet, "Join My Pillow CEO Mike Lindell for a never-before-seen report breaking down election fraud evidence ..." OAN also tweeted: "Growing evidence of election fraud reveals that the Presidency of the United States has been stolen from the American people. Join My Pillow Mike Lindell for an exclusive report" (*Smartmatic USA Corporation v. Herring Networks, Inc.* Complaint, 2021, p. 74).

Coomer v. Donald J. Trump for President

Dominion Voting Systems' Director of Product Strategy & Security was Dr. Eric Coomer, who had a doctorate in nuclear engineering from the University of California at Berkeley and held several patents with Dominion. In Colorado, *Conservative Daily* podcast host and founder of Faith Education Commerce United Joe Oltmann made unsubstantiated claims that he had infiltrated an "Antifa conference call" in September 2020 and heard a man named "Eric" who said, "Don't worry about the election; Trump's not going to win. I made f—king sure of that." (*Coomer v. Donald J. Trump for President,* Complaint, 2021, p. 7).

Oltmann acknowledged that he had no recording of this phone call and no knowledge of the identities of the participants. But Oltmann singled out Dominion and Eric Coomer, at which point Coomer and his Dominion colleagues began receiving death threats and other forms of harassment. (*Coomer v. Donald J. Trump for President,* Complaint, 2021, p. 8). The death threats against Coomer were so serious that Coomer could no longer go to Dominion's Denver office. A man showed up at Coomer's house, shouting at Coomer about election fraud. Coomer could not stay in his own home because so many people on social media were calling for Coomer to be executed that he ultimately had to go into hiding for six months (*Coomer v. Donald J. Trump for President,* Complaint, 2021, p. 8). Oltmann posted the following taunt on his Parler account: "Eric Coomer ... want to chat with you but you are too scared .... Everyone is watching you, Eric ... everyone" (*Coomer v. Donald J. Trump for President,* Complaint, 2021, pp. 9–10). Coomer later commented that Oltmann's Parler post "made it clear that Oltmann had sent someone to my house, knew that I feared for my life, and did not care" (*Coomer v. Donald J. Trump for President,* Complaint, 2021, pp. 8–10). On November 13, 2020, Michelle Malkin invited Oltmann as a guest on her YouTube program #MalkinLive. Oltmann accused Coomer of rigging the 2020 election, adding, "I think [Coomer's] treason is punishable by death." (*Coomer v. Donald J. Trump for President,* Complaint, 2021, p. 10).

Malkin also invited Oltmann to appear on her Newsmax television show *Sovereign Nation* in which she described Coomer as an "Antifa radical" and tweeted to promote her interview with Oltmann to her 2 million Twitter followers (*Coomer v. Donald J. Trump for President*, 2022, p. 28). James Hoft, owner of the right-wing online publication *The Gateway Pundit* published Oltmann's accusation that an Antifa activist had made sure that Trump would not win the election. Donald Trump's son Eric Trump tweeted a link to *The Gateway Pundit's* article to Eric Trump's .5 million Twitter followers, who retweeted it 11,000 times (*Coomer v. Donald J. Trump for President*, Complaint, 2021, p. 13).

OAN White House correspondent Chanel Rion invited Oltmann for an interview on her program, accused Coomer of "Dominion-izing the vote," and then tweeted: "#Eric Coomer. Trump won't win. I made f—king sure of that" to her 445,000 followers. Rion also attached to her own tweet a tweet from Ron Watkins, former administrator of 8chan, claiming that Dominion's software could adjust the vote tally. Donald Trump was so pleased with Rion's interview that he retweeted her "Dominion-izing the Vote" segment to all 88 million of his Twitter followers. The segment also had 1.2 million views on Trump's YouTube channel (*Coomer v. Donald J. Trump for President*, Complaint, 2021, pp. 16–17). Donald J. Trump for President (the Trump campaign), Sidney Powell and Rudy Giuliani also repeated Oltmann's lies.

In December 2020, Coomer also filed a defamation suit against Newsmax, but reached an out-of-court settlement with Newsmax in April 2021, the terms of which were confidential. Newsmax issued a retraction and an apology, posting the following statement on its web site:

> Newsmax subsequently found no evidence that such allegations [that Eric Coomer had manipulated the election results] were true. Many of the states whose results were contested by the Trump campaign after the November 2020 election have conducted extensive recounts and audits, and each of these states certified the results as legal and final. (Birkeland, 2021, para. 2)

Despite Newsmax' retraction, the Donald J. Trump Campaign refused to issue a retraction or an apology. Coomer suffered severe emotional distress and gave up his job with Dominion in May 2021. Even six months after the election, people who believed Joe Oltmann's lies were threatening to harm or murder Coomer each day. In addition to suing Donald J. Trump for President, Coomer's defamation suit named Joe Oltmann's group Faith Education Commerce United. Oltmann's attorneys filed a motion to dismiss the case, but in May

2022, Denver County District Court Judge Marie Moses held that the case could proceed to trial. Oltmann appealed, but the court has not yet scheduled oral arguments; thus, the case is pending (Birkeland, 2023, para. 11).

Threats of Violence against Dominion and Smartmatic Employees

Although most social media posts expressed outrage, some angry viewers also posted threats. Dominion and Smartmatic employees received numerous death threats (*Smartmatic v. Fox Corporation*, 2022). For example, Woody James (@WoodsonTJames) tweeted, "Why isn't every single Dominion employee in jail for their election fraud?!" (*US Dominion, Inc. v. Fox Corporation*, Complaint, 2021, p. 108). Another person, "lionslovestrump" (@leonkhanin1234) tweeted, "Jail Dominion. Find them. Ask allies to track them down" (*US Dominion, Inc. v. Fox Corporation*, Complaint, 2021, p. 108). OAN viewer Mike Grieco (@mikeysfunplace) tweeted: "They [Dominion and Smartmatic employees] all should be in jail for election interference." And "Raider TonyRyo13" tweeted, "All those involved in this fraud, check out their new address: Guantanamo Bay Detention Camp, Prison in Cuba" (*Smartmatic USA Corp. v. Herring Networks*, Complaint, 2021, p. 183).

Arizona State Senator Wendy Rogers (@WendyRogersAZ) tweeted, "I would like to know if we have enough solitary confinement cells in Arizona available for the entire Maricopa Board of Supervisors and the execs at [Dominion]." Several months after all the verbal threats, someone threw a brick through the window of a Dominion office (*US Dominion, Inc. v. Fox Corporation*, Complaint, 2021, p. 109). In the examples above, social media users Woody James, Leon Hanon, Mike Grieco, and Tony Ryo called for Dominion employees to be imprisoned. While these four men may have had influence with others, Arizona State Senator Wendy Rogers would have had far more influence when she echoed their calls for Dominion executives to be thrown in jail. The sad reality is that verbal threats *can* result in physical violence; when someone threw a brick through the window of a Dominion office, it was sheer luck that no employees were injured.

In December 2022, someone posted on TikTok, "Defamation case against Fox has been steadily progressing in Delaware." In response, "bigredone4" posted, "Dominion just lost its case yesterday versus Rudy [Giuliani]." In response, "dhstokyo" posted, "Nice try. [The Dominion] case hasn't been resolved yet. You just keep crossing those fingers." In response, "michaelcollins1760" (2022) posted, "We still have bullets."

Posts on Social Media Two Years after Trade Libel Suits Were Filed

Among Trump supporters who were duped and believed the lies about Dominion, Smartmatic, and Eric Coomer, there was still strong interest in the outcome of the trade libel suits in 2022, two years after Dominion, Smartmatic, and Eric Coomer had filed their lawsuits. For example, the following comments were posted on Facebook in December 2022:

> Dominion will not like the way this ends (George Pierson).
> Rudy [Giuliani] shouldn't worry .... He said he could prove Dominion voting machines were corrupted. Bring the proof, Rudy. This is your big chance (Stephen M. Beshens).
> Let's have a close examination of the machines designed to flip votes! Dominion already lost one lawsuit! Counter-sue into oblivion!" [Dominion has not actually lost any lawsuits.] (Duane Reynolds).
> But [Dominion and Smartmatic] haven't won, have they? Thank God there's plenty of proof that Dominion committed fraud! (Patricia Pearson).
> Yes, this is bullshit as usual, just Dominion trying to cover their ass for their bullshit ripoff machines (Daniel Ocker).
> Same old dirty tactics. I hope Fox wins (Walter Lauinger).
> Now we can force Dominion to disclose all info about the [voting] machines and show the fraud (James C. Braico).

The following comments were posted on Instagram in December 2022:

> It was a rigged election (Christopher Cianicullo).
> Maybe someone can look into what truly happened with those results (2005qpb).

Economic Loss Due to Viral Disinformation Campaign

In its trade libel suit against the Fox Corporation, Dominion charged that, "With Fox' global platform, an audience of hundreds of millions, and the ... republication and dissemination of the falsehoods through social media, these lies deeply damaged Dominion's once-thriving business" (*US Dominion v. Fox Corporation*, Complaint, 2021, p. 4). Over a three-hour period on December 21, 2020, the terms "Dominion" together with "fraud" were tweeted out by 2,200 Twitter users with 8,750,000 followers (*US Dominion v. Fox Corporation*, Complaint, 2021, p. 106). After the disinformation campaign against Dominion went viral, the company spent more than $600,000 on private security to protect its employees (*US Dominion v. Fox Corporation*, Complaint, 2021, p. 110). State legislators where Dominion had contracts such Arizona, California, Colorado, Florida, Michigan, Ohio, and Pennsylvania informed Dominion that they are reassessing these contracts due to pressure from constituents due to the lies from Fox News, Newsmax, and OAN. (*US Dominion v. Fox Corporation*, Complaint, 2021, p. 111). For example, the state of Louisiana reneged on a $100 million contract that it had awarded Dominion. Louisiana's Republican Secretary of State Kyle Ardoin explained that there had been "damage to voter confidence" in Dominion (*US Dominion v. Fox Corporation*, Complaint, 2021, p. 112). Officials in San Luis Obispo County in California also discontinued their contract with Dominion; one official e-mailed his explanation: "I don't trust Dominion Voting Systems at all" (*US Dominion v. Fox Corporation*, Complaint, 2021, p. 114).

Just as Dominion's employee Dr. Eric Coomer received death threats, Smartmatic claimed that its employees had received hate mail and death threats from Trump supporters who believed the lies about Dominion and Smartmatic, which claimed that the damage to its reputation amounted to $2.7 billion in future lost contracts (*Smartmatic USA Corporation v. Fox Corporation*, 2022).

Discussion

As a result of the viral disinformation campaigns on social media, Dominion and Smartmatic have clearly suffered economic loss. After going into hiding due to numerous death threats, Dr. Eric Coomer gave up his employment with Dominion in May 2021 and now suffers from severe anxiety and depression (*Coomer v. Trump*, Complaint, 2021, p. 24). Nearly two years after Dominion filed its defamation suit, Fox News host Sean Hannity testified under oath that he did not believe "for one second" Sidney Powell's lies about Dominion voting machines (Peters, 2022, pp. B1, B3). In addition to Sean Hannity, Tucker Carlson, and Laura Ingraham "repeatedly insulted and mocked Trump advisers … Sidney Powell and Rudolph Giuliani in text messages" among themselves (Peters & Robertson, 2023a, p. B1). Fox News' owner and chief executive officer Rupert Murdoch called Donald Trump's voter fraud claims "really crazy stuff" (Peters & Robertson, 2023, pp. B1, B3).

In rare instances, social media platforms would flag the false accusations of election fraud with the note "This claim is disputed," but in the vast majority of posts on social media, there was no attempt to moderate or to distinguish facts from lies. Of course, the social media platforms operate with impunity because Section 230 of the Communications Decency Act of 1996 provides them with immunity from liability for the content of what their users might post, whether or not it is truthful or harmful.

For example, the U.S. Supreme Court has recently decided two cases, *Twitter, Inc. v. Taamneh* (2023) and *Gonzalez v. Google, LLC* (2023), involving Section 230's guarantee of immunity for social media platforms. In 2017 Islamic State terrorists murdered Nawras Alassaf in Istanbul. Alassaf's family filed suit against Twitter, challenging Section 230's provision of immunity for social media platforms and arguing that Twitter had allowed the Islamic State in Iraq and Syria (ISIS) to use its platform to recruit and train terrorists (*Taamneh v. Twitter, Inc.* 2018). Islamic State terrorists in Paris had also massacred college student Nohemi Gonzalez in 2015. Her parents filed suit against Google, Facebook and Twitter, arguing that these platforms did not bother to remove Islamic State videos that incited violence in France (*Gonzalez v. Google, LLC*, 2021).

The U.S. Supreme Court upheld Section 230's provision of immunity for social media platforms in both *Twitter* and *Gonzalez* in May 2023 (*Twitter, Inc. v. Taamneh*, 2023; *Gonzalez v. Google, LLC*, 2023). With *Twitter* and *Gonzalez* as recent precedents, it seems clear that if Dominion and Smartmatic had attempted to file suit against the social media platforms themselves for allowing users to re-post Fox News' false and defamatory accusations, courts would have dismissed their cases. As a result of Section 230's guarantee of immunity, social media platforms can get away with being casual or entirely absent when it comes to flagging false information because they face no legal consequences when they ignore dangerous disinformation or death threats that their users post.

As is mentioned above, when Fox News lost viewers to Newsmax and One America Network (OAN), its hosts began "promoting outlandish claims of a ... voter fraud conspiracy involving Dominion" (Peters & Robertson, 2023a: B1, B3).

As is mentioned above, Dominion reached an out-of-court settlement with Fox News in April 2023, but the cases of Smartmatic and Eric Coomer are pending. Smartmatic and Coomer will have to be able to prove that the defendants such as the hosts of Fox News, Newsmax and OAN *knew* that their allegations against the plaintiffs were false or were made with reckless disregard for the truth.

The defendant media companies have argued that they were merely reporting the "news" that Trump attorneys Sidney Powell and Rudy Giuliani were making. Journalists can possibly avoid liability for false statements if they claim a "qualified privilege" to accurately and fairly report charges and countercharges, but they cannot claim a qualified privilege if they knowingly *promote* false and defamatory statements (Peters & Robertson, 2023a, p. B3). In his deposition under oath, Fox News owner Rupert Murdoch acknowledged that some Fox News hosts had "endorsed" Donald Trump's lies; this admission served to undercut Fox News' defense (Peters & Robertson, 2023b, A1, p. A20). Dominion's attorneys also had reams of internal documents showing that numerous Fox News employees *knew* that the "Dominion election conspiracy was pure fantasy. That extended to the network's highest ranks—right up to Rupert Murdoch himself" (Rutenberg & Robertson, 2023, p. A20).

The poet John Milton argued that "Though all the winds of doctrine were let loose to play upon the earth, so truth be in the field, we do injuriously, by licensing and prohibiting, to misdoubt her strength" (Milton, 1644). Milton's argument that "truth will win out" became the basis of our Founding Fathers' "marketplace of ideas." Later, Justice Louis Brandeis acknowledged the "marketplace of ideas" in his plea for "more speech."

> If there be time to expose through discussion, the falsehoods and fallacies, to avert the evil by the processes of education, the remedy to be applied is more speech, not enforced silence. (*Whitney v. California*, 1927)

We would naturally hope that "truth will win out in the end," as John Milton and Justice Louis Brandeis had suggested, but they could not have anticipated the impact of social media in spreading the "big lie" that led to the January 6, 2021, storming of the U.S. Capitol. John Milton and Justice Brandeis could not have anticipated the profound damage to the reputations of Dominion, Smartmatic, and Dr. Eric Coomer that resulted when Trump supporters echoed and repeated the "big lie" on social media.

In June 2021, a year and a half after the November 2020 election, poll after poll indicated that 70% of Republicans do not believe that Joe Biden is the legitimate winner (Greenberg, 2022). Donald Trump's "big lie" and its proliferation on social media has done profound damage, not only to Dominion, Smartmatic, and Dr. Eric Coomer, but to the general public's trust in the validity of elections in our representative republic.

In our legal system, there is a "presumption" against prior restraint, meaning that the First Amendment prevents the U.S. government from censoring content on cable television news programs. Of course, our legal system permits redress of grievances, meaning that Dominion, Smartmatic, and Dr. Eric Coomer can file suit against the cable news companies who have caused so much damage to them, but only after the fact. The problem, however, is that trade libel suits may be tied up in litigation for years before they are resolved. In the meantime, unscrupulous television news hosts scrambling for higher Nielsen ratings do not care how much damage they inflict with their malicious lies about an individual employee such Dr. Eric Coomer. When these vicious lies are amplified on social media platforms, the ensuing death threats are terrifying. The cable news companies will claim that they were merely covering "newsworthy" accusations of election fraud and that they were merely reporting Donald Trump's accusations. The cable news companies may or may not face consequences, depending on whether or not a jury finds that they acted with malice (meaning that they knew that they were airing false accusations, or acted with reckless disregard of whether their accusations were false). In contrast, the social media platforms will face no consequences for amplifying the vicious lies about Dominion, Smartmatic, and Dr. Eric Coomer because Section 230 provides them with immunity. Even if they face no legal consequences, the social media platforms have a lot to answer for.

References

Agiesta, J., & Edwards-Levy, A. (2023, August 3). CNN Poll: Percentage of Republicans who think Biden's 2020 win was illegitimate ticks back up near 70%. *CNN.* https://www.cnn.com/2023/08/03/politics/cnn-poll-republicans-think-2020-election-illegitimate/index.html

bgolf45. (2020, November 12). Instagram. https://www.instagram.com/p/CHgkRWyBBus/

Birkeland, B. (2021, April 30). Newsmax issues retraction and apology to Dominion employee over election stories. *NPR.* https://www.npr.org/2021/04/30/992534968/newsmax-issues-retraction-and-apology-to-dominion-employee-over-election-stories

Birkeland, B. (2023, April 29). Former Dominion Voting employee waits for his day(s) in court on multiple suits. Colorado Public Radio.

Business Wire. (2021, January 25). Fox News digital network delivers record year. https://www.businesswire.com/news/home/20210125005734/en/FOX-News-Digital-Network-Delivers-Record-Year

Coomer v. Donald J. Trump for President, Complaint, No: 2020-CV-034319 (District Court, Denver County, Colorado, filed September 17, 2021).

Coomer v. Donald J. Trump for President, Order Regarding All Defendants' Special Motions to Dismiss pursuant to C.R.S. § 13-20-1101, No: 2020-CV-34319 (District Court, Denver County, Colorado, filed May 13, 2022).

danayelavich. (2020, November 30). Instagram. https://www.instagram.com/p/CIO6-KVBKb8/

Dobbs, L.. [@loudobbs]. (2020a, November 12). [Twitter]. Twitter. https://twitter.com/LouDobbs/status/1327024215887851521

Dobbs, L. [@loudobbs]. (2020b, November 16). [Twitter]. Twitter. https://twitter.com/LouDobbs/status/1328469195550576645

Dobbs, L. [@loudobbs]. (2020c, November 19). [Tweet]. Twitter. https://twitter.com/LouDobbs/status/1329553227046588417

Dobbs, L. [@loudobbs]. (2020d, November 30). [Tweet]. Twitter. https://twitter.com/LouDobbs/status/1333547266032984064

Gonzalez v. Google, LLC. 2 F. 4th 871 (9th Circuit, 2021).

Gonzalez v. Google, LLC. 2023 U.S. LEXIS 2059.

Greenberg, J. (2022, June 16). Most Republicans still falsely believe Trump's stolen election claims. Here are some reasons why. *Poynter Institute*. https://www.poynter.org/fact-checking/2022/70-percent-republicans-falsely-believe-stolen-election-trump/

Kennedy, I., Wack, M., Beers, A., Schafer, J. S., Garcia-Camargo, I., Spiro, E. S., & Starbird, K. (2022). Repeat spreaders and election delegitimization: A comprehensive dataset of misinformation tweets from the 2020 U.S election. *Journal of Quantitative Description: Digital Media, 2.* https://doi.org/10.51685/jqd.2022.013

Mastrangelo, D. (2022, August 2). OAN's troubles spark questions for conservative cable news. *The Hill.* https://thehill.com/homenews/media/3583306-oans-troubles-spark-questions-for-conservative-cable-news/

michaelcollins1760. (2022, December 11). TikTok.

Milton, John. (1644, November 23). *Areopagitica.* The John Milton Reading Room. https://milton.host.dartmouth.edu/reading_room/areopagitica/text.shtml

Pampuro, A. (2024, January 30). Trump campaign appeals to throw out defamation suit over 2020 election fraud claims. *Courthouse News Service*. https://www.courthousenews.com/trump-campaign-asks-colorado-court-of-appeals-to-throw-out-defamation-suit-over-2020-election-fraud-claims/

Peters, J. W. (2022, December 22). In testimony, some at Fox voiced doubt on vote plots. *The New York Times*, B1, B3.

Peters, J. W., & Robertson, K. (2023a, February 17). Fox stars voiced voter fraud doubts. *The New York Times*, B1, B3.

Peters, J. W., & Robertson, K. (2023b, April 19). Fox and Dominion abruptly settle for $787.5 million: No apology by network for election lies. *The New York Times*, (A1, A20).

Rutenberg, J., & Robertson, K. (2023, April 19). Network's deal avoids a fight, but not scars. *The New York Times*, (A1, A20).

Smartmatic USA Corporation v. Fox Corporation, No. 151136/2021 (Supreme Court of New York, New York County, filed November 9, 2022).

Smartmatic USA Corporation v. Giuliani, No. 151136/2021 (Supreme Court of New York, New York County, filed April 8, 2021).

Smartmatic USA Corporation v. Herring Networks, Inc. 2022 U.S. Dist. LEXIS 109645 (D.D.C., filed June 21, 2022).

Smartmatic USA Corporation v. Herring Networks, Inc. Complaint. No. 1:21-cv-02900 (D.D.C., filed November 3, 2021).

Smartmatic USA Corporation v. My Pillow, Inc. & Michael J. Lindell, Case No. 0:22-cv-00098-WMW-JFD (U.S. District Court, District of Minnesota, filed March 21, 2022).

Smartmatic USA Corporation v. Newsmax Media, Inc., Case No. N21C-11 (Superior Court of Delaware, filed November 3, 2021).

Smartmatic USA Corporation v. Powell, Case 1:21-CV-02995 (D.D.C., filed November 12, 2021).

Taamneh v. Twitter, Inc., 343 F. Supp. 3rd 904 (U.S. District Court, Northern District of California, filed October 29, 2018).

Twitter, Inc. v. Taamneh, 2023 U.S. LEXIS 2060.

US Dominion, Inc. v. Byrne, 2022 U.S. Dist. LEXIS 72634 (D.D.C., filed April 20, 2022).

US Dominion, Inc. v. Fox Corporation, Complaint. No. N21C-11-082 EMD (Superior Court of Delaware, New Castle County, filed November 8, 2021).

US Dominion, Inc. v. Fox News Network, LLC. 2021 Del. Super. LEXIS 706 (Superior Court of Delaware, New Castle County, December 16, 2021).

US Dominion, Inc. v. Giuliani, No. 1:21-cv-00213 (D.D.C., filed January 25, 2021).

US Dominion, Inc. v. Herring Networks, 2022 U.S. Dist. LEXIS 203413 (D.D.C., filed November 7, 2022).

US Dominion, Inc. v. My Pillow, Inc. 2022 U.S. App. LEXIS 7649 (D.D.C., filed January 20, 2022), cert. denied, My Pillow, Inc. v. US Dominion, Inc., 2022 U.S. LEXIS 3826 (U.S. Oct. 3, 2022).

US Dominion, Inc. v. Newsmax Media, Inc., Civil Action N21C-08-063 EMD (Superior Court of Delaware, filed June 16, 2022).

US Dominion, Inc. v. Powell, 554 F. Supp. 3d 42 (D.D.C. filed August 11, 2021).

Whitney v. California, 274 U.S. 357 (1927).

· 13 ·

NORMALIZING NEW IDENTITIES IN POLITICAL ROLES: AN EXAMINATION OF THE SOCIAL MEDIA OF PETE AND CHASTEN BUTTIGIEG

Christopher J. McCollough

Political communication is multichannel, and the messengers are not always the elected officials or political appointees that advocate for administration agendas or issues. Often, it is the spouses and other administration and party members who work most effectively to help advance the dialog about administrative positions in public discourse. In the case of 2020 Democratic presidential candidate Pete Buttigieg and his husband Chasten Buttigieg, we see two individuals gifted in issue advocacy and political surrogacy work. Additionally, both present a means of comparatively examining how they work on matters of issue advocacy, surrogacy, and serving to normalize members of the LGBTQ community in political administration and public and civic life.

Political communication literature offers a body of literature that explores how political surrogates (Wright, 2016) play a critical role in advocating for policy agendas and issues with bipartisan audiences that elected officials and political appointees cannot reach. The Biden administration's commitment to establishing a diverse group of public officials in its administration offers an opportunity to explore efforts to normalize diverse people in leadership roles and in political public life (Tremblay, 2022). Finally, Chasten Buttigieg presents a unique opportunity to examine how a gay political spouse performs in comparison to heteronormative political spouses who have historically performed as issue advocates (Bickersham, 2020) and political surrogates (Wright, 2016). The following study analyzes the first year of tweets of both Pete and Chasten Buttigieg to explore their work on surrogacy, issue advocacy, and in normalizing nontraditional individuals in prominent political and public roles.

Research Context

The focus of the study is Secretary of Transportation, Pete Buttigieg, and his spouse, Chasten Buttigieg. Both are public figures with a record in politics and activism that merit brief examination before the focus of the chapter turns to relevant theory and analysis.

Pete and Chasten Buttigieg

Pete Buttigieg currently serves as the Secretary of Transportation and has several political accomplishments of note that mark his record. He successfully won election as Mayor of South Bend, Indiana and took office in January of 2012 at the age of 29, becoming the second youngest man to serve in the role (Fuller, 2014). In 2014, Buttigieg took a seven-month leave of absence to serve in the United States Navy Reserve in Afghanistan (Bell, 2014) before returning to office from leave in October of 2014. Buttigieg would win re-election and serve a second term as mayor of South Bend, Indiana, carrying 80 percent of the vote (Peterson, 2015), earning him the standing nickname "Mayor Pete" in the process.

During his reelection bid in 2015, Indiana Senate Bill 101 emerged as a major issue in the state and became a focus of debate for the statewide election. The original version of which was widely criticized for allowing discrimination against lesbian, gay, bisexual, and transgender people. Buttigieg emerged as a leading opponent of the legislation (Catanzarite, 2015). Amid his reelection campaign, Buttigieg came out as gay and expressed his solidarity with the LGBTQ community (Buttigieg, 2015).

In his editorial piece in *The South Bend Tribune*, Buttigieg expressed that being gay was simply a part of who people are, "like having brown hair," rather than a choice to be made, including how they decide to share that part of their identity. He noted that each time he came out to a friend or family member, they would reassure him it was simply a part of him, rather than a choice. He also took great care to explain that while it was a big decision to share this part of himself publicly at the time, being gay did not define his public service:

> Being gay has had no bearing on my job performance in business, in the military, or in my current role as mayor. It makes me no better or worse at handling a spreadsheet, a rifle, a committee meeting, or a hiring decision. It doesn't change how residents can best judge my effectiveness in serving our city: by the progress of our neighborhoods, our economy, and our city services. (Buttigieg, 2015, para. 9).

Buttigieg's second term in office included several environmental and infrastructure projects. The City of South Bend entered a partnership with the state of Indiana and private developers to begin a $165 million renovation of the Studebaker factory complex, transforming it into a technology hub, stoking industrial and housing developments (Colombo, 2017). The project led to South Bend's ranking 39 on the 100 best small cities in the United States in 2020 (Resonance, 2020). Beyond development, Buttigieg initiated projects to establish a smart sewer program that made their system more efficient and environmentally sound (Gardner, 2019), a city climate plan in April 2019 to make South Bend carbon neutral by 2050 to meet the terms of the Paris Agreement (Parrott, 2019), and a plan to move the city's South Shore Line station from South Bend International Airport to the city's downtown in August of 2018 (Parrott, 2018), while initiating a transportation benefit program that brought local and national business together with the city government to support citizens while advancing environmental initiatives (Semmler, 2019).

Buttigieg pursued national roles in the Democratic Party quickly on the heels of his growing profile in the party and LGBTQ community. In January of 2017, he announced his candidacy for the chair of the Democratic National Committee, seen as a dark horse candidate who sought to empower the millennial votes in the party. He would withdraw as a candidate without endorsing an opponent (Seitz-Wald, 2017).

On January 20, 2019, Buttigieg announced he was forming an exploratory committee to run for the presidency during the 2020 election (Merica, January 23 2019). If elected, he would have been the youngest and first openly gay American president (Merica, January 23, 2019). Buttigieg officially launched his campaign on April 14, 2019, in South Bend, Indiana (Merica, April 14 2019). Initially seen as an unlikely candidate (Gambino, 2019), Buttigieg became a serious contender by December of 2019.

Buttigieg's appeal reflected a mix of appealing characteristics and demonstrated skill. His youth, lack of established constituency, and limited personal wealth served to bolster his profile. He was a polished speaker and performer in public, and skilled in persuasion as be built a strong national network of supporters during his run. Notably, Buttigieg built platform on issues affecting every American and ensured his sexuality was incidental to his candidacy, by design. The first legitimate gay candidate for president in American history was notable for how secondary his sexuality was (Altman & Alter, 2020). In February of 2020, Buttigieg achieved the apex of his candidacy, garnering the highest percentage of votes among voters in the Iowa Caucus, becoming the first openly gay candidate to win a state presidential primary (Keith, 2020). Buttigieg would follow his performance in Iowa with a second-place finish in New Hampshire (Nilsen, 2020), but following a fourth-place finish in South Carolina, Buttigieg withdrew from the race on March 1, 2020, and endorsed Joe Biden (Epstein & Gabriel, 2020).

Following his improbable run in the presidential primary, Buttigieg focused on supporting down-ballot Democrats by launching a new leadership political action committee named With the Era PAC to raise money and distribute among candidates (Merica, 2020). In addition to fundraising, Buttigieg became a prominent and effective political surrogate for Biden's campaign in the general election (Verhovek & Nagle, 2020). Following Biden's election, Buttigieg was in the running for multiple cabinet posts, before being nominated for secretary of transportation on December 15, 2020 (Laris et al., 2020).

Pete Buttigieg was one among several members of the Biden administration who represented a diverse group of individuals marking the first in their roles in government. For example, Kamala Harris became the first African American and Asian American to serve as vice president, in addition to being the first woman to serve as vice president (Kalita, 2020). Her husband, Douglas Emhoff, became the first second gentlemen of the United States, and the first of Jewish descent (Deliso, 2020). Deb Haaland became the first cabinet secretary of Indigenous descent after being confirmed as the secretary of the interior (Lakhani, 2021). Finally, Emily Voorde was also appointed to serve as the senior advisor in the office of public engagement, becoming the first transgender member of a presidential administration.

Chasten Buttigieg, Pete Buttigieg's husband, is an arts educator, writer, and activist. They were engaged in December 2017, and married on June 16, 2018, in South Bend, Indiana making Chasten the first "first gentleman" of South

Bend, Indiana (Trebay, 2018). Chasten served as a spokesperson, advisor, and social media campaigner for Pete Buttigieg (Weiss, 2019). Chasten was called Pete's "not-so-secret public relations weapon" (Petrow, 2020). Chasten made the case for his agenda as First Gentleman of the United States during the primary, committing to focus on improving public schools, arts education, and mental health (Relman, 2019). Chasten was also a vocal advocate for LGBTQ rights (Igoe, 2019; Zavaleta, 2019). Following Pete Buttigieg's withdrawal, Chasten Buttigieg embraced a role as political surrogate for the Biden campaign (Bowden, 2020; Oliver, 2020). In concert with his past role as a first first gentleman, Chasten Buttigieg made fast friends with Kamala Harris and Doug Emhoff, the first woman to serve as vice president and the first second gentlemen, respectively (Ring, 2020). With perspective on the research figures established, the focus now turns to relevant literature on the topic.

Literature Review

Normalization

Recent scholarship offers a wealth of examples of normalization of nontraditional roles in politics, specifically in popular culture and literature. Within politics, we also see some relevant scholarship that offers perspective relevant to this study.

Looking at representation in public office as a means of normalizing the underserved, scholars have established the role this plays in multiple contexts. For example, Tremblay (2022) noted that simply serving in political roles as a member of the LGBTQ community helps to put a face on the community with those who often misunderstand and mistakenly assign hate or fear, helping to mediate the relationship between the community and state, combatting the well-established notion that prejudice is a learned practice (Allport, 1954).

Media outlets and their role in political communication have also been a focus of recent scholarship in normalizing underserved populations in political and civic settings. Mahadeen (2021), for instance, examined the role of the first Jordanian LGBTQ web platform, Mykali, and its use to combat moral panics related to queer culture in Jordan. The scholar noted the historic role of moral panics in enforcing social control with the Jordanian government, and Mykali's presentation as a queer counter public and use of pop-activism to challenge Jordan's homophobic stances to establish Jordan's LGBTQ community as part of Jordan's authentic identity.

The literature also offers insights about the challenges those who are normalizing underserved populations in leadership roles face. Bates et al. (2017) found in an experimental analysis that a hypothetical candidate's identification with the LGBTQ community still played a mitigating role in their electability, regardless of political ideology among those in the experimental sample. Krzyżanowski and Ekström (2022) also pointed to the competing narratives of far-right populism and nativist rhetoric's rising prevalence in western media, and the threats they pose to underserved populations and democratic politics, calling for deeper inquiry about their prevalence and impact on western media and public opinion.

Recent literature on normalization of politicians from underserved populations serving in top political roles remains limited. This paper provides an opportunity to explore how the first full generation of individuals outside of heteronormative, racial, and ethnic backgrounds are engaged in public and political communication, their role in political surrogacy, and their approach to engaging in issue advocacy. Normalization is a key consideration, given Pete Buttigieg's role as an openly gay cabinet member, as well as the need to normalize several administration members fulfilling key roles as women, people of color, and members of the LGBTQ community for the first time. With normalization discussed in brief, the focus will now shift to a discussion of political surrogacy in political communication.

Political Surrogacy

Political surrogacy is a critical role in political campaign communication and was no less significant during the 2020 presidential election. Pye and Taylor (2024) examined the effective use of a two-for-the-price-of-one (2-for-1) narrative in explaining the relative strength of two qualified candidates in Joe Biden and Kamala Harris on the Democratic ticket, drawing parallels to the unsuccessful use of the same strategy by Hillary Clinton during the 2016 election (Taylor & Pye, 2019). The authors contended that Harris was effective through her use of artful political communication and digital platforms to articulate her readiness for service, in building identity with women voters, and drawing a connection to the Obama and Biden tickets of 2008 and 2012 to help bolster the 2-for-1 approach.

Taking a broader look at political surrogacy on digital platforms, Goodwin et al. (2020) analyzed the strategic use of paid influencers (specifically micro-influencers) in political campaign communication by political action committees (PACs). The decision to leverage these individuals is because of the strength of their perceived trustworthiness, and subsequent ability to influence public opinion among their followers. The researchers characterized paid influencer use as a highly sophisticated form of digital propaganda. The findings present a new understanding of the use of digital platforms and influencers in political campaigns and the shifting landscape of surrogacy in political campaigns.

First Ladies and Political Communication

Research examining the role of first ladies in political communication illustrates a diverse set of roles that are critical in supporting a presidential agenda. Over time, the Office of the First Lady has become an extension of the machinery of the White House, and first ladies are used to strategically benefit their husband's administration (Beasley, 2010; Burns, 2008; Grimes, 1990). First ladies can serve both as political surrogates and as issue advocates.

Speaking to surrogacy work, first ladies are often more popular than the sitting president and appeal as less or nonpartisan in comparison to the president making them an effective conduit for direct appeals to the American public than the sitting president (Burrell, 2001; Burrell et al., 2011). Wright (2016) similarly argued that first ladies may be more effective communicators on issue advocacy in this polarized era because of their less partisan positioning and wider appeal. Wright (2016) also noted that presidential administrations strategically use the remarks of first ladies to draw attention to or gain support for policy issues and to make credible bipartisan appeals. First ladies can balance the partisan tone of an administration and appeal to broader audiences. Presidents and first ladies can coordinate their remarks so that presidents may benefit from the popularity of their wives. Mueller (2008) found that a presidential surrogate who is perceived as neutral will have a stronger public reception to administration talking points than those more subject to daily fluctuations, like elected officials.

Borrelli (2011) revealed through historical analysis that even when first ladies are not accepted as representatives of the electorate, they still find a way to reinstate themselves as interpreters and mediators in the executive branch. Relatedly, Jeffrey Cohen (2000) emphasized first ladies are critical in the institutional presidency due to their institutionalized "political, popular, and/or policy making benefit to the president" (p. 374).

First Ladies are also free to leverage more personalization and role stereotypes as they are free to construct an image defined by compassion and caring, and that is unobjectionable to voters (Fu & Savel, 2020). In Fu and Savel's (2020) study examining the public comments on policy of Hillary Rodham Clinton, Laura Bush, and Michelle Obama, the researchers found a division of labor along gender lines consistent with past research showing that first ladies are free to lean into gender stereotypes and focus wholeheartedly on issues that female politicians have long been seen as experts in, like education, family, and health care (Bauer, 2015; Dolan, 2010, 2014; Fridkin and Kenney, 2009; Koch, 2000), without spending much time discussing issue areas that have been traditionally thought of as "masculine," like the economy or foreign policy (Dolan, 2014; Holman et al., 2016; Huddy & Terkildsen, 1993; Lawless, 2004; Sanbonmatsu, 2002). They also found that first ladies do so in a nonpartisan manner, while also using language that crosses partisan lines for broader appeal.

The body of research on how first ladies are leveraging digital platforms is also growing, demonstrating political nuance, and considering their relationship to their political partners. Looking at the effectiveness of first ladies on digital platforms, Bickersham (2020) examined the strategic nuance and sophistication of Michelle Obama's capacity to be effective in traditional and contemporary forms of digital and social media in engaging the public and the press. The literature illustrates the value of spouses and partners as political surrogates in the most traditional definition of the role. What the literature lacks is perspective on the influence of nontraditional partnerships, marriages, and gender roles of those spouses or partners on approach to and impact of political surrogacy in supporting a political figure or in efforts to advocate for political and social issues. This study seeks to offer some perspective on the matter.

Research Questions

Based on previous literature on political surrogacy (Pye & Taylor, 2024; Taylor & Pye, 2019), the following research question are posed:

RQ1: What core themes did Pete Buttigieg present in his tweets as secretary of transportation?

Based on the previous literature on political spouses (Bickersham, 2020; Borrelli, 2011; Burrell, 2001; Burrell et al., 2011) and their approaches to political advocacy (Fu & Savel, 2020; Wright, 2016), the following research questions are posed:

> RQ2: How did Chasten Buttigieg engage in issue advocacy in his tweets?
> RQ3: How did Chasten Buttigieg engage in political surrogacy in his tweets?

Based on the previous literature on normalization (Tremblay, 2022), the following research questions are posed:

> RQ4: How did Pete Buttigieg engage in normalization in his tweets?
> RQ5: How did Chasten Buttigieg engage in normalization in his tweets?

Method

Platform

To comparatively study the approach of both Pete and Chasten Buttigieg, Twitter was selected as the platform for analysis. This is due to the robust presence both have maintained on the platform with Pete Buttigieg having been present on the platform since December of 2010 and Chasten establishing an active profile in September of 2015. It is important to note that Pete Buttigieg established an official page for his role as secretary of transportation in February of 2021, but that page is not analyzed for this study, as the goal is to explore Pete Buttigieg in the broader lens as an individual beyond the cabinet role.

Sample Period

The sample collected for analysis included tweets from the inauguration of President Joe Biden on January 20, 2021, through January 20, 2022. The goal was to examine the first year of Secretary Buttigieg in his role as a member of the Biden administration, as well as to explore the approach of Chasten Buttigieg in his new role as a spouse to a prominent political figure and established role as a political advocate in public life.

Means of Analysis

The researcher used qualitative textual analysis to identify themes (Patton, 2002) to better understand their presence in the body of each subjects' tweets.

The qualitative textual analysis took place in four stages: decontextualization of the data, recontextualization of the data, categorization of the data into substantive themes, and compilation of findings in the write-up to ensure a thorough examination of the tweets (Berg, 2001; Neuendorf & Kumar, 2016). The intent of the four-stage examination was to achieve a latent analysis and to consider deeper meaning and motivations behind the tweets of both Pete and Chasten Buttigieg (Berg, 2001).

The researcher performed the four-stage analysis by performing multiple readings of the body of both Pete and Chasten Buttigieg's tweets over the period of analysis to meet saturation and to better ensure trustworthiness (Nowell et al., 2017). On the first reading, the researcher performed simple annotation of potential themes present in each tweet. Following the first reading, the research examined the potential themes identified, and established some dominant topics for each individual's feed. Following the initial examination of themes, the researcher performed a second read of the tweets to permit for identification of instances of emergent themes identified during the initial read across the entire body of tweets analyzed, and to revisit each tweet to reexamine for annotated themes in each tweet to clarify meanings and to facilitate consolidation around the most central themes present in each individual's feed. Following the second full read, the researcher reexamined the body of themes identified to determine the body of macro-themes present in reference to each research question, and sub-topics related to each theme. Finally, the researcher performed a final read-through of the tweets, by theme and subtopic to consider the tweets in relation to key events, administrative and personal issue positions, and in terms of each individual.

On saturation of the themes (Bernard & Ryan, 2010), the researcher examined a universal sample of each individual's tweets to perform the comparison, eliminating the possibility of excluding themes in tweets absent from analysis. Moreover, the researcher allowed for the possibility of emergent themes of topics at each reading and would re-examine the body of tweets for additional instances of the emergent theme or topic to guard against omission of themes, and to get firm grasp on volume and orientation of topics relative to the larger themes present in each individual's feed.

Prior literature informed the researcher's perspective in organizing themes for both individual's tweets. Secretary Buttigieg offered the opportunity to explore his approach as a surrogate (Taylor & Pye, 2019) as a part of the new president's cabinet and as an emerging figure of prominence in his part. Specifically, the key themes the Biden administration prioritized following election in 2020, or issues Buttigieg wanted to prioritize that are relevant to his long-term political aspirations. Chasten Buttigieg, by contrast, offered a unique opportunity to examine a political partner's role in public forums (Bickersham, 2020; Borrelli, 2011; Burrell, 2001; Burrell et al., 2011), particularly on Twitter (now X) as a public communication platform (Fu &Savel, 2020). In Chasten's case, it was important to establish how his approach compared to past political spouses and partners, given his unique role as one of the first high-profile same-sex partners in the executive branch of American government. Consistent with analyzing some forms of latent analysis (Berg, 2001), the researcher performed some simple tallies in which tweets contained topics related to the identified themes, adding a quantitative dimension to this qualitative study. While not conventional in qualitative research methods, much qualitative data can easily be counted to help illustrate frequency and prevalence of themes (Morgan, 1993).

In combining a simple tally of occurrences of each theme in the larger body of tweets for each individual with a qualitative approach to examining and organizing topics into themes, readers can see how key themes are discussed across the body of tweets for each individual, while also seeing the frequency with which each theme is present across each individual's body of tweets. The researcher adopted this approach to analysis due to the brevity of the tweets limiting the potential for deeper qualitative analysis within tweets and the potential value of quantification in explaining frequency and prevalence over time.

Results

In reviewing the body of tweets over the year analyzed, the researcher sees a distinctive contrast in presentation between Pete and Chasten Buttigieg. In Pete Buttigieg, the body of tweets serve to demonstrate an active political appointee engaged in public service and surrogacy, while also articulating efforts to meet many of the campaign promises pertaining to transportation infrastructure articulated by Biden on the campaign trail, with few notable exceptions. For Chasten Buttigieg, we see three narratives coming to the forefront in his body of tweets during the year analyzed: (1) public activism for LGBTQ rights; (2) normalizing a gay family unit; and (3) normalizing nontraditional firsts in public service roles in the Biden administration. The following is a comparative breakdown of both the Buttigiegs' tweets.

Pete Buttigieg

When examining Secretary Buttigieg's tweets over the sample year (see Table 13.1), he utilized his personal social media for three core functions, directly focused on his new role as Secretary of transportation and serving as a political surrogate for President Biden, aligning with previous literature explaining the role of political surrogates in reinforcing political candidates' and administration's agenda (Pye & Taylor, 2024; Taylor & Pye, 2019). First, a broad focus on advancing the Department of Transportation's agenda on infrastructure, using several key initiatives that incorporated some unconventional appeals. Second, a strong surrogacy focused on promoting President Biden's Build Back Better program and its value to transportation and infrastructure. Third, a strategic focus on demonstrating his engagement and productivity as a cabinet member in visiting and connecting with state departments of transportation as secretary of transportation and Biden surrogate at Build Back Better program events. The following is a focused discussion of each of these

Table 13.1: Pete Buttigieg tweets, January 20, 2021–January 20, 2022

Tweet Theme	Tweets	
	N	%
Direct Surrogacy	90	34.4
Build Back Better	20	7.6
Biden Admin/Party	70	26.7
Indirect Surrogacy	68	26
Infrastructure	34	13
Bridges	12	4.6
Supply Chain	22	8.4
Shipping Support	15	5.7
Electric Vehicles	25	9.5
Job Creator	12	4.6
Climate Change	8	3.1
Equity	5	1.9
Effective Work	67	25.6
Personalization	32	12.2
LGBTQ	1	.4
Family	31	11.8
Normalization	5	2
Total	262	100

elements, as well as the one clear break that had a dual function of personalizing Secretary Buttigieg and advancing Biden administration issue positions.

Direct Surrogacy in Promotion

Buttigieg's made some notable effort to reconnect with the Biden campaign's theme relevant to his agency's operations. Secretary Buttigieg presented a healthy number of posts (20 tweets, 7.6%) related to promoting President Biden's Build Back Better plan in his tweets during the year of analysis. For Buttigieg, the plan's connection to infrastructure, environmental improvements, and support for achieving Department of Transportation objectives made being a surrogate and advocate for the campaign promises essential. The tweets were typically clips from Buttigieg media segments advocating for the plan, graphics explaining benefits, or retweets of President Biden or Biden administration members making the case for the policy.

Focusing on his broader surrogacy on behalf of the Biden administration and other members of the Democratic Party, Secretary Buttigieg posted 70 tweets and retweets (26.7%) during the observation year. The tweets included direct retweets from the political figures in the party, video segments of his appearances to comment on administration policy and issues, and individual tweets expressing concern and support for American citizens in times of crises. In this regard, Secretary Buttigieg tends to align with the more neutral forms of surrogacy (Mueller, 2008) by not drawing too personal a tie to Biden in expressing a workman-like accomplishment of administrative goals.

Indirect Surrogacy through Discussion of Action

The most robust content in terms of tweets, retweets, and replies focused on critical initiatives to the Department of Transportation during Secretary Buttigieg's first year in the role. Thematically much of the discussion centered around infrastructure, which was in keeping with campaign promises put forward by the Biden administration and aligned with Buttigieg's political history as mayor of South Bend, Indiana. In total, Buttigieg posted 68 tweets or retweets (26%) focused on infrastructure policy points, problems, and the efforts of the Biden administration in addressing concerns with infrastructure.

Among the most common related topics to infrastructure were concerns with roads and bridges (12 tweets, 4.6%), and supply chain related to shipping concerns during the first year coming out of the COVID-19 pandemic (22 tweets, 8.4%). The supply chain tweets grew in focus during late 2021 as the holidays approached (17 of 22 tweets on or following Thanksgiving) with increased oppositional criticism of the Biden administration and claims of lack of progress on shipping and supply chain, and the risks it posed at Thanksgiving and for Christmas.

An emergent subtheme in response to criticism on supply chain centered on rapid response to and refutation of claims. Secretary Buttigieg posted seven tweets and retweets that served as direct means of debunking these claims, boasting about 91% capacity in stocked shelves in stores, and shrinking numbers in backlogged inventory at ports waiting to be shipped out. Beyond these responses, Secretary Buttigieg also posted 15 tweets (5.7%) focused on supporting truck drivers and how logistical support for roads and shipping included in the Biden administration led budget plans would help contribute to battling supply chain issues.

A specific topic that carried a strong emphasis in discussing the subject was the potential value of strategically aligning infrastructural planning with environmentally friendly approaches to renewable energy, with a specific emphasis on electric vehicles (25 tweets, 9.5%), including cost reductions and increased access to charging stations. As a means of expanding the appeal of electric vehicles, Secretary Buttigieg made specific references to the potential value of supporting expansion of electric vehicle production and logistical support for electric vehicles as a potential job creator (12 tweets, 4.6%) and as a means of combating climate change (8 tweets, 3.1%).

Equity also emerged as a critical subtheme in examining Buttigieg's surrogacy work in tweeting about administrative policy and the work of the Department of Transportation. A small, important portion of the discussion around infrastructural planning for the Department of Transportation was about how more equitable planning for access to transportation, roadways, and other resources were essential to bettering the quality of life in historically underserved communities in the United States (5 tweets, 1.9%). The small number of tweets focused on this area came early in the review period but signaled that equity of access was one appeal among many used by the Biden administration and Secretary Buttigieg to advance budget and legislative efforts in support of infrastructure and transportation.

The integration of administrative priorities like infrastructure, supply chain issues, the environment, and equity through the lens of agency action serves to advance the administration's agenda, while making the case for the agency's effectiveness on behalf of the American public an Buttigieg's role as its leader. This dual functionality is indicating a surrogate mindful of future political aims, while performing effectively in supporting the current administration's agenda.

An Engaged Cabinet Member in the Field

Another strong thread of tweets for Buttigieg in the year analyzed were tweets that focused on demonstrating his effectiveness as a a cabinet secretary executing administrative priorities. Buttigieg posted 67 tweets and retweets (25.6%) demonstrating his efforts to promote and explain the Department of Transportation, including tweets about his site visits to state and federal entities, programs focusing on Biden administration initiatives, and his video segments of his on-air appearances discussing department efforts.

In one sense he was effectively demonstrating he was an active member of the administration, and competently leading the agency in execution of the administration's priorities in meeting political promises, through tweets of photo opportunities and press releases related to each public event and factory tour. In another sense, he was presenting himself as an advocate for and educator about the work of the agency by teaching people in his tweets and interviews about the kinds of work the Department of Transportation is responsible for and were performing. On one level, he was actively trying to demonstrate that the agency was working for the American public. On another level, it was clearly implied he was an effective, competent administrator in demonstrating his active presence on agency matters throughout the year.

Personalization and Limited Normalization

Secretary Buttigieg's approach to his social media during his first year in the role was dominated by political messaging and public service, which reflected his emergence as a prominent member of the Biden administration as Secretary of Transportation and the prominent role that infrastructure and transportation concerns played in the 2020 election and the first year of the Biden presidency. That said, Buttigieg did present a few key moments that reflected his firsthand experiences. Posts wishing people well during the holidays, posts about family, and humorous segments on late night talk shows were among his personalizing tweets.

One tweet, dated September 20, 2021focused on the tenth anniversary of "Don't Ask, Don't Tell." In it, he said, "Ten years after the end of Don't Ask Don't Tell, I'm reflecting on the courage of LGBTQ+ servicemembers who answered the call, both before and since it became possible to serve openly—as well as those who fought to ensure all could wear the uniform as their whole, full selves" (Buttigieg, 2021). Buttigieg presents a dual identification with his military service and membership in the LGBTQ community, directly honoring and acknowledging the contributions of LGBTQ+ service members, while implicitly criticizing the original policy. Despite this moment of personal identification with the issue, it was his one occasion posting about the subject during the year studied.

The strongest set of personalization tweets served as a vehicle for Secretary Buttigieg to promote the Biden administration's legislative agenda supporting parents and their children. Pete and Chasten Buttigieg adopted two children in August of 2021. His first tweet announcing their adoption of twins came on August 17, Buttigieg posted a second tweet on September 4, 2021, showing him and Chasten with their children, expressing thanks to followers who commented on the initial announcement. He posted 31 total tweets and retweets (11.8%) of Chasten's comments talking about parenting, health scares, and holiday events discussing parenting experiences during the final 5 months of 2021. Tweets on parenting illustrated both humorous and affectionate comments about their first experiences with parenting the infant twins, including naps, feeding, and getting them to sleep. Secretary Buttigieg also took a moment on Christmas of 2021 to tweet out a family photo with Chasten and the twins, wishing a happy holiday season to followers from his own family. In these tweets, we see an example of Buttigieg personalizing himself and bringing his followers and potential supporters into his life and around his family. It helps the public identify with him as a person and not simply a public figure. Further, he is normalizing same sex adoption, albeit implicitly, through this personalization and sharing warm, affectionate home dynamics on Twitter.

Not all tweets and retweets included happy moments of parenting. On November 5, 2021, Pete retweeted his husband Chasten, who shared they had just gotten their son home following a 3-week stay in the hospital following an ambulance trip and extended stint on a respirator. In 2023, Buttigieg would elaborate and share his son was battling a severe case of Respiratory Syncytial Virus (RSV), which infects an individual's lungs and breathing passages. It is particularly difficult for infants. In retweeting his husband, Buttigieg said, "Thankful, relieved, and reflecting a great deal on the mixture of joy, terror, and love that is parenting" (Buttigieg, 2021). In this scare, his decision to share the experience offered another form of personalization, showing that he and Chasten were coping with the same challenges parents experience.

Further discussion related to this health scare and other family experiences enabled Buttigieg to reconnect with political surrogacy in advocating for legislation aimed at supporting American families struggling to support their children. Buttigieg posted nine tweets connecting those his experiences with childcare and his son's health scare with a key component of the Biden administration's Build Back Better program: the reconciliation bill. The legislation proposal intended to provide increased support for parents and children to help close the gap on childhood poverty, including health care. In a retweet of a November 8 interview he granted on the bill, specifically about provisions related to funding for paid parental leave and childcare, he drew a critical distinction about parental leave being more than "time off," characterizing it as "time to do work—good work, joyful work, meaningful work—but it's time to do important work" (Hutzler, 2021). His personalization of experiences as a new parent of twins with his husband presented an opportunity to identify with American citizens most directly affected by the legislative proposal, and to concretely demonstrate how the legislation could help those not as fortunate as him, Chasten, or their adopted children.

The Biden administration's cabinet appointments and selection of Kamala Harris as his Vice President enabled Biden to make the claim that his administration was opening the door for Americans of all walks of life to be the first to serve. Despite his role as one of those firsts and some notable efforts at personalization that include some themes of normalization, Secretary Buttigieg offered rare commentary on the subject on Twitter in his first year. During the year of analysis, Buttigieg made five total tweets (1.9%) on the matter. One tweet acknowledged the diversity of the cabinet in a comparison of photos of Franklin Delano Roosevelt's first cabinet to the Biden administration's cabinet. Another tweet complimented Deb Haaland on her appointment as the first cabinet member of Indigenous descent, and others making minor comments on these accomplishments. With an analysis of the primary theme of tweets and retweets by Secretary Buttigieg addressed, the focus will now shift to how Chasten Buttigieg approached his role as the spouse of a political figure in a prominent role.

Chasten Buttigieg

In reviewing Chasten Buttigieg's posts over the course of the reviewed year, there was a distinctively different approach in presenting himself and the issues he chose to discuss in comparison to Pete Buttigieg's approach (see

Table 13.2: Chasten Buttigieg tweets, January 20, 2021–January 20, 2022

Tweet Themes	Tweets	
	N	%
LGBTQ Advocacy	120	62.8
Fundraising Promotion	46	24.1
Trevor Project	24	12.6
Don't Say Gay Bill	30	15.7
Texas Bill	20	10.5
Family	46	24.1
Adoption	31	16.2
Issue Connection	10	5.2
Other	5	2.6
Normalizing Diversity	25	13.1
Total	191	100

Table 13.2). In Chasten's approach, the clear focus was on advocacy for the LGBTQ community, a strong focus on personalizing his family and advocating for a same sex parented family, as well as a concerted effort to normalize diversity in key roles in government and public life.

LGBTQ Advocacy

It is clear in reviewing Chasten Buttigieg's tweets during the analysis year that he embraced a similar role to past literature that tells us about first ladies and political spouses and embracing an active role in advocacy for not only their partners (Burrell, 2001; Burrell et al., 2011), but also as advocates for issues under less severe scrutiny than elected or appointed officials (Fu & Savel, 2020; Wright, 2016). For Chasten Buttigieg, there was a concerted focus on speaking out against legislation that targets members of the LGBTQ community. Buttigieg posted 120 total tweets and retweets (62.8%) focusing on LGBTQ issues, events, and days of recognition during the year of analysis. For example, a focal point was a series of tweets promoting fundraising and events supporting the Trevor Project (24 tweets and retweets, 12.6%), in addition to 46 tweets (24.1%) promoting other fundraising and advocacy events supporting LGBTQ rights.

During the first year of the Biden presidency, the Florida Parental Rights in Education act was proposed in the Florida state legislature, prohibiting instruction or discussion on matters of sexual orientation and gender identity. The controversial bill earned the colloquial moniker "the Don't Say Gay bill." For Buttigieg, this became a focus of personal criticism for him in tweets and retweets. All told, Buttigieg posted 30 tweets and retweets (15.7%) criticizing the bill during the 2021 legislative session. The posts included video clips from interviews, sound bites from individuals testifying against the bill in committee hearings, and retweets from members of the community and allies speaking out against it. At the same time of the Florida bill's discussion, Texas was considering a similar body of legislation intended to target trans kids, including access to equitable facilities and healthcare. In this case, Buttigieg offered 20 tweets and retweets (10.5%) including criticism about the impact of the legislation on the lives of transgender youth.

It is notable to compare the approach of both Buttigiegs in tweets focused on issue advocacy. Chasten was consistently supportive of Pete's work as Secretary of Transportation, retweeting and offering simple, positive messaging that was often similar or restating the position offered by Pete. In terms of content, they both made effective use of news clips, video clips, and graphics provided by the Biden administration. In terms of their discussion of the reconciliation bill, Chasten's messaging mirrored Pete's. In this regard, we saw a lot of commonalities that reflected the administration's, party's, and Secretary Buttigieg's approach to strategic political messaging.

Of more interest is the contrast in focus on certain issues where Chasten was more visible and vocal. Noted above, Chasten offered 120 distinct tweets speaking out in support of LGBTQ organizations, nonprofits, and issues like adoption, reflecting his firsthand experiences. This is consistent with his history of being a visible advocate for LGBTQ rights (Igoe, 2019; Zavaleta, 2019). Speaking to tone of tweets, Chasten also presented a more enthusiastic, direct tone criticizing legislators and political figures advancing legislation that can inhibit the quality of life for LGBTQ. During the 2022 deliberation of Florida's Parental Rights in Education bill, Chasten Buttigieg offered strong criticism of the bill as he had on previous bills in Florida and Texas targeting LGBTQ citizens. In a January 20, 2022, tweet, Buttigieg said of the bill:

> This will kill kids, @RonDeSantisFL. You are purposefully making your state a harder place for LGBTQ kids to survive in. In a national survey (@TrevorProject), 42% of LGBTQ youth seriously considered attempting suicide last year. Now they can't talk to their teachers? (Buttigieg, 2022)

The strong language and focus on the bill being a matter of challenging the survival of LGBTQ youth presents a more aggressive approach to advocacy.

In contrast, Secretary Buttigieg is notable for a relative absence of discussion about LGBTQ issues on his feed. Except for his comments on "don't ask, don't tell" on the tenth anniversary of its repeal. Secretary Buttigieg did not engage in dialog around LGBTQ issues. All told, Chasten Buttigieg demonstrated in his first year the capacity to push issue advocacy in ways that elected officials often do not or can not for strategic purposes, in keeping with past literature on political surrogacy among spouses (Fu & Savel, 2020; Wright, 2016).

Family

Chasten was comparatively stronger than Pete Buttigieg in posting about family and personalizing himself and Pete on Twitter. In total, Buttigieg posted 46 distinctive tweets and retweets (24.1%) that served multiple functions. Posts including photos of Pete, Chasten, and their children helps to personalize them with the public, and helped bring levity to their mutual identities in public life. As was the case with Secretary Buttigieg, the September 4 post showing their first photo with their adopted children was a major touch point in his dialog about family with the public, yielding 31 total tweets and retweets (16.2%). In this regard, Chasten's practice mirrored some normative practices of spouses serving a humanizing function in showing political figures around the home and in personal settings (Beasley, 2010; Bickersham, 2020; Borrelli, 2011; Burns, 2008; Grimes, 1990).

A key secondary effect, further reinforcing past literature on the capacity for political spouses to engage in issue advocacy (Wright, 2016), was the role that their adoption of two children played in helping establish his role as an advocate for normalizing adoption for same sex couples. Beyond the humanizing effect of posting pictures and quips about learning to parent, the posts helped to normalize the idea of same sex couples adopting children and forming families, by drawing on shared experiences with new parents and veteran parents alike. In posting about their struggles, successes, and concerns, they helped show the experience and mindset of gay and heterosexual parenting couples do share a lot of commonalities.

A third function that was common with Secretary Buttigieg was the focus on advocating for affordable childcare that was a focus in the Biden administration's Build Back Better plan. All told, 10 of his 46 posts (5.2%) shifted focus from his personal experience to how what was proposed could help people in similar situations, but with fewer resources to overcome challenges. This again reinforces some of the traditional literature about the role of political spouses as surrogates for their partners (Bickersham, 2020; Borrelli,

2011; Burrell, 2001; Burrell et al., 2011), as well as the Biden administration as Chasten Buttigieg was consistent in his messaging with those serving in the Biden administration, including Secretary Buttegieg. Interestingly, in this body of tweets, Chasten is embracing some key issue positions normatively associated with women in politics or female political spouses (Bauer, 2015; Dolan, 2010; 2014; Fridkin and Kenney, 2009; Koch, 2000). In this regard, it does offer an interesting perspective deserving of further exploration about how same sex political partnerships impact advocacy roles of issues previously defined in perception on basis of gender.

Normalizing Diversity in Government and Public Life

While Secretary Buttigieg offered a select few posts supporting peers who achieved firsts in key roles in government, Chasten Buttigieg made a point of supporting friends and allies who were breaking barriers in key roles. All told, Buttigieg posted 25 tweets and retweets (13.1%) focusing on celebrating key members of the Biden administration and their partners filling first-time roles in public life. Tweets focused on Deb Haaland, the first secretary of the interior of Indigenous descent, Doug Emhoff as the first second gentlemen, Vice President Kamala Harris as the first woman and African American vice president, and Emily Voorde as the first member of the White House staff from the transgender community. These posts were in addition to personal tweets of support of his husband, Pete Buttigieg, serving as the first openly gay secretary of transportation. This mix of public congratulations and support also reflects some normative practices among political spouses and first ladies dedicated to public congratulations and showing of support, even in more contemporary political couples (Wright, 2016) and even as there is an implicit element of advocacy for diversity in equity in recognizing these individuals in their respective roles (Fu & Savel, 2020), and reflecting the importance of normalization (Tremblay, 2022) among political figures and their surrogates.

Discussion

This study presents a preliminary examination of a unique situation that is emerging in American politics where individuals of different genders, sexual orientation, racial, and ethnic backgrounds are fulfilling key roles in government and public life for the first time. As a preliminary study, it is by no means an exhaustive analysis, and there is a need for deeper examination of each of these unique contexts and how different situations may impact everyone's approach, as well as how they share commonalities. That said, there are some insights that connect the findings of this study with past research looking at political spouses, surrogates, advocacy, and normalization.

Addressing the first research question on political surrogacy (Pye & Taylor, 2024 Taylor & Pay, 2019.), specifically Pete Buttigieg, it is clear he adopted a robust role as a surrogate for the Biden administration in his role as the Secretary of Transportation. In many ways, it is his strongest practice on Twitter, and a reflection of his adopted role during the 2020 presidential campaign and television and digital platforms. He used the platform to reinforce critical agenda items with direct ties to the work of the Department of Transportation. This reflects past literature on the value of political surrogacy and illustrates how Buttigieg effectively uses it to illustrate his effectiveness and advance the mission of the Department of Transportation.

Speaking on political spouses, specifically first ladies, we see compelling evidence of parallels and differences with what past studies demonstrated about the role and approach of first ladies in comparison to their presidential partners. For Chasten Buttigieg, he was able to embrace a more proactive role as an issue advocate on behalf of members of the LGBTQ community and leverage his prominence to bring visibility to ongoing legislation and issues on his Twitter page. Chasten Buttigieg's consistent discussion of these issues reflects recent scholarship acknowledging the ability of first ladies to address positions on issues than their political partners may not be able to address (Fu & Savel, 2020; Wright, 2016). Of note is the contrast from past literature indicating that likeability and the ability to be more nonpartisan enables a political spouse to be more effective (Wright, 2016), when seeing the body of critical tweets and retweets against legislatures and politicians put forward by Chasten Buttigieg on LGBTQ issues—particularly his use of data and firm language to equate some of the policy positions on matters like the "Don't Say Gay" bill in Florida as something that will only lead to needless deaths among LGBTQ youth. In terms of surrogacy (Borrelli, 2011; Burrell, 2001; Burrell et al., 2011), it is clear that Chasten was effective in elevating the profile of members of the Biden administration, and vocal in support of the administration's position on LGBTQ rights. A deeper comparison of Chasten's approach to advocacy and surrogacy in comparison to other notable political spouses in history would offer greater insight into the contrast and parallels you can draw about him as one of the first prominent same sex political spouses and other notable political spouses in history (e.g., Hillary Rodham Clinton, Michelle Obama, Nancy Reagan, and Eleanor Roosevelt).

Speaking to the research questions on normalization (Tremblay, 2022), merely being in nontraditional roles is important in normalizing diversity in traditional political roles and roles in public life. That said, the effort to normalize members of the Biden administration and their spouses were a much stronger part of Chasten Buttigieg's social media content on Twitter than it was Pete Buttigieg's Twitter page. This may, in part, reflect the freedom political spouses enjoy, enabling them to branch out and be more vocal about important issues (Fu & Savel, 2020; Wright, 2016). In addition to the prevalence of the posts, Chasten Buttigieg was more critical, particularly in response to legislative efforts in Texas and Florida that would harm the quality of life of trans children and promote ignorance about LGBTQ culture, respectively. A larger analysis of nontraditional political figures and their spouses would provide greater context to help identify if this pattern holds, if there is a clear strategy within this administration, or if this is unique to the Buttigiegs.

References

Allport, G. W. (1954). *The nature of prejudice*. Addison-Wesley.
Altman, A., & Alter, C. (2020, March 1). "Pete Buttigieg's history-making campaign fell short, but he leaves the race a star". *Time*. https://time.com/5793275/pete-buttigieg-ends-campaign/
Bates Bailey, M., Nawara, S., & Burgess, S. (2017). Gay and lesbian candidates, group stereotypes, and the news media: An experimental design. In M. Brettschneider, S. Burgess, & C. Keating (Eds.), *LGBTQ politics: A critical reader* (pp. 334–350). New York University Press. https://doi.org/10.18574/nyu/9781479849468.003.0024
Bauer, N. M. (2015). Emotional, sensitive, and unfit for office? Gender stereotype activation and support female candidates. *Political Psychology, 36*(6), 691–708. https://doi.org/10.1111/pops.12186
Beasley, V. B. (2010). The rhetorical presidency meets the unitary executive: Implications for presidential rhetoric on public policy. *Rhetoric and Public Affairs, 13*(1), 7–35. https://doi.org/10.2307/41955589
Bell, K. (2014, September 24). Mayor Buttigieg reports being back on U.S. soil. *South Bend Voice*. https://southbendvoice.com/2014/09/24/mayor-buttigieg-reports-being-back-on-us-soil/
Berg, B.L. (2001). *Qualitative research methods for the social sciences*. Allyn and Bacon.
Bernard H.R., & Ryan G. W. (2010). Analyzing qualitative data: Systematic approaches. Thousand Oaks, CA: Sage; 2010.
Bickersham, S. B. (2020). Michelle Obama and the effective use of strategic communication: The art of messaging across multiple media platforms. In L.M. Burns (Ed.), *Media relations and the modern first lady: From Jacqueline Kennedy to Melania Trump* (pp. 245–264). Lexington Books.

Borrelli, M. (2011). *The politics of the president's wife.* Texas A&M University Press.

Bowden, J. (2020, August 31). Chasten Buttigieg to talk husband's presidential bid, coronavirus in new memoir. *The Hill.* https://thehill.com/blogs/in-the-know/in-the-know/514496-chasten-buttigieg-to-talk-husbands-presidential-bid-coronavirus-memoir

Burns, L. M. (2008). *First ladies and the fourth estate: Press framing of presidential wives.* Northern Illinois University Press.

Burrell, B. (2001). *Public opinion, the first ladyship, and Hillary Rodham Clinton.* Routledge.

Burrell, B., Elder, L., & Frederick, B. (2011). Polls and elections: From Hillary to Michelle: Public opinion and the spouses of presidential candidates. *Presidential Studies Quarterly, 41*(1), 156–176. https://doi.org/10.1111/j.1741-5705.2010.03835.x

Buttigieg, C. [@Chasten] (2022, January 20). This will kill kids, @RonDeSantisFL. You are purposefully making your state a harder place for LGBTQ kids to survive in. In a national survey (@TrevorProject), 42% of LGBTQ youth seriously considered attempting suicide last year. Now they can't talk to their teachers? [Post]. X. https://twitter.com/Chasten/status/1484281974441316353

Buttigieg, P. [@SecretaryPete] (2021, September 21). Ten years after the end of Don't Ask Don't Tell, I'm reflecting on the courage of LGBTQ+ servicemembers who answered the call, both before and since it became possible to serve openly—as well as those who fought to ensure all could wear the uniform as their whole, full selves. [Post]. X. https://twitter.com/SecretaryPete/status/1439975810652418051

Buttigieg, P. [@SecretaryPete] (2021, November 5). Thankful, relieved, and reflecting a great deal on the mixture of joy, terror, and love that is parenting. [Post]. X. https://twitter.com/PeteButtigieg/status/1456712775137431562

Buttigieg, P. (2015, June 16). South Bend mayor: Why coming out matters. *South Bend Tribune.* https://www.southbendtribune.com/news/local/south-bend-mayor-why-coming-out-matters/article_4dce0d12-1415-11e5-83c0-739eebd623ee.html

Catanzarite, M. (2015, March 27). SB mayor, business owners speak out against religious freedom act. *WNDU-TV.* https://web.archive.org/web/20190330200546/https://www.wndu.com/home/headlines/SB-mayor-business-owners-speak-out-against-religious-freedom-act-297838631.html

Cohen, J.E. (2000). The Polls: Public Favorability toward the First Lady, 1993-1999. *Presidential Studies Quarterly, 30:* 575-585. https://doi.org/10.1111/j.0360-4918.2000.00130.x

Colombo, H. (2017, October 12). Some national Democrats swoon over South Bend Mayor Pete Buttigieg. *Indiana Business Journal.* https://www.ibj.com/articles/65820-some-national-democrats-swoon-over-south-bend-mayor-pete-buttigieg

Deliso, M. (2020, November 7). Vice President-elect Kamala Harris's husband Doug Emhoff set to become 1st second gentleman. *ABC News.* https://abcnews.go.com/Politics/vice-president-elect-kamala-harris-husband-doug-emhoff/story?id=74076409

Dolan, K. (2010). The impact of gender stereotyped evaluations on support for women candidates. *Political Behavior, 32,* 69–88. https://doi.org/10.1007/s11109-009-9090-4

Dolan, K. (2014). Gender stereotypes, candidate evaluations, and voting for women candidates: What really matters? *Political Research Quarterly, 67*(1), 96–107. https://doi.org/10.1177/1065912913487949

Epstein, R. J., & Gabriel, T. (2020, March 1). Pete Buttigieg drops out of Democratic presidential race. *The New York Times.* https://www.nytimes.com/2020/03/01/us/politics/pete-buttigieg-drops-out.html

Fridkin, K. L., & Kenney, P. J. (2009). The role of gender stereotypes in US Senate campaigns. *Politics & Gender, 5*(3), 301–324. https://doi.org/10.1017/S1743923X09990158

Fu, S., & Savel, M. (2020). Policy without partisanship: The direct appeals of first ladies. *Presidential Studies Quarterly, 50*(4), 736–761. https://doi.org/10.1111/psq.12678

Fuller, J. (2014, March 10). The most interesting mayor you've never heard of. *The Washington Post.* https://www.washingtonpost.com/blogs/the-fix/wp/2014/03/10/the-most-interesting-mayor-youve-never-heard-of/

Gambino, L. (2019, March 23). Pete Buttigieg for president? Long-shot stands out in crowded field. *The Guardian.* https://www.theguardian.com/us-news/2019/mar/23/pete-buttigieg-democrat-2020-presidential-election

Gardner, D. (2019, April 14). How has South Bend changed under Mayor Buttigieg's leadership? *WBND-LD.* https://www.abc57.com/news/how-has-south-bend-changed-under-mayor-buttigiegs-leadership

Goodwin, A., Joseff, K., & Woolley, S. C. (2020). Social media influencers and the 2020 US election: Paying 'regular people' for digital campaign communication. *Center for Media Engagement.* https://mediaengagement.org/research/social-media-influencers-and-the-2020-election/

Grimes, A. (1990). *Running mates: The making of a first lady.* William Morrow & Company.

Holman, M. R., Merolla, J. L., & Zechmeister, E. J. (2016). Terrorist threat, male stereotypes, and candidate evaluations. *Political Research Quarterly, 69*(1), 134–147. https://doi.org/10.1177/1065912915624018

Huddy, L., & Terkildsen, N. (1993). Gender stereotypes and the perception of male and female candidates. *American Journal of Political Science, 37*(1), 119–147. https://doi.org/10.2307/2111526

Hutzler, A. (2021, November 8). Pete Buttigieg says paid family leave isn't just time off: "It's time to do important work". *Newsweek.* https://www.newsweek.com/pete-buttigieg-says-paid-family-leave-isnt-just-time-off-its-time-do-important-work-1647108

Igoe, K. (2019, April 17). Chasten Buttigieg, Mayor Pete's husband, just gave his first major interview. *Marie Claire.* https://www.marieclaire.com/politics/a27179973/chasten-buttigieg-interview-pete-buttigieg-campaign/

Kalita, S. M. (2020, August 12). Kamala Harris' Indian roots and why they matter. *CNN.* https://edition.cnn.com/2020/08/11/politics/harris-indian-roots/index.html

Keith, J. (2020, February 6). "Pete Buttigieg's Iowa Victory A Milestone in U.S. History; America On-Track to Elect Its First Gay President". LGBTQ Victory Fund. Retrieved from https://victoryfund.org/news/pete-buttigiegs-iowa-victory-a-milestone-in-u-s-history-america-on-track-to-elect-its-first-gay-president/

Koch, J. W. (2000). Do citizens apply gender stereotypes to infer candidates' ideological orientations? *The Journal of Politics, 62*(2), 414–429. https://doi.org/10.1111/0022-3816.00019

Krzyżanowski, M., & Ekström, M. (2022). The normalization of far-right populism and nativist authoritarianism: discursive practices in media, journalism, and the wider public sphere/s. *Discourse & Society, 33*(6), 719–729. https://doi.org/10.1177/09579265221095406

Lakhani, N. (2021, March 15). Deb Haaland confirmed as first Indigenous US cabinet secretary. *The Guardian*. https://www.theguardian.com/us-news/2021/mar/15/deb-haaland-interior-secretary-first-indigenous-native-american-cabinet

Laris, M., Duncan, I., & Kim, S. M. (2020, December 16). Biden to name Pete Buttigieg as transportation secretary. *The Washington Post*. https://www.washingtonpost.com/local/trafficandcommuting/biden-transportation-secretary/2020/12/15/cf1b7456-3a41-11eb-98c4-25dc9f4987e8_story.html

Lawless, J. L. (2004). Politics of presence? Congresswomen and symbolic representation. *Political Research Quarterly*, 57(1), 81–99. https://doi.org/10.1177/106591290405700107

Mahadeen, E. (2021). Queer counterpublics and LGBTQ pop-activism in Jordan. *British Journal of Middle Eastern Studies*, 48(1), 78–93. https://doi.org/10.1080/13530194.2021.1885850

Merica, D. (2019, April 14). Pete Buttigieg officially announces presidential campaign. *CNN*. https://www.cnn.com/2019/04/14/politics/pete-buttigieg-presidential-campaign/index.html

Merica, D. (2019, January 23). Pete Buttigieg, mayor of South Bend, Indiana, jumps into 2020 race. *CNN*. https://www.cnn.com/2019/01/23/politics/pete-buttigieg-2020-president/index.html

Merica, D. (2020, April 3). Pete Buttigieg launches a new PAC aimed at helping down-ballot Democrats. *CNN*. https://www.cnn.com/2020/04/03/politics/pete-buttigieg-pac/index.html

Morgan, D. (1993). Qualitative content analysis: A guide to paths not taken. *Qualitative Health Research*, 3(1), 112–121. https://doi.org/10.1177/104973239300300107

Mueller, J. E. (2008). *Tag teaming the press: How Bill and Hillary Clinton work together to handle the media*. Rowman & Littlefield Publishers.

Neuendorf, K. A., & Kumar, A. (2016). Content analysis. In G. Mazzoleni (Ed.), *The International encyclopedia of political communication*. https://doi.org/10.1002/9781118541555.wbiepc065

Nilsen, E. (2020, February 11). Bernie Sanders just won the all-important New Hampshire primary. *Vox*. https://www.vox.com/2020/2/11/21133087/bernie-sanders-new-hampshire-democratic-primary-winner-2020

Nowell, L. S., Norris, J. M., White, D. E., & Moules, N. J. (2017). Thematic analysis: Striving to meet the trustworthiness criteria. *International Journal of Qualitative Methods*, 16(1). https://doi.org/10.1177/1609406917733847

Oliver, D. (2020, August 31). Chasten Buttigieg talks Biden, quarantine and new memoir: 'I wanted to write my real story'. *USA Today*. https://www.usatoday.com/story/entertainment/books/2020/08/31/chasten-buttigieg-opens-up-joe-biden-quarantine-new-memoir/5656609002/

Parrott, J. (2019, November 26). South Bend council approves Pete Buttigieg climate plan, while activists urge going further. *South Bend Tribune*. https://www.southbendtribune.com/story/news/local/2019/11/26/south-bend-council-approves-pete-buttigieg-climate-plan-while-activists-urge-going-further/46368465/

Parrott, J. (2018, April 9). Souther Bend mayor says study on new South Shore station will be 'worth it' despite delays. Retrieved from https://www.southbendtribune.com/story/news/

local/2018/04/09/south-bend-mayor-says-study-on-new-south-shore-station-will-be-worth-it-despite-delays/46347693/

Patton, M. Q. (2002). *Qualitative research & evaluation methods*. Sage.

Peterson, M. (2015, November 3). South Bend Mayor Pete Buttigieg wins re-election. WNDU-TV. Retreived from https://web.archive.org/web/20170221081921/https://www.wndu.com/home/headlines/Buttigieg-vies-for-second-term-as-South-Bend-mayor-340002362.html

Petrow, S. (2020, August 31). Chasten Buttigieg's 'I Have Something to Tell You' is refreshingly candid, but a missed opportunity. *The Washington Post*. https://www.washingtonpost.com/entertainment/books/chasten-buttigiegs-i-have-something-to-tell-you-is-refreshingly-candid-but-a-missed-opportunity/2020/08/31/97f80f54-e634-11ea-970a-64c73a1c2392_story.html

Pye, D., & Taylor, M. A. (2024). Backward and in converse: Artful political communication; How the Biden/Harris presidential ticket reverses the 2-for-1 campaign. *American Behavioral Scientist, 68*(1), 56–79. https://doi.org/10.1177/00027642211000391

Relman, E. (2019, April 19). Meet Chasten Buttigieg, Pete Buttigieg's husband, who is a junior high school teacher, a dog dad, and very online. *Business Insider*. https://www.businessinsider.com/pete-buttigiegs-husband-chasten-buttigieg-2020-candidate-2019-4

Resonance. (2020). America's best small cities. https://www.edawn.org/wp-content/uploads/2020/08/Resonance-2020-Americas-Best-Small-Cities-Report-Part-1.pdf

Ring, T. (2020, December 16). Buttigieg speaks on his historic cabinet role, proposing to Chasten. *Advocate*. https://www.advocate.com/politics/2020/12/16/buttigieg-speaks-his-historic-cabinet-role-proposing-chasten

Sanbonmatsu, K. (2002). Gender stereotypes and vote choice. *American Journal of Political Science, 46*(1), 20–34. https://doi.org/10.2307/3088412

Semmler, E. (2019, October 19). South Bend ride-sharing program solves transportation problems for workers. *South Bend Tribune*. https://www.southbendtribune.com/story/business/2019/10/19/south-bend-ride-sharing-program-solves-transportation-problems-for-workers/46498859/

Seitz-Wald, A. (2017, February 25). DNC race: Democrats elect new leader Saturday. *NBC News*. https://www.nbcnews.com/politics/elections/dnc-race-democrats-elect-new-leader-saturday-n725596

Taylor M. A., & Pye D. (2019). Hillary through TIME: The (un)making of the first woman president. *American Behavioral Scientist, 63*(7), 807–825. https://doi.org/10.1177/0002764217711801

Trebay, G. (2018, June 18). Pete Buttigieg might be president someday. He's already got the first man. *The New York Times*. https://www.nytimes.com/2018/06/18/fashion/weddings/mayor-peter-buttigieg-wedding-democratic-party.html

Tremblay, M. (2022). "Standing for" representation: LGBQ politicians as symbolic agents. In M. Tremblay (Ed.), *LGBQ legislators in Canadian politics: Out to represent* (pp. 135–185). Palgrave Macmillan. https://doi.org/10.1007/978-3-030-91301-4_4

Verhovek, J., & Nagle, M. (2020, October 21). Joe Biden campaign deploys top surrogates while candidate preps for final debate. *ABC News*. https://abcnews.go.com/Politics/joe-biden-campaign-deploys-top-surrogates-candidate-preps/story?id=73720943

Weiss, J. (2019, March 29). Chasten Buttigieg is winning the 2020 spouse primary. *Politico*. https://www.politico.com/magazine/story/2019/03/29/pete-buttigieg-husband-chasten-226335/

Wright, L. A. (2016). *On behalf of the president: Presidential spouses and White House communications strategy today*. ABC-CLIO.

Zavaleta, L. (2019, September 13). Chasten Buttigieg visited Montrose Center prior to dem debate. *OutSmart Magazine*. https://www.outsmartmagazine.com/2019/09/chasten-buttigieg-visits-montrose-center-prior-to-dem-debate/

· 1 4 ·

HASHTAG POLITICS: #STOPTHESTEAL AS RHETORICAL STRATEGY

Joseph P. Zompetti

Recently, the bipartisan joint House select committee published its investigative report on the insurrection of January 6, 2021 (also referred to as "J6"). The 845-page document attempts to make the case that President Trump was directly responsible for the violent attack on the Capitol (Thompson et al., 2022). At the conclusion of their investigation, the committee confidently initiated four criminal referrals against Trump to the Department of Justice (DOJ) (Schnell, 2022). As a result, special prosecutor Jack Smith of the Department of Justice has indicted the former president with multiple criminal charges, including obstruction and conspiracy to defraud the U.S. (Diaz, 2023; O'Kruk & Merrill, 2024).

Of nearly 550 criminal indictments for those who participated in the J6 Capitol insurrection, many have testified and pleaded "not guilty" under the auspices that they believed protesting and engaging with Congress on that fateful day was part of their patriotic duty, since they believed the election was stolen and put democracy in jeopardy (Hsu, 2021). From their point of view, hypothetical voter fraud in key battleground states, deficient oversight at precinct voting places, and coordinated attempts by Democrats to count votes from improperly registered voters were all reasons that did not just suggest that Democrat votes were intentionally inflated, but also that the election was literally stolen from Trump as a result (Cuthbert & Theodoridis, 2022). According to this logic, closer monitoring, intensified voting challenges at voting venues, and amplified challenges to Democrat votes could prove what Trump supporters firmly believed—that the election was "stolen" from the former president.

As a result, the concept—and then the movement—signified by the hashtag #StopTheSteal was an effort to promote fair and equal elections, which is the *sine qua non* for a functioning democracy. In this way, liberal voices claiming that Trump and his followers were placing American democracy in peril simply did not address the opposing perspective. Both sides of the debate were like two ships passing each other in the night—there was no direct argumentative exchange of opposing ideas to generate areas of compromise, but instead it was two sides locked into their own ideological and insular framework. In this chapter, a rhetorical thematic analysis will be employed to comb through instances of the #StopTheSteal hashtag on Twitter as a rhetorical strategy to mobilize support for the former president. The purpose of the chapter is to explore not only the use of the hashtag as a rhetorical strategy to generate interest and support for Trump, but to also investigate how such social media messages perpetuate polarization among the electorate. The possible implications of this type of social media use on the January 6 insurrection will also be discussed.

Given their myopic perspective, rightwing pundits and Trump supporters, for their part, not only believed their position was correct and crucial for preserving democracy, but they also portrayed themselves as victims—the aggrieved party who had their election stolen from them. After all, if the election was not rigged according to this thinking, then Trump would have naturally and unquestionably won. It is understandable that if a group begins with this premise, then the election outcome as reported by mainstream media would be infuriating. In fact, the rightwing anger was so intense as to manifest itself into a refusal to believe Trump's loss unless some orchestrated and nefarious conspiracy was at work that stole the election from the president. As such, many followers resurrected a hashtag used by Trump's sycophant, Roger Stone, during the 2016 election—#StopTheSteal—as a way to quickly and emphatically disseminate the frustration over the election results (Rucker & Costa, 2016).

A rhetorical analysis helps us locate embedded meanings in texts, such as hashtags. In this chapter, Twitter messages containing the hashtag #StopTheSteal will be analyzed to uncover possible themes associated with the phrase that appear in tweets relating to the J6 insurrection (Adam et al., 2005). Identifying these themes can be extremely important since they "articulate or describe a particular social phenomenon" (Aguinaldo, 2012, p. 769). The categories are meant to represent the text as a whole, functioning as synecdoche. Examining the themes can help us understand the text holistically about particular social or cultural issues, such as the themes emanating from #StopTheSteal.

Framework

Hashtags have the potential to be very potent. They facilitate the transmission of a political viewpoint that can spread rapidly across social media platforms. Hashtags also pack complex political meaning into a single and simple word or phrase. Much like McGee's (1980) notion of an ideograph or Jamieson's (1982) concept of the ideologeme, a hashtag can contain all of the political, ideological meaning that is signified by the word or phrase. Political ideologies typically entail nuance and intricacy. And in the case of hashtags, the involved ideology relates to a number of other political arguments, concepts, and positions. As a result, the simple, single word or phrase functions as a container, in the sense of semiotics, for multiple signifieds. In general, the way a hashtag operates conjoins byzantine elements with a straightforward word or phrase that enables easy recollection as well as linguistically linking the various political concepts that are involved.

To identify, interpret, and assess the significance of hashtag politics, scholars can use a type of rhetorical criticism that targets particular themes emerging from a text that function as rhetorical strategy. A rhetorical strategy, as differentiated from a tactic, is the precise goal of persuasion, whereas tactics are the different ways that support and enable the overarching strategy (Bezzemelnaya, 2021, p. 174). For instance, a rhetorical strategy might be to influence specific online groups that require the use of certain tactics (e.g., appeals to tradition, vilifying a perceived enemy, calcifying an us versus them logic, etc.). Tactics, then, are subordinate to strategies insofar as they support and justify the strategy in operation.

Persuasive strategies and tactics are not new concepts in the rhetorical tradition. For example, in around 300 BCE Sun Tzu (2000) declared, "All men can see the tactics whereby I conquer, but what none can see is the strategy out of which victory is evolved" (p. 23). Additionally, rhetorical concepts appeared in Africa, especially in the Egyptian region, long before Aristotle and the origins of Eurocentric rhetorical theory (Blake, 2009). However, what is novel in our current conjuncture is how strategies and tactics are operationalized in our digital terrain, including social media. Unlike mainstream media, our digital media world encourages user-generated content, relies on hyper-fast data transmission, and facilitates intertextual relationships among different platforms, which can overwhelm us with information overload as well as expand our horizons of what we consider "authentic" and "legitimate" by converging different media.

Scholars can problematize the countless connections between media while simultaneously exploring the core political meanings with online messages. In this way, their task is to identify, interpret, and evaluate the common and most significant themes within a particular mediated text. Indeed, thematic analysis can be a very important exercise in locating hidden or underlying logics of meaning. Subsequently, the identified themes can be interrogated for their potency as well as their potential.

For example, Kreiss (2016) utilized a qualitative content analysis to uncover the ways in which political operatives used messages to influence different audiences in the 2012 presidential election. Part of the analysis included the different types of messages—or themes—that the presidential campaigns used in their persuasive messages. Relatedly, Parmalee and Bichard (2012) discussed how "political Twitter" is a specialized form of political communication that is occurring more frequently on the popular social media platform.

Furthermore, Lee and Young-Shin (2016) explored the different public relations strategies of Trump and Clinton during their campaigns. Their study revealed "significant differences in many aspects of their or their teams' tweeting styles" that were largely based on gendered characteristics (p. 853). Similarly, Zompetti (2019) examined the key themes that are buttressed by the different rhetorical techniques from Trump and Clinton in their use of Twitter. In addition, a study by Yaqub et al. (2017) used a data analytic approach to examine the behavior of Twitter users during the 2016 campaign, but it did not look at the specific tweets from candidates. While these studies have advanced our knowledge and conversation regarding digital media and politics, they have not examined the specific utility of the hashtag, which is a gap this study hopes to fill.

When researchers consider the impact of online digital media on our political consciousness, they should note a crucial distinction between digital media and mainstream media. Mainstream media refer to the pre-digital landscape of information dissemination, such as television, radio, newspapers and magazines. Digital media include online information via the Internet, websites and social media. An obvious difference is the speed of information dissemination, with digital media transmitting data almost instantaneously from one place to a user on the other side of the planet. A consequence of absorbing information in this manner is shorter attention spans along with an insatiable desire for more and more stimuli. Another difference is that digital media encourage, if not require, user activity, such as user-generated knowledge (e.g., Wikipedia), citizen journalism, amateur video production, audience feedback (e.g., reviews, "likes," re-posts, and retweets), and individual postulations (e.g., blogs and vlogs). While other distinctions between mainstream and digital media exist, it is sufficient for our purposes to note the speed of information transmission as well as how such information is transmitted—namely that everyone has the possibility of taking part in information exchange instead of the traditional top-down notion that information is solely generated from elites who then direct it downward to the populace.

Thematic analysis requires careful attention and self-reflexivity. Some themes are more easily spotted than others, and not all themes in a rhetorical act are worth exploring (Campbell, 2014). Once a theme has been identified, the rhetorical critic discerns the worthwhile themes from the mundane or trivial. Based on the critic's perspective and orientation, the consequential themes are interpreted and evaluated by excavating the explicit and latent meanings. In this way, the critic can make arguments about the possible meanings of a text as well as how the polysemic nature of a text relates to or influences our social or cultural condition.

Method

Using a specially-developed R script (called RTweet) from our Social Media Analytic Command Center (SMACC), tweets that contained #StopTheSteal were located by aggregating various databases, such as the Twitter archive and Twitter application programming interface (API). The RTweet application allows researchers to see original posts of #StopTheSteal, its retweets, as well as screen grabs. With the use of a specialized R script, the aggregate posts of a particular hashtag can be identified, which for purposes of this study was #StopTheSteal (or, #STS for short). Consequently, the specified hashtag in a precise date range can be located and examined. Nearly 12,000 tweets were uncovered with the STS hashtag in just three days of use—from January 5 to January 7, 2021. On a single day—on January 5—there were 4,346 tweets that included #StopTheSteal. The next day, when the insurrection occurred on the Capitol, 5,411 references to #STS appeared in the Twittersphere. Additionally, over 1,500 tweets relating to #StopTheSteal were identified on January 7.

For the purposes of this study, #StopTheSteal functions as both a text itself as well as a signifier that represents a larger text. In other words, the phrase "#StopTheSteal" is itself a text, but so too is the actual tweet that has the hashtag linked to it. A rhetorical thematic analysis allows both to be examined since they are both texts, and their content relates to each other. To be sure, the hashtag and the larger text it signifies are mutually reinforcing in terms of content and context (matter and form). As such, this project explores the use of #StopTheSteal on and around J6so that scholars can uncover meanings that might be significant for our political and cultural understanding of the insurrection specifically, and for a larger understanding of polarized political discourse more generally.

Surveying #StopTheSteal: Uncovering Contentious Politics

By now, we know that #StopTheSteal did not begin with the 2020 presidential election, although the concepts and philosophy behind the hashtag certainly became pronounced after November, 2020, when virtually all news outlets and every state verified, but had not yet certified, a Biden victory. The logic behind #StopTheSteal was premised on offensively shifting the burden of the election results on everyone except Trumpworld such that Trump and his surrogates could question the validity of every vote in every precinct in every state *ad nauseum*. Questioning all minutiae in their various contexts served multiple purposes: it delayed any final declaration because each potential instance of fraud requires an inordinate amount of time; it required that opposition to Trump must devote time and resources to responding to each query; and, at a minimum, it continued to cast doubt that every aspect of our democratic elections was secure. This last point may be the most important since it continued to add frustration to every Trump supporter who simply did not want to concede or acknowledge the possibility that Trump lost.

Given the scope of these contestations, the #StopTheSteal movement included many different arguments for various audiences. The overall strategies, then, of #STS were to force recounts, weaken the opposition with attrition, secure legal victories, and provide enough doubt that Trump would not need to concede to Biden and, as a result, demonstrate to the world that Trump was, in fact, the vanquisher. All of these strategies required a rhetorical dimension since they were premised on the idea that citizens could be persuaded that Trump was ultimately the victor.

Although similar themes occurred, each day also revealed unique themes. In general and as might be expected, the distinct themes on January 5 leading up to the so-called "Save America Rally," depicted actual behavior and real-time observations on January 6, building a crescendo up until the Capitol attack, and then the MAGA, pro-insurrection voices rapidly waned on the day after J6. Since each day exposed discrete thematic messages concerning #StopTheSteal, the subsequent analysis will occur in chronological order. Given the sheer volume of data and concomitant themes from the data set, not all themes will be analyzed here, and repetitive tweets and messages are automatically purged from the data set. A comprehensive list is available from the chapter author.

January 5, 2021

The day before the J6 insurrection, a series of content themes were attached to #StopTheSteal, all of which favored Trump and the planned rally. There were 16 distinct themes, but 13 will be discussed here for their overall significance relating to the J6 event. The first theme expressed alarm that the presidential election was rigged and riddled with fraud. For instance, twitter user grandmaXs3 (2021) stated, "The only way Democrats know how to win is cheat!," which was also echoed in this tweet: "Liberals are ALWAYS on the wrong side of history. Plus, cheating is the only way they can win - at anything! You'd have to be a complete blind moron not to admit Trump won the Election!" (LiberalsLeaving, 2021). Instead of blaming the Democrats directly, another user declared, "For the record, I still believe what I said following election night. It was rigged, stolen. Will be overturned. The evidence has been pouring in from citizens all over the place for weeks. Sworn affidavits, documents, video evidence etc. Every American should care. #stopthesteal" (brentinrome, 2021). These sentiments were not uncommon from Trump supporters, because—apparently—massive voter fraud occurred despite no single shred of evidence supporting this notion. Even when the Trump cadre were exposed to copious studies, testimonies, and voting location video footage explicitly countering accusations of fraud, they doubled down with their impassioned claims concerning what they were convinced was overwhelming evidence of a rigged election. In a puzzling way, such conviction was predicated on inuendo and gossip; yet such "evidence" somehow sufficiently responded to the contrary facts in the minds of Trumpians.

Relatedly, a second theme revealed how many users believed the evidence was overwhelming that supported the accusations of election fraud. One notable tweet announced, "Anyone who says there is no evidence of fraud in this election is either lying or willfully ignorant" (KeithCRogers, 2021). Although no actual evidence was ever produced, a tweep—a person who uses Twitter (Merriam-Webster, 2023)—exclaimed, "I don't care about anything else that's going on in Congress while the Constitution is burning. You need to stand with #Stopthesteal now or forever lose trust. There is even video evidence of the fake ballots being brought out from under the table in Georgia. Paying attention?" (joenors, 2021). And, another user said, "There is a mountain of evidence nationwide and state-by-state of record level election fraud of various types and styles," even though no evidence was presented (FrancaiPolitics, 2021). Interestingly, another user likened the way people believed Biden won to the brainwashing methods performed by cults (waytruthlife07, 2021).

Moreover, because election fraud believers perceived the "stolen" election as a threat to their way of life, it is not surprising to see the emergence of the discursive theme of "fighting" to save their country. In particular, one tweep characterized their overall position in a way that also captured the spirit of the #StopTheSteal movement: "No WAY!! #StopTheSteal we ARE 80 million strong, fighting for this Country. Founding Fathers fought for this Country, WE WILL TOO" (FoxytailRedhead, 2021). Tweets like this used allusions to the Founding Fathers as a form of position legitimization. The vehement posturing linking January 6 motivations to the democratically-inspired stances of the pioneers of our nation's origin also extended the logic that challenging the electoral certification process as a result of voter fraud were acts of patriotic defiance based on the political tradition of life and liberty. Some of the tweets within this theme were moderately balanced when compared to more extreme messages and simply expressed excitement about supporting Trump: "Conservatives are no longer laying down at the feet of the crazy left. WE ARE FIGHTING BACK! Tons in DC today to support the President!" (RepublicanUS_A, 2021). Other posts were more sanguine: "This isn't about an election, this is about saving our republic! #stopthesteal rally in DC" (TheRealKeean, 2021). Still others expressed a clear patriotic commitment to preserve election integrity, as one noted, "WE WILL NEVER ACCEPT A STOLEN ELECTION" (LanieMV, 2021), while another echoed, "We will not be silenced. We will not quit. #STOPtheSTEAL" (rodriQuez, 2021). Indeed, many January 6 rioters claimed it was their "obligation or patriotic duty to ensure the saving of the republic" (Reilly, 2023, para. 7). Of course, several tweets in this theme were alarming, especially now that—in hindsight—we know what happened the day after these tweets were posted. One Twitter user said, "DO WHATEVER IT TAKES! #STOPTHESTEAL #PATRIOTS #TRUMPWON" (JuddDunning, 2021). Yet another declared, "Hear the drumbeat?? Move to the sounds of battle .... Assemble" (TrumpsMustache, 2021). And, perhaps most frightening of all, was this post: "WE ARE IN A COLD CIVIL WAR .... DON'T LET ANYONE TELL YOU OTHERWISE. #StopTheSteal" (moonglow63092, 2021).

Since the predominant sentiment attached to #StopTheSteal was that there was ample evidence that the election was rigged, many users advocated that it was their duty—and the responsibility of all Americans—to stand up against the fraudulent election. Many users also characterized this position as a natural and obligatory belief couched in patriotism. For example, one Twitter operator emphatically expressed, "Praying for all you PATRIOTS going to WASHINGTON to Support President Trump's America; to TAKE BACK OUR COUNTRY from the LYING, TREASONOUS, CORRUPTED POLITICIANS. #STOPTHESTEAL PRAYING FOR ALL PATRIOTS, President Trump's AMERICA" (KristieWelch17, 2021). With the perception that those attending the rally were pro-Trump in their opposition to the so-called "rigged" election, one tweep simply said, "Thank you American Patriots!!! #FightForTrump #StopTheSteal #SaveAmerica" (MissyLee1967, 2021).

Similarly, users aligned with the rigged election perspective noted how the opposition (namely Biden and the Democrats) were actually radical leftists, even communists, who represented the "evil" the liberals "must not advance" (AndyWHumphreys, 2021). Some alt-right conservatives evidently believed that Biden and the Democrats were puppets of the Chinese Communist Party. As one Twitter user declared, "Anyone who is a Conservative that is not objecting to the certification of electoral votes for Biden is just proving that they are owned by the CCP and, therefore, not a Conservative at all. @HouseGOP @SenateGOP @GOP #StopTheSteal" (mrsrogers2270, 2021). Additionally, after Trump tweeted that voting machines "deleted" votes or "switched" them to count for Biden, many conservatives lost faith in the machines built by Dominion (Swenson et al., 2020, para. 1). As a result, some tweeps posted comments like this: "A vote on a #Dominion machine is a vote for SOCIALISM" (Jimmcnary, 2021). Of course, no explanation or evidence was offered to support such claims.

By framing the rigged election perspective as a noble and patriotic pursuit, Twitter users tagged #StopTheSteal as a way of uniting like-minded believers. For example, one tweep sent a message directed to Trump with an obvious message to everyone else who might read it: "@realDonaldTrump #MAGA2020 #STOPTHESTEAL We the People, Have Ur Back Cuz U Have Ours!!!" (JosephAmazing14, 2021). This type of unity through loyalty appeared frequently, especially on January 5 and 6. Another example of this theme occurred with this simple tweet: "This is my post where I am using my voice to stand in solidarity" (e_verhage, 2021). This tweet exemplified how Trump followers remained loyal by means of "a complex interplay of class and racial antagonism, aggravated by despair and social drift and amplified by new communication platforms, converging to what some see as a troubling psychological phenomenon" (Lempinen, 2020, para. 3).

Viewing rivals as enemies is the next logical extension of trying to unify the electorate. Using #StopTheSteal already implies that someone is to blame for the theft of the presidential election and must be stopped. Of course, the obvious enemy was Biden and the Democrats. Hence, the next theme emerging on January 5 was the "us versus them" rhetorical appeal. Although many us/them tweets surfaced on January 5, one in particular serves as an exemplar: "@GOP It's 'Find out who the #RINOtraitors are in America tomorrow!' If your Republication Senator does not help #STOPTHESTEAL by standing AGAINST voter fraud, then you'll know that they are really DEMOCRAT in Republican clothing. If @GOP does nothing, you'll know about them too" (OldSargeUSAF, 2021). With a combination message that conjoins otherizing with a scare tactic, one user declared, "#StopTheSteal #FreedomPlaza #HoldTheLine WE THE PEOPLE WILL NOT FORGET THOSE WHO DID NOT STAND BEHIND THIS @POTUS" (moeanon03a, 2021). And yet another tweep highlighted that, "Republicans can support democracy or Trump. There's no middle ground" (mcleoda, 2021). In addition to reinforcing an "us" versus "them" perspective, this is a false dilemma fallacy, which is when an audience is given two unsatisfactory options when actually more than two exist. According to Paul and Elder (2006), "People are often ready to accept a false dilemma because few feel comfortable with complexity and nuanced distinctions. They like sweeping absolutes. They want clear and simple choices. So, those skilled in manipulating people, face them with false dilemmas . . . . They present arguments in *black* or *white* form (p. 25). As a false dilemma fallacy, it allowed Trump's followers to manipulate the situation in order to coax—or intimidate—people to support their cause.

Another theme *qua* rhetorical strategy that happened on January 5 was the use of fear appeals. Typically, if reasons and evidence fail to persuade an audience, then using an affective approach, namely scare tactics, can be extremely effective. Politicians who were not yet on board the "Trump train" experienced a unique form of scare tactic. Members of the Trump establishment would, on occasion, threaten to "primary" politicians who refused allegiance. This meant, of course, that alt-right Republicans would find more extreme conservatives to oppose the more moderate Republicans during primary elections. For example, kattastic007 (2021) tweeted, "Take note @GOP If you're not onboard to support President Trump on January 6 to #StopTheSteal and vote against certifying the electoral college vote, you will be primaried! #DecertifyTheVotes." Similarly, another pro-Trump tweep posted that Republicans not aligned with Trump were cowards, and their political ambitions—whether in terms of primaries or some other circumstance—were in jeopardy. Indeed, kapd131 (2021) stated it this way: "@realDonaldTrump @gop #FightForTrump #stopthesteal or your political careers are over. 'Surrender Caucus' are cowards."

Since those who proffered the rigged election thesis were already positioning themselves as crusaders for fair elections and combatants against the communist leftists, many users in this camp already saw themselves as on the "correct" or "moral" side of the issue. The ultimate backing for this philosophical perspective would be if God also endorsed or inspired these beliefs. Believing one's cause is aligned with the Almighty can also function as a fear appeal to those who opposed Trump's claim to victory since no one wants to fight against God. For instance, Damon J. Gray tweeted this scare tactic: "When a nation has become degenerate and corrupt, as ours has, God's response (if he even chooses to respond) is almost always a painful 'purge and restore' operation. Pain is coming. Either this nation devolves into pure chaos and death, or God's purge is coming. Get ready" (@DamonJGray, 2021). Some of the tweets within the religious theme also offered a false dilemma, as noted above. Here is an exemplar of this type of tactic: "To all the Dems and RINOS, here is where we are at. RESISTANCE TO TYRANNY IS OBEDIENCE TO GOD! Better to die standing than bow to the Tyrants" (MarksManVA, 2021). Other religious tweets attempted to turn over to God the entire election debacle: "May we be able to restore our nation to the land it once was. I pray for truth, and that light overcomes darkness. In the name of Jesus, amen" (Ealeeyellama, 2021). Finally, some simply declared, "Praying for God's purging!! #MAGA #stopthesteal #JesusIsComing" (SavyTruthSeeker, 2021). Certainly, even if some Trump followers had some reservations about the former president's decorum or particular policy positions, aligning Trumpian politics with God created the ultimate "trump" card in that any opposition automatically was framed and perceived as politically and religiously heretical.

The reason the "Save America Rally" was planned for January 6 in Washington, D.C., was because that day marked the significant event when Congress certified the Electoral College ballot count, with the vice president—in this case, Mike Pence—validating each state ballot's certification. While the majority of Americans were certain that Joe Biden won the election, tens of millions of other Americans thought there were serious election irregularities that should call into question the veracity of electoral votes, and, even worse, many others believed the election was outright stolen by Biden and the Democrats. Despite over 60 lawsuits filed by the Trump campaign that alleged "massive" voter fraud, multiple state and federal courts ruled against Trump in all but one case—and that single case ultimately had no bearing on the election outcome (Cummings et al., 2021). For those Americans who still clung to the belief that the election was rigged and stolen, the only legal recourse left was to implore to, and pray for, Mike Pence to not certify the election. As a result, on January 5 there were many pleas to Pence on Twitter, such as "FIGHT FOR US @Mike_Pence!!! Stand with us! Stand with Trump!" (DCdecals1, 2021). Some tweeps seemed worried that Pence might not support Trump during the certification process. For instance, one posted: "HOLD THE LINE MIKE PENCE!!" (xgudwilx, 2021). In a more alarming tone, a user exclaimed, "@Mike_Pence Praying you stick to your word and have a backbone! The people elected you to fight for America not coward to dark side. #STOPTHESTEAL #TRUMP2020 #FIGHTFORTRUMP" (c0f1041f0f4e4fc, 2021). An additional user added something similar, along with reiterating how the election was awash with fraud: "@realDonaldTrump @Mike_Pence Please do the right thing and save our country from tyranny. Free and fair elections are the cornerstone of our country. We had neither of those in 6 swing states where fraud and state law was disregarded entirely. #stopthesteal please to save our country!" (defaziojim, 2021). Another example of this theme holistically captured the frustration and anxiety regarding Pence's role in the certification process: "@Mike_Pence please do the right thing! Biden will ruin America.

We know that you know more than we do, you must have seen at least some of the evidence. #StopTheSteal" (StyleCleverly, 2021).

In a related way, pro-Trump Twitter users attached the #StopTheSteal hashtag to arguments about protecting the legitimacy of the American election system and American democracy as a whole. Interestingly, while Democrats argued that alt-right forces were jeopardizing our democracy (especially after the J6 insurrection), many Republicans also vehemently believed they were fighting for the survival of our democracy. Simply put, they felt that if the election was rigged or fraudulent, then our votes were meaningless and, by definition, that threatens democracy. Indeed, the rhetorical power of the hashtag #StopTheSteal embodied this notion. As such, tweets such as this were quite common leading up to January 6: "Americans stand for the integrity of our electoral system and the future success of the US by working to #StopTheSteal. Together we will save our country and end China's 'Hundred Year Marathon' as outlined by @mikepillsbury" (admolon, 2021).

Finally, some Trumpian followers predicted possible altercations during the "Save America Rally." In anticipation, they pre-empted any perceptions that violent overtures would come from die-hard patriots who love America and who love Donald Trump. In terms of a rhetorical maneuver, if the pro-Trump group could instill in the minds of viewers that they were not initiating violence, then it provided a strategic opportunity to also undermine opposing cultural groups—namely the Black Lives Matter (BLM) movement, a national group fighting for anti-racism and causes that address racial disparities, and Antifa, which is a decentralized movement that protests against people and institutions who are perceived to contribute to fascist forces in the United States. For instance, one Trump supporter tweeted that, "Ok so BlmAntifa are at the #stopTheSteal Protest to keep an eye out for these troublemakers they are watching you #ProudBoys #Patriots #DCProtests" (fluffyMcFluff, 2021). Additionally, this tweep contrasted the #StopTheSteal movement to the insidious actions of BLM and Antifa, thereby portraying the pro-Trump supporters as more democratic: "WE HAVE NO DEMOCRACY. We have Antifa and BLM. Also a bias media that does not show the truth and democrats who would rather vote Biden just to get at Trump. Also judges that DO NOT look at cases. They throw them out without [sic] a thought. They are the cowards. #stopthesteal" (Nic_Radd, 2021). At the very least, most #STS advocates were priming Twitter followers to think the pro-Trump crowd was non-violent, as in this case: "America Patriots engaging in a nonviolent vigil Rally to #stopTheSteal" (BeeNewsDaily, 2021).

January 6, 2021

As Trump supporters gathered for the "Save America Rally," many eagerly took to Twitter to express their feelings. The excitement only grew stronger once Trump took the stage to give his energetic speech on the Ellipse at President's Park. Toward the end of the speech, when Trump was building his crescendo, he raised his voice as the crowd became louder and louder to ultimately say, "we need to fight like hell" (Wade, 2021). He also promised his followers that he would walk with them to the Capitol building, although he, supposedly due to pressure from his Secret Service detail, failed to accompany them (Dawsey, 2022). Yet, Trump's supporters marched onward to the Capitol where Congress and Mike Pence were well underway in the certification process.

Once the Trumpian mass reached the building, hundreds of people encouraged by rabble rousers with bullhorns and pure adrenaline broke through windows and doors to trample inside the Capitol. As all of this was occurring, the rioters expressed themselves on Twitter.

Of the twenty themes associated with #StopTheSteal that day, most repeated the sentiments from the previous day, albeit the January 6 tweets were more excited and vociferous. For example, one pro-Trump voice wrote, "Over half the country is now at war with the Left and the Democrat party. We are fighting for our votes and our voice which is being stamped out a little more each day. If we don't hold our ground now we may never get it back. Resist" (TheNKO, 2021). In a similar passionate plea, a tweep declared, "NO JUSTICE, NO PEACE!!! FIGHT FOR OUR COUNTRY FELLOW AMERICANS!!! DON'T LET THEM RAVAGE OUR GREAT NATION TO THE GROUND!! DON'T ALLOW THEM TO CHEAT!!!" (kamala_and, 2021). These strategic tweets were posted online as the crowds assembled around the Capitol—as the mob grew ever more agitated, irrational, and violent.

Of course, during the J6 ordeal, insurrection participants—and those watching from the sidelines or from home—continued their rallying cry for engaging in a type of "righteous conflict," premised on principles of freedom, morality, and constitutionalism, which was similar to the rationale used to justify the American Revolutionary War against Britain (Ortega, 2024). In fact, many Twitter users drew this comparison: "How does this end in anything less than a second American Revolution?" (Ryan_Myers, 2021), and then the pronouncement that "The REVOLUTION is NOW!" (NOcosignMiKE, 2021), and ultimately tweets like this: "Looks like The Revolution began January 6, 2021" (Colby67353751, 2021). One tweep went so far as to post: "Protestors stormed the capital. NOW is the time America to take the damn country back. #Stopthesteal" (lookforvalue, 2021).

Believers in the #StopTheSteal movement persisted with messages of unity while simultaneously reinforcing their us versus them philosophy against Biden, the Democrats, and all other Americans who did not join their cause. As the insurrection forces were gaining momentum outside of the Capitol, many #STS Twitter users were trying to justify what the crowd was inevitably going to do next, which was attack the Capitol. While many Americans believe—and continue to believe—that no justification exists for an attempted coup, many pro-Trump followers characterized their activities on J6 as a stand for freedom. At the very least, according to some #StopTheSteal supporters, the mass demonstrations and the eventual insurrection was a line in the sand, since, "Communism has infiltrated every conceivable sphere of activity. It must be exposed" (AuyrnNetwork, 2021). This sentiment seemed popular, as many pro-Trump supporters genuinely felt the country was at risk: "AMERICA IS AT A DARK MOMENT DEMORATS STOLE 2020 AND WE WILL NEVER ACCEPT CHINA JOE AS OUR PRESIDENT. I WILL PRAY FOR HIS DOWN FALL. THIS IS A REPUBLIC NOT SOCIALIST COUNTRY AND DEFINITELY NEVER TO BE RAN BY CHINA AND A SICK MAN WITH DEMENTIA. #STOPTHESTEAL" (minnymoo2662, 2021). And, since many believed that the "USA HAS GONE FULL COMMUNIST. FREedom [sic] of speech no longer exists. This election was a takeover by communist China. #stopthesteal," it is no surprise that hundreds ended up attacking the Capitol (strive4best1, 2021). In fact, if their interpretations were not so warped and predicated on manipulated lies, the J6 protesters might be seen as embodying the original revolutionary spirit upon which America was founded.

While some #StopTheSteal users laid the groundwork to blame BLM and Antifa for any violence, once the rally turned into an insurrection the contrasts with BLM and Antifa became starker. In other words, some Trumpians explicitly blamed BLM and Antifa for the violence as a sort of "false flag" operation, which argues "the violence was secretly orchestrated by Trump's opponents in an attempt to make Trump look bad" (Dale & Cohen, 2022, para. 30). For example, one person—who's sentiment was echoed by many others—speculated: "Looks like #ANTIFA has infiltrated the @realDonaldTrump protests. They are the ones in the violence, seeking to demonize the #Stopthesteal demonstration. Hey @SpeakerPelosi @SenSchumer and @JoeBiden you should tell your boys to go home!" (martinssempa, 2021). And another user simply noted that, "It was ANTIFA who undermined the peaceful #StopTheSteal vigil" (QNCTHRNHRH, 2021). Of course, not a single shred of evidence to support these claims was ever presented or recovered. Additionally, many users compared their freedom of expression and passionate pleas for change to the recent efforts of BLM when they marched and rioted in the streets for racial justice. As one user remarked, "You had ZERO issue with Antifa and BLM BURNING DOWN OUR CITIES, but you blame Trump for Patriots Protesting an invalid and illegal election! Are you kidding me? You are CORRUPT and YOU are a TRAITOR to the United States of America! #Traitor #CorruptDemocrats #stopthesteal" (SweetPea_leepher, 2021). In this way, we can see how a single theme—blame BLM/Antifa as scapegoats—morphed into another, albeit related, theme, such as the *tu quoque* ("and this applies to you too") fallacy—if it is acceptable for "them" (BLM/Antifa) to engage in riotous behavior, then it should be acceptable for #STS individuals as well. While the *tu quoque* fallacy typically is applied to instances of hypocrisy, it can also apply to *quid pro quo* situations, when if one side does something, it justifies the opposition to do something similar (Kaptein, 2002).

Additionally, #StopTheSteal advocates continued to invoke God's providence in their efforts to protect freedoms and morality in their God-fearing nation that, according to their philosophy, was formed as a Christian nation. The tweets with the attached hashtag of #StopTheSteal put a great deal of faith into Trump to protect and save America. Two examples exemplify this ideal. One Twitter user expressed, "God Bless our president @realDonaldTrump. A good man in a swamp filled with evil vipers. #WashingtonDC #PresidentTrump #StopTheSteal" (Crosseyed, 2021). In a relatively overt way, this tweet positioned Trump as a fighter against evil. The other example implored followers to pray for Trump's success: "Dear Lord, I am praying for our country, for our @GOPLeader @GOPChairwoman @senatemajldr and @VP to do the right thing and stand behind this President and make sure he stays in office as the voters have made their choice #HoldTheLine #StopTheSteal Lord hear our Prayers" (moeanon03b, 2021). Since January 6 was certification day, some Trump supporters may have felt that time was running out, and they may have tweeted these sorts of messages in desperation.

Lastly, while some users held onto hope that Pence would save the day, most of the others in the pro-Trump mob finally realized that Pence, in Trump's terms, "lacked the courage" to de-certify the election results (Morgan & Chiacu, 2022). Many tweets with #StopTheSteal exclaimed with conviction that, "@CodeMonkeyZ Mike Pence punked out and has stopped following president @realDonaldTrump #PencePunkedOut #HeNeverWasForAmericans #CallinNationalGuard #StopTheSteal" (67_rie, 2021), and "@Mike_Pence You caused this by not #StopTheSteal and bear the responsibility for it" (dandsme, 2021). Of course, we now know that Vice President Pence did certify the election results, which in the minds of many Trump supporters was an act of treason.

One other important theme to note that occurred on January 6 was the existence of some anti-Trump, anti-rally Twitter users who also attached #StopTheSteal to their tweets. Critics or opposition to the J6 rally were not prominent in the tweets from January 5. But seemingly because some users saw how the insurrection would fail or simply that some users were disgusted by what they saw at the Capitol that day, many critical tweets began to surface. Some tweets merely reported on the facts on the ground, such as, "Videos Show Rioters in Support of #StopTheSteal Have Breached the Capitol Building, Capitol Now On Lockdown" (TAsterisk, 2021). Others were more forceful in their condemnation and labeling of the protestors: "MAGA terrorists have invaded the U.S. Capitol" (mcleodb, 2021), and then this: "Trumpistas are nothing but seditious domestic terrorists—as is Trump, Cruz & the Representatives & Senators opposing the Electoral College certification! Lock 'em all up!" (KruzeTed, 2021). Additionally, many other tweets directly blamed Trump for the violence and chaos: "trump incited this, he and his followers should be arrested, prosecuted and locked behind bars. #stopthesteal #trumplost #bidenwon" (abigpersonality, 2021). Similarly, another tweep that laid the responsibility directly on Trump stated, "Donald J Trump has now officially incited a riot and insurrection against the United States of America #losergate #trumpForPrison2021 #EndTheSteal #StopTheSteal #YoureFired" (ChuckSpringborn, 2021). All of these tweets connected to #StopTheSteal are extremely significant since it was the first time in American history that the Capitol was stormed at the behest of a President of the United States.

January 7, 2021

Despite the insurrection's failure and the apparent backlash from the majority of Americans, many Trump followers continued anchoring their positions with the hashtag #StopTheSteal that included messages about election fraud, evidence of corruption, appeals to God, and reiterations about how the insurrection was a false flag operation from BLM and Antifa. Additionally, although the coup attempt failed miserably, some Trumpian Twitter users remarked how the "rigged" 2020 election already destroyed democracy, as demonstrated in this tweet: "#Election2020 was the assault and death of our democracy #stopthesteal" (TAmerican23, 2021). They also emphatically noted that the "Trump movement" would continue to move forward after J6, perhaps hinting their support for a Trump re-election. Hence, this tweet from January 7 exemplifies how MAGA supporters did not feel defeated: "The Republicans lost most of their base. We are Trump #PatriotParty members moving forward. That's the truth. The wave is coming. #freedom #Constitution #stopthesteal #Trump2020 @realDonaldTrump @RudyGiuliani" (PatriotMinded, 2021). And, of course, there were proclamations like this: "Trump did not lie. He won in a landslide. Ask God right now for the truth. The Truth is Joe Biden is a criminal. Remember it was Obama and Biden's Administration that illegally spied on Trump's campaign. They stole multiple Elections & were caught. #Trumpwon #StopTheSteal" (JesusCh74101301, 2021). Sentiments like these were widespread among Trump's followers that, at least in part, attempted to justify their seditious behavior (Morgan & Chiacu, 2022). As such, these tweets display the rigid, on-going allegiance of Trumpians despite the mountain of evidence to the contrary.

However, a noticeable difference from the previous two days was the amount of anti-Trump denunciations. Some described how the insurrection was clearly not the work of BLM or Antifa. Instead, to most observers—especially those who were critical of Trump—alt-right conservatives who were aligned with QAnon, the Proud Boys, and the Oath Keepers were obviously the groups who orchestrated and then implemented the Capitol uprising. QAnon is a radical group of conservatives who "falsely claims that former President Trump is facing down a shadowy cabal of Democratic pedophiles" (Roose, 2021, para. 1). Similarly, the "Proud Boys are a right-wing extremist group with a violent agenda. They are primarily misogynistic, Islamophobic, transphobic and anti-immigration. Some members espouse white supremacist and antisemitic ideologies and/or engage with white supremacist groups" (ADL, 2023, para. 4). Additionally, the Oath Keepers "are an anti-government, right-wing political organization committed to supporting and defending their interpretation of the U.S. Constitution against all enemies," while also aligning with various militia groups to defend and protect natural rights and liberties enshrined by the Constitution (McQueen, 2021, para. 1). While other radical conservative groups exist, these three have loosely aligned with each other and were the face of the January 6 insurrection. Their ideologies are connected during this unique conjuncture, as this tweet noted: "Tarrio and the Proud Boys are gearing up for a #StopTheSteal protest in Washington D.C. Wednesday to support President Trump's desperate and futile effort to overturn the election results" (SabDigitalWitch, 2021). Furthermore, some users went so far as to argue that Trump himself was to blame for the turmoil since he had been using incendiary language for weeks, which were exemplified when Trump said "we need to fight like hell" during his Ellipse speech. For example, this tweet did not sugarcoat the author's feelings on the matter: "Fuck #stopthesteal. #stopthecoup is more like it. Trump is seditious and anyone who still supports him after he caused the capitol to be invaded is a poor excuse for a human being, let alone an American. Y'all truly are deplorable and tonight proves it" (Mercstappen, 2021). Additionally, some Trump critics intuitively proclaimed that if there was no evidence of a rigged election, it was actually Donald Trump who was trying to "steal" the election, such as this tweet: "#stopthesteal Don't be so stupid! You've been fed lies by #DonaldTrump and you've fallen for them. It is he who threatens American democracy and Twists the truth endlessly to suit his aims. He tricks people into following him blindly like the 'Emperor's New Clothes'. Very sad" (SmokeySmith100, 2021). If we want to simplify all of this, we could straightforwardly say that to secure Biden's victory or to support Trump's insurrection as efforts at preserving our democracy boil down to a question of perspective. However, as this analysis has shown, the ideologies and behaviors relating to the 2020 election were hardly "simple," nor were they just based on differing perspectives.

Conclusion

This thematic rhetorical study offers several important and interesting insights. By focusing on a hashtag (#StopTheSteal) instead of a larger text like song lyrics, slogans, speeches, etc., this project reveals how a single textual marker, the hashtag, can not only provide social media users an issue-based, searchable label, but it also relays important messages that are attached to it (Reinwald, 2021). In this way, hashtags might be considered a unique rhetorical trope that conjoins content and form in digital discourse (Bonilla & Rosa, 2015). As a result, it should not be surprising that hashtags—like #StopTheSteal— were a key rhetorical strategy for the Trump campaign (Riggins, 2022).

Of course, in terms of the specific #StopTheSteal hashtag, it becomes clear that there was a major shift in perspective in just three short days. On January 5, most of the users and activity on Twitter connected to #STS were excited and preparing for the "Save America Rally" scheduled for the next day. Then, on January 6, there was both praise and condemnation for those involved in the insurrection. Given the general attitude of the country, the Twitter activity changed almost entirely on January 7 to reflect positions of disgust, sadness, and denunciation of the J6 events. In this way, by monitoring a hashtag temporally, users and researchers can examine how shifts in meaning can occur with the content accompanying the hashtag.

Furthermore, this study reaffirms the importance of studying the rhetorical and political communication occurring on social media. Very little research has been done focusing on hashtags; therefore, this study significantly adds to the conversation about the role of social media in political discourse. Interestingly, most of the work involving hashtags has explored their potential for progressive causes and movements (Ames & McDuffie, 2023; Bonilla & Rosa, 2015; Cannon, 2020; Jackson et al., 2020; Rho & Mazmanian, 2019). This present study reminds us that rhetoric from elites, conservative populists, and hegemonic entities can also harness the power of social media and hashtags (Johnson, 2022). As a result, ignoring how people in positions of power and privilege use hashtags would be a serious mistake for those interested in preserving democracy (Donovan et al., 2022).

References

@67_rie. (2021, January 6). *Tweets*. Retrieved from https://http://backtweets.com/
@abigpersonality. (2021, January 6). *Tweets*. Retrieved from https://http://backtweets.com/
Adam, B. D., Husbands, W., Murray, J. & Maxwell, J. (2005). AIDS optimism, condom fatigue, or self-esteem? Explaining unsafe sex among gay and bisexual men. *The Journal of Sex Research*, 42(3), 238–248. https://doi.org/10.1080/00224490509552278
@admolon. (2021, January 5). *Tweets*. Retrieved from https://http://backtweets.com/
Aguinaldo, J. P. (2012). Qualitative analysis in gay men's health research: Comparing thematic, critical discourse, and conversation analysis. *Journal of Homosexuality*, 59, 765–787. https://www.doi.org/10.1080/00918369.2012.694753
Ames, M., & McDuffie, K. (2023). *Hashtag activism interrogated and embodied: Case studies on social justice movements*. Utah State University Press.
@AndyWHumphreys. (2021, January 5). *Tweets*. Retrieved from https://http://backtweets.com/
Anti-Defamation League (ADL) (2023, December 11). *Proud Boys*. ADL Backgrounder. https://www.adl.org/resources/backgrounder/proud-boys-0

@AuyrnNetwork. (2021, January 6). *Tweets*. Retreived from https://http://backtweets.com/
@BeeNewsDaily. (2021, January 5). *Tweets*. Retreived from https://http://backtweets.com/
Bezzemelnaya, O. A. (2021). Semantics of strategies and tactics in political discourse. *Russian Linguistic Bulletin*, 4(28), 174–177. https://cyberleninka.ru/article/n/semantics-of-strategies-and-tactics-in-political-discourse-based-on-analysis-of-h-clinton-and-d-trump-s-election-speeches/viewer
Blake, C. (2009). *The African origins of rhetoric*. Routledge.
Bonilla, Y., & Rosa, J. (2015). #Ferguson: Digital protest, hashtag ethnography and the racial politics of social media in the United States. *American Ethnologist*, 42(1), 4–17. https://doi.org/10.1111/amet.12112
@Brentinrome. (2021, January 5). *Tweets*. Retreived from https://http://backtweets.com/
@c0f1041f0f4e4fc. (2021, January 5). *Tweets*. Retreived from https://http://backtweets.com/
Campbell, K. K., Huxman, S. S., & Burkholder, T. A. (2014). *The rhetorical act: Thinking, speaking, and writing critically* (5th ed.). Cengage Learning.
Cannon, M. E. (2020). *Beyond hashtag activism: Comprehensive justice in a complicated age*. InterVarsity Press.
@ChuckSpringborn. (2021, January 6). *Tweets*. Retreived from https://http://backtweets.com/
@Colby67353751. (2021, January 6). *Tweets*. Retreived from https://http://backtweets.com/
@Crosseyed. (2021, January 6). *Tweets*. Retreived from https://http://backtweets.com/
Cummings, W., Garrison, J., & Sergent, J. (2021). By the numbers: President Donald Trump's failed efforts to overturn the election. *USA Today*. https://www.usatoday.com/in-depth/news/politics/elections/2021/01/06/trumps-failed-efforts-overturn-election-numbers/4130307001/
Cuthbert, L., & Theodoridis, A. (2022, January 7). Do Republicans really believe Trump won the 2020 election? Our research suggests that they do. *The Washington Post*. https://www.washingtonpost.com/politics/2022/01/07/republicans-big-lie-trump/
Dale, D., & Cohen, M. (2022, January 5). Fact check: Five enduring lies about the Capitol insurrection. *CNN Politics*. https://www.cnn.com/2022/01/04/politics/fact-check-capitol-insurrection-january-6-lies/index.html
@DamonJGray. (2021, January 5). *Tweets*. Retreived from https://http://backtweets.com/
@dandsme. (2021, January 6). *Tweets*. Retreived from https://http://backtweets.com/
@DCdecals1. (2021, January 5). *Tweets*. Retreived from https://http://backtweets.com/
Dawsey, J. (2022, April 7). Trump deflects blame for Jan. 6 silence, says he wanted to march to Capitol. *The Washington Post*. https://www.washingtonpost.com/politics/2022/04/07/trump-interview-jan6/
@defaziojim. (2021, January 5). *Tweets*. Retreived from https://http://backtweets.com/
Diaz, J. (2023, August 2). The charges facing Trump in the Jan. 6 investigation, explained. *NPR*. https://www.npr.org/2023/08/01/1191493880/trump-january-6-charges-indictment-counts
Donovan, J., Dreyfuss, E., & Friedberg, B. (2022). *Meme wars: The untold story of the online battles upending democracy in America*. Bloomsbury.
@Ealeeyellama. (2021, January 5). *Tweets*. Retreived from https://http://backtweets.com/
@e_verhage. (2021, January 5). *Tweets*. Retreived from https://http://backtweets.com/

@fluffyMcFluff. (2021, January 5). *Tweets*. Retreived from https://http://backtweets.com/
@FoxytailRedhead. (2021, January 5). *Tweets*. Retreived from https://http://backtweets.com/
@FrancaiPolitics. (2021, January 5). *Tweets*. Retreived from https://http://backtweets.com/
@grandmaXs3. (2021, January 5). *Tweets*. Retreived from https://http://backtweets.com/
Hsu, S. S. (2021, August 4). Not patriots, not political prisoners – U.S. judges slam Capitol riot defendants at sentencing. *The Washington Post*. https://www.washingtonpost.com/local/legal-issues/capitol-riot-political-prisoners/2021/08/04/9b6adb84-f54d-11eb-9068-bf463c8c74de_story.html
Jackson, S. J., Bailey, M., Foucault Welles, B., & Lauren, G. (2020). *#Hashtag activism: Networks of race and gender justice*. The MIT Press.
Jamieson, F. (1982). *The political unconscious: Narrative as a socially symbolic act*. Cornell University Press.
@JesusCh74101301. (2021, January 6). *Tweets*. Retreived from https://http://backtweets.com/
@Jimmcnary. (2021, January 5). *Tweets*. Retreived from https://http://backtweets.com/
@joenors. (2021, January 5). *Tweets*. Retreived from https://http://backtweets.com/
Johnson, P. E. (2022). *I the people: The rhetoric of conservative populism in the United States*. University of Alabama Press.
@JosephAmazing14. (2021, January 5). *Tweets*. Retreived from https://http://backtweets.com/
@JuddDunning. (2021, January 5). *Tweets*. Retreived from https://http://backtweets.com/
@kamala_and. (2021, January 6). *Tweets*. Retreived from https://http://backtweets.com/
@kapd131. (2021, January 5). *Tweets*. Retreived from https://http://backtweets.com/
Kaptein, H. (2002). *Tu quoque? Fallacy and vindication in appeal to other people's "wrongs." Rozenberg Quarterly*, ISSA Proceedings 2002. https://rozenbergquarterly.com/issa-proceedings-2002-tu-quoque-fallacy-and-vindication-in-appeal-to-other-peoples-wrongs/
@kattastic007. (2021, January 5). *Tweets*. Retreived from https://http://backtweets.com/
@KeithCRogers. (2021, January 5). *Tweets*. Retreived from https://http://backtweets.com/
Kreiss, D. (2016). Seizing the moment: The presidential campaigns' use of Twitter during the 2012 electoral cycle. *New Media & Society, 18*(8), 1473–1490. https://doi.org/10.1177/1461444814562445
@KristieWelch17. (2021, January 5). *Tweets*. Retreived from https://http://backtweets.com/
@KruzeTed. (2021, January 6). *Tweets*. Retreived from https://http://backtweets.com/
@LanieMV. (2021, January 5). *Tweets*. Retreived from https://http://backtweets.com/
Lee, J., & Young-Shin, L. (2016). Gendered campaign tweets: The cases of Hillary Clinton and Donald Trump. *Public Relations Review, 42*(5), 849–855. https://doi.org/10.1016/j.pubrev.2016.07.004
Lempinen, E. (2020, December 7). Despite drift toward authoritarianism, Trump voters stay loyal. Why? *Berkeley News*. https://news.berkeley.edu/2020/12/07/despite-drift-toward-authoritarianism-trump-voters-stay-loyal-why
@LiberalsLeaving. (2021, January 5). *Tweets*. Retreived from https://http://backtweets.com/
@lookforvalue. (2021, January 6). *Tweets*. Retreived from https://http://backtweets.com/
@MarksManVA. (2021, January 5). *Tweets*. Retreived from https://http://backtweets.com/
@martinssempa. (2021, January 6). *Tweets*. Retreived from https://http://backtweets.com/

McGee, M. C. (1980). The "ideograph": A link between rhetoric and ideology. *The Quarterly Journal of Speech*, 66(1), 1–16. https://doi.org/10.1080/00335638009383499
@mcleoda. (2021, January 5). *Tweets*. Retreived from https://http://backtweets.com/
@mcleodb. (2021, January 6). *Tweets*. Retreived from https://http://backtweets.com/
McQueen, E. (2021, June 17). Examining extremism: The Oath Keepers. *Center for Strategic & International Studies*. https://www.csis.org/blogs/examining-extremism/examining-extremism-oath-keepers
@Mercstappen. (2021, January 6). *Tweets*. Retreived from https://http://backtweets.com/
Merriam-Webster (2023). *Tweeps*. Merriam-Webster Dictionary. https://www.merriam-webster.com/dictionary/tweep
@minnymoo2662. (2021, January 6). *Tweets*. Retreived from https://http://backtweets.com/
@MissyLee1967. (2021, January 5). *Tweets*. Retreived from https://http://backtweets.com/
@moeanon03a. (2021, January 5). *Tweets*. Retreived from https://http://backtweets.com/
@moeanon03b. (2021, January 6). *Tweets*. Retreived from https://http://backtweets.com/
@moonglow63092. (2021, January 5). *Tweets*. Retreived from https://http://backtweets.com/
Morgan, D., & Chiacu, D. (2022, June 17). Trump criticizes Pence's actions on Jan. 6, 2021, says he lacked 'courage.' *Reuters*. https://www.reuters.com/world/us/trump-criticizes-pences-actions-jan-6-2021-says-he-lacked-courage-2022-06-17/
@mrsrogers2270. (2021, January 5). *Tweets*. Retreived from https://http://backtweets.com/
@Nic_Radd. (2021, January 5). *Tweets*. Retreived from https://http://backtweets.com/
@NOcosignMiKE. (2021, January 6). *Tweets*. Retreived from https://http://backtweets.com/
O'Kruk, A., & Merrill, C. (2024, February 6). Donald Trump's criminal cases, in one place. *CNN Politics*. https://www.cnn.com/interactive/2023/07/politics/trump-indictments-criminal-cases/
@OldSargeUSAF. (2021, January 5). *Tweets*. Retreived from https://http://backtweets.com/
Ortega, M. (2024, January 31). Hollywood's foray into dystopian civil unrest a reflection of us. *Stumbling Down*. https://stumblingdown.com/p/hollywoods-foray-into-dystopian-civil
@QNCTHRNHRH. (2021, January 6). *Tweets*. Retreived from https://http://backtweets.com/
Parmelee, J. H., & Bichard, S. L. (2012). *Politics and the Twitter revolution: How tweets influence the relationship between political leaders and the public*. Lexington.
@PatriotMinded. (2021, January 7). *Tweets*. Retreived from https://http://backtweets.com/
Paul, R., & Elder, L. (2006). *The thinker's guide to fallacies: The art of mental trickery and manipulation*. Foundation for Critical Thinking. http://www.brahmakumaris.info/download/Cult%20related/Fallacies.pdf
Reilly, R. J. (2023, November 30). Jan. 6 rioter asks for early release, says he was 'manipulated' by Trump and Fox News. *NBC News*. https://www.nbcnews.com/politics/justice-department/jan-6-rioter-manipulated-trump-fox-news-rcna127404
Reinwald, J. J. (2021). *Doing hashtags: Identifying hashtag's role in the rhetorical tool kit* [Doctoral Dissertation, University of Pittsburgh.] http://d-scholarship.pitt.edu/41595/
@RepublicanUS_A. (2021, January 5). *Tweets*. Retreived from https://http://backtweets.com/
Rho, E. H. R., & Mazmanian, M. (2019). Hashtag burnout? A control experiment investigating how political hashtags shape reactions to news Content. *PACM on Human-Computer Interaction*, 3(197), 1-25. https://doi.org/10.1145/3359299

Riggins, G. (2022). *From #StopTheSteal to an Insurrection: A Fantasy Theme Analysis of the Discourse Surrounding the 2020 U.S. Presidential Election* [Master's Thesis, Arkansas State University]. https://www.proquest.com/openview/f261cbd86022ac4cfd5d9ba280b49877/1
@rodriQuez. (2021, January 5). *Tweets*. Retreived from https://http://backtweets.com/
Roose, K. (2021, September 3). What is QAnon, the viral pro-Trump conspiracy theory? *The New York Times*. https://www.nytimes.com/article/what-is-qanon.html
Rucker, P., & Costa, R. (2016, April 17). While the GOP worries about convention chaos, Trump pushes for 'showbiz' feel. *The Washington Post*. https://www.washingtonpost.com/politics/while-the-gop-worries-about-convention-chaos-trump-pushes-for-showbiz-feel/2016/04/17/482cc914-0322-11e6-9d36-33d198ea26c5_story.html
@Ryan_Myers. (2021, January 6). *Tweets*. Retreived from https://http://backtweets.com/
@SabDigitalWitch. (2021, January 6). *Tweets*. Retreived from https://http://backtweets.com/
@SavyTruthSeeker. (2021, January 5). *Tweets*. Retreived from https://http://backtweets.com/
Schnell, M. (2022, December 19). Jan. 6 committee unveils criminal referrals against Trump. *The Hill*. https://thehill.com/homenews/house/3780865-jan-6-committee-unveils-criminal-referrals-against-trump/
@SmokeySmith100. (2021, January 7). *Tweets*. Retreived from https://http://backtweets.com/
@strive4best1. (2021, January 6). *Tweets*. Retreived from https://http://backtweets.com/
@StyleCleverly. (2021, January 5). *Tweets*. Retreived from https://http://backtweets.com/
@SweetPea_leepher. (2021, January 6). *Tweets*. Retreived from https://http://backtweets.com/
Swenson, H. Y., Swenson, A., & Seitz, A. (2020). AP fact check: Trump's claims of vote rigging are all wrong. *Associated Press*. https://apnews.com/article/election-2020-ap-fact-check-joe-biden-donald-trump-technology-49a24edd6d10888dbad61689c24b05a5
@TAmerican23. (2021, January 7). *Tweets*. Retreived from https://http://backtweets.com/
@TAsterisk. (2021, January 6). *Tweets*. Retreived from https://http://backtweets.com/
@TheNKO. (2021, January 6). *Tweets*. Retreived from https://http://backtweets.com/
@TheRealKeean. (2021, January 5). *Tweets*. Retreived from https://http://backtweets.com/
Thompson, B. G., Cheney, L., Lofgren, Z., Schiff, A. B., Aguilar, P., Murphy, S. N., Raskin, J., Luria, E. G., & Kinzinger, A. (2022). *Final report of the Select Committee to Investigate the January 6th Attack on the United States Capitol*. U.S. Government Publishing Office. https://www.govinfo.gov/content/pkg/GPO-J6-REPORT/pdf/GPO-J6-REPORT.pdf
@TrumpsMustache. (2021, January 5). *Tweets*. Retreived from https://http://backtweets.com/
Tzu, S. (2000). *The art of war* (L. Giles, Trans.). Allendale Online Publishing. https://sites.ualberta.ca/~enoch/Readings/The_Art_Of_War.pdf
Wade, P. (2021, December 11). Trump says his 'fight like hell' speech before capitol riot was actually 'extremely calming.' *Rolling Stone*. https://www.rollingstone.com/politics/politics-news/trump-fight-like-hell-speech-extremely-calming-1270504/
@waytruthlife07. (2021, January 5). *Tweets*. Retreived from https://http://backtweets.com/
@xgudwilx. (2021, January 5). *Tweets*. Retreived from https://http://backtweets.com/
Yaqub, U., Ae Chun, S., Atluri, V., & Vaidya, J. (2017). Analysis of political discourse on Twitter in the context of the 2016 US Presidential elections. *Government Information Quarterly, 34*, 613–626. https://doi.org/10.1016/j.giq.2017.11.001

Zompetti, J. P. (2019). Rhetorical incivility in the Twittersphere: A comparative thematic analysis of Clinton and Trump's tweets during and after the 2016 presidential election. *Journal of Contemporary Rhetoric*, 9(1/2), 29–54. http://contemporaryrhetoric.com/wp-content/uploads/2019/02/Zompetti9_1_2_3.pdf

ABOUT THE EDITORS

John Allen Hendricks (Ph.D., The University of Southern Mississippi) is Chair and Professor of the Department of Media & Communication at Stephen F. Austin State University in Nacogdoches, Texas. He has held the department leadership role since 2009.

He has published numerous books on the topics of media/politics, social media/new media technologies, and the media industry, including: *Social Media Politics: Digital Discord in the 2020 Presidential Election* (with Dan Schill, Routledge, 2024), *The Presidency and Social Media* (with Dan Schill, Routledge, 2016), *Presidential Campaigning and Social Media* (with Dan Schill, Oxford University Press, 2014), *Social Media and Strategic Communications* (with Hana Noor Al-Deen, Palgrave MacMillan, 2013), *Social Media: Usage and Impact* (with Hana Noor Al-Deen; Lexington Books, 2012), *Techno Politics in Presidential Campaigning* (with Lynda Lee Kaid; Routledge, 2011), and *Communicator-in-Chief: How Barack Obama Used New Media Technology to Win the White House* (with Robert E. Denton, Jr.; Lexington Books, 2009).

He has received book awards from the National Communication Association and the Broadcast Education Association. Dr. Hendricks is founding editor of the book series, "Studies in New Media," for Rowman & Littlefield/Lexington Books.

Dan Schill (Ph.D., University of Kansas) is a Professor in the School of Communication Studies and Affiliate Professor in Political Science at James Madison University (JMU), where he teaches courses in advocacy, political communication, research methods, and media and politics. He holds numerous teaching awards including the Carl Harter Distinguished Teacher Award, JMU's top award for teaching excellence, and the School of Communication Top Teacher Award from the JMU student body. Schill previously worked on Capitol Hill as an American Political Science Association (APSA) Congressional Fellow and often conducts dial focus groups for news organizations.

His research focuses on communication, politics, media, and technology. He has published five books on political communication topics, including *Social Media Politics: Digital Discord in the 2020 Presidential Election* (with John Allen Hendricks, Routledge, 2024), *The Presidency and Social Media* (with John Allen Hendricks, Routledge, 2018), *Political Communication in Real Time* (with Rita Kirk and Amy Jasperson; Routledge, 2017), *Communication and Midterm Elections* (with John Allen Hendricks; Palgrave Macmillan, 2015), *Presidential Campaigning and Social Media* (with John Allen Hendricks; Oxford University Press, 2014) and *Stagecraft and Statecraft: Advance and Media Events in Political Communication* (Lexington Books, 2009). Other work has appeared in the *Journal of Political Marketing, American Behavioral Scientist, Mass Communication & Society, Argumentation and Advocacy, Review of Communication*, and *PS: Political Science & Politics*.

He has also received top paper awards from the Political Communication Divisions of the International Communication Association, National Communication Association, and the Central States Communication Association.

ABOUT THE CONTRIBUTORS

Ariana Aquino (M.A., University of Arkansas) studied the intersection of environmental, organizational, and strategic communication. Her research has been presented at the National Communication Association's annual conference.

Kathleen Coyle (M.A., University of Arkansas) studied gender & sexuality rhetoric and political rhetoric. Her research has been presented at the National Communication Association's annual conference.

Juliet Dee (Ph.D., Temple University) is an associate professor in the Department of Communication at the University of Delaware. She teaches courses in First Amendment law, mass media and culture, broadcast programming and television production. She has been director of the Legal Studies Program at the University of Delaware, has been an editor of the *Free Speech Yearbook*, and is a co-author of *Mass Communication Law in a Nutshell* (2020). She has published articles or book chapters on First Amendment issues involving controversial artwork funded by the National Endowment for the Arts, copyright and trademark law, anonymous defamation on the Internet, objectionable lyrics in rock music and hip-hop, media liability for violent content, media liability for classified ads for hitmen, the Occupy

Wall Street movement, hate speech, intentional infliction of emotional distress, the right to heckle at baseball games, images of violence against women in advertising, cyber-harassment and cyberbullying, and the tension between free exercise of religion and maintaining public health during the corona virus lockdowns.

Randall Fowler (Ph.D., Maryland) is assistant professor and Foundational Course Director in the Department of Communication & Sociology at Abilene Christian University. His research examines presidential rhetoric, the rhetoric of religion, and U.S. foreign policy in the Middle East. A 2013–2014 Fulbright Award grantee to Jordan, he is author of *More Than a Doctrine: The Eisenhower Era in the Middle East* (Nebraska, 2018), *Something to Fear: FDR and the Foundations of American Insecurity, 1912–1945* (Kansas, 2023), *Securing the Prize: Metaphor, Presidential Rhetoric, and U.S. Intervention in the Persian Gulf from Twin Pillars to the Axis of Evil* (South Carolina, 2024), and *Reagan's Doctrines: How the Great Communicator Transformed U.S. Relations with the Middle East* (Bloomsbury, 2025). His work has appeared in *Quarterly Journal of Speech, Rhetoric & Public Affairs, Journal of Communication & Religion, Journal of Arab & Muslim Media Research,* and other academic outlets.

Jacob Groshek (Ph.D., Indiana University Bloomington) has a long list of research and teaching appointments, which currently include the Executive Director of the Institute for Representation in Sports and Media, the Chair of Emerging Media at Kansas State University, as well as Honorary Associate Professor in the Department of Communication and Arts at Roskilde University (Denmark). He earned his Ph.D. in media research at Indiana University Bloomington, where he specialized in international, political, and health communication networks and advanced econometric methods. Topically, his areas of expertise now address online and mobile media technologies as their use may relate to sociopolitical and behavioral health change at the macro (i.e., national) and micro (as in individual) levels. His work also includes computational, data-driven analyses of sports and culture in media content along with user influence in social media.

Freddie J. Jennings (Ph.D., University of Missouri) is an assistant professor in the Department of Communication at the University of Arkansas. His research has been published in *Argumentation & Advocacy, Social Media+ Society, Communication Monographs, American Behavioral Scientist,* and *Information, Communication and Society*. His research focuses on the emerging political communication landscape, political polarization, and the cognitive processing of political messages.

Kalah Kemp (Ph.D., Regent University) is an associate professor at College of the Ozarks, located in Branson, Missouri, where she also consults local organizations on digital marketing. Her Burkean cluster analysis of Trump's tweets was published in Stephen Perry's *Pro Football and the Proliferation of Protest* (2019). She has also presented research on social media activism at NCA's annual conference and participated in conference panels on media portrayals of persons with disabilities. Kemp's research interests include the effects of social media on political discourse and social media activism.

Sarah Krongard (Ph.D., Boston University) is the Vice President of Programs at the Organization for Social Media Safety. She is a researcher and learning designer, exploring the intersection of education, media, and technology. Sarah has authored studies related to the civic implications of streaming television engagement, including a co-authored chapter in the book, *Media and the 2016 Election: Discourse, Disruption, and Digital Democracy*.

Tyler Martinez (M.A., Arizona State University) is an independent scholar interested in the rise in global populism. Martinez is also interested in intercultural communication and human development.

Christopher J. McCollough (Ph.D., Louisiana State University) joined the faculty at Jacksonville State University as an accomplished educator and scholar, having earned 5 Top Paper awards, earned 2 outstanding Faculty Service Awards for his work in community outreach and shared governance, and has a reputation as a visible member of the faculty community, performing pro bono public relations consultation as part of Columbus State University's Non- Profit and Civic Engagement (NPACE) Center. His research blends the applied practice of public relations, the teaching and learning of public relations, and various forms of impact on communities through the application of high-impact learning practices. Within the study of public relations and political communication, Dr. McCollough focuses on the historical and working relationships between state government public information officers and journalists. He's consistently presented award-winning work at the Southern States Communication Association, the Association for Education in Journalism and Mass Communication, and the National Communication Association.

Madeleine Montgomery (M.A., University of Arkansas) focused her research on feminist studies, as well as the intersection of organizational, interpersonal, and mass communication. Her research has been presented at the National Communication Association's annual conference.

Malloree Murdock (M.A., University of Arkansas) studied political rhetoric and the criminalization of Critical Race Theory. Her research has been presented at the National Communication Association's annual conference.

Majia Nadesan (Ph.D., Purdue University) is a professor in the School of Social and Behavior Sciences at Arizona State University. Nadesan is a multidisciplinary scholar whose publications examine (1) biopolitical risk governance of human and ecological life; and (2) the growing populist mobilizations responding to the decoupling of system and lifeworld. Nadesan's monographs and edited collections have most recently focused on populism, pluralism and the challenges of forging sustainable and democratic energy transitions, particularly under "crisis" conditions.

Myrna Roberts (Ph.D., Regent University) is the founder and curator of the Tatums Museum of History in Oklahoma. She often presents her research on African American cultural identity and the Tulsa race massacre. Additionally, Roberts and her colleagues authored a book chapter on peace journalism, examining terrorism, extremism, and radicalization. She is an independent scholar, writer, rhetorician, and behavioral scientist. Roberts' research interests include triangulating journalism, intercultural communication, and communication theory.

Emily Sauter (Ph.D., University of Wisconsin-Madison) is working at Minnesota State University-Mankato and her research focuses on transnational media flows, digital rhetorics, and popular culture. In her work she explores how political identity is formed and performed by the online communities in which people participate. Her research is primarily rhetorical and includes examination of public address texts, sports communication, new media, as well as critical analyses of the multitude of visual and oral texts generated by social media participants. She recently published a paper titled "Validity and the Art of Rhetorical Criticism" in the Annals of the International Communication Association in which she and her co-authors examine Rhetoric as a methodology. She also has an article in the *Journal of Tourism and Leisure Studies* titled "Discursive Constructions of South African

Cities Through Tourism Websites" that examines the impacts of online discourse on physical spaces.

Xavier Scruggs (M.S., Texas Christian University) is a doctoral candidate in the Department of Communication at the University of Missouri. He researches the intersection of family and political communication, specifically how differing political beliefs/attitudes can create division and conflict within families.

Todd R. Vogts (Ph.D., Kansas State University) is an assistant professor of media and department co-chair at Sterling College in Kansas. At Kansas State, his research focused on how mis- and disinformation spread in rural America by looking at the pathways to news for rural citizens.

Benjamin R. Warner (Ph.D., University of Kansas) is an associate professor of Communication and Director of Graduate Studies at the University of Missouri. One of the nation's leading experts in political polarization and partisan media effects, he has published articles and book chapters examining the polarizing effects of partisan media, new media echo-chambers, and presidential debates. He also studies the effects of viewing political comedy and discussing politics on social media.

Ben Wasike (Ph.D., Louisiana State University) is a professor in the Communication Department at the University of Texas Rio Grande Valley. He teaches classes in visual communication, communication theory, and research methods, among others. His research focuses on social media communication, social media misinformation, political communication, and law and policy issues.

Yanjun Zhao (Ph.D., Southern Illinois University at Carbondale) is an associate professor in Communication at Cameron University. Her research interest is the irrational nature of information processing. Her most recent research is a conference paper about AI's impact on people's misconception of reality, presented at WJEC (World Journalism Education Council) in 2022. In 2021, she got third place in the AEJMC teaching contest and got her teaching practice published in *Best Practices in Teaching Skills Courses Online*. She is also interested in persuasion and perception of visual messages.

Joseph P. Zompetti (Ph.D., Wayne State University) is a professor in the School of Communication at Illinois State University. He is author of the book, *Divisive Discourse: The Extreme Rhetoric of Contemporary American Politics* (2018), articles on political rhetoric on social media published in the *Journal of Contemporary Rhetoric*, and a co-author of the article "Twitter, Incivility, and Presidential Communication: A Theoretical Incursion into Spectacle and Power" published in *Cultural Studies*. His research interests focus on rhetorical theory and political covmmunication, particularly the polarization of political rhetoric.

INDEX

active citizen engagement 7
Affordable Care Act 26, 47
agriculture- related industries 132
AMA (Ask Me Anything), Yang's 79
Apparatgeist Theory 184, 202–3
artificial intelligence (AI) 5, 19, 253
   confirmation bias 262
   critical thinking skills 265
   Deep Neural Networks 255
   democracy, impact on 264–5
   diversity 256–8
   division and polarization 258–60, 264
   echo chamber effect 258, 260
   filter bubbles 253–4, 260, 267
   group polarization 261
   human ethics 255
   information cocoons 257
   invisibility of the algorithms 256
   offensive content 263–4
   people, impact on 260–1
   political discourse, impact on 262–4
   predictive algorithms 266
   satisfaction and comfort 261–2
   social media AI 254–5, 257
   YouTube's algorithm, impact on 259
asyndeton 27

belief gap hypothesis (BGH) 101, 104–5
   media exposure 105
   partisan divide 104
Bernie Bros 15, 68–9, 84
big data 5
big lie 102, 122, 273, 280–2, 284, 291–2
binge- watching
   horror genre 202
   motivations for 184–5
   news and informational content 202
   and political participation and talk 191–8, 201–2
   television 201–2
Black Lives Matter (BLM) movement 67, 335

cause- effect relationships 27, 30

Celebrity Politics (Orman) 69
celebrity politics/politicians 49, 52, 59, 69, 70
  actions 70
  celebritization of politics 69
  communication 61, 62
  definition 70
  foundation of 69
  influence 49
  policies 59
  and traditional politician, difference 69–70
  usage of social media 61
ChatGPT 39
citizen-fan 15, 69–73
  affective and emotional bonds 75
  categories 72–3
  characteristics 76
  description 69
  fan behavior 91
  fandom communities 76
  knowledge of policy 80–1
  parasocial relationship and intimacy 82
  separation from citizen-stan 88
  specialized knowledge of 79
  see also citizen-stan; fandom; fan materials
citizen-stan
  act of stanning 87
  anti-fan, behavior 88
  anti-fandom 88
  conspiracy theories 89
  election denialism 89
  Pizzagate 89
  stan, definition 88
  standom 89
communication, political 5–7
  declined trust in traditional media 7–8
  definition 3, 5–6
  echo chamber 10, 12–3, 19, 21, 123, 127, 143, 159, 258, 260
  exploitation of social and political tensions 11
  false or misleading information 11
  filter bubbles 10

  fundamentals of 4
  intersection of technology and politics 5
  media outlets 8
  partisan news outlets 7–9
  persuasive 3
  political *see* participation, political
  public opinion formation 6
  selective exposure 8, 50, 143, 214, 260, 262
  traditional and digital media, combination 6
  see also disinformation; misinformation
Communications Decency Act of 1996 290
Computer- Mediated Communication (CMC) 131
Convergence Culture (Jenkins) 71
cosplay 73, 75, 85–6
couch potato stereotype 183
COVID- 19 pandemic 18, 26, 32, 35, 38, 103–4, 144, 168, 171, 209, 223, 234, 260, 307
cultivation theory (CT), applicability 124, 129–30
cultural citizenship 70
cultural competence 4

Dark Brandon meme 90
Deep Neural Networks 255
defamatory accusations
  big lie 102, 122, 273, 280–2, 284, 291–2
  Coomer and Trump for President 285–7
  death threats against Coomer 285
  documentaries, 284
  Dominion and Smartmatic defamation suits 272, 274–5
  Fox news hosts 276–80
  loss, disinformation campaign 288–9
  newsworthy accusations of election fraud 292
  objective reporting 273
  One America News (OAN) hosts 283–5
  out- of- court settlement with Fox News 291
  posts on social media, after Trade Libel Suits 288

republication of falsehoods 275
threats of violence 287–8
see also Newsmax
Democratic National Convention 26
digital culture/platforms 28–9, 39–40
  dominance of 124–5
  effectiveness of first ladies on 302
  in political campaigns 301–2
  political surrogacy on 300
  see also polysyndeton
discourse theory of citizenship 71
disinformation
  definition 128
  dissemination of misinformation 16
  influence of online platforms 17
  and media 140–2
  and misinformation, distinction 11–2
  news consumption 17
  rural population behavior 17
  spread of 129
  threat to democratic institutions 12
  see also misinformation
disruptive technology 40
Dominion v. Fox News 271–2, 276, 279–80, 377–8
Dominion Voting Systems Corporation 19, 271–3, 274, 275, 279, 281, 283, 285, 289

echo chamber 10, 12–3, 19, 21, 123, 127, 143, 159, 258, 260
Elaboration Likelihood Model 18, 210, 215, 222–3
2020 election
  assault against U.S. Capitol building 157
  campaigns 14, 25–6, 33, 35, 38, 85
  conspiracies/controversy 105, 122–3
  Dominion and Smartmatic defamation suits 272
  exploratory committee 297
  false claims about 259
  fan studies 90–1
  filter bubbles 258
  hashtags 264
  hate speech and aggressive messages 263

  presidential campaign rhetoric 28
  September 14 address 38
  social media, role of 21
  third rally, Trump's 25–6, 33
  trust in traditional media 7
  TV *see* TV and political participation
  Twitter use, influence of 45, 52, 69
  see also polysyndeton; theDonald.win
Election Integrity Partnership 273
elections- related misinformation 16, 101–2, 106, 112–4
empathy
  components 186, 191
  dimensions of 198–201
  hierarchical linear regression of 200
  perspective- taking 198–9
  theory of narrative empathy 186–7
  see also 2020 election; TV and political participation
everyday political celebrities 49
  see also celebrity politics/politicians

Facebook 4, 6–7, 14–5, 19, 27–9, 39, 68, 83–5, 102, 137, 144, 159, 168, 254, 257, 262, 272, 275, 278, 280, 283–4, 290
Fairness Doctrine 125–6
Faith Education Commerce United 285, 287
fan- based citizenship, theory of 71–2, 85
  see also fan communities; fandom
fan communities 15, 69, 82–5
  acquiring a community name 83
  Berniebros. 84
  community of imagination 82
  KHive 84–5
  MAGA 84
  slogans 83–4
  subreddit 82
  Yang Gang 85
  YouTube channels 85
fandom 15–7
  affect, bodily displays of 73–4
  anti- fandom 88
  behavior 68, 91

bodily performance 73–4
boundaries 77, 80
communities 76, 81–3, 88–9
contemporary American political behavior 68
digitally mediated 163
emotional and affective relationships 73–5
engage in politics 88
growth 90
identity 75
MAGA 84, 87
mode of participation 82
mode of political engagement 88, 90
to motivate fans 68
narratives binding 160
negative sides 88, 91
online fan behavior 68–9
participatory cultures of 89
personal information about the candidates 81
polarized 176
policy detailed knowledge 79–80
political 160
and politics, link between 71
skills for political participation 67
source of creativity 88
tools for civic engagement 90
see also theDonald.win
fan materials
affirmational engagement 86
cosplay 86
fan content for Trump 87
fanfiction/memes, remixes, and videos 85
images of fan- object 86
memes 87
popular 86
transformational engagement 86
fan practices
as citizenship practices 72
common 72
cosplay 75
normative 71
transformative or affirmational 85

filter bubbles 10, 13, 21, 123, 159, 253–4, 256
  consequences of 260
  daily media consumption 257
  and echo chamber 10, 12–3, 19, 21, 123, 127, 143, 159, 258, 260
  effect on beliefs and opinions 258
  elections, 2016 and 2020 258
  factors for future 267
  media bubbles 10
Fox News 122, 125, 136–7, 136–8, 141, 260, 271, 274–5, 281
  Bartiromo, Maria 276–7
  big lies 102, 122, 273, 280–2, 284, 291–2
  Dobbs, Lou 277–80
  Dominion v. Fox News 271–3
  false and defamatory accusations 271, 290
  hosts 275–80
  party- aligned sources 122
  Pirro, Jeanine 280
  Republicans 8
  right- leaning news organization 8, 108
gender
  in campaign communication 18–9
  candidate communication 245
  differences 91
  division of labor 302
  gendered characteristics 326
  influence of attitudes about 230–2, 234
  in political communication 242
  role in perceptions of campaign communication 18–9, 230
  sexual orientation 313, 315
  stereotypes 302
Gonzalez v. Google, LLC (2023) 290
Google Forms 132
Gravitational Black Holes of Information, concept of 254–5

hashtag politics
  anti- Trump denunciations 339–40
  blame on Trump 341
  election as a threat 330

framework 325–7
God's providence 338
impact of online digital media 326–7
January 5, 2021 329–35
January 6, 2021 336–9
January 7, 2021 339–41
messages of unity 337
method 327–8
Pence's role in the certification process 334–5
pro- Trump crowd 334–5
public relations strategies 326
qualitative content analysis 326
qua rhetorical strategy 333
racial justice 338
rigged election, impact 331–2, 340
R script 327
Save America Rally 329, 334–6, 342
shift in perspective in three days 341–2, 342
significance 325, 341
#StopTheSteal 324, 328–9
thematic analysis 327
viewing rivals as enemies 332
hierarchical linear regression (HLR) analysis/models 55, 192–3, 195–201
homogeneity 232–3, 243
homogeneous communication environments 232–3, 244
homogenous media environments 232
horror and news / informational programming 17–8, 196
hostile sexism 231–2, 236, 243–5
and racial resentment correlation *see* racial resentment

identity- motivated elaboration 216
immigration 55, 101, 101 41, 104–5, 107, 113, 161, 261, 340
incidental news exposure 125
independent media 137
Inflation Reduction Act 41
infographics 4
informed decision- making 7
informed electorate 7, 214

Instagram 4, 6–7, 19, 29, 83–4, 168, 272, 277–9, 288
Institutional Review Board (IRB) 132
interactive websites 4
interviews
  friendly 35
  in- depth 17, 122, 124
  qualitative 132
  video and/ or audio recording 133
Islamic State in Iraq and Syria (ISIS) 290

J6 Capitol insurrection *see* U.S. Capitol, assault
journalism 4–5, 28, 123, 125, 128, 140, 264, 281, 327

Kansas Farm Bureau 132
KHive 15, 68–9, 78–80, 83–4, 88, 91
knowledge gap hypotheses (KGH)
  BGH *see* belief gap hypothesis (BGH)
  COVID- 19- related information 103
  dynamics at a specific point in time 114
  education- based knowledge gaps 103
  effect of right- leaning media exposure 113
  elections- related knowledge 107, 111
  ideological orientation 107–8
  implications 114
  internet- driven knowledge 103
  interpersonal discussion 103–4, 108–9, 113
  limitations 114
  method 106–10
  online interactions 103–4
  partisan media use 108–10
  questions 105–6, 109
  results 110–3
  sampling and data collection 106–7
  self- reported responses 114
  social media engagement 110, 112
  socio- economic factors 113
  Twitter meme depicting misinformation 106
  variables 107
K- pop fans 67

legacy media
  distrust of 161
  information directly to voters. 27
LIFT Act 80
live streams 4

Make America Great Again (MAGA) 46, 69, 91, 172, 278–9, 329, 334, 339–40
  fandom 69, 82–4, 84, 87, 90–1, 172
  fans 68, 69, 82
  rhetoric 47
  slogan 47
  subreddit by supporters 82
  supporters and Trump 69
Maternal CARE Act 80
mean world syndrome 129
Mechanical Turk (MTurk) 53
media bubbles 10
Meta 6
misinformation 11–2
  definition 128
  dissemination of 16
  elections- related 16, 101–2, 106, 112–4
  influence of online platforms 17
  political 16–7
  risks of 14
  via social media engagement (SME) 101
  see also disinformation
motivated reasoning 18, 210, 216, 222, 223–4
  accuracy goals 213
  identity- congruent partisan cues 222
  identity- motivated elaboration 216
  interpret favorable information 233
  limiting exposure to information 213
  partisan motivated reasoning 214
MSNBC 8, 84, 110, 122, 125, 136, 144, 260

narcotizing dysfunction, concept of 40
narrative empathy, theory of 186–7, 191–2
  see also empathy
networked publics, theory of 185
news
  CMC, role of 131

Conservatives, cable television networks 123
consumption habits 123, 125–6
controversy of 2020 election 122–3
cultivation theory (CT), applicability 124, 129–30
disbelief in election 122
disinformation and media 140–2
distrust in 123, 128
dominance of digital platforms 124–5
echo chamber and filter bubbles *see* echo chamber; filter bubbles
incidental exposure 125
interviews, semi- structured, in- depth 122
journalism and communication 128
literature review 124–31
mean world syndrome 129
media use, categories 130–1
methods 131–3
mis- and disinformation 129
national outlets plant media distrust 138–40
news consumption habits 123, 125–6
news sources 122
non- television- related research 129
partisan cable, channels 126
party- aligned sources 122
political socialization 131
radio, conservative talk 126–7
results 133–5
rural Americans 121–44
sources 122
television, interpersonal mistrust 129
television journalism 125
thematic analysis 133
trust 127–8
Uses and Gratifications Theory (U&G) 124, 129–30
Newsmax 19, 122, 136–7, 141, 271–5, 281, 289–90
  defamation suit against 286
  media, hosts and tweets 281–2, 286
normalizing new identities

affordable childcare 314–5
Buttigieg, Chasten 311–5, 315–7
Buttigieg, Pete 306–11
  diversity in government and public life 314–5
  down-ballot Democrats 297
  environmental and infrastructure projects 297
  first ladies and political communication 301–2
  first openly gay secretary 315
  gay political spouse performance 295
  LGBTQ advocacy 312–4, 316
  means of analysis 303–5
  national roles in the Democratic Party 297
  political surrogacy 295, 300–1, 316
  reelection bid 296
  research questions 302–3
  sample period 303
  tweets and retweets 312, 314
Nvivo coding 166

One America News Network (OAN) 258, 271–5, 281, 283–4, 286–7, 289–90
  agenda setters 273
  false accusations against Dominion 273
  lies about Dominion and Smartmatic 274
  spike in viewership 258
over-the-top (OTT) TV 183, 185, 203

panels
  conference panels on media 353
  opt-in 188
  Qualtrics 106
parasocial interaction 15
  and identification with Trump see Twitter
Parler 19, 159, 161, 176, 272, 285
participation, political 15, 17–8, 67, 70, 158, 169, 176, 183–5, 187–9, 201–2
  and binge-watching see binge-watching
  online 189, 192–5
  TV see TV and political participation

party-aligned sources 122
perceptions of Trump's Twitter (PTT) 48, 54, 56
Plandemic (video) 144
podcasts 4, 84–5, 125, 266, 285
polarization 8–10, 9–10, 12, 14, 16–21, 91, 121
  artificial intelligence and algorithms 19
  binge-watching see binge-watching
  confirmation bias 262
  description 9–10
  group 261
  impact of communication environment 19
  influence of partisan cues 18
  informational programming 17–8
  LGBTQ+ advocacy 20
  in media consumption 259
  negative affective 40
  partisan antipathy 9
  party identification 18
  political communication 20
  presidential debates 18
  of public opinion 260
  race and gender 19–20
  social 157
  societal dynamics and governance 9
  societal segmentation 265
  suspicion and scrutiny 8
political rhetoric 6–7, 12, 14–6, 39–41, 160, 209
polysyndeton 14–5
  and Biden see polysyndeton and Biden's campaign
  dynamics of online digital culture 28–9
  foreign affairs 41
  function of 28
  normalcy model 35
  police violence 36
  and political culture 27–9
  racial discrimination 36
  reliance on polysyndeton as an organizational logic 38
  shovel-ready jobs 36

trope of online digital culture 28–9, 40
and Trump *see* polysyndeton and Trump's campaign
Trump's COVID-19 leadership 35
polysyndeton and Biden's campaign
  campaign rhetoric 38
  crisis rhetoric 37, 39
  criticism 37
  early childhood education 36
  effects of COVID-19 in speech 35
  foreign affairs 41
  interdependent solutions 37
  normalcy model 35
  plea to support him on healthcare and racial justice 37
  police violence 36
  racial discrimination 36
  reliance on polysyndeton as an organizational logic 38
  shovel-ready jobs 36
  Trump's COVID-19 leadership 35
polysyndeton and Trump's campaign
  amplification for rally speeches 29–30
  chronological sequencing of issues 33
  impromptu lists 29
  media coverage 33
  online ubiquitous presence 34
  order/tactical use of issues list in speeches 31–4
  2020 presidential campaign 33
  rhetorical strategies of association 31
  September 10 address in Freeland, Michigan 30
  September 3 rally in Latrobe 31
popular culture 68–9, 71–2, 75, 183, 299
@POTUS 52, 55, 332
2024 presidential campaign 21, 39, 40, 59, 86, 176
Public.com (Sunstein) 266

race/racial/racism 36, 164, 231–2, 240, 244
  antagonism 332
  attitude about 19, 230–2, 232, 234, 243, 245–6
  difference/discrimination/inequality 18, 36, 91, 209, 335
  fighting for anti-racism 335
  inequality 18
  injustice 36–8
  justice 26, 36–9, 261, 338
  protests 223
  resentment *see* race/racial/racism
  riots 230
  role in campaign communication 18, 230, 243
racial resentment 230, 236, 239
  attitudes about race and gender 230–2, 241
  communication environment, effect on 232–4, 240, 242–5
  correlation between 240
  data analysis 237–8
  debate performance 232–4, 237
  gender 230
  Harris brand image 236–7
  homogeneous communication environments 232–3, 244
  hostile sexism 19, 230–2, 234, 236, 238–44, 243–5
  image perceptions of Harris 237
  motivated reasoning 233–4
  participants 235–6
  pre-debate questionnaire 235
  procedure 234–5
  racial resentment 230, 236, 239
  Republican or Republican leaning 235
  results 238–42
  video-conferencing technology 230
  violence and aggression toward women 231–2
radio 5, 17, 83, 110, 123.126–7, 131–2, 135–6, 141, 143, 327
@realDonaldTrump 47, 52, 55, 277–8, 283, 332–4, 337–40
Rent Relief Act 80
Reuters Institute 8
rigged election 288, 330–3, 341
right-wing populism, rise of 157

INDEX

Roe v. Wade 124
R script 327
RTweet (specially- developed R script) application 327
Rumble 19, 272, 283
Russia- backed meddling, 2016 U.S. elections 102

same- sex marriage 101
Save America Rally 329, 334–6, 342
selective exposure 8, 50, 143, 214, 260, 262
sex education 101, 104–5
SGO Corporation Limited 275
short- form videos 4
Smartmatic Corporation 19, 271–4, 271–92
   conspiracy 280
   damage to the reputations 291–2
   economic loss 287–8, 289–90
   focus on Fox News 275–8, 275–9, 281
   lies about 283
   rigged 2020 election 281–2
   SIH 275
   of siphoning off votes 274
   suit against the social media platforms 290, 292
   SUSA 275–6
   switched votes 284
   violence against 287–9
Smartmatic Corporation (SGO Corporation Limited) 19, 271–4
Smartmatic International Holding B.V. (SIH) 275
Smartmatic USA Corporation (SUSA) 275–6
social cohesion 4
social identity
   definition 211
   in- group favoritism 212
   out- group derogation 212
   positive in-group bias 212
   self- identified in- group and out- group 211
   theory (SIT) 18, 210–5, 221–3
social isolation 67

socialization, political 131
social media
   ability of 13
   attempted insurrection of the United States Capitol 13
   attitudinal congruence, influence of 219–20
   decline in traditional news consumption 13
   discussion 222–4
   Elaboration Likelihood Model 210
   features 13
   hypothesized model 216–7
   identity- consistent elaboration 215
   impact on democracy 13
   limitations 224
   media literacy 14
   message- consistent/ inconsistent elaboration 219
   motivated reasoning 212–4
   negative implications 14
   partisan cues on 121–45
   partisan social identity hypothesis 219–20, 223
   platforms 5, 12–4, 18–21, 29, 82–3, 105, 126, 137, 159, 168, 175, 253, 256, 258–9, 263, 271–3, 275, 290, 292, 325–6
   and political communication 12–4
   process analysis 221
   results 219–21
   risks of polarization and misinformation 12, 14
   self- report partisanship 218
   SME *see* social media engagement (SME)
   social identity theory (SIT) 211–2
   theory of identity- motivated elaboration (TIME) 210, 214–5, 222
   valenced elaboration, effect of 221
Social Media Analytic Command Center (SMACC) 327
social media engagement (SME) 59, 101, 105, 109
   and elections- related misinformation 111–2, 112, 114

and interpersonal discussion
 questions 109
 questions 109
 see also social media
social presence theory (SPT) 60
 communication and perceptions of
  closeness 50
 effects of politicians' Twitter
  communication 50
 increased social presence 51
specialized fan knowledge
 backstory and history 76–7
 detailed knowledge 76
 excessive readers 76
 fanon 81
 history of engagement 77
 policy based 79
 policy detailed knowledge 80
 sense of intimacy 82
 Trump's record of success in
  business 77–8
Stop the Steal movement (STS) /
 #StopTheSteal 14, 20–1, 324–5,
 327–42
 see also hashtag politics
storytelling 30, 185
superstar and everyday celebrity
 politician 70

television
 binge-watching *see* binge-watching
 cable networks 123–6, 132
 cope with stress and uncertainty 17
 depictions of violence 129
 influence on politics 5, 17
 interpersonal mistrust 129
 journalism 125
 mis- or disinformation spreads 141, 327
 news 136, 271, 274, 282–3, 292
 on-demand television ecosystem 183
 online discourse 185
 and participation *see* TV and political
  participation
 reality and series, shows 46, 49, 72, 76
theDonald.win

argumentation and verification 163
August 31, 2020, themes 166, 167–9
Big Tech 168–9
censorship by technology
 companies 173–4
communication research 176
Democrats as cheaters 166–7
discussion 173–7
economic dislocations 157
emergent themes 167
enlightenment faith 162
fake news 159
hyperreality, concept of 162–3
internet as liberational technology 158
lack in faith in democratic
 institutions 174
mail-in voting fraud 170–1
marginalization 157
methodology 165–6
narratives of electoral fraud 17, 171, 176
November 4 themes 171–3
Nvivo coding 166
October 31, 2020, themes 170–1
online discussion forums, analysis of 159
paranoid rhetoric 161
polarization, social 157
political fandom 160, 163–5
political polarizations 158–60
post-truth digital commons 161–3
responses to threats 169
stolen election 171–3
Theory of Identity-Motivated Elaboration
 (TIME) 210, 214, 222–3
TikTok 4, 14–5, 27, 29, 68, 73–4, 77, 81,
 84–6, 266, 287
transformational engagement 86
TV and political participation
 Apparatgeist Theory's perpetual
  contact 202–3
 binge-watching *see* binge-watching
 civic engagement 185–6
 demographics 188
 discussion 201–3
 empathy *see* empathy
 entertainment content 186

Interpersonal Reactivity Index (IRI) 191
limitations 203
political antecedents 188–9
political talk/participation, offline and online hierarchical linear regression 192–3, 194–5, 197–8
research questions and hypotheses 187–8
social media 189–90, 194
theory of narrative empathy 191–2
theory of networked publics 185, 203
Twitter 4, 6, 12, 14–5, 19–20, 27–9, 33–4, 39, 45–56, 59–61, 68, 76, 78, 82–5, 102, 106, 137, 161, 168, 175, 245, 256, 258, 272, 274–7, 279–80, 283–4, 286, 289–90, 303, 305, 310–1, 314, 316–7, 324, 326–32, 334–42
 appeal to voters 46
 archive 327
 behavior and political issues 55
 celebrity-persona identification 46, 50, 54
 celebrity politician 49
 controversial statements 47
 credibility 48, 54, 60–1
 divisive rhetoric 52
 HLR analysis 56–8
 identification theory (IDT) 49–50, 54, 59–60
 limitations 61–2
 loyalty to the U.S.'s historical enemies 48
 MAGA rhetoric 47
 measurements 53
 method 53–5
 parasocial interaction (PSI) 48–9, 53–4, 59
 perceived credibility 51
 Presidency 46–7
 presidential candidacy in 2015 46
 presidential Twitter account 52
 psychological closeness 60
 public involvement 52
 research questions 52
 selfdisclosure through 60–1
 social presence theory (SPT) 50–1, 54, 60
 survey 53, 55–9
 symbols 49
 and Trump 46–51
 tweets, informal, celebrity-styled 46
Twitter, Inc. v. Taamneh (2023) 290
two-for-the-price-of-one (2-for-1) narrative 300

U.S. Capitol, assault 17, 20–1, 45, 121, 127, 157, 159, 165, 175, 209–10, 217, 219, 224, 258, 263–4, 291, 323, 328–9, 336–7, 339–41
U.S. Election Assistance Commission (EAC) standards 273
Uses and Gratifications Theory (U&G) 124, 129–30, 184
The Uses of Argumentation (Toulmin) 161

video-conferencing technology 230

Working Families Party (WFP) 88

X (formerly as Twitter) *see* Twitter

Yang Gang 15, 68–9, 78, 85–6, 91
YouTube 4, 14–5, 19, 27, 77, 85, 168, 254–5, 272, 283, 285–6

General Editors
Mitchell S. McKinney and Mary E. Stuckey

At the heart of how citizens, governments, and the media interact is the communication process, a process that is undergoing tremendous changes as we embrace a new millennium. Never has there been a time when confronting the complexity of these evolving relationships been so important to the maintenance of civil society. This series seeks books that advance the understanding of this process from multiple perspectives and as it occurs in both institutionalized and non-institutionalized political settings. While works that provide new perspectives on traditional political communication questions are welcome, the series also encourages the submission of manuscripts that take an innovative approach to political communication, which seek to broaden the frontiers of study to incorporate critical and cultural dimensions of study as well as scientific and theoretical frontiers.

For more information or to submit material for consideration, contact:

    editorial@peterlang.com

To order other books in this series, please contact our Customer Service Department:

    peterlang@presswarehouse.com (within the U.S.)
    orders@peterlang.com (outside the U.S.)

Or browse online by series:

    WWW.PETERLANG.COM

www.ingramcontent.com/pod-product-compliance
Ingram Content Group UK Ltd.
Pitfield, Milton Keynes, MK11 3LW, UK
UKHW022238230426
12048UKWH00018BA/1323